Palgrave Studies in Adaptation and Visual Culture

Series Editors
Julie Grossman
Le Moyne College
Syracuse, NY, USA

R. Barton Palmer
Atlanta, GA, USA

This series addresses how adaptation functions as a principal mode of text production in visual culture. What makes the series distinctive is its focus on visual culture as both targets and sources for adaptations, and a vision to include media forms beyond film and television such as videogames, mobile applications, interactive fiction and film, print and nonprint media, and the avant-garde. As such, the series will contribute to an expansive understanding of adaptation as a central, but only one, form of a larger phenomenon within visual culture. Adaptations are texts that are not singular but complexly multiple, connecting them to other pervasive plural forms: sequels, series, genres, trilogies, authorial oeuvres, appropriations, remakes, reboots, cycles and franchises. This series especially welcomes studies that, in some form, treat the connection between adaptation and these other forms of multiplicity. We also welcome proposals that focus on aspects of theory that are relevant to the importance of adaptation as connected to various forms of visual culture.

Marc C. Conner • Julie Grossman
R. Barton Palmer
Editors

Screening Contemporary Irish Fiction and Drama

palgrave
macmillan

Editors
Marc C. Conner
Skidmore College
Saratoga Springs, NY, USA

Julie Grossman
Le Moyne College
Syracuse, NY, USA

R. Barton Palmer
Clemson University
Clemson, SC, USA

ISSN 2634-629X   ISSN 2634-6303   (electronic)
Palgrave Studies in Adaptation and Visual Culture
ISBN 978-3-031-04570-7   ISBN 978-3-031-04568-4   (eBook)
https://doi.org/10.1007/978-3-031-04568-4

© The Editor(s) (if applicable) and The Author(s), under exclusive licence to Springer Nature Switzerland AG 2022
This work is subject to copyright. All rights are solely and exclusively licensed by the Publisher, whether the whole or part of the material is concerned, specifically the rights of translation, reprinting, reuse of illustrations, recitation, broadcasting, reproduction on microfilms or in any other physical way, and transmission or information storage and retrieval, electronic adaptation, computer software, or by similar or dissimilar methodology now known or hereafter developed.
The use of general descriptive names, registered names, trademarks, service marks, etc. in this publication does not imply, even in the absence of a specific statement, that such names are exempt from the relevant protective laws and regulations and therefore free for general use.
The publisher, the authors and the editors are safe to assume that the advice and information in this book are believed to be true and accurate at the date of publication. Neither the publisher nor the authors or the editors give a warranty, expressed or implied, with respect to the material contained herein or for any errors or omissions that may have been made. The publisher remains neutral with regard to jurisdictional claims in published maps and institutional affiliations.

Cover illustration: Fox Searchlight/Photofest.

This Palgrave Macmillan imprint is published by the registered company Springer Nature Switzerland AG.
The registered company address is: Gewerbestrasse 11, 6330 Cham, Switzerland

Contents

1 **Introduction**   1
   Marc C. Conner, Julie Grossman, and R. Barton Palmer

2 **Filming Global Ireland: Roddy Doyle's *The Commitments***   21
   Marc C. Conner

3 **The Riddle of the Models of John Carney's *Sing Street***
   (2016)   43
   Julieann Veronica Ulin

4 **The Women Incarnate of *Words Upon the Window Pane***   65
   Matthew J. Fee

5 **Mouth Not Eye: On Jordan's Adaptation of Beckett's *Not I*** 83
   Eyal Amiran

6 **"The Joyce of Filum: Cinematic Accounts of *Ulysses*"**   99
   Michael Patrick Gillespie

7 **"One Beetle Recognizes Another": Translation,**
   Transformation, Transgression in Cartoon Saloon's Film
   The Secret of Kells   113
   Lisabeth C. Buchelt

v

vi CONTENTS

8 Bad Da's: Rewriting Fatherhood in *Breakfast on Pluto* 137
Nicole R. McClure

9 *What Richard Did*: Sort of Adapting Irish History 155
R. Barton Palmer

**10 Plagues of Silence: Adaptation and Agency in Colm
Tóibín's and John Crowley's *Brooklyn*s** 181
Kathleen Costello-Sullivan and Julie Grossman

11 *The Program*, *Seven Deadly Sins*, and Stephen Frears 199
Lesley Brill

**12 The Immutable and Un-retrievable in the Diasporic
Films of John Michael and Martin McDonagh** 215
Eamonn Jordan

**13 "How should we remember what happened?": Cultural
Representations of Institutional Abuse in Jim Sheridan's
*The Secret Scripture*** 239
Tara Harney-Mahajan

Index 265

Notes on Contributors

Eyal Amiran is Professor of Comparative Literature at UC Irvine and Editor of the journal *Postmodern Culture* (Johns Hopkins). He has published *Wandering and Home: Beckett's Metaphysical Narrative* (1993) and Modernism and the Materiality of Texts, and co-edited the collection *Essays in Postmodern Culture* (1994). His recent essays on the relation between contemporary literature and electronic culture have appeared in *Cultural Critique* (on "pornocracy" in popular media), *Discourse* (on utopian digital architecture), *TDR* (on Stelarc), *Ex-position* (on "the open" in the age of Big Data), *parallax* (on digital ontology and the echosphere), and in *Humanities, Provocateur: Toward a Contemporary Political Aesthetics* (on weaponization of the body). He is working on psychological ideas of society in modern comics.

Lesley Brill Emeritus Professor of English and Film Studies at Wayne State University in Detroit, has published four books on filmmakers and cinema, and many essays on film, photography, and literature. His most recent books are *Crowds, Power, and Transformation in Cinema* (2006) and *The Ironic Filmmaking of Stephen Frears* (2017).

Lisabeth C. Buchelt specializes in medieval and nineteenth-century British and Irish literary and cultural studies at the University of Nebraska, Omaha, and is the Albert W. and Helen J. Jefferis Chair of English Literature. She has published on tenth-century Old English poetry, gospel book design in ninth-century Ireland, early medieval Hiberno-Latin poetry, modern Irish visual arts, nineteenth-century vampire narratives, and occult imagery in the drama of W.B. Yeats. Her article "'Delicate

viii   NOTES ON CONTRIBUTORS

Fantasy' and 'Vulgar Reality': Undermining Romance and Complicating Identity in Bram Stoker's *The Snake's Pass*" won *New Hibernia Review*'s Roger McHugh Award for Outstanding Article in 2012, and her research on twelfth-century Irish monastic intellectual culture won a fellowship from the National University of Ireland—Galway Moore Institute for Research in the Humanities and Social Sciences. She is at work on a monograph examining the intersection of Irish literary narratives and the Neoplatonic philosophic revival of the twelfth century.

Marc C. Conner is the President of Skidmore College in Saratoga Springs, New York, where he is also professor of English. His books include *The Aesthetics of Toni Morrison: Speaking the Unspeakable* (2000), *Charles Johnson: The Novelist as Philosopher* (2007), *The Poetry of James Joyce Reconsidered* (2012), *The New Territory: Ralph Ellison and the Twenty-first Century* (2016), *Screening Modern Irish Fiction and Drama* (Palgrave/Macmillan 2016), and *The Selected Letters of Ralph Ellison* (2019). He has produced three lecture series with the Great Courses program: *How to Read and Understand Shakespeare* (2012), *The Irish Identity: Independence, History, and Literature* (2016), and *Touring Ireland and Northern Ireland* (2020).

Kathleen Costello-Sullivan is Professor of Modern Irish literature and former Dean of the College of Arts and Sciences at Le Moyne College in Syracuse, New York. She holds an MA and PhD degree from Boston College. Kate is the author of two monographs: *Mother/Country: Politics of the Personal in the Fiction of Colm Tóibín* (2012) and *Trauma and Recovery in the Twenty-first-Century Irish Novel* (2018). She has also edited critical editions of J. Sheridan Le Fanu's novella *Carmilla* (2013) and *Norah Hoult's Poor Women!* (2016) and has authored a number of articles on contemporary and nineteenth-century English and Irish novels. Kate is the president of the American Conference for Irish Studies (ACIS) and sits on the Executive of the International Association for the Study of Irish Literature (IASIL). Since 2018, she has served as the (first female) Series Editor of the prestigious Irish line of Syracuse University Press. Her research is on recuperative narrative representations of the embodied parent-child bond.

Matthew J. Fee is a lecturer and director of the Integral Honors Program at Le Moyne College. His primary areas of research and specialization are Irish cinema, Irish studies and film genres. He has presented and published on Irish cinema, contemporary documentary, horror films and post-9/11 cinema.

NOTES ON CONTRIBUTORS ix

Michael Patrick Gillespie After receiving his PhD from the University of Wisconsin in 1980, he taught for twenty-nine years at Marquette University as an assistant, associate, and a full professor and finally as the inaugural Louise Edna Goeden Professor of English. He has written fourteen books (on the works of James Joyce, Oscar Wilde, William Kennedy, Chaos Theory, Classic Hollywood Cinema, and Irish Film) and two monographs. He has edited eight other works, including two volumes in the Norton Critical Edition of authors. He has also written over eighty articles and book chapters relating to English and Irish studies. He has been on the advisory boards of a half dozen scholarly journals and has served as a reader for thirteen university presses. He has received fellowships or grants from the National Endowment for the Humanities, the American Philosophical Society, the Humanities Research Center, the William Andrews Clark Library, the American Council of Learned Societies, the Wisconsin Humanities Council, and Marquette University. He has been named as a featured speaker in the Joseph Schick Lecture Series and gave one of the Lawrence McBride Memorial Lectures. He is the only American recipient of the Charles Fanning Medal for Distinguished Work in Irish Studies. He came to Florida International University in the fall of 2009 and serves there as a professor of English having directed the Center for the Humanities in an Urban Environment for five years. He has been named a Distinguished Scholar by Florida International University and is a STEM Institute Fellow. Gillespie has been on the Board of Trustees of the International James Joyce Foundation and on the Board of Consultants for the Zurich James Joyce Foundation. He has been Secretary, Vice-President, and President of the American Conference for Irish Studies. He has most recently published *Film Appreciation Through Genres* (2019).

Julie Grossman is Professor of English and Communication and Film Studies at Le Moyne College, USA. She is author of *Rethinking the Femme Fatale in Film Noir: Ready for Her Close-Up* (Palgrave, 2009); *Literature, Film, and Their Hideous Progeny: Adaptation and ElasTEXTity* (Palgrave, 2015); and *The Femme Fatale* (2020). She is co-author (with Therese Grisham) of *Ida Lupino, Director: Her Art and Resilience in Times of Transition* (2017) and co-author (with Will Scheibel) of *Twin Peaks* (2020). She is co-chair (with Kamilla Elliott) of the Association of Adaptation Studies and founding co-editor (with R. Barton Palmer) of the book series *Adaptation and Visual Culture* (Palgrave). With R. Barton Palmer, she co-edited the essay collection *Adaptation in Visual Culture: Images, Texts, and Their Multiple Worlds* (Palgrave, 2017).

NOTES ON CONTRIBUTORS

Tara Harney-Mahajan is Assistant Professor of English at Caldwell University, where she teaches courses on Irish literature and Global Anglophone literature. Her research specializes in modern and contemporary Irish and South Asian literature, with a focus on women writers, and her scholarship has been published in journals such as *Women's Studies* and *New Hibernia Review*. Most recently, she co-edited *Post-Celtic Tiger Ireland and Contemporary Women's Writing*, published by Routledge in 2021. She is also co-editor of the literary studies journal *LIT: Literature Interpretation Theory*.

Eamonn Jordan is Professor in Drama Studies and former Subject Head (2011–2014) at the School of English, Drama and Film, University College Dublin. His book *The Feast of Famine: The Plays of Frank McGuinness* (1997) is the first full-length study on McGuinness's work. In 2000, he edited *Theatre Stuff: Critical Essays on Contemporary Irish Theatre*. He co-edited with Lilian Chambers *The Theatre of Martin McDonagh: A World of Savage Stories* (2006). His book *Dissident Dramaturgies: Contemporary Irish Theatre* was published in 2010 by Irish Academic Press. In 2012, he co-edited with Lilian Chambers *The Theatre of Conor McPherson: 'Right beside the Beyond'*. In 2014 his monograph *From Leenane to LA: The Theatre and Cinema of Martin McDonagh* was published by Irish Academic Press. In 2016 he introduced and selected with Finola Cronin *The Contemporary Irish Theatre and Performance Studies Reader for Carysfort Press*, a publication with over 70 essays. September 2018 saw the publication of *The Palgrave Handbook of Contemporary Irish Theatre and Performance*, a work he co-edited with Eric Weitz. *The Theatre and Film of Conor McPherson: Conspicuous Communities* has been published by Methuen Bloomsbury in February 2019. In 2020, *Justice and the Plays and Films of Martin McDonagh* was published by Palgrave as part of its Pivot series of publications.

Nicole R. McClure is an assistant professor of English at Kutztown University, where she teaches film adaptation, documentary cinema, feminist film theory, and international cinema among other film courses. Her work in Irish film studies includes research on Troubles cinema and survivor representation, historical revisionism/adaptation, and more recently explorations of contemporary feminism in Irish film. She serves on the Executive Board of the American Conference for Irish Studies as the Web and Communications Director.

R. Barton Palmer is the Calhoun Lemon Professor of Literature emeritus at Clemson University, where he taught from 1995 to 2019 after a previous stint as Professor of English and Communication at Georgia State University, where he helped establish the film program. At Clemson, Palmer was the founding director of the World Cinema program. Palmer has published widely in both literary and film studies, with a special interest in both film noir and American film history. Among his most recent publications on film are several edited collections: *The Other Hollywood Renaissance*, with Dominic Lennard and Murray Pomerance (2020); *French Literature on Screen*, with Homer Pettey (2019); *Rule Britannia! The Biopic and British National Identity*, with Homer Pettey (2018); *Adaptation in Visual Culture: Images, Texts, and Their Multiple Worlds*, with Julie Grossman (Palgrave, 2017); *Film Noir* and *International Film Noir*, with Homer Pettey (2016, 2014). Palmer serves as the editor of the *South Atlantic Review* and *The Tennessee Williams Annual Review*. He is the general editor of the following book series: with Julie Grossman, of the series *Adaptations and Visual Culture* at Palgrave; with Linda Badley, of the series *Traditions in American Cinema* and *Traditions in World Cinema* at Edinburgh; with Matthew Bernstein, of the series *The South on Screen* at Georgia; with Tison Pugh, *New Perspective on Medieval Literature* at Florida; with Homer Pettey, of the series *International Film Stars* at Edinburgh and *Global Film Directors* at Rutgers.

Julieann Veronica Ulin is Associate Professor of Transatlantic Modernism at Florida Atlantic University. She received her PhD in English from the Keough-Naughton Institute for Irish Studies at the University of Notre Dame, where she was the Edward Sorin Postdoctoral Fellow in the Humanities from 2007 to 2009. She holds her MA in English from Fordham University and a BA in English from Washington and Lee University. Her Irish studies scholarship has appeared in *Joyce Studies Annual, James Joyce Quarterly, New Hibernia Review, WSQ, Hungry Words: Images of Famine in the Irish Canon* (2006), *Open Graves, Open Minds: Representations of Vampires and the Undead from the Enlightenment to the Present* (2013), *Screening Modern Irish Fiction and Drama* (2016), and *The Edinburgh Companion to Irish Modernism* (2021). She co-edited *Race and Immigration in the New Ireland* (2013). Her monograph *Medieval Invasions in Modern Irish Literature* (2014) explores the recurrence of twelfth-century Irish history in Ireland's modern literature.

LIST OF FIGURES

Fig. 3.1	*Sing Street* recalling *The Commitments*	46
Figs. 3.2 and 3.3	Duran Duran's "Rio" and *Sing Street*'s Raphina	52
Figs. 3.4 and 3.5	"Rio" influences Raphina's makeup	52
Figs. 3.6 and 3.7	Images of bifurcated selves in "Rio" and *Sing Street*	53
Figs. 3.8 and 3.9	The Holyhead ferry emerging suddenly out of the rain and fog	56
Fig. 3.10	Connor and Raphina, resonating with Molly and Bloom in *Ulysses*	58
Fig. 3.11	The DVD cover of *Bloom* (2003)	58
Fig. 7.1	Vikings on the march in *The Secret of Kells* (2009)	127
Fig. 7.2	Brendan and Aisling in the oak tree	128
Fig. 7.3	Crom Cruach trapped	129
Fig. 9.1	In an intimate moment, Richard (Jack Reynor) confesses to his father (Lars Mikkelsen), who cannot deal with the situation	163
Fig. 10.1	Eilis's assertion, "I am Eilis Fiorello!"	182
Fig. 10.2	Eilis on the train, gazing out the window	185
Fig. 10.3	Eilis and Tony, embodied charismatically by Saoirse Ronan and Emory Cohen	187
Fig. 10.4	Rose's silent tear	188
Fig. 10.5	Eilis's eyes, her stare signifying an alert mind	188
Fig. 10.6	Eilis and her sunglasses, catching the attention of passers-by on her return to Enniscorthy	192

xiv LIST OF FIGURES

Fig. 10.7	Eilis and Jim Farrell (Domhnall Gleeson) on the beach in Ireland	193
Fig. 10.8	Eilis and her bright yellow dress	193
Figs. 10.9 and 10.10	Crowley using a rack focus to redirect viewer attention	196

CHAPTER 1

Introduction

Marc C. Conner, Julie Grossman, and R. Barton Palmer

The trajectory of the Irish film industry interestingly parallels the story of Ireland's economic and cultural development following its independence from Great Britain, which was achieved at the conclusion of the Civil War in 1922. In the century that has followed the establishment of the Republic, the Irish cinema, virtually non-existent during the last years of British rule, has become a thriving commercial enterprise, as well as an essential vehicle for the expression of national (and sometimes counter-national) narratives. It is certainly the case, as Lance Pettitt argues at convincing length in his *Screening Ireland*, that "film is now the preeminent

---

M. C. Conner
Skidmore College, Saratoga Springs, NY, USA
e-mail: mconner@skidmore.edu

J. Grossman (✉)
Le Moyne College, Syracuse, NY, USA
e-mail: grossmjj@lemoyne.edu

R. B. Palmer
Clemson University, Clemson, SC, USA
e-mail: ppalmer@clemson.edu

© The Author(s), under exclusive license to Springer Nature
Switzerland AG 2022
M. C. Conner et al. (eds.), *Screening Contemporary Irish Fiction
and Drama*, Palgrave Studies in Adaptation and Visual Culture,
https://doi.org/10.1007/978-3-031-04568-4_1

1

medium through which Ireland both examines itself and projects itself to the wider world" (xvi).

In recent years, the cinematic projection of Ireland has had little to do with the continuing political division of the island into two separate political entities: the independent Republic in the south and Northern Ireland in the north, a part of the UK. In the 1980s and 1990s, internecine political conflicts ("the Troubles") were a dominant subject for Irish filmmakers, north and south. Since the signing of the Good Friday Peace Accords in 1998, however, and the elimination of the militarized border that once divided the Republic from Northern Ireland, the sense among the Irish that they belong to two separate societies has weakened into near irrelevance. There is considerable film production in the North but only in a quite technical rather than cultural sense can this filmmaking and the infrastructure that supports it be considered a separate cinema. Ireland's writers, directors, performers, and technical workers ply their trades in both parts of the country, and of course overseas in international co-productions. In this volume, the term "Irish Cinema" refers to all the filmmaking connected with this talented cadre.

The Irish today are as proud of their cinema as they are of their literature, and with good reason. Ireland's emergence, starting in the 1990s, as a model EU economy (for better and for worse) has thus been matched by the emergence of a film culture that reflects the European rather than the Hollywood model, with a productive interdependence of the private and public sectors at its base.

A remarkable series of acclaimed and profitable domestic productions during the past three decades has accompanied, while chronicling, Ireland's struggle with self-identity, national consciousness, and cultural expression, such that the story of contemporary Irish cinema is in many ways the story of the young nation's growth pains and travails. Whereas Irish literature had long stood as the nation's foremost artistic achievement, it is not too much to say that film now rivals literature as Ireland's key form of cultural expression. The proliferation of successful screen versionings of Irish fiction and drama shows how intimately the contemporary Irish cinema is tied to the project of both understanding and complicating (even denying) a national identity that has undergone radical change during the past three decades (see, e.g., the account of what can without exaggeration be called this "new Ireland" in O'Dowd; for a longer historic perspective, see Pettitt). Few other national cinemas, however, including those of other EU members, are as dependent on the national

1 INTRODUCTION 3

literary establishment for their source material (including original scripts by prominent novelists and dramatists). It would be an understatement to say that literary adaptation has played a substantial role in the success achieved by the Irish cinema, which is in important ways a literary cinema, as the essays collected in this volume illustrate.

The film business in the US is just that: a private industry that operates independently of any government control or oversight, protected and regulated, if only to a minimal extent, by trade organizations, pre-eminently the MPA, the Motion Pictures Association (see https://www.motionpictures.org/). Film culture in Ireland today, by way of contrast, has positioned itself as a public good, its accomplishments to be celebrated as part of an ever-evolving national patrimony (see https://www.screenireland.ie). Consider, as an indication of the affection of the Irish for their cinema, Kevin Rockett's *Ten Years After: The Irish Film Board 1993–2003*. An American counterpart of this book is literally impossible to imagine. *Ten Years After* is a lavishly illustrated, unabashedly promotional narrative of artistic accomplishment and commercial success of the Irish cinema that emerged in the wake of transformative legislation in 1993 that re-established the Irish Film Board (Bord Scánnan), chronicling its first ten years of operation. The Bord, as Rockett recounts, has enthusiastically overseen a generous grants program of start-up financing that is readily available to aspiring filmmakers, while providing other necessary services to the industry.

Originally instituted in 1980 in order to help Ireland develop a proper film industry and culture, the Bord at first proved largely ineffective, with its only real success being Neil Jordan's debut film *Angel* (1982). When it shut down operations in 1987, this seemed to ratify the inability of the national culture to produce and support a fully functioning cinema. By 1993, however, the country's circumstances had changed with the incipient economic growth of the Celtic Tiger, and the Bord came to a quite different second life under the leadership of one of the country's most dynamic politicians, Michael D. Higgins, who is also an important figure in the Arts community. Rockett observes:

> It is hard to imagine from the vantage point of 2003 how complete the transformation of the institutional and cultural landscapes for film in Ireland has been, not just in the last decade presented here, but in the two decades prior to that, when the very term 'Irish Cinema' had yet to be coined or used with any confidence. …During this decade, the Board supported one

hundred feature films and television series, and almost three hundred short dramas, documentaries, and animation, while over five hundred film projects received development money. (ix)

In the nearly two decades since the publication of *Ten Years After*, fulfilling the promise that Rockett had identified, Irish filmmaking has continued to flourish, surviving changes in government and the considerable challenges posed by the financial crisis of 2008–2009, which brought the Tiger to a screeching halt. In fact, the Bord (renamed as Fis Éireann, literally "Screen Ireland," in 2018), re-organized and expanded in 2009, along with associated state institutions devoted to the film sector such as the Irish Film Institute, has continued to play a significant role, with a guiding principle being that the film industry should serve as the national means of expression for a people that had previously been deprived of the ability to fashion the images of their own culture. As Síle de Valera observed in a Dáil debate in 1997 about proposed amendments to the 1993 Film Board act:

> The Irish people have been on the receiving end of images of Ireland and Irishness since time immemorial. The significance of the Irish Film Board's achievements is that Irish film makers are now able to speak directly to an audience at home and our best work can be exported abroad in an epoch of increasing globalization. (Dáil Éireann Debate 25 May 1997)

The ability to "speak directly" imagined by de Valera has meant that Irish cinema not only promotes projects based on original screenplays (often authored by writer/directors in the mold of John Michael McDonagh and Conor McPherson), but also offers adaptations of significant Irish prose fiction and drama. Many above the line creative personnel in the industry work regularly in the other arts, including the theater and television, as the Irish film industry has become multi-layered and interdisciplinary, with deep connections throughout the national arts scene. This has been, as Pettitt suggests, a kind of "Second Coming" (see his detailed account, 115–133).

This present volume offers itself as a sequel of sorts to the multi-authored survey of film adaptations of modern Irish literary works in Palmer/Conner *Screening Modern Irish Fiction and Drama*, published in this same series in 2016. As the planning and production of that earlier book proceeded, it became increasingly obvious to the editors that a

1 INTRODUCTION   5

further collection of essays was needed in order to assess in more depth the increasing prominence of adaptation in Irish filmmaking since 1991, particularly of contemporary Irish literature. Central to the cultural mission of this state-supported, but not state-controlled, cinema has been the screen re-versioning of the national literature, with the authors themselves often playing a significant role in project conception and production.

The different chapters that follow, through their focus on individual films, address how adaptation has figured in this Irish cinema, and in some overseas productions, for the last three decades. With deftness and perspicacity, leading figures in government, especially Higgins, have taken full advantage of the country's most noteworthy cultural resource: its writers and their internationally acknowledged achievements in both fiction and drama. (This is a stark contrast to the history of film adaptation of earlier modern Irish literature, particularly the great achievements of the first half of the twentieth century. As Palmer and Conner note, "the drama and fiction of the period of the Irish Renaissance, that great flowering of Irish literature and culture that runs from roughly 1890 to 1940, has proven curiously resistant to adaptation to film" [1].) In a fortunate parallel development, a generation of talented directors, their careers supported by the Bord, soon emerged who, like their counterparts in the US Independent sector such as Steven Soderbergh and the Coen brothers, were willing to make limited budget art films for that exhibition niche, even as they sometimes lent their talents to larger, more mainstream commercial projects. They often have worked in television as well, in line with another global trend. To be sure, what might be called the New Irish Cinema (not unlike a number of other national/cultural cinematic movements in the new millennium) reflects the ethos of auteurism that has been prominent on the international scene since the 1960s, when so-called New Waves, first in France and then elsewhere, emphasized the central role of the director in production and also as a critical touchstone. What distinguishes contemporary Irish filmmaking is its promotion of the other kind of authorship that, thanks to adaptation, can figure prominently in the way that a national cinema draws upon, even as it represents, its sponsoring culture.

Chance had little or nothing to do with the emergence of this extended moment of excellence. The closing years of the last century were notable for the success, both with critics and at the box office, achieved by three films produced abroad but taking full advantage of Irish talent: *My Left Foot* (1989, Jim Sheridan), *The Commitments* (1991, Alan Parker), and *The Crying Game* (1992, Neil Jordan). Jordan and Sheridan emerged as two of Ireland's most notable writer/directors (see Gilbert in Palmer/Conner 2016). An international figure born in the UK, Parker succeeded in bringing to the screen the first in a trilogy of films drawn from the works of Roddy Doyle, one of contemporary Ireland's leading fiction writers (see Ulin in Palmer/Conner 2016, and Conner in the present volume). The profits from these three films were realized elsewhere, while Ireland received only a reflected glory for the accomplishments of its émigré talent. This sense of a lost opportunity prompted a number of figures in the arts and business communities to lobby successfully for the re-commissioning of the Bord, which had ceased operations several years earlier, as well as an expansion of its role in project development. It was fortunate that at the time Higgins happened to be the Minister for Arts, Culture and the Gaeltacht; consequently, he was able to make sure that all institutions of government were supportive of the results. As films developed with financing and other forms of assistance, the Bord began successful and critically acknowledged releases, and official reaction was strongly positive. As Senator Quill observed in the 1997 Seanad debate over amendments that modified the original act:

> The film industry is very important to the future of this country, not alone to our cultural development and understanding of our identity but to our economic development, directly and indirectly. When shown abroad, Irish films invite curiosity about the country. They often project an interesting and appealing image of Ireland and prompt tourists to visit and industrialists to invest here and thereby generate jobs. These are indirect benefits which should not be overlooked. There are direct benefits such as the growing number of people who are gaining interesting and exciting employment in filmmaking. When we invest taxpayers' money in the film industry, we invest wisely....Senator Mooney spoke passionately on the importance of making indigenous films. *Young people in particular have the ability to make films based on our stories, because we have good stories to tell. We also have great scriptwriters.* (emphasis ours) (Seanad)

Since the early 1990s, committed to making films "based on our stories," the Irish cinema has become one of the most artistically and financially successful of the national cinemas that have achieved a global presence through the somewhat paradoxical policy of cultivating attractive alternatives to Hollywood, while also contributing substantially (especially through joint ventures) to international projects that enjoy considerable, often spectacular, success. Cooperation with US/UK/EU filmmakers, producers, and distributors has proven mutually beneficial to all concerned. Ireland, so it has been argued, has taken advantage, like Spain, of being on the late-modernizing periphery of the European cinema-scape, away from other members of the common market, notably France and Germany, with their long-established vertically coordinated industries and established urban habits of cinema-going and appreciation. (These issues are discussed in Holohan.)

A signal change that has also contributed to the rise of contemporary Irish cinema has been the expansion of its audience market. Since the last decade of the twentieth century, native filmmakers in Ireland have not been hampered by the limited scale of the national film audience. As of early 2021, Ireland's population is a mere 5 million, about the size of suburban Atlanta or one of Mumbai's expanding neighborhoods, with more rural (especially small village) rather than urban patterns of settlement and cultural life; it was in cities and small towns in North America and elsewhere that the "movies" established themselves as a commercially successful popular art in the early decades of the previous century. Consequently, for much of Ireland's history post-independence, being on the periphery of town and city development ensured Ireland's failure to develop a national cinema, a rejection of modernity that was consonant with its cultural and political circumstances, of which more later. The country's small size would today still preclude any plan for its cinema, including television production, to base its operations on the economic power of domestic exhibition in the face of the daunting expenses now involved in producing and marketing "A" features, as well as quality serialities for the rapidly expanding global television market.

The advent of television as an alternative source of financing and exhibition provided further support to traditional filmmaking, as has the streaming sector of a digitizing cinema economy—technical and industrial developments also supported by the FIS, as series television production in Ireland, most often with government sponsorship, has flourished, often with the participation of prominent filmmakers, often working with literary sources. The most notable recent example is *Normal People*, produced by Ireland's Element Pictures in partnership with BBC3 and the streaming service Hulu. This 12-part series is based on the novel of the same name by Sally Rooney (b. 1991), who is one of the leading literary lights of a younger generation strongly committed to the useful interplay between the literary arts and visual narrative. *Normal People* was published in 2018 and named "Irish Novel of the Year," in addition to winning other awards.

This popularity virtually guaranteed a screen version, with the series modality proving a canny choice for all concerned, allowing the full breadth of the novel's exploration of a complex nexus of relationships to figure in the adaptation.

Rooney wrote the screenplay with Alice Birch (a British playwright and screenwriter), while Dublin born-and-bred Lenny Abrahamson, perhaps Ireland's hottest young director, split directing chores with the UK's Hettie MacDonald. Abrahamson also served as one of the project's executive producers. With a focus on the sometimes turbulent romantic relationship between two secondary schoolmates in County Sligo, the series follows them to Trinity College, engaging with a number of current social issues: her kookiness, their sexual connection, the bullying she endures from others, their difficulties with parents. Intimate scenes between the couple featured some nudity (prompting the occasional complaint during the Irish broadcast run), but the production had been wise in employing an "intimacy coordinator" who proved successful in overseeing what many thought were some of the steamiest scenes ever a part of a television series in Ireland. *Normal People* successfully balances its detailed depictions of the suburban culture that is an increasingly prominent element of the national experience with a more general contemporary vibe, avoiding thorny political issues for the most part. The production team proved agile in creating a product that was sophisticated enough to appeal to upscale narrowcast audiences in the US, UK, and Ireland, without closing out possibilities for even wider distribution in other countries. The series is, perhaps, just Irish enough to satisfy the demonstrated taste for Irishness of both domestic and international audiences, in that balancing of national and universal themes Síle de Valera has argued the industry should promote.

The success of *Normal People*, among many other similar Irish productions, suggests that Ruth Barton is correct in stating that international "co-productions are now the backbone of the industry" (Barton 2019 1). Some of these films (Abrahamson's *Room* [2015], e.g.) are Irish in terms of their creative team and production circumstances even though the stories they tell are not. The project that would become *Room* was developed with initial financing from the Bord. Production was overseen by one of Ireland's most successful directors, with a script adapted from the novel by Irish-émigrée writer Emma Donoghue. The promotion of the film by distributor Universal Pictures was crucial to its success. The story is set in North America and makes no reference to Irish culture. Nominated for the Academy Awards Best Picture, *Room* won that award in both the Canadian and Irish competitions, confirming its powerful sense of transnationality, which almost earned it an unusual trifecta of appreciation had it succeeded in all its nominations. *Room* deals in themes that easily crossed cultural and linguistic borders; *Normal People* does much the same, but its fictional world references its County Sligo location, while the manners and accents of the characters are unambiguously Irish (even if the show's dialogue carefully avoids regionalisms not easily comprehensible to those who are not).

Such successful productions prompt Barton's claim that "the understanding of what constitutes a national cinema is ever more elusive," but this is perhaps true only if the parameters of nationality are too narrowly defined at a time when a certain political indeterminacy usefully prevails in both "parts" of the island itself (Barton 2019 1; for a different view see Gillespie). And yet Barton, and those of similar mind within the Irish critical establishment, have a point. The Irishness of Irish filmmaking is threatened not only by the emergence of "Europudding" cinema, whose releases feature a bland mixing of national styles, traditions, and themes, and what Iain Robert Smith usefully terms the "Hollywood meme" as a force for insipid bastardization in trans-national adaptation (see Selznick; Smith). Still, the pervasive trans-nationality of the current world cinema requires a flexible definition of national affiliation, and one that undergirds the choice of topics for the different chapters that constitute this present volume. These essays focus on how, since the 1990s, Irish literature has become an important, arguably essential, presence, a key attraction, both domestically and globally, in an exciting run of artistically complex and profitable films, with the changes to theatrical exhibition imposed by the COVID-19 pandemic less likely to create serious difficulties for the industry, given how adroitly the industry has already adapted to new modes of creation, production, and distribution. In the new millennium, no other national cinema can make a similar claim on a multi-layered literariness that enhances rather than displaces the more purely filmic qualities for which directors and other creative personnel are responsible.

It is striking how different the present situation is from the not-too-distant past in Irish cinema. For the first nine decades or so of the previous century Ireland was, with only few exceptions, a cinematic desert. Had it not been for American and British producers willing for their own reasons to take on the cultural task, prior to 1980 or so there would have been no "Irish" films as such, including any that were adapted from stories from

10   M. C. CONNER ET AL.

native fiction and drama, providing them with an extended second life. No masterpieces of the Irish literary tradition, a collective treasure of considerable world renown, had a screen presence except in films directed, produced, and distributed by others. This was especially remarkable, given the extraordinary richness and artistic achievement of the Irish Renaissance writers. With only a handful of exceptions (most notably, John Huston's 1987 adaptation of "The Dead"), the great literary works of Joyce, Yeats, Synge, Gregory, Shaw, Wilde, and O'Casey were underserved by filmmakers who could claim an Irish identity. As many have observed, this inability of the Irish film industry to successfully adapt and interpret Ireland's literary achievements was a defining failure of that industry (see Palmer and Conner, 2–3). This was a regrettable irony that cut deeply for ardent nationalists eager to promote their culture. What passed for an Irish cinema for the first 90 years or so of world cinema history was, both metaphorically and in fact, yet another form of extra-territorial diaspora, yet another mournful sign of the failure of what Edna O'Brien, writing as a refugee from a culture that had condemned her Europeanist views and shunned her for them, still nostalgically and ironically refers to as "mother Ireland" (see O'Brien). In part, the blame for this artistic failure must be ascribed to the near-theocracy established during the early years of the Republic. The Irish church fully endorsed Pius XI's intense wariness about the power of the cinema as expressed in his encyclical *Vigilanti Cura* (1936), a screed about the dangers of modern media that unfortunately served as the foundational document of the Irish Film Institute, established in 1943 under the leadership of Archbishop Charles McQuaid, for some decades the unofficial moral spokesman of the nation who figures as a controversial, even negative figure in recent revisionist histories of the period (see O'Dowd and Brown).

The "film madness" that took Europe by storm by 1900 never affected Ireland, then still largely a nation of small villages and very conservative social values, as promoted by the nation's first *Taoiseach*, Eamon de Valera, in a radio address that became a foundational document of post-Civil War identity (see de Valera). De Valera's economic nationalism and commitment to Ireland's self-sufficiency included a cultural program that insisted upon Ireland's unique moral character, what Terence Brown has described as "a conviction that the life of an Irish small farm represented a purity and decency of life that could set Ireland apart from the more commercial societies that surrounded her" (Brown 133). In his famous St. Patrick's Day radio address of 1943, de Valera evoked an image of the Irish homestead that would become almost comical in its naiveté, were it not for the power that this image would exert over Irish cultural life for the decades to follow:

> That Ireland which we dreamed of would be the home of a people who valued material wealth only as a basis of right living, of a people who were satisfied with frugal comfort and devoted their leisure to the things of the spirit; a land whose countryside would be bright with cosy homesteads, whose fields and villages would be joyous with sounds of industry, the romping of sturdy children, the contests of athletic youths, the laughter of comely maidens; whose firesides would be the forums of the wisdom of serene old age.

This vision of Irish life made no room for the urban modernism of the cinema. The impact of de Valera's cultural program on the arts was extraordinary. Censorship, including banned books and a suppression of the film industry, was an omnipresent element in Irish life well into the 1970s. As Brown explains, "an almost Stalinist antagonism to modernism, to surrealism, free verse, symbolism, and the modern cinema was combined with prudery (the 1930s saw opposition to paintings of nudes being exhibited in the National Gallery in Dublin) and a deep reverence for the Irish past" (135). This decision to remain disconnected from the most prominent artistic/commercial innovation of the early twentieth century should have put native literary arts at a distinct disadvantage, but this collective artistic energy could not be suppressed. In other European countries, at least since the 1920s, the national literature found a place on national screens, even if the nature of the commercial medium meant that filmmakers in other countries at times could adapt the same texts (e.g., *Madame Bovary* [1934, Jean Renoir, France] and [1949, Vincente Minnelli, US]), putting into question the "nationality" of the films involved.

However, the quality of Irish fiction and theater, even when publicly presented (as in the case of writers like Bernard Shaw and Beckett) in other countries, was too extraordinary to remain unexplored by the cinema. In the absence of a native filmmaking industry, acclaimed and appealing fiction and drama produced in Ireland were provided overseas with the "screening" that would allow these works to reach a wider audience in Ireland itself and globally. For decades, the only Irish cinema was what Gillespie has identified as an "Irish-themed" cinema. In the absence of a vibrant national industry that would cultivate and utilize the gifts of the native-born, would-be filmmakers were forced to seek work abroad, even if occasional runaway productions did film in the country (such as Michael Anderson's UK-produced version of Rearden Conner's novel *Shake Hands with the Devil* [1959]), thus enacting another version of the sad trope of emigration that has so deeply marked the national experience. For most of the history of the cinema, Ireland exported its talent, while the domestic economy profited little from the many successes at the box office of "Irish" films that re-versioned works from a literary culture of world renown and influence.

Consider one of the most famous of this series of overseas productions: John Ford's *The Quiet Man* (1952). Based on a short story by the Kerry writer Maurice Walsh, the film earned nearly $4 million, making it one of Hollywood's most profitable films that year. Location shooting in Ireland (County Galway and County Mayo) provided some boost to the local economy, and the production offered cameos and minor roles to many of the notable performers from the Abbey Theatre (including Arthur Shields and Eileen Crowe) and even an ex-patriate or two like Séan McClory, as well as third billing to Barry Fitzgerald, at the time one of the most famous Irish-born actors on stage and in Hollywood. A key writer in the crucial period of the 1930s, that decade in the wake of the tragically inconclusive finale of the Civil War, Walsh was a perceptive observer of, and passionate partisan in, an ever-shifting political climate where an Irish national identity was being shaped. His romantic ruralism (in line with official policies supported by de Valera) was an important voice in that national conversation (consider the role played by the Grierson documentary unit during the same period in the UK, in which film "spoke" for and made visible aspects of communal life then ignored or silenced by modernization). But without a native Irish film industry, and no state-level support of such an industry, writers such as Walsh and films such as Ford's required extra-national production. As a result, they created only extra-national profit. At the time, the country possessed no governmental institutions or relevant NGOs that could sponsor the kind of national self-portrait produced of the UK by Grierson with the support of the Empire Marketing Board. Today, under the sponsorship of the Bord, documentary filmmaking in Ireland offers richly diverse perspectives of national life.

Because Hollywood came to dominate the international film scene after the end of the Great War, other cinemas, especially in Europe, even if they had developed initially in free market circumstances, were all forced eventually to depend on state intervention, from protectionist quota systems to the provision of seed money or completion financing. and even in some instances government development of production and post-production infrastructure if they were to survive and prosper. Some countries, to be sure, had an unfortunate experience with state control, with government efforts in the UK, for example, failing to prevent during the period 1920–1970 a continuing Hollywood domination of the exhibition sector that resulted in a series of crises for domestic producers. Some government policy, in fact (particularly the 1927 Cinematograph Films Act) arguably made the problem worse rather than better. But this does not suggest that intervention in the film sector is always unwise; a Friedmanian criticism of controlled and regulated markets does not universally apply. If not a creation of state policy alone (one cannot discount the role played by a vibrant national arts community), the contemporary Irish cinema certainly would not have had the quick, substantial success that it has enjoyed since 1993 without effective government assistance. It seems certain that the conditions of the nation's cultural market could not have nurtured and supported filmmaking even in the midst of the freewheeling capitalism of the Tiger in the 1990s and early 2000s. It is also true, however, that the rapid cultural and political changes of the past three decades have provided a social landscape in which the cinema, particularly one in which the nation's literary voices play a prominent role, has been able to thrive.

The extraordinary success and production of Irish film in the period of roughly 1990–2020 that, as noted earlier, Rockett describes as "the transformation of the institutional and cultural landscapes for film in Ireland" occurred alongside, and often in a causal relationship to, a series of seismic social and cultural changes in the country whose effects are still being felt today. Put alongside the economic eruption of the Tiger and the significant transformations it has wrought in Irish social life and economic experience, one sees the intensity of the transformation in Ireland right during this time of growth and production in the film industry. These events are all intertwined in the contemporary Irish experience. As Brown has argued, "the early 1980s…was the end of an era in Ireland," as the old "Gaelic, Catholic, and Republican" national identity finally receded and a global, multicultural, and cosmopolitan array of identities offered themselves to the nation (318–319). These multiple identities offered a fruitful landscape for the new achievements in Irish film that are discussed in this volume.

The main areas of transformation occurred within gender roles and their associated laws, and with the role and authority of the Catholic church in Irish life. The extent to which traditional hetero-normative gender definitions dominated Irish culture can be understood by the fact that it was not until the 1977 Employment Equality Act that it became illegal to bar married women from the Civil Service and the local authorities and health boards (Brown 291). The emergence of a women's liberation movement in the 1970s eventually fueled the abortion amendment debates of the 1980s, and the divorce referenda of the mid-1980s and 1990s. These major, highly contentious public debates eventually issued in the 15th amendment to the constitution in 1996, which made divorce legal, and finally the climactic passage of the 36th constitutional amendment in 2018, which made possible the legalization of abortion in the Republic. (This included a repeal of the 8th amendment, approved in 1983, which had recognized the equal right to life of the unborn.) The 34th amendment of 2015, which legalized same-sex marriage in Ireland, is of course a key part of this progression. Seeing the 8th amendment in 1983 and the 36th amendment in 2018 as the "bookends," as it were, of the current volume, we form a good idea of the immense transformation in Irish life contained in that 35-year period.

The challenges and transformations in the Irish Catholic Church were equally groundbreaking. A slow disentanglement of the nation from the church was signaled in 1972, when the national referendum resulted in the removal from the Irish Constitution of the clause that specified the Catholic church's special relation as the national "guardian of the Faith" (Brown 294). Further indications of Ireland's shift away from the near-theocracy of de Valera's vision included the exponential growth of multi-national popular culture (the meteoric rise of Ireland's own U2 beginning in the early 1980s was part of this), the appearance of clearly secular and indeed anti-Catholic literature (Edna O'Brien's writing long exemplified this, though many other examples accrued), and of course cinematic works, perhaps best illustrated by the film version in 1991 of Roddy Doyle's 1989 novel, *The Commitments* (the subject of Conner's chapter to follow, and the first film, chronologically, treated in the present volume). The modernizing transformations of the church in the wake of Vatican II were also taking hold, although more slowly in Ireland than in much of the rest of the world.

But of far greater impact on the major role of Catholicism in Irish life were the terrible scandals that rocked the Church over the past 30 years, such as the Brendan Smyth case, the Bishop Casey scandal, the Magdalene sisters' revelations, and multiple other sexual abuse scandals. As Louise

1 INTRODUCTION   15

Fuller has pointed out, the ethical reversal that came about after these revelations was such that whereas "previously the church monitored the moral behavior of the state [now] the state was acting as moral policeman in areas that were the church's own domain" (183). The resulting loss of authority in the very areas of sexual morality and family teaching for the church created a vacuum of public moral direction for a society that had traditionally held itself accountable to an institutionally directed code of behavior. The resulting uncertainty is the very terrain that so many Irish films and works of literature examine, from Doyle's *Barrytown Trilogy* to Patrick McCabe's *The Butcher Boy* (novel in 1992, film in 1997) to *Song for a Raggy Boy* (book in 1999, film in 2003). The most poignant and shocking cinematic dramatization of the effect on small village Irish life of clerical pedophilia among other forms of cruel manipulation of the "flock" has been *Calvary* (2014), written and directed by John Michael McDonagh, one of the country's most acclaimed playwrights (see Chap. 12 in this volume). Indeed, it is only in the contemporary period that thoughtful and provocative film studies of Irish religious life have emerged at all. Prior to this time, as Gillespie has noted, "getting a sense of how films reflect Irishness through representations of religion and religious attitudes becomes even more difficult than it is in other aspects of Irish society because of the paucity of motion pictures on the subject" (170). But in the current moment, literature and films that deal with the decline of the Catholic church's authority specifically, and with the overall fragmentation and disunity in spiritual life more generally, have become much more pervasive, as several of the chapters in the present volume attest.

Of course, perhaps the most signal alteration in Irish identity and cultural life over the 30-year period from the 1990s to the present moment is the shift in the political structure of the North, beginning with the Good Friday Agreement of 1998 and continuing in the various fits and starts of power-sharing and devolved government in the decades to follow. Northern Ireland has seen the police barricades, armored vehicles, and British Army presence nearly disappear over this period, a remarkable change to daily life in the North, the region of intense conflict since Independence whose particular culture, one might argue, is yet to be adequately assessed and expressed in both literature and film. Exceptions include not only the impressive oeuvre of Derry-born writer/director Tommy Collins, and, in general, "Troubles" films such as Jim Sheridan's *The Boxer* (1997) and, more recently, the action-thriller *The Foreigner* (2017, Martin Campbell), both of which examine the simmering resentments that pre-dated the Good Friday Accords (1998) and, sadly, have not been extinguished by the coming of peace. Gilbert's film, like those of Collins more generally, is more international than Irish. *Foreigner* is an American-British-Chinese co-production, starring Jackie Chan, Pierce Brosnan, and a mostly Irish cast, with a script adapted from the novel by Stephen Leather. It is similar to the Irish-themed historical representations and interpretations of the great events of the 1920s that established the Republic that dominated Irish film as a whole in the 1990s, especially Neil Jordan's *Michael Collins* (1996) and Ken Roach's *The Wind That Shakes the Barley* (2003). Emerging in an age of nationalist reconsideration, these films, as Gillespie points out, "[foreground] multiplicity as the basis for understanding the social context of the narrative" (215), insisting that unified historical/nationalist narratives almost by definition simplify and obscure the full complexity of Ireland's national story. But Gillespie also argues convincingly that a coherent thread in such films is the decrying of violence as a solution to the national questions: such work, he writes, "underscores the inherent contradictions in supposedly moral individuals taking up physical force, and it suggests the inadequacy of exclusionary thinking in comprehending these antinomies" (220–221).

Finally, among the signal changes in Irish society brought about by the Tiger is the subsequent internationalizing of Irish life and the new multicultural and multi-racial identities the waves of migration to Ireland have wrought, as a country that had long known the unwilling export of its people became, much like all other Western European nations, a net importer. The "new" Irish are not only political refugees, of course, but immigrants looking for a better life, most of whom have re-located from other EU countries and, now post-Brexit, the UK. As Conner discusses in the opening chapter of this book on Roddy Doyle, the emergence in Ireland and in Dublin especially of migrant workers from eastern Europe and China, and of refugee communities from Africa and elsewhere, have wrought in Ireland a heretofore unimagined blending of race, ethnicity, religion, cuisine, music, and language that before the 1980s, the Irish could have hardly conjured in their wildest imaginings.

Doyle's work as a short-story writer and journalist for the Metro Éireann project is exemplary of this newly multicultural Irish identity. Such stories as "The Deportees" include African, Eastern European, American, Russian, and every other nationality Doyle can report that will represent the cultural excitement he sees in Dublin in the wave of the Celtic Tiger, a new Ireland that the novelist lovingly describes:

The Forum was a surprise. Jimmy had walked and driven past it but he'd never seen it. It didn't look like a pub; it was more like a café and, as far as Jimmy was concerned, there were enough of those things in Dublin already. But, once he was inside, it was a real pub, and a good one. Portuguese-looking barman, Spanish-looking lounge-girl, Chinese-looking girl on the stool beside him, good-looking pint settling in front of him, REM's new album on the sound system—sounded good, though maybe a bit too like an REM album—African locals chatting and laughing, Irish locals chatting and laughing. Jimmy tasted his pint. Grand—and just as well, because it wasn't fuckin' cheap. (39)

Such perspectives and representations seek to depict, not a unified Irish identity nor even one that seeks to achieve such unification, but rather a new concept of Irishness that is multiple, polyglot, cosmopolitan, and international (similar, e.g., to Paula Kehoe's *Assimilation* [2013], whose subject is an Irish-Aboriginal culture in Australia).

Many of the works of literature and film discussed in this volume struggle with understanding how these emerging concepts of Irish identity can co-exist with still-powerful ideas of Irishness that remain rooted in long-standing definitions of what makes Irishness so. But in truth, such multiple and contested understandings of the Irish identity in many ways date back to the coming of the Normans and the Vikings, and so the current scene is situated in literally a centuries-long ongoing effort to understand what it means to be Irish and express Irishness. Contemporary Irish film is the latest effort to express and chronicle this fluid and oft-metamorphosing nation and its many elusive identities.

* * *

If this introduction has emphasized a resistance to fixity in contemporary film adaptations' understanding of Irish culture and identity, the same may be said of the following chapters' treatment of textuality itself. Participating in the movement in current adaptation studies to see texts as inherently multiple and unending (see Palmer, 2017), the chapters in this volume establish an analogy between the broadening of local to global audiences in contemporary Irish cinema and extending a focus on "local" or single sources to identifying and exploring the multiple and hybrid "scripts" that undergird adaptations (see Leitch). The contributors explore contemporary Irish cinema in conversation with multiple texts, histories, and audiences, showing how new perspectives emerge from a broad view of the stretched canvas of sources that can determine or influence these texts. Marc C. Conner establishes this volume's emphasis on a diverse contemporary Irish arts culture resistant to summary and cliché in his study of *The Commitments*. Julieann Veronica Ulin follows in Chap. 3 with the analysis of the "cross-directional flows and exchanges across multiple platforms" that inform another popular Irish musical film, John Carney's *Sing Street*. Similarly focused on a wide range of sources, Lisabeth C. Buchelt shows in her chapter how multiple viewpoints and texts, as well as multicultural sensibilities, combine to create the rich animated visual landscape of *The Secret of Kells*.

Several of the chapters contained herein combine discussion of the uncanniness attending to intermedial adaptation (modern drama, e.g., adapted to contemporary cinema), challenging conventional views of modern literature (in particular, Yeats, Beckett, and Joyce). Matthew J. Fee's exploration of Mary McGuckian's *Words Upon the Window Pane* exemplifies how gender conventions are recast in contemporary cinematic language, as McGuckian's film adapting W.B. Yeats establishes female agency in a newly imagined landscape. Eyal Amiran also explores shifts in agency, as the physical "Mouth" in Beckett's staged *Not I* is transposed to image in the film adaptation and subject to Neil Jordan's radical cinematic montage. Further investigating the possibilities of adapting what has conventionally been seen as an unfilmable modern literature, Michael Patrick Gillespie surveys a surprising 2004 documentary seeking to re-present an iconic work of fiction, reinforcing the multiplicity of Joyce's *Ulysses*.

The "immense transformation of Irish life" referenced earlier appears as a central theme in many of the chapters that follow. Nicole R. McClure's essay on "bad da's," for example, links the power of textual reprise in adaptation with a revisionary look at fatherhood in Neil Jordan's *Breakfast on Pluto*. Kate Costello-Sullivan and Julie Grossman similarly draw an analogy between the migration of text to film in Colm Tóibín's novel and John Crowley's film *Brooklyn* and the story's interest in movement and shifts in identity brought to bear by change. And Eamonn Jordan's chapter on the work of John Michael and Martin McDonagh explores the adaptation of religion into contemporary representations of redemption and self-sacrifice that reflect a world haunted by traditions but acutely aware of a present that feels inoculated from the solace that religion provided in Ireland's past.

Several essays explore in particular the tensions that arise in contemporary Irish films' adaptation of history. Chapters by Lesley Brill on Frears's *The Program*, R. Barton Palmer on Abrahamson's *What Richard Did*, and Tara Harney-Mahajan on Sheridan's *The Secret Scripture* study these films' interest in engaging and conversing, often collaborating, with source texts about real events and the political or cultural uses to which representations may be put. In the case of Jim Sheridan, as Harney-Mahajan explores, an equivocal desire to ameliorate subject matter through representation comes inevitably into conflict with the costs of so doing when history and real trauma are adapted. These films' focus on scandal and unstable power structures foreground the complexity and multiplicity of textual, individual, and multicultural identities in Ireland that its contemporary cinema has highlighted and brought creatively into relief.

WORKS CITED

Barton, Ruth. *Irish Cinema in the Twenty-First Century*. Manchester: Manchester University Press, 2019.

Brown, Terence. *Ireland: A Social and Cultural History, 1922–2002*. New York: HarperCollins, 2004.

Dáil Éireann Debate 23 April 1993. https://www.oireachtas.ie/en/debates/debate/dail/1993-04-29/11/.

Dáil Éireann Debate 25 May 1997. https://www.oireachtas.ie/en/debates/debate/dail/1997-04-08/36/.

de Valera, Eamon. 1943 Radio address. "On Language & the Irish Nation." https://en.wikipedia.org/wiki/The_Ireland_That_We_Dreamed_Of#:~:text=%22On%20Language%20%26%20the%20Irish%20Nation%22%20was%20the,it%2C%20or%20the%20%22comely%20maidens%22%20speech%2C%0Aa%20misquotation.

Gillespie, Michael Patrick. *The Myth of an Irish Cinema: Approaching Irish Themed Films*. Syracuse: Syracuse University Press, 2009.

Holohan, Conn. *Cinema on the Periphery: Contemporary Irish and Spanish Film*. Dublin: Irish Academic Press, 2010.

Leitch, Thomas. *The History of American Literature on Film*. New York: Bloomsbury, 2019.

O'Brien, Edna. *Mother Ireland: a Memoir*. New York: Plume, 1999.

O'Dowd, Niall. *A New Ireland: How Europe's Most Conservative Country Became Its Most Liberal*. New York: Skyhorse Publishing, 2020.

Palmer, R. Barton. "Continuation, Adaptation Studies, and the Never-Finished Text." *Adaptation and Visual Culture: Images, Texts, and Their Multiple*

Worlds, eds. Julie Grossman and R. Barton Palmer. London: Palgrave Macmillan, 2017. 73–99.

Palmer, R. Barton and Marc C. Conner, eds. *Screening Modern Irish Fiction and Drama*. London: Palgrave Macmillan, 2016.

Pettitt, Lance. *Screening Ireland: Film and Television Representation*. Manchester: Manchester University Press, 2000.

Rockett, Kevin. *Ten Years After: The Irish Film Board 1993–2003*. Dublin: The Irish Film Board, 2003.

Screen Ireland. http://www.screenireland.ie/.

Seanad Debate 18 December 1997. https://www.oireachtas.ie/en/debates/debate/seanad/1997-12-18/8/.

Selznick, Barbara Wilinsky. "Europudding: International Co-Productions and Televisual Representation." *Spectator* 20 no. 2 (2000): 53–62.

Smith, Iain Robert. *The Hollywood Meme: Transnational Adaptations in World Cinema*. Edinburgh: Edinburgh University Press, 2017.

CHAPTER 2

Filming Global Ireland: Roddy Doyle's
The Commitments

Marc C. Conner

One of the iconic lines from Alan Parker's 1991 film *The Commitments* occurs when Jimmy Rabbitte, the visionary and manager for the Dublin soul-band of that name, informs his band members that they in fact bear a striking similarity to the African-American musicians who created the genre of soul music. When Dean, the sax player, asks him, after viewing a vibrant James Brown video and being told, "That's what ya got to measure up to, lads," "Do ya not think, uh, well, we're like, maybe we're a little *white* for that kind of thing?" Jimmy responds: "Do ya not get it lads? The Irish are the blacks of Europe. And Dubliners are the blacks of Ireland. And the northside Dubliners are the blacks of Dublin. So say it once, say it loud, I'm black, and I'm proud." The moment evokes one of the film's main arguments: that the downtrodden, impoverished, disenfranchised condition of the Irish, particularly the status of the Dublin youth of the film, is akin to the condition and status of African-Americans. The film's scrupulous attention to the poverty, the unemployment, and the poor

M. C. Conner (✉)
Skidmore College, Saratoga Springs, NY, USA
e-mail: mconner@skidmore.edu

© The Author(s), under exclusive license to Springer Nature Switzerland AG 2022
M. C. Conner et al. (eds.), *Screening Contemporary Irish Fiction and Drama*, Palgrave Studies in Adaptation and Visual Culture, https://doi.org/10.1007/978-3-031-04568-4_2

21

housing conditions of its characters reinforces this argument, and so the fledgling group turns to soul music as an expression to which they can make some legitimate claim, based on their shared experience of being an oppressed people. Seen in this way, "blackness" is a synecdoche for suffering and not having a foothold in society—to be disempowered and frustrated economically and socially is what it means to be black, and the Irish youth share this experience and hence can turn with credibility and an almost racial legitimacy to soul music as an outlet and expression of their frustrations and their aspirations.

Now, of course such a definition of being African-American is rife with problems, and it would be an easy exercise to deny and denounce such an identification of blackness with poverty and suffering (to say nothing of the easy appropriation of an African-American art form by white European youth). One could start with Zora Neale Hurston's and Ralph Ellison's rejection of all definitions of the black experience that focus only on suffering.[1] But such an exercise would miss the opportunity to explore the more interesting claims being made in the film about race, gender, class, and culture across, not just Dublin or Ireland, but the entire globe. For ultimately what Parker aims to express in *The Commitments* is a society in Dublin that is remarkably isolated and cut off from the global scene, but that is showing the early signs of stirring into a globalism, both artistically and economically, that foreshadows the remarkable transformation of Irish culture in the very decade that would follow the film's release.

For the Ireland emerging in the very period of Doyle's novel and Parker's film, to say nothing of the Ireland of the twenty-first century, would be in many ways unrecognizable from the Ireland depicted in the novel and the film. Diverse, polymorphous, cosmopolitan, modernized economically and culturally, the Ireland of the twenty-first century would both glory in and face the unique challenges of global diversity and multiculturalism. As Terence Brown writes in his monumental study of Irish cultural change, *Ireland: A Social and Cultural History, 1922–2002*:

---

[1] See Hurston's 1928 essay, "How it Feels to be Colored Me," and Ellison's seminal 1963–1964 rebuttal of Irving Howe's reductive characterization of African-American life, "The World and the Jug." In 2008 Charles Johnson published "The End of the Black American Narrative," in which he forcefully argued that "the old black American narrative of pervasive victimization" does not adequately describe African-American life: although of course injustice and suffering persist, it "simply is no longer the case that the essence of black American life is racial victimization and disenfranchisement" (37–38).

2 FILMING GLOBAL IRELAND: RODDY DOYLE'S *THE COMMITMENTS* 23

"In the early 1980s a sense developed among social commentators and analysts that the end of the 1970s was the end of an era in Ireland, and this view may have reflected an emerging public consensus. It was felt that the period inaugurated by Sean Lemass in the late 1950s had somehow drawn to a close." Brown goes on to ascribe this sense of transformation as a crisis of self-identity for Ireland: "the underlying Irish problem was the lack of a satisfactory, workable self-image after the economic and social change of the 1960s and 1970s had destroyed the once-serviceable version of the national identity of Ireland as Gaelic, Catholic, and Republican" (Brown 318–319). *The Commitments* serves as a harbinger of the New Ireland that is about to emerge, and indeed helps us see the needs and causes of that transformation within the world of the film.

The film is based on the novel of the same name by Roddy Doyle, which appeared just a few years earlier in 1987. This was Doyle's first novel, and its vivacity, energy, and iconoclasm gave some indication that more exciting work was on the horizon for the author. In the years to follow Doyle would emerge as one of the most successful and innovative fiction writers not just in Ireland but on the global literary scene. Just in the years between the novel and the film, Doyle would publish two more novels that would join *The Commitments* as his "Barrytown Trilogy," three novels all set in the fictional region of northside Dublin that depict the struggles and triumphs of that working-class community as the great transformations in Irish and global culture begin to happen all around them. He followed this trilogy with *Paddy Clarke Ha Ha Ha* in 1993, which would win the Booker Prize that year, announcing Doyle's arrival as a world-class novelist.[2] In the years to follow, Doyle published several other novels, branching out from his themes and topics from the early books for a broader historical spectrum and increasingly experimental fictional styles.[3]

Then beginning in 2000, Doyle began writing his *Metro Éireann* stories, depicting the transformations in Dublin as an influx of immigrants

---

[2] *Paddy Clarke* announced a new direction in Doyle's writing, leaving behind the Rabbitte family that had been the focus of the Trilogy. "There are no more Rabbittes," Doyle announced, "I've eaten them" (White 5).

[3] Brian Donnelly asserts that *A Star Called Henry* in 1999 "marked a radical departure from the world and the themes that had interested Roddy Doyle in his works up to its publication," mainly the Rabbitte novels that "portray aspects of contemporary, working-class, urban life without the obligation to explore more fully the bleaker consequences of much of that reality" (28, 20).

and new cultures arrives to participate in the Celtic Tiger, Ireland's remarkable economic boom at the start of the century. In these stories—the first eight of which were collected in *The Deportees*, published in 2008—Doyle engages with the newly multicultural Ireland and tries to portray the clashes as well as the opportunities for community that the new Ireland brings. As *Metro Éireann* editor Chinedu Onyejelem describes these contributions, "To us and many of our readers, Roddy's writings in *Metro Éireann* are more than work of fiction. They are shaped by and reflect events within multicultural Ireland—and continue to truly help us in our continued pursuit to achieve our mission, to be a channel through which the diverse peoples of Ireland will inform, challenge, understand and learn to respect each other" (Metro). I will say more about these remarkable stories, and particularly the ways in which the title story signifies upon both the novel and film *The Commitments*, at the end of this essay.[4]

Doyle's novel and Parker's film share a number of aspirations, not least to reject the confining narratives and tropes of so-called traditional Ireland and replace them with highly contemporary, pop- and youth-culture-based, revisionist perspectives on Ireland. Kevin Rockett has argued that this is one of the signal achievements of the film, to shift representations of Irishness from the rural countryside to the urban city and especially to representations of contemporary Dublin, which had been rare in Irish cinema until the 1980s. "In part this was a response by a new generation of film-makers to the changes in Irish society, most notably increased urbanization and its cultural expression, which made it apparently quite different to its rural literary predecessors" ("Cinema and Irish Literature," 556). Parker's film, Rockett claims, "signaled a very different type of Irish urban sensibility" than other contemporary treatments of Dublin. It shows "a cosmopolitan Dublin" with a "vibrancy" and "cultural hybridity" that was "marked by a modern secular humanism and … a sense of exuberance and pleasure, and delight in their Irishness, if not through place, then through language" (557). The representation of working-class Irish communities as somehow conveying the new authentic Irishness would subsequently be seen in "many literary, cinematic and television representations of urban Ireland" (557).

Importantly, Doyle's novel accomplishes this through an aesthetic of absence: throughout the novel, one struggles to find conventional

---

[4] For a helpful reading of Doyle's efforts to engage new racial registers in Ireland in the *Metro Éireann* stories, see Reddy.

representations of Irishness. There are no pastoral scenes, no immigrant narratives, no idealized family gatherings (although there is a rough camaraderie in the Rabbitte family that is an alternative to the sentimental presentations of family in traditional Irish film), and especially no sign whatsoever of the Catholic church. Rockett describes this as an absence of "particularity," arguing that the northside urban settings are "devoid of history or memory, an unremarkable place which has the sameness of other nameless working-class estates anywhere else in the world" (558).[5] Perhaps the most striking demonstration of this aesthetic of absence comes in the novel's engagement with music. All the musical elements of the book come from the African-American soul tradition; there is not even a hint of traditional Irish music in the book—not a fiddle, uillean pipe, bodhran, or harp anywhere in sight.

As some critics have pointed out, this aesthetics of absence is characteristic of Doyle's style at least in the Barrytown novels. Doyle's novel demonstrates a disregard for the usual novelistic means of cultivating a sense of place—he simply leaves out the details that would typically lead to a composition of place. Caramine White describes this as "an unobtrusive literary style" that uses "common, everyday language, which includes a great deal of profanity and slang, little description of any sort, and almost no authorial commentary" (3). As a result, the main content of Doyle's early novels is speech, a carefully rendered north Dublin vernacular, primarily of the youth culture that Doyle knew well from his years as a teacher at the Greendale Community School in Kilbarrack on the northside of Dublin, which became his fictional Barrytown. White explains that this is key to understanding how his novels function: "understanding the characters' speech is crucial because there is so little description or authorial commentary. The novels at times read like screenplays" (9). Doyle himself has stated that "I deliberately just let the words do the talking and it didn't seem necessary to describe places" (9). Or as Noel McFarlane put it in his review of *The Van*, the third novel in the Barrytown trilogy, "No significant effort is expended on physical description of character or locale.... There were unkind thoughts that this department was being left to some cinematographer fellow in California with dark specs and a ponytail"

---

[5] Julieann Ulin argues that in each of the Barrytown novels and in their film adaptations, the characters "repeatedly resist their representations by an exclusively internal Irish cultural framework, instead selectively employing music and film as a vehicle for self-definition, communication and community-formation" (192–193).

26   M. C. CONNER

(McFarlane, quoted in White 3–4). Although Alan Parker sports neither dark specs nor a ponytail, this is a remarkably apt summary of the challenge that Parker faced when he turned to adapt Doyle's novel to film. How would Parker render the sense of place, the *mise en scene*, that Doyle's novel connotes? What filmic techniques could he use to convey the sense of Dublin in the late 1980s, both in its own current particularity and to show it as a harbinger of the near future, a city on the cusp of remarkable change?[6]

When Parker approached the book to render it in film, he faced the challenge of showing a shift from traditional Irish tropes to a new concept of Irishness that abandoned all such representations. In the film's opening scene, Jimmy is making his way through the Smithfield Market on the northside of Dublin, a scene that would readily conjure up traditional Irish imagery. And Parker shows the horse traders, the street balladeer, and the fiddle player as Jimmy walks through the crowd, oblivious to and uncaring of these elements. Jimmy's focus is on swapping cassette tapes, underground T-shirts, and videos to a youth culture that could care less about throwback Irish imagery. Similarly, when Jimmy is holding the auditions for the band in his family home, this scene is quickly described in the novel (not even a full page [21]), whereas Parker amply depicts the various musicians who show up (a full 6:25 of film time), a number of whom offer traditional Irish instruments, vocals, and performances. Jimmy's scorn for this traditional culture is shown by his preference for those whose influences bear no resemblance to this antiquated culture—particularly when Joey "The Lips" Fagan appears and presents a litany of soul influences that stands as a kind of alternative cultural authority: "Screamin' Jay Hawkins, Martha Reeves, Sam Cooke—poor Sam—Otis Redding—may the Lord have mercy on his sweet soul—Joe Tex, the Four Tops, Stevie Wonder—he was only eleven, a pup—Wilson Pickett." Joey explains that he has come to Dublin to bring soul to the Irish because "The Lord sent me. The

---

[6] Doyle's fidelity to the highly particular lived experience of the north Dublin world marks him as in the vein of Patrick Kavanagh's famous concept of "parochialism" as opposed to being "provincial." Kavanagh stated of Ireland and Irish writers, "the provincial has no mind of his own; he does not trust what his eyes see until he has heard what the metropolis—towards which his eyes are turned—has to say on any subject. This runs through all activities. The parochial mentality on the other hand is never in any doubt about the social and artistic validity of his parish. All great civilizations are based on parochialism—Greek, Israelite, English.... In Ireland we are inclined to be provincial not parochial, for it requires a great deal of courage to be parochial."

Lord blows my trumpet." "See," he continues, "the Lord told me the Irish brothers needed some soul. Well, Ed Winchell, a Baptist reverend on Lenox Avenue in Harlem, told me. But the Lord told him to tell me. He said the Irish brothers wouldn't be shootin' the arses off each other if they had soul." In the novel, it is at this moment that Jimmy realizes "that everything was going to be alright. The Commitments were going to be. They had Joey the Lips Fagan. And that man had enough soul for all of them. He had God too" (26). In effect, "soul," and its claim even upon "God," resides in Joey, in his true affinity for Soul music, and in his spiritual genealogy with African-American street culture.[7]

Perhaps the most concise expression of this rejection of traditional Irish trappings for contemporary Irish reality occurs when the band is posing for its publicity poster photo. The photographer suggests a better backdrop than the alleyway lane and abandoned tenements Jimmy has chosen—"wouldn't the Custom House be a better background?"—and Jimmy responds, "I'm not going for a bleedin' tourist poster, I'm goin' for urban decay!" In the novel, the group photograph occurs almost as an afterthought after the band's first performance in the church hall. Here Joey is the centerpiece of the photograph, and there is no emphasis on the larger Dublin scene and idea that surrounds them:

> Joey The Lips sat on a chair. The Commitments kneeled and stood around him. Bernie sat on his knee. Imelda lay in front of him, leaning on an elbow, chin in her hand, hair in her eyes. Natalie did the same, in the opposite direction. Jimmy, Mickah, the caretaker and Mrs. Foster stood at the sides, like football managers and magic-sponge men. That way they all fitted. (113)

This is an important contrast from the novel. Whereas Doyle is focused on the group and its own self-obsession, Parker seeks in the film to broaden the scope of the story, and to show how the group is emblematic of the larger context of Dublin, and ultimately of the larger surrounding world.[8]

---

[7] In Doyle's novel, Joey delivers this full speech just to Jimmy (25–26); but Parker splits this into two scenes: the first just with Jimmy, but the second, beginning with "See," he speaks to the band as a whole. This is part of Parker's effort to explore the implications of the soul affinity with the larger group, not just with Jimmy alone.

[8] In the documentary "The Making of Alan Parker's Film The Commitments," Parker states: "In the end it's about young kids who use music to get out of the world that they're in, in order to give them something else, give them a hope and a dream. And that's pretty relevant wherever you are in the world, I think" ("The Making").

28 M. C. CONNER

This effort to show the distance between traditional Irish film elements and the world that the young people in The Commitments know is perhaps best evidenced in one of the film's most iconic moments, a brief scene that does not appear in Doyle's novel but was created by Parker just for the movie. About one-third into the film, Jimmy goes to visit Bernie to find out why she has been missing rehearsals. Parker shows the impoverished life in the northside housing projects like the Ballymun Towers, a gritty Dublin realism that illustrates what the young people are trying to express and to escape.[9] As Jimmy is waiting for the lift to take him up to Bernie's floor, a young boy is also waiting, with an old, tired, half-white horse. Jimmy exclaims, "Hey! Yer not takin' that into the lift?" And the boy replies, "I have to. The stairs would kill him." It is a comic moment, of course, but at the same time it shows the persistence of the old Irish ways—few things could be more discordant than a horse in this urban setting, and yet the horse is there, almost like the old Irish traditions that cannot quite be gotten rid of. This scene is revisited a year later in the Jim Sheridan/Mike Newell Irish film, Into the West, in which the young traveler boys living in the Ballymun projects bring a magnificent white stallion into their tenement flat; the horse turns out to be a mythic creature that will reunite the boys with their Traveler past and their deceased mother, and by extension, with the spiritual essence of the authentic Ireland. The two films talk to each other, and Into the West in many ways was made possible by the example of The Commitments, which showed how the traditional trappings of Irish film were no longer available in the easy manner of the past but needed to be reworked and reconceived for a legitimate film expression by the late twentieth century.[10]

Consistently the film is faced with this challenge of rendering place and context for a novel that blithely abandons any such effort. This becomes

[9] It is important to note that although the tenement scenes, here and elsewhere, do show the reality of grinding Dublin poverty, they are also filled with energetic children who are running, biking, skateboarding, playing, jumping; in short, Parker clearly aims to show both the impoverished conditions as well as the positive energy and potential of the young people in Dublin at the time. There is a sense of incipient energy about to burst forth in creative and meaningful expressions.

[10] Michael Gillespie discusses The Commitments in the context of working-class Irish identity, and Into the West as an example of films focusing on reconstructions of the Irish family. But the connections between the two films are pronounced, especially in the latter film's "artistically complex explorations of family identity in contemporary Ireland" and its significance for "exploring the range of Irishness that films can convey" (160–161).

rather contentious in the way Parker decides to portray the presence of the Irish Catholic church in the film. Whereas in Doyle's novel the Catholic Church seems wholly absent from Irish life, Parker reinserts the Church in ways that are alternatingly humorous and cynical, and that again suggest a defining Irish characteristic giving way to a contemporary reality that is strikingly different from what has come before. In a brief segue scene, Parker depicts Natalie and Imelda walking out of mass and talking about the band and their new celebrity. This suggests that the meaning the Church promises to provide is shifting to the meaning provided by the band—certainly a telling interpretation of how the band functions in both novel and film. Another scene, also unique to the film, shows Steven and Jimmy in church as Steven practices on the organ. He is playing "A Whiter Shade of Pale" by Procol Harum, and as they talk about its lyrics and music, Jimmy exclaims, "Great intro, huh? They nicked it from Marvin Gaye," and Steven retorts, "HE nicked it from Bach!" This is a complex signification on the musical argument of the film: Parker suggests that soul music actually traces part of its lineage to European classical music, all in the context of sacred/church music. At that moment Father Molloy appears and remarks on the "very peculiar lyric," "One of sixteen vestal virgins / Leaving for the coast"—a moment of humor as the three young men seem to share an understanding that the strict, censorial world of the Catholic church is evolving to be able to accommodate the spiritual possibilities of new musics and vocabularies emerging from the global world.[11]

This shared understanding is reinforced in a later scene in which Steven goes to confession. He admits to the lustful thoughts he is having about the girls in the band, and then states that "when I studied I used to sing hymns, but now I'm always humming 'When a Man Loves a Woman' by Marvin Gaye." At that point Father Molloy corrects him: "Percy Sledge. It was Percy Sledge did that particular song. I have the album." Here again the fact that the priest, in the moment of spiritual counsel, is teaching the penitent the details of soul music suggests that the aptly named soul music is filling the need for spiritual meaning that the Catholic church—at least in its repressive, authoritarian, censorial mode that still

---

[11] Ironically, this scene occurs in St. Francis Xavier's Church on Gardiner Street on Dublin's northside. This church is the setting for James Joyce's great short story *Grace* from Dubliners (1914), perhaps Joyce's most vicious satire on the hypocrisy and materialism of the Catholic Church. It may also be worth noting that Parker changes Steven's name from the novel, where his name is James Clifford.

30   M. C. CONNER

dominated Ireland in the 1980s—is no longer providing. And there is evidence in the novel that Doyle shared something of this view: the only mentions of religious life in the novel are references to the "folk mass choir" that some of the characters used to sing in, whereas now they sing in The Commitments: "Imelda, Natalie and Bernie could sing though. They'd been in the folk mass choir when they were in school but that, they knew now, hadn't really been singing" (34). This shift from an orthodox church choir to seeing themselves as what Jimmy describes as "the saviors of soul" is a key point of emphasis in Parker's film.[12]

Yet these elements of religious fusion and expansion in the film were not pleasing to Doyle. He felt they introduced elements of religious life that would not have been apparent in the world of 1980s Dublin youth culture:

> One thing in The Commitments film which made me uncomfortable was the religious scenes and holy statues and such. The confession scene, very funny lines, but it annoyed me—I didn't write that scene—you know, where he goes in and starts talking about the temptation of women and the soul music and the priest contradicts him....It's funny, but it annoyed me. That kid would not have gone to confession. Kids do not go to confession anymore....None of those kids in the film would have gone near a confession box. (White 34)

This is an odd objection from Doyle. To be sure, he is chronicling the period when the Catholic Church's cultural and political authority was beginning to recede, and the relation of the younger generation to that religious authority was undergoing a profound change. This had begun in the 1970s, as the transformations of Vatican II became apparent in Ireland and as a number of religious challenges were worked out in Irish society. In the Papal visit to Ireland in 1979, in the abortion amendment debates of the early 1980s, and in the divorce referendum issue of 1985–1986, the contest between a conservative Church associated with traditional values and a questioning, if not yet a rejection, of that church particularly by the younger generations had begun. As Brown describes, "despite these

---

[12] Importantly, "When a Man Loves a Woman" is referred to in the novel as one of the songs the new band will be performing—accurately attributed to Percy Sledge (p.28). The song is not performed in the film.

compelling indications of the social influence of a conservative Catholicism still vigorously at work in the country, the process of secularization, observed in the 1960s and 70s, was continuing into the 1980s." Brown quotes sociologist Liam Ryan who wrote in 1983, "A picture emerges of a people largely believing in God and in the Church, but in possession of a belief which had little impact, not just on the wider world of business and politics, but also in many areas of private morality" (Brown 339–340). Whereas Doyle's novel makes the Catholic Church conspicuous by its total absence—an absence that indeed seems extreme for the Dublin of this period—Parker works to more carefully chronicle this important element in the decade of transition for Catholicism that was the 1980s. Parker seems to be interested in portraying a thicker understanding of Dublin culture at this time, and in showing an evolving relationship between the characters and, not the Catholic Church only but also, the roles of the spiritual world in the lives of young people desperate for meaning and significance. This is ultimately what the soul music offers to the group, after all, as one scholar asserts: "Parker seems to suggest that American soul music may foster more reverence, devotion, and inspiration, than religion has among the Irish" (Kunz 56).[13]

In this, both Doyle's novel and, to an even greater extent, Parker's film share in the effort to render Irish identity in greater complexity than it had heretofore seen in Irish film treatments, and particularly to reject simplistic or singular conceptions of Irishness that had tended to dominate Irish film up to the late 1900s. Gillespie has argued that the defining feature of Irish film in the late twentieth century—almost dating to Parker's *The Commitments*—has been precisely to render this increasingly complex presentation of Irish identity. Gillespie argues against "the conception of Irish identity as a monolithic temperament," when in fact "Irishness as a stable category finds itself under assault" (xii) due to the very social and historical pressures that Parker's film presents:

---

[13] One wonders if Doyle's own well-documented antipathy to the Church colors his sense of the Dublin world here. Just a few years after publishing *The Commitments*, Doyle became quite involved in the mid-1990s second divorce referendum: "It basically was the Catholic Church against everyone else. It was this insistence that if you're Irish, you're white and you're Catholic as well, and if you're not both of those things then you're not fully Irish.... I felt that it was a real fight, a fight for the future of my children and the future of the country"(White 38). Doyle's view of the Catholic Church as an enemy in a war may well influence his desire to write the Church out of the spiritual domain of his characters.

32   M. C. CONNER

> Rapidly changing demographics, emerging social concerns, and shifting economic assets often make the most accurate representations of contemporary Irish life the ones that are least dependent on conventional Irish cultural markers....To complicate circumstances, the institutions that have traditionally defined "Irishness" are changing or becoming obsolete. This condition of flux does not mean that viewers should cease to take Irishness into consideration when interpreting specific films, but it does demand a refinement of one's point of view. Recognizing that mutability, fragmentation, and pluralism have led to a range of diverse entities, all valid representations of Irishness, negates the impulse for a monolithic perception and calls for an acknowledgement of multiple perspectives applicable to the term. (xii–xiii)

The litany of key themes and modes in Irish film that Gillespie sees as undergoing a profound revision, questioning, and complicating are all present to a greater or lesser extent in *The Commitments*: the strong presence of the working class, the rejection of a simplified and nostalgic rural story, the challenges to singular concepts of the family, and questioning of religious beliefs, all find expression in Parker's film, indeed to a greater extent than they do in Doyle's novel, though the novel provides the essential framework for the film.

In this, Parker's film participates in a more far-reaching unsettling of "Irishness" that Gillespie sees in Irish film more generally and indeed in Irish culture, as I have argued above. Far from presenting a unified, simplified, nostalgic idea of Irishness, Irish film over the past three decades "undermines an overarching sense of Irishness" (xiv). This reflects the fact that contemporary Ireland reveals "the instability of national identity in a country undergoing rapid social, cultural, and economic changes" and hence the most representative Irish films in fact "replace a monolithic sense of Irishness with an awareness of uncertainty" (17). It is not too much to say that Parker's film is the first that accomplishes this rejection of unified Irishness in favor of a cultural presentation of, as Gillespie describes the films of the early 2000s, "an Irish environment devoid of Irishness" (67).

However, it is important to note that whereas Gillespie suggests that many contemporary Irish films struggle to replace the void caused by the absence of traditional markers of Irishness—"exchanging its distinctive parochialism for a vapid cosmopolitanism" (68)—Parker resists such an extreme evacuation of meaning. In place of the traditional Irish tropes, he follows Doyle in filling this void with the meaning-filled expressions of

2 FILMING GLOBAL IRELAND: RODDY DOYLE'S *THE COMMITMENTS* 33

African-American soul music. Doyle's concept in the novel is extraordinary: to take a group of disaffected Dublin youth and show their affinity with African-American culture, and for that culture to provide, at least for a short period, the meaningful expression of their lives and indeed of their very nation. Doyle's choice of songs in the novel and his means of conveying the band's relation to those songs is of signal importance. The defining song of The Commitments in the novel is "Night Train," the James Brown signature song that was central to Brown's live performances. In Brown's performances he would replace the lyrics of the song with his own shouted-out list of the cities in which his band was performing on that particular tour (Smith 95, 115). Doyle makes "Night Train" the most popular song that The Commitments perform in their concerts, with the local crowd responding with glee when the band shouts out, not the American cities from Brown's performances but, the all-too-local place-names of north Dublin that their audience alone would recognize:

> Deco let the other Commitments go on without him. The important part was coming.
> Dublin Soul was about to be born....
> Deco growled: —STARTIN' OFF IN CONNOLLY—
> The train in the hall stopped as they waited to hear what was going to follow that.
> Deco was travelling north, by DART.
> —MOVIN' ON OU' TO KILLESTER—
> They laughed. This was great. They pushed up to the stage.
> —HARMONSTOWN RAHENY—
> They cheered.
> —AN' DON'T FORGET KILBARRACK—THE HOME O' THE BLUES—
> Dublin Soul had been delivered.
> —HOWTH JUNCTION BAYSIDE—
> —THEN ON OU' TO SUTTON WHERE THE RICH FOLKS LIVE—
> OH YEAH—
> NIGH' TRAIN—
> His voice went but he got it back.
> —EASY TO BONK YOUR FARE—
> Wild, happy cheers.
> —NIGH' TRAIN—
> AN ALSATIAN IN EVERY CARRIAGE—
> NIGH' TRAIN—
> LOADS O' SECURITY GUARDS—

NIGH' TRAIN—
LAYIN' INTO YOUR MOT AT THE BACK—
NIGH' TRAIN—
GETTING' SLAGGED BY YOUR MATES—
NIGH' TRAIN—
GETTING' CHIPS FROM THE CHINESE CHIPPER—
OH NIGH' TRAIN—
CARRIES ME HOME—
THE NIGH' TRAIN—
CARRIES ME HOME—(105–106)

In place of Brown's list of U.S. cities, The Commitments proffer a cartography of Dublin's northside, following the DART line from the city center all the way out to Sutton, the last stop before Howth and the seaside community of golf courses and country clubs that is a different world from the Dublin northside city-dwellers. And the central stop, Kilbarrack, is where Roddy Doyle was born; hence the title "the home o' the blues" carries additional signification, connecting Doyle's very local home area to the genesis of the novel itself.

As we have seen, for Doyle the "local" is at the very heart of his aesthetic and even his sense of vocation as an author. Deco and the group stumble upon the inspiring genius of the local in one of their early rehearsals, as Deco slips in a local Dublin reference in the middle of the Jimmy Ruffin song, "What Becomes of the Brokenhearted?":

—I'LL BE SEARCHIN' EVERYWHERE—
JUST TO FIND SOMEONE TO CARE—
I'VE BEEN LOOKIN' EVERY DAY—
I KNOW I'M GOIN' TO FIND A WAY—
I WILL FIND A WAY SOMEHOW—
They all stopped. The record faded quickly there. They didn't know how they were going to end it.
Deco kept singing.
—I'LL SEARCH FOR YOU DOWN ON THE DOCKS
I'LL WAIT UNDER CLERY'S CLOCK—
They cheered.
Deco stopped.
—Wha' was tha' abou'? Jimmy asked.
—A bit o' local flavor, said Deco.
—Tha' was deadly, said Derek.
—Yeh said we were goin' to make the words more Dubliny, said Deco. (54)

2 FILMING GLOBAL IRELAND: RODDY DOYLE'S *THE COMMITMENTS* 35

The entire band immediately approves of Deco's addition. "It's good," Billy says, and James echoes, "Very soul," to which Joey affirms, "Soul is the people's music." There is an authenticity to the soul music, and its organic connection to the people, less through its identification with African-American culture than its northside Dublin particularity.

This helps address the fact that the band only performs covers of other songs—they do not write their own material. Midway through the novel Outspan laments, "It's a pity we don't do anny songs of our own, isn't it?" Joey intones, "A song belongs to no man…The Lord holds copyright on all songs." But Derek gives the more meaningful response: "We have the Dublin bits," to which Outspan replies, "True" (82).

All of this is left out of the film. Parker does not include the song "Night Train"; the band does not add "Dublin bits" to the songs they do perform—indeed, Parker chooses a very different set of songs for the film than what Doyle focuses on in the novel. Parker's goal in the film is to capture the same essential northside Dublin particularity, without sacrificing a more universal and broad-ranging vision that is not lost on anyone not of the Kilbarrack world. We have looked at several examples of this already: the opening scene at the market square; the horse-in-the-lift scene at the housing development; the scene of Jimmy visiting Bernie that shows the desperate straits of many working-class Irish; and the more expanded scenes of the Irish church and its changing role in Irish life. One of the most important moments of this occurs when Jimmy explains to the fledgling band what "soul" is really about. In Doyle's novel, the group gathers in Joey's mother's garage, to rehearse, but also to hear Jimmy's "lectures" on the true meaning of soul. Here Jimmy explains that soul and sex are intertwined: "The rhythm o' soul is the rhythm o' ridin'….The rhythm o' ridin' is the rhythm o' soul" (36). He then explains that the politics of soul is that of the working person: "Soul is the politics o' the people….Our people. —Soul is the rhythm o' sex. It's the rhythm o' the factory too. The workin' man's rhythm. Sex an' factory." He concludes by asserting that institutional politics is meaningless to soul: "Party politics… means nothin' to the wokin' people. Nothin'. —Fuck all. Soul is the politics o' the people….The Labour Party doesn't have soul. Fianna fuckin' Fail doesn't have soul. The Workers' Party ain't got soul. The Irish people—no.—The Dublin people—fuck the rest o' them. —The people o' Dublin, our people, remember need soul. We've got soul" (39–40). Here the politics, the very Dublin particularity, the sexual drive, and the music all come together in a single expression by Jimmy.

Parker preserves the essential conjoining of soul with sex and with the rhythm of the factory; but he abandons the tighter connection to Dublin, and especially to the particularities of Irish politics. But in order to retain that connection to Dublin locale, he shifts this scene to the group riding on the DART at night, presumably through the very station stops that Deco vocalizes in the live versions of "Night Train" in the novel. Jimmy begins by prescribing the music the group should not and should listen to as they begin their immersion in soul: "I want ya on a strict diet o' soul. James Brown for the growls, Otis Redding for the moans, Smokey Robinson for the whines, and Aretha for the whole lot put together." He then denies that "soul is sex," but clarifies that "the rhythm o' soul is the rhythm o' ridin'." He goes on: "Soul is the rhythm o' sex, and it's the rhythm o' the factory too. The workin' man's rhythm." But he then explains that even though soul is "basic and simple," it is also "honest": "There's no fuckin' bullshit. It sticks its neck out and says it straight from the heart" [grabbing his crotch]. "It takes ya somewhere else. It grabs ya by the balls and lifts you above the shite." This is analogous to a later moment when Jimmy chastises Outspan and Derek about their high-minded concerns about "the direction" the band is taking. He cries to them, "Why'd ya want to be in a band in the first place?" When they can't answer, he states: "You want to stand out from the rest o' the tossers. You want to get up and shout, 'I'm Outspan fuckin' Foster,' and 'I'm Derek fuckin' Scully, and I'm not a tosser!' Isn't that it?" They assert, "That's it, Jimmy," and he concludes, "Well don't forget it." This scene does appear in the novel (5–6), but without the harsh admonition that Jimmy delivers here, which asserts a crucial element in Parker's film that distinguishes it from Doyle's novel: Parker wants the young people to find self-expression and self-worth in the soul music and in the group's efforts; but for Doyle, the emphasis is more on the group's identification with the very local Dublin world from which they emerge. Parker seeks to retain that Dublin particularity through the multiple filmic techniques we have discussed, but will ultimately place his greatest creative emphasis on the self-expression that he feels is actually the most fundamental desire of each member of the group.

This is fundamentally what is behind Parker's selection of the songs he will feature in the film, especially those few songs that become defining elements in the film's portrait of the band. Parker abandons several of the major songs to which Doyle devotes significant space in the novel: "Night Train," "What Becomes of the Broken-Hearted?," "Superbad," "Walkin' in the Rain," and "Knock on Wood," among others. Instead, Parker focuses on songs that emphasize the interpersonal and the romantic, that bring to the surface the desire of the characters to find expression, fulfillment, and affection above and beyond the sex-politics emphasis that Jimmy describes. Hence the key songs for the group in the film are "Destination Anywhere" (which they sing on the DART ride immediately following Jimmy's speech, suggesting the desire for direction and transformation they seek), "At the Dark End of the Street" (performed in their first paid public performance, a song focused entirely on a romantic encounter that transcends its particular moment), "Chain of Fools" (performed in the pub while Jimmy and Mickah fight back against the Dublin hood who tries to take their money—a scene that's only in the film), and of course, "Try a Little Tenderness," which is the band's great triumph song and also their final song before their dissolution.

The band's final performance in the film occurs with Dublin press observing and writing with praise about them; the representative from Idiot/Eejit Records appears, offering them a contract and recording studio time; and throughout the scene there lingers the hoped-for visit by Wilson Pickett that would confer legitimacy on their soul aspirations. But the dissension and resentments among the group are rife, and by the end of the song's performance they are literally at each other's throats and the band has dissolved just when it seems on the cusp of a public stardom. But the performance of "Try a Little Tenderness" for this 4:30 segment is without question the climactic moment of the film.

The group's version closely follows the legendary Otis Redding version of 1966, in which the song opens almost a capella, with Deco evoking the opening lines in his best Joe Cocker slightly spasmodic, expressive style. The song builds slowly as Mickah enters lightly on the drums, Steven's piano increases ever so carefully, and Outspan's short guitar strokes begin to move the song forward. The Commitmentettes begin to sway in rhythm to Deco's singing, and they look at him with anticipation as the first climax approaches. Then, at "all you gotta do / is try a little tenderness," suddenly the group erupts, with the girls singing in chorus, the trumpet and sax crying out together, and at that point the camera cuts to the audience where we see the northsiders bursting into applause, singing along, and crying out for more from their band. As the song continues, Parker shows each of the band members performing, smiling, all in unison, evincing an unmistakable joy in their performance. Importantly, this is a revision of the Redding version, which has no backup vocals, no harmonies, and no sense of a group lifting each other through the mutual expression of the song. They end together, smiling and laughing and looking at one another with real affection. The audience explodes into applause, and the moment is the high point of their performing careers. At this moment, it seems the band is completely triumphant in its fulfillment of its mission. Soul has been brought to the people of Dublin.

Then the band goes upstairs, and the dissension is immediate and unforgiving. Deco and Mickah are ready to fight, the girls are spitting at each other over Joey's affection, and Jimmy is outraged at Joey because Wilson Pickett has not come to jam with the band. Joey's response—"I'm sorry ya doubt me, Brother Rabbitte,"—is indicative of the band's failure of faith. They return to sing one last encore, but we know the band cannot sustain its unity beyond the stage. The imminent breakup is all the more ironic, because as they perform, Jimmy is sealing a deal with Idiot Records for recording time and the next step in their professional careers. But when he sees them fighting and expressing hatred toward each other—the very antithesis of his aspirations for the band—his response is final: "Fuck youse. Fuck the lot o' youse."

Parker's selection of songs that are less Dublin-specific and more personal, romantic, and ultimately more of a single soul's expression is also reflected in one of the band's other high point performance songs, "At the Dark End of the Street," which they sing midway through the film, as their confidence is growing along with the fan response to their music. It is a rare slow song for the group, and features Deco singing along with Natalie, whose darkly expressive eyes and intensity with the song reveal how the song expresses her own desires for Jimmy and for a romantic relationship that would take her away from the debasing nature of her current life, "guttin' fish" in the factory. The response of the audience is palpable, as they look on in powerful empathy with the song's expression of a secret, fleeting, but transcendent love:

> *You and me, at the dark end of the street*
> *You and me…*
> *It's a sin and we know it's wrong*
> *Ohhhh, but our love keeps comin' on strong*
> *Steal away, to the dark end of the street,*
> *You and me.*

2 FILMING GLOBAL IRELAND: RODDY DOYLE'S *THE COMMITMENTS*   39

This is emblematic of Parker's intention with the music he selects, to use the songs to convey the individual longings of the characters, longings that are shared by their audience and that explain the audience's powerful identification with the group. Deco even introduces the song by saying, "What I'd like to do for my fans now is a nice slow song." The song is in signal ways intended for the Dublin audience.[14]

This is what makes the film's ending profoundly hopeful for the Dubliners who will no longer be able to hear the now-disbanded group. In his final meeting with Jimmy immediately after the breakup, Joey urges him not to be discouraged: "O sing unto the Lord a new song, for he's done marvelous things—Psalm 98." Jimmy doesn't want to hear it, but Joey persists: "Look I know you're hurtin' now. In time you'll realize what you've achieved.... The success of the band was irrelevant. You raised their expectations of life! You lifted their horizons! Sure, we could've been famous and made albums and stuff, but that would have been predictable. This way—it's poetry." The "their" to whom Joey refers is clearly not just the members of The Commitments; it includes all the Dubliners who for a brief time were lifted up in their performances and expressions.

In this, Parker clearly departs from Doyle's novel, which ends with the core of the group re-forming to become a country band: "'Dublin country,' said Jimmy. 'That's fuckin' perfect.... We're a Dublin country group'" (165). In the novel, there is an ongoing effort to find a musical form that best expresses the Irish identity. And indeed this is a continuing obsession for Doyle: he returns to The Commitments in his 2005 story *The Deportees*, in which Jimmy Rabbitte returns, now a middle-aged father and husband, trying to put together a new band that can give adequate expression to the Dublin experience in the twenty-first century. Called The Deportees, it will include African, Eastern European, American, Russian, and every

---

[14] Don Kuntz has argued that the film, even more than the novel, turns "the formation and disintegration of the band into an allegory on the Irish 'Troubles,'" a reading he supports by describing Parker's selection of songs as encoding references to the Northern struggle: "In his film, Parker excludes 'Night Train' and emphasizes two songs which lyrically express Irish despair over the 'Troubles' and the hope of escaping them: 'At the Dark End of the Street' and 'Destination Anywhere.'...the dark end of the streets [becomes] a visual metaphor for terrorism" (Kunts 54). Although it's an intriguing way to read the film, ultimately I find this reading unconvincing, partly due to the novel's and the film's consistent disinterest in any form of actual political action or position, but especially because the songs in the film are about individual desire and hope, not about a public or political action.

40   M. C. CONNER

other nationality Jimmy can find that will represent the cultural excitement he sees in Dublin in the wave of the Celtic Tiger, a new Ireland that Doyle lovingly describes:

> The Forum was a surprise. Jimmy had walked and driven past it but he'd never seen it. It didn't look like a pub; it was more like a café and, as far as Jimmy was concerned, there were enough of those things in Dublin already. But, once he was inside, it was a real pub, and a good one.
>
> Portuguese-looking barman, Spanish-looking lounge-girl, Chinese-looking girl on the stool beside him, good-looking pint settling in front of him, REM's new album on the sound system—sounded good, though maybe a bit *too* like an REM album—African locals chatting and laughing, Irish locals chatting and laughing. Jimmy tasted his pint. Grand—and just as well, because it wasn't fuckin' cheap. (39)

This story, like the other stories collected in the 2008 volume *The Deportees*, and like a range of other short fiction Doyle has written in the past decade, was published in *Metro Éireann*, the Dublin newspaper aimed at and emerging from the newly multicultural populations of Ireland. *Metro Éireann* describes itself as follows: "Metro Eireann is Ireland's first and only weekly multicultural newspaper set up by two Nigerian journalists, Chinedu Onyejelem and Abel Ugba in April 2000. Published by Metro Publishing and Consultancy Limited, metro eireann is the primary source of news and information on Ireland's fast-growing immigrant and ethnic communities. Apart from supplying up-to-date news and analysis, metro eireann has become a forum for inter-cultural communication, showcasing the rich cultural diversity of Ireland" ("About"). Doyle began publishing short fiction in the newspaper beginning in its early stages in the early 2000s and, as noted above, founding editor Onyejelem views Doyle's contributions as definitive of the paper's aims for expressing the new Ireland. The *Metro Éireann* stories are a logical extension of the expanding view of Dublin and Ireland that Doyle first gestured toward in *The Commitments*, his debut novel now over 30 years ago. To situate Dublin in the growing multicultural world that had not yet truly arrived in Ireland, but whose emergence was only a decade away, was a visionary achievement for Doyle. Parker's film takes up the idea of that emerging global Ireland, connecting it in subtle ways to the Dublin particularity so dear to Doyle, while simultaneously aiming for a more universal and wide-ranging expression that may very well connect Doyle's novel more intimately and accurately to the ever-expanding world that Doyle's subsequent work addresses. Ruth Barton has recently argued that Irish film in the twenty-first century has worked to complicate and resist "the binaries of local/global." Many Irish films now continue to engage and define "Irishness" but without abandoning global production practices and transnational creation in every aspect of the film process: "Creating taxonomies of Irishness are, in a medium such as film that is inherently global, a waste of energy. More productive is understanding Irish film production as inherently transnational" (224). Parker's adaptation of Doyle's novel, two decades before the twenty-first century arrived, is one of the first forays into a concept of Irishness that is both highly particular and resolutely global, foreshadowing and influencing the Irish films that would follow.

WORKS CITED

"About Metro Eireann." http://www.metroeireann.com/pages/about-us.html. Accessed 2 February 2020.

Barton, Ruth. *Irish Cinema in the Twenty-First Century*. Manchester: Manchester UP, 2019.

Brown, Terence. *Ireland: A Social and Cultural History, 1922–2002*. London: Harper Collins, 2004.

Donnelly, Brian. "Roddy Doyle: From Barrytown to the GPO." *Irish University Review* 30:1 (Spring-Summer 2000). 17–31.

Doyle, Roddy. *The Commitments*. London: Vintage/Random House, 1998.

———. *The Deportees*. London: Vintage, 2008.

Ellison, Ralph. "The World and the Jug." *The Collected Essays of Ralph Ellison*. Ed. John F. Callahan. NY: Random House, 1995: 155–188.

Gillespie, Michael Patrick. *The Myth of an Irish Cinema: Approaching Irish-Themed Films*. NY: Syracuse UP, 2008.

Hurston, Zora Neale. "How it Feels to be Colored Me." *The Norton Anthology of African American Literature*. Eds. Henry Louis Gates, Jr., and Nellie Y. McKay. New York: W.W. Norton, 1997. 1008–1011.

Johnson, Charles. "The End of the Black American Narrative." *The American Scholar* 77:3 (Summer 2008): 32–42.

Kavanagh, Patrick. "The Parish and the Universe." *Collected Pruse* 1967. London: MacGibbon & Kee.

Kunz, Don. "Alan Parker's Adaptation of Roddy Doyle's *The Commitments*." *Literature/Film Quarterly*. 29:1, 2009. 53–57.

McFarlane, Noel. "Raucous Days in Barrytown." *Irish Times Limited*, 8.10.1996.

Metro Eireann. "Roddy's Back and in Time for '2016.'" http://www.metroeireann.com/news/364/roddys-back-and-in-time-for-2016.html, accessed 15 December 2019.

Reddy, Maureen T. "Reading and Writing Race in Ireland: Roddy Doyle and *Metro Eireann.*" *Irish University Review* 35:2 (Autumn-Winter 2005). 374–388.

Rockett, Kevin. "Cinema and Irish Literature." *The Cambridge History of Irish Literature.* Eds. Margaret Kelleher and Philip O'Leary. Cambridge: Cambridge UP, 2006. https://doi.org/10.1017/CHOL9780521822237.013.

Smith, R.J. *The One: The Life and Music of James Brown.* New York: Gotham Books, 2012.

"The Making of Alan Parker's Film *The Commitments*" (1991). YouTube. 1 Feb 2018. https://www.youtube.com/watch?v=5YspKXhi2FA.

Ulin, Julieann Veronica. "Roddy Doyle's The Barrytown Trilogy and Filming Ireland's 'New Picture.'" *Screening Modern Irish Fiction and Drama.* Eds. R. Barton Palmer and Marc C. Conner. Cham, Switzerland: Palgrave Macmillan, 2016: 191–211.

White, Caramine. *Reading Roddy Doyle.* NY: Syracuse UP, 2001.

CHAPTER 3

The Riddle of the Models of John Carney's *Sing Street* (2016)

Julieann Veronica Ulin

Critical reviews of John Carney's *Sing Street* (2016) repeatedly characterized the film as "a mini-*Commitments*," noting its similarities to the 1991 film adaptation of Roddy Doyle's novel and viewing Carney's film as a "complementary companion piece" (Lodge; Clarke "The Reel Dublin"). Both films focus on the formation of bands in Dublin in the midst of the economic crisis and mass emigration of the 1980s, though Doyle's Northsiders on the dole and the pupils of Carney's Synge Street Christian Brothers School hail from opposite sides of the Liffey. Reviewers saw both the casting of *The Commitments*'s Maria Doyle (who played singer Natalie Murphy) as the mother in *Sing Street* and band member Eamon's numerous pet rabbits as nods to Jimmy Rabbitte Jr.'s management of the Dublin soul band, two interpretations Carney rejected forcefully in his remarks on his own film:[1]

---

[1] In addition, Glen Hansard played Outspan in *The Commitments* and starred in Carney's *Once*.

J. V. Ulin (✉)
Florida Atlantic University, Boca Raton, FL, USA

© The Author(s), under exclusive license to Springer Nature Switzerland AG 2022
M. C. Conner et al. (eds.), *Screening Contemporary Irish Fiction and Drama*, Palgrave Studies in Adaptation and Visual Culture, https://doi.org/10.1007/978-3-031-04568-4_3

43

44   J. V. ULIN

> There's genuinely no relationship to *The Commitments* in this film, other than the fact that it does have songs in it. There really is no homage to *The Commitments*, no connection to it.... *The Commitments* was never a significant movie to me. It's a perfectly good film, and a good script. But it wasn't something that moved me as a kid. I was a film snob when I was that age. I would have steered away from *The Commitments* when I was 19 or 20, whenever it came out. Obviously people are going to draw comparisons, because there are so few films made in Ireland, and so few musicals.... *The Commitments* and *Sing Street* couldn't be more different. In *The Commitments*, they're a cover band, doing cover versions of old soul songs. That's fine, and it's very funny and enjoyable. But we're telling the story of a creative process, and of fashioning and shaping and hammering love songs to get the girl to improve your life, to get off the island, and to be a success. And what's great about *The Commitments* is that the band isn't a success. They implode, which is a very truthful story. *Sing Street* is a fantasy film about the American Dream, in a sense. It's just dressed up as an Irish film, but he's punching the air and heading off, in his head. (Robinson)

Carney affords quite a bit of space above to a film he claims has "no connection" to his own. What follows will push against Carney's comments here and elsewhere in his discussion of *Sing Street* that deliberately reject or obscure its indebtedness to and adaptation of key Irish cinematic, literary, and cultural narratives.[2] *Sing Street* not only revises aspects of *The Commitments* but engages with longstanding literary tropes of family and institutional entrapment within cycles, structures that thwart the individual's potential, and the Irish artist's exile in response to the "nets flung at [the soul] to hold it back from flight" (Joyce 220). While adaptation theory initially focused upon fidelity to a literary source text as the core of the analysis, viewing the cinematic version as purely derivative, more recent work in the field has considered the impact of non-narrative sources and intertexts and replaced a one-direction model of source to adaptation with cross-directional flows and exchanges across multiple platforms.[3] While the film itself celebrates influences both visual and musical, Carney both

---

[2] Carney reiterated this critique in an *Irish Times* interview in which he stated, "*The Commitments* had a great script and it was a very funny book, but the problem for me was that they were doing cover versions.... Where's the creativity? The band we had in school wrote the songs" (Clarke "Sing Street Director John Carney").

[3] Cf. Deborah Cartmell and Imelda Whelehan, *Screen Adaptation: Impure Cinema* (London: Palgrave Macmillan 2010), Thomas Leitch, *Film Adaptation and its Discontents: From Gone with the Wind to The Passion of the Christ* (Baltimore, Johns Hopkins UP 2007), Jay David Bolter and Richard Grusin, *Remediation: Understanding New Media* (MIT Press 1998).

overstates the originality of protagonist Conor Lawlor's "creative process" and disguises his own indebtedness to the origin story of U2, a band whose formation in Mount Temple Comprehensive School, now-legendary early gigs at the school in 1976–1978, and initial consultation with Carney on *Sing Street* belie his characterization of *Sing Street* as a "fantasy film about the American Dream." While *Sing Street* is indeed deeply enthralled with fantasy, particularly as it is enabled for Conor Lawlor by the revolutionary medium of the music video, the film's full power emerges only when those escapist elements are seen as a response to the specifically Irish contexts with which it engages.

Despite Carney's emphatic denial of any resemblance between *Sing Street* and *The Commitments*, whole sequences in his movie have counterparts in *The Commitments*. These include the audition scene featuring a range of traditional Irish instruments alongside standard rock instruments (played in *The Commitments* by a host of would-be band members and in *Sing Street* by the singularly talented Eamon), a sustained focus on family and economic turmoil that makes the band a respite for its members, the quest for privacy for band meetings in a house where someone is always bringing in the tea, performances in school gymnasiums, and the conversion of the local bully to band security/roadie. Carney's decision to have *Sing Street* shoot their video for the song in a depressed back alley recalls the scene in which The Commitments take promotional photographs in a similar location, the images that became the most associated with Parker's film (Fig. 3.1). Carney's attitude toward Parker's film adaptation of Doyle's novel blinds him to how the two films explore the transformational power of music to break free of the tyranny of social determinism, whether meted out by an economic system that renders Doyle's characters powerless or by the familial patterns and institutional structures designed to crush individual expression as in Carney's film. Carney's working title for the film that preceded *Sing Street* was "Can a Song Save Your Life?", a title that gives a clear indication of the life-altering power of music on the lives of Carney's protagonists in *Once*, *Begin Again*, and *Sing Street*. In writing off *The Commitments* as merely "funny and enjoyable," Carney neglects how, in the words of Joey "The Lips" Fagan, Jimmy Rabbitte's decision to form the band "raised their expectations of life [and] lifted their horizons" (Robinson; *The Commitments*). Just as Doyle's *The*

Fig. 3.1 *Sing Street* recalling *The Commitments*

Barrytown Trilogy and the film adaptations of the novels show characters recognizing and resisting imposed social and cultural roles through the use of entertainment, Carney's *Sing Street* shows Conor Lawlor, his enigmatic love interest and would-be model Raphina, and to a lesser extent his bandmates engaging in self-refashioning through remixing elements from music videos and fashion from bands ranging from Duran Duran to The Cure to Michael Jackson. In doing so, they are able to construct self-representations that defy the roles imposed upon them by familial or institutional structures, allowing for an emergence of "explicitly oppositional alternatives to imagined dominant cultures" (Collins 11).

In *Sing Street*, the economic recession that drives emigration and the institutional structure of the Christian Brothers School to which Conor transfers as a consequence of his family's declining finances work to restrict his "expectations of life" (*The Commitments*). The opening of the film finds Conor playing guitar in his room, the lyrics supplied by quotes from his parents' argument over the financial stress of his father Robert's vanishing commissions and his mother Penny's reduction to a three-day work week. The next scene elevates their domestic economic crisis to the national level through a news broadcast covering the "enormous increase" of Irish headed to London in search of work: "Many take the boat with barely enough money to survive a few days in London but still they emigrate because they see hope across the sea, hope they cannot see in Ireland." Conor watches the broadcast while wearing a scarf and sweater indoors and the camera captures his mother pulling a sweater more tightly around her for warmth. In announcing their decision to transfer Conor to Synge Street Christian Brothers School, Robert and Penny employ the same language used to explain their reduction in the workforce, explaining that "we're transferring you" due to "cuts in the budget" following "a look at the accounts." Conor's older brother Brendan quickly punctures their rhetorical spin on the change. Brendan says the Christian Brothers are known for "the systematic beating of their young charges" and when Robert asks Conor if he knows what the motto "Virlitar Age" ("Act Manly") means, Brendan suggests the translation "Let's rape our students."

The release of the *Report of the Commission to Inquire into Child Abuse* (2009) called widespread attention to the endemic abuse that took place in Ireland's industrial schools, day schools, and orphanages. Though Synge Street is not an industrial school Carney uses the character of Brother Baxter to capture the threat of physical and sexual abuse present.[4] Baxter does nothing to curb the violence meted out by the school bully Barry Bray, who holds Conor hostage with a slingshot while forcing him to perform a range of dances in the bathroom. Conor becomes the target of Brother Baxter for wearing brown rather than black shoes and their conflict culminates in a scene in which Baxter orders Conor to remove the makeup he is wearing in Baxter's own private bathroom. When Conor refuses, Brendan's interpretation of the school's motto very much in mind, Baxter violently attacks him in the school bathroom, immersing his face in the sink and forcibly removing the makeup. Brother Baxter concludes his assault with the declaration "No more Ziggy Stardust," a Bowie reference that makes clear that his violation of Conor is not only physical but aesthetic. Baxter wants to eliminate the potential for Conor to have Bowie as a model; while it was Bowie who famously chose to retire Ziggy Stardust in 1973, Baxter wants to take this choice from Conor.

Carney's representation of the abuse tolerated and perpetrated at the Synge Street Christian Brothers School generated some controversy as well as some powerful personal memories from alumni.[5] The school was

[4] Cf. http://www.childabusecommission.ie/rpt/. For the specific section on the institutions run by the Christian Brothers, see http://www.childabusecommission.ie/rpt/01-06.php.

[5] Cf. McNally, Frank. "Brothers Disarmed: An Irishman's Diary on the memories unleashed by 'Sing Street.'" April 2, 2016. *Irish Times.* https://www.irishtimes.com/opinion/brothers-disarmed-an-irishman-s-diary-on-the-memories-unleashed-by-sing-street-1.2595475. Cf. https://presspack.rte.ie/2016/08/09/last-orders-with-gay-byrne/

featured in RTÉ's *Last Orders with Gay Byrne* in which Byrne recalled the daily brutality of life at the school. Of his own time in a Christian Brothers School, Neil McCormick writes in his memoir that it was run by "an order of repressed sadists who operated a policy of beating the fear of God into you. Violence was deemed a healthy way for boys to occupy their time. Certainly the pupils…did little else but fight, usually under the approving supervision of their teachers" (McCormick 5). *Sing Street*'s closing credits includes a caveat noting the school's transformation from the mid-1980s to the year 2016: "This is a period film. Synge Street School, like much of Ireland, was a very different place in the 1980s than it is now. Today Synge Street School is a progressive, multi-cultural school with an excellent academic record and a committed staff of teachers." At least one viewer felt the statement to be "an insufficient remedy" to the representation of the school in the film: "It should have been on the screen at the start of the film, or at least at the beginning of the credits. Synger, like the rest of us, has moved on" (de Bréadún). The claim to have "moved on" is especially curious coming at the end of an article that discusses the author's own "searing memory" of the beatings meted out by the Brothers.[6] The recent investigations into state and religious-run institutions in Ireland have shown the limits of "moving on" for survivors and Carney's own reservations about the title of his film *Begin Again* suggest his own skepticism: "We don't believe in beginning again in Ireland…We fester until we die" (Setoodeh 16). *Sing Street* turns a 2016 gaze upon 1985 and acknowledges the festering wounds that such a school experience might create. While Carney's film leaves the sexual and physical abuse in Synge Street primarily off screen (Conor avoids an encounter in a bathroom stall with Barry Bray and Baxter's physical assault of Conor in the school bathroom stands in for the assumed sexual assault that would have taken place in his private bathroom), in Baxter's attempt to kill off Ziggy Stardust Carney directly represents how such institutions destroy the creative impulse and the choice to emulate artists that challenge the conventional.

Carney's commitment to representing the singular vision of the artist in contrast to often hostile surroundings may be seen across his work. In

---

[6] Roddy Doyle's novel *Smile* (2017) captures the difficulty of acknowledging the effects that remain long after the victim has aged out of the school abuse and the compulsion by some victims to defend the schools.

Once, Begin Again, and *Sing Street,* Carney embeds scenes that capture the musician's (or producer's in *Begin Again*) capacity to hear fully realized music in contrast to an indifferent or uninspired audience (or viewer) that hears little to nothing special. The juxtaposition of these divergent musical experiences is a hallmark of Carney's aesthetic, in which the sound and vision in the creator's mind is superimposed over the actual. It fails miserably in *Begin Again* (in an alienating sequence in which Mark Ruffalo watches as violins begin to play themselves) but works perfectly in Carney's rendering of the vividness of Conor's imagination in his American high school film inspired concept for his "Drive it Like You Stole It" video. Carney offers a nod to an earlier cinematic use of this juxtaposition between what the artist/musician sees and hears against what the audience experiences in a scene in which Brother Baxter tells Conor that he cannot wear makeup to school, one of many instances in which the strictly imposed gender roles evident in the school's motto ("Act Manly") are enforced. Unwavering, Conor replies that Mozart wore makeup to which Baxter replies, "So you're Mozart now? I guess that makes me Salieri." Here Carney incorporates a reference to Peter Shaffer's play *Amadeus,* which was released as an award-winning feature film directed by Milos Foreman in 1984, the year before *Sing Street* is set. In a scene in which Mozart serenely composes in his mind over the muted shrieks of his mother-in-law's reprimands, Foreman's film captures Mozart's ability to superimpose music over the mundane aspects of everyday life.

Carney's reluctance to acknowledge *The Commitments* and his dismissal of the cover band emerges from this interest in the singular vision of the artist. He embeds a characterization of cover bands as tragic, backward-looking, nostalgic, and ineffectual for wooing women within the film through Conor's older brother Brendan. Conor internalizes this critique as he recruits members for his band. In Conor's first meeting with Eamon, he argues for the importance of originality:

Eamon: What are you into?
Conor: I'm a futurist.
Eamon: What does that mean?
Conor: Like no nostalgia. Not like your da's [cover] band. Not looking backwards, just forwards. (*Sing Street*)

While those auditioning for The Commitments have ready answers for Jimmy's question, "Who are your influences?" Conor stakes his artistic

50   J. V. ULIN

credibility on the claim to not have any. Carney is quick to undercut this as posturing; the degree to which Conor adapts the influential fashion, style, and sound of a range of 1980s' bands under his older brother Brendan's tutelage makes clear that he is deeply indebted to contemporary musical influences. In response to Eamon's subsequent question about Conor's opinion of Duran Duran, he delivers nearly verbatim his brother's assessment of the band, suggesting the limitations of his argument for radical, future-facing originality. Carney is far more accepting of his protagonist's tendency to use the music and the ideas of others to forge a path forward than he is for Doyle's characters; while *Sing Street* introduces original music in contrast to *The Commitments*'s cover songs, the music videos Conor creates borrow heavily from the work of others.

Seeking a means to resist the pervasive threat of violence at Synge Street and retreat from his parents' crumbling marriage, Conor seizes upon the escapist and potentially revolutionary power of the music video. Both *The Commitments* and *Sing Street* include an instructional sequence in which viewing a recorded performance initiates the band's direction away from established musical norms. In *The Commitments*, this well-known scene occurs when Jimmy plays James Brown's performance of "Please, Please, Please" from the *T.A.M.I. Show* (1964) concert film as a way of illustrating "what ye have to measure up to lads" (*The Commitments*). In *Sing Street*, this instruction happens through the anachronistic music video for Duran Duran's "Rio" (1982), which both shapes Conor's subsequent music videos and provides him with an alternative to the tragic symbolic structure that aligns Dublin's boats and piers with economic depression and emigration. In one of the few scenes of family togetherness featured in *Sing Street*, the Lawlors assemble at 7 pm to watch Duran Duran's Russell Mulcahy-directed music video "Rio" (1982) on *Top of the Pops*. For A.O. Scott, the inclusion of the "Rio" music video in a film set in 1985 causes him to "feel old and a little cranky" and to "pick nits about [the film's out-of-sync] musical choices" but Carney's choice is structurally purposeful in its introduction of the film's elevation of the music video to art (Scott). Michael Hurll's lead in to "Rio" highlights the power of the music video to circulate an image of the band beyond the restrictions of the stage, concert film, or sound studio. Duran Duran, he notes, "can't be here because they're in the US so we'll have to go to 'Rio.'" *Sing Street* is a departure from *The Commitments* less because the title band is writing original songs than because Conor learns from watching *Top of the Pops* with his brother how developments in recording techniques enable the visual spectacle offered by the music video to supplant live performance as a key marketing vehicle and potential route to a record deal. In *The Commitments*, the theatricality of James Brown's performance becomes the key to the audience's fervor. "Rio" sells its audience on a set of visual images that have nothing to do with the song itself. Shot in Antigua, the color-saturated video shows the band members infatuated with London-based model Reema Ruspoli. The video opens with her being photographed on a pier and alternates between the band singing on a sailboat and their pursuit of her attention. Duran Duran's John Taylor attributes the growth of music videos for hit songs to the fact that "bands didn't want to keep showing up to play the song on *Top of the Pops*. That was the motivation within the UK market" (Marks and Tannenbaum 8). Of the visual impact of the video, the band's Nick Rhodes has said, "'Rio' was a day or two days of shooting. We were on the boat for three possibly four hours. And that image is engrained upon a generation of MTV viewers" (95). The depiction of the band members on the boat was termed by them "the most significant visual of our career" (94). Carney's inclusion of "Rio" is not an anachronistic mistake but rather a purposeful incorporation of what becomes a key internal visual structure within Carney's film, which repeatedly returns to a core set of images from the music video as Conor evolves from the leader of a band playing a cover of "Rio" to adapting and remixing elements from Duran Duran's video into his own Dublin-based creations. In response to his father's question of what the band is trying to hide by not playing live, Brendan states, "It's a video, Robert. It's art. Everybody's making them these days. Look at it…. These last forever. It's the perfect mixture of music and visuals. It's short and to the point. Look at it. I mean, what tyranny could stand up to that?"

"Rio" shapes Conor's romantic interest in Raphina, his aesthetic choices in his own videos, and his rebellion against the tyrannical institutional structure of Synge Street (Figs. 3.2 and 3.3). Carney emphasizes aspiring model Raphina's (Lucy Boyton) striking resemblance to Reema Ruspoli through the low-angle shot that frames Conor's first conversation with her and that mirrors a shot in "Rio". The correspondence between Raphina and the model in "Rio" in their use of dramatic makeup may well account for Conor's attraction to her and for his strategy for approaching her by promising to cast her in a music video for his nonexistent band. Crucially, the similarity between Raphina and Reema Ruspoli suggests not only that the visual medium of the music video shapes Conor's desire but Raphina's as well. One of the strengths of the film lies in how it avoids

Figs. 3.2 and 3.3   Duran Duran's "Rio" and *Sing Street*'s Raphina

Figs. 3.4 and 3.5   "Rio" influences Raphina's makeup

casting Raphina solely as the object of Conor's gaze but instead shows her as equally engaged in navigating the process of self-construction through a series of models. Carney's composition of the scene in which Conor first sees Raphina suggests that Raphina also watched "Rio" on *Top of the Pops* the previous evening and adapted her look accordingly, an idea confirmed by her makeup application for the music video they make for the band's first original song, "The Riddle of the Model" (Figs. 3.4 and 3.5).

While the song "The Riddle of the Model" is inspired by his first encounter with Raphina, Conor's statement to her that the song is "not about you, it's about another model I know" is not entirely untrue. In making the video, Conor adapts the models offered to him by Duran Duran and other pioneers of the music video format. Conor's instructions to Darren (Ben Carolan) to shoot Raphina using a low-angle shot indicates how much he has absorbed from "Rio." He directly lifts a sequence in which John Taylor uses a compact mirror to show a bifurcated self that gives way to a split image of him with Reema (Figs. 3.6 and 3.7). Though Darren mocks another band member for bringing toy fangs to wear in the video, telling him "We're making a video, not a bleedin' horror film,"

Figs. 3.6 and 3.7 Images of bifurcated selves in "Rio" and *Sing Street*

Conor incorporates them into the video's homage to Michael Jackson's "Thriller" video. Conor's reenactment with Raphina of Jackson's pursuit of Ola Rey reminds the audience that "Thriller" had already collapsed the boundaries between horror film and music video. Conor's capacity to mix seemingly incongruous visual styles and sounds from a range of 1980s music and fashion speaks to his desire to continually reinvent himself and the band, enabling what John Joseph Hess terms "the remix of self."[7] The significance for Conor of "the self-making possibilities inherent in new developments in music technology in the 1980s" such as the music video is underscored when he compares his individual development to art captured in an endless video in the lyrics to his song "Girls" (Hess 175): "Sometimes I pull myself apart / I shift my shape the way I change my colors/ Guess I'm a human work of art / A never ending video."

By retaining "Rio" as a key influence upon Conor's artistic vision for his music videos, Carney creates a film in which boats and piers are free from the narrative and visual iconography of exile and emigration established by the opening newsreel. This is seen most clearly when the band leaves the city center and journeys to Dún Laoghaire to shoot the video for their song "Like the Sea." In describing his concept for the video as "a guy standing on a pier [when] a beautiful woman walks past him… [and] disappears," Conor essentially lifts the opening sequence of the video for "Rio." Raphina's alternative narrative, that the woman is a mermaid returning to the sea after having been captured in a fishing net, is inspired

---

[7] While the focus of the present chapter is on how adapting visual elements of the music video frees Conor to recreate his surroundings in Carney's film, it is indebted to explorations of how music enables a "remix of self" in contemporary literature in John Joseph Hess's "Music Consumption and the Remix of Self in Colson Whitehead's *Sag Harbor*" in *Write in Tune: Contemporary Music in Fiction* (2014).

by a visual sequence from "Rio" in which one of the band members is pulled ashore in a fishing net but makes a clear narrative departure. The image of Raphina walking along the Dún Laoghaire Harbour East Pier enclosing herself within an oversized picture frame mirrors the opening of "Rio" in which Ruspoli is photographed on the pier and a black box circumscribes the dimensions of the shot. "Rio"'s multiple shots of band members falling into the water are collapsed into the scene in which both Conor and Raphina jump from the pier into the sea after Raphina refuses to be satisfied with merely the illusion of immersion. The repeated use of the pier and the boat in "Rio" is significant for how these settings acquire new symbolic associations for Conor beyond their more typical links with the Irish emigrant experience. While these borrowings might suggest that Conor is overly influenced by the visual media he has consumed to the detriment of his artistic vision, his—and by extension Carney's—capacity to reimagine settings more typically associated with the pain of exile and emigration speaks to the freedom afforded by escaping limited visual and narrative structures.

Despite Carney's comment that *Sing Street* is not an Irish film, its focus on Conor's musical evolution from playing a cover of "Rio" to writing original lyrics and electing to journey with Raphina to London invokes the particular exilic condition of a number of Irish artist precursors. After the shoot, Conor and Raphina walk along the Dún Laoghaire Harbour East Pier, deeply significant for its connection to Irish emigration to England. The destination of Holyhead across the Irish Sea prompts the following from Conor: "My brother says all the great artists had to get off this island. The ones who stayed got depressed and turned into alcoholics." Here, in another moment of indebtedness to his older brother's pronouncements, Conor rehearses a commonplace about Ireland's hostility to its artists. Raphina has already made a similar claim about the necessity of leaving when she announces at their first meeting that, "I'm going to London soon...There's no real work for models in Dublin." Neither the prospect of leaving nor the sites associated with embarking for elsewhere fills either of them with any discernable sadness. The pier at Dalkey features twice in the film, the Dún Laoghaire Harbour East Pier serves as the setting for "Like the Sea," and there are two journeys by boat—one to Dalkey Island and one to Holyhead. The same structures and vessels imbued with deep meaning in terms of the Irish emigrant experience are, for Conor, significant only for how he can adapt them to achieve the effect of Duran Duran's "Rio" in Dublin and secure a record deal based upon his videos.

In the same scene in which Conor tells Raphina of the fate awaiting artists who stay in Ireland, he tells her of his older brother's plan years earlier to go to Germany, a plan thwarted by their mother. Raphina theorizes that their mother loved Brendan too much to let him go. Having revealed aspects of her own history—her mother's institutionalization, her father's alcoholism and death, her life in a group home for girls—slowly over the course of multiple conversations with Conor, she makes the fullest disclosure here. Comparing her situation to that of Brendan, she says that during her mother's hospitalization her father would force her to stay home whenever she dressed up to go out with friends: "And afterward he'd say, I love you too much is all. And the thing is me ma's much better looking than I am so I don't really know why he'd bother with me. It's a strange kind of love, isn't it? Parents." Much of the abuse of Raphina's life is contained in the word "afterward" and the phrase "bother with me," which both conceal and reveal sexual abuse. Her character shares some features with Eveline from James Joyce's *Dubliners*—the absent, mentally unwell mother, the threatening father, the romantic promise of a more experienced man who could remove her from Dublin. Though Raphina's older boyfriend Evan seduces and abandons her rather than fulfill his promise to take her to London, precisely the possible threat posed by Frank in "Eveline," Raphina escapes a tragic narrative structure in which she is ruined. Instead, she displays the same capacity for reinvention as Conor, both in her initial attempt to avoid embarrassment at her return by introducing herself as Raphina's twin and in beginning again the trip to London to pursue her dream of becoming a model.

Among the most recognizable Irish narratives upon which *Sing Street* draws are the familial entrapments that threaten the individual's, and particularly the artist's, sense of freedom. Perhaps the clearest indication of the threat posed by Conor's parents to his artistic vision comes in the person of his older brother, Brendan. The cost of this discovery and the abortion of Brendan's plans to go to Germany are made clear in Carney's film, which depicts the close connection between Brendan and his mother as damaging to his own individual development. Brendan is uniquely attuned to his mother's behavior, deducing her affair with a coworker from surveilling her rides home and regularly watching her smoking on their back porch from the interior stairway of the house. As Conor sits beside him as he observes her through the opened back door, Brendan explains that these moments in the sun are the limit of their mother's happiness. Later in the film, Brendan takes her place on the back porch, a position that makes clear how the orbit of his life is closing in.[8] It is perhaps the character of Brendan, whose character remains trapped in Dublin, haunted by the sense of what was once possible, that makes *Sing Street* so much an Irish film. When Brendan says, "I wish I'd done this" as he drops Conor and Raphina at the pier at Dalkey in the film's conclusion, there is no sense that he still can. His earlier rant to Conor that culminates in his embittered "Once I was a jet engine" is tragic because of the contrast between the once promising version of himself planning his escape to Germany and his current stagnation. Despite this recognition, Brendan is not so corrupted by his own lost dreams and opportunities that he cannot support his brother's chance, driving him to the pier to leave with Raphina. What part of Brendan that can accompany Conor on the journey out of Ireland will be in the lyrics he scrawls on the yellow legal paper to give to Conor as he departs. Brendan ends the film sitting as a passenger in the backseat of a driverless car, watching his brother captain the boat that will take him and Raphina away from Ireland.

The economic concerns that drive the emigrant experience highlighted in the opening news broadcast return in the closing sequence of the film through the image of the Holyhead ferry. As Conor and Raphina take his grandfather's boat from Dalkey and set off for London to seek a modeling contract for Raphina and a record contract for Sing Street, the Holyhead ferry emerges suddenly in front of them out of the rain and fog (Figs. 3.8 and 3.9). The image recalls the reported waves of emigrants seeking hope

Figs. 3.8 and 3.9 The Holyhead ferry emerging suddenly out of the rain and fog

---

[8] There's an echo here of the ending of McDonagh's *The Beauty Queen of Leenane* when Maureen ends the play in her mother's rocking chair.

outside of Ireland even as it emphasizes Conor and Raphina's separateness from their fellow emigrants through the color composition of the shot, their boat bright white in contrast to the industrial gray of the ferry. Conor and Raphina's upward gaze turns upon the darkened figures lining the ferry's railings, and while they exchange waves with passengers on the ferry the shot emphasizes the difference and the distance between the teenagers in the boat brimming with confidence and the spectral figures along the ferry railings. The closing shot of the ferry's wake into which Conor steers recalls Brendan's tragic monologue from earlier in the film, in which he claims that his own struggles paved the way for Conor's achievements. Carney signals his own indebtedness to his late brother in the dedication of the film "To Brothers Everywhere."

That Carney makes leaving Ireland a precursor to Conor and Raphina's ability to attain success accounts for the several Joycean echoes in the film. The closing image of Conor and Raphina escaping Dublin on a boat named Jim is certainly tempting to read as a nod to Joyce and Nora's departure, though the name of the boat is in fact a tribute to Carney's brother. The Joyce family's own diminished finances led to James Joyce's transfer to a Christian Brothers School. Like Stephen Dedalus, Conor develops his own artistic credo. Asked by Darren to define his description of himself and his music as "happy-sad," Conor acknowledges the challenges of creating in a destructive institution: "It means that I'm stuck in this shithole full of morons and rapists and bullies and I'm gonna deal with it, okay? It's just how life is. I'm gonna try and accept it and get on with it and make some art." When Conor takes Raphina by boat to Dalkey Island, their kiss while consuming crackers reenacts Molly and Bloom's as recalled in the Lestrygonians and Penelope episodes of *Ulysses* and mirrors the cover of the DVD of Sean Walsh's *Bloom* (2003) (Figs. 3.10 and 3.11). In his eventual choice not to accept being stuck and to instead leave Ireland with Raphina, Conor follows in the wake of Ireland's "great artists," not only literary ones such as Joyce but musical ones such as U2.

In the special features included in the DVD version of *Sing Street*, singer Adam Levine notes the distinction between its ending and the endings of Carney's *Once* and *Begin Again*. In response to Levine's "Look at you with your happy ending…It took three movies," Carney looks visibly uncomfortable. In interviews about the film, Carney has equivocated about the ending, citing it as a fantasy sequence that is all in Conor's head and defending an alternate version in which the two drown:

58   J. V. ULIN

Fig. 3.10 Connor and Raphina, resonating with Molly and Bloom in *Ulysses*

Fig. 3.11 The DVD cover of *Bloom* (2003)

I sort of hope the scene at the end would look a little like a fantasy sequence. You're supposed to wonder where the reality ends and the pop video begins. But people are actually taking it very seriously, and people are presuming it's fully real, which is interesting. That wasn't the intention.... I wish they had [drowned], in a way. I'm sorry! But there is a side of me that wishes they had. Given the difficulty of people who are making journeys, and end up dying....I mean, I don't think it's supposed to be a fully real sequence. I think they're supposed to be quite brave, setting off. But it's supposed to be... it's funny. Maybe I do want to have my cake and eat it. Maybe I do want to have a winning sequence, but... there's an element of it that could be a music video, or a fantasy. They're in a boat together, and it's dangerous, and they're being rocked by the sea, and he's like the brave captain, but it's kind of all in his head. (Robinson)

Carney's efforts to interpret the film's conclusion as a "pop video," "music video, or a fantasy" that exists only in Conor's head simply cannot be justified within the world of the film; the "Drive It Like You Stole It" performance is a pop video-inspired fantasy entirely within Conor's head and bears no relation to the closing section of the film. Carney's inability to acknowledge the possibility of a happy ending conceals a final key cultural and entertainment narrative adapted in the film, the origin story for U2. That securing a record deal seems possible for Conor's band owes much to the obvious ways in which the film's plot tracks U2's start as a high school band and their subsequent global success. As Bono has said in numerous interviews over the years, "...a long time ago I started to date this girl who was in Mount Temple, Ali Stewart, and it was the same week I joined U2. It was a very, very good week" (Gittens). Far from "a fantasy film about the American Dream...dressed up as an Irish film," *Sing Street* adapts a number of key story elements from the band that would become "the most famous Irish export since Guinness" (Robinson, McCormick 9).

Speaking of *Sing Street*, a Synge Street graduate remarked that "we were delighted with it—and it's an honour to have our very own movie. Mount Temple, where U2 went, didn't get a movie—but Synge Street did!" (Nolan). In fact, Mount Temple did get its own movie, *Killing Bono* (2011), based on Neil McCormick's memoir *Killing Bono: A True Story*. McCormick traces the early days of U2 at a time when *Top of the Pops* was watched "with something akin to religious veneration" and he was a student and musician at Mount Temple along with the four future members of U2 (McCormick 2). In its meditation on what might have been, McCormick's memoir poignantly captures something of Brendan's character in Carney's film. In the forward, Bono writes that McCormick "fully inhabits the great line out of Marlon Brando's mouth in *On the Waterfront*...'I could have been a contender'" (ix). In a phone call with Bono, Neil reflects some of Brendan's resentment of the possibilities available for Conor when he tells Bono "The problem with knowing you is that you've done everything I've ever wanted to do. I feel like you've lived my life" (xiv).

U2's formation as a high school band in fall of 1976 followed a notice posted on a board by drummer Larry Mullen Jr. As in *Sing Street*, meetings about the band name took place in the kitchen "over tea and crackers" and for rehearsals Larry "opened the kitchen doors to create space in which to set up his drum kit, half in the kitchen and half in a small conservatory precariously attached to the back of the house" (18, 19). McCormick recalls Bono and Adam Clayton acting out through fashion and Bono's pursuit of Alison Stewart, a girl with "a sort of aura of impermeability about her" that McCormick describes as "way out of my league" (11). As in *Sing Street*, school provides the venue for the band's first performance where the band wins over the student crowd though not the teachers. In their first performance, the band that would become U2 played "cover versions on some rickety school tables held together by sticky tape in the Mount Temple gymnasium" (xvii). In what could be a description of the final *Sing Street* performance in Carney's film, in which the band plays to great success, thwarting the school rules and driving Baxter out of the gymnasium, McCormick writes, "When their slot came, the group started to hoist their equipment on to the stage. It took them about ten minutes to set up, an extended period of inactivity in which any last remnants of discipline in the room evaporated" (25). By the end of the set, however, "The gym was in a complete uproar, with kids singing, yelling, screaming, clapping, dancing" (26). The administrative response is likewise similar and Eamon Dunphy writes that "The teachers who sat as judges didn't give the band the prize; that would have been inappropriate, not to mention an affront to the teacher who walked out in disgust during the set. But everyone left Mount Temple that night talking about the four lads" (Dunphy 79).

Though U2 is curiously and conspicuously absent in the 1985 world of *Sing Street*, both Bono and The Edge consulted Carney on the film and early reports on it cited them as the film's songwriters. A 2014 article noted that *Sing Street* "has already generated a great deal of publicity thanks to the involvement of U2. Bono and The Edge have agreed to

3 THE RIDDLE OF THE MODELS OF JOHN CARNEY'S *SING STREET*... 61

write some songs for the piece and are helping corral other musical talent into the party. It turns out that Mr. Hewson has been at John's shoulder intermittently over the last eight years" (Clarke "John Carney goes urban musical"). For U2, this period coincided with the release of their 2014 album *Songs of Innocence*, a deeply personal retrospective album featuring songs about the influence of punk rock on the band ("The Miracle (Of Joey Ramone)"), enduring high school love ("Song for Someone"), fractured home life ("Iris"), abuse by priests ("Sleep Like a Baby Tonight"), and the promise of America ("California (There is No End to Love")"). David Fricke's *Rolling Stone* review describes the album as "turning back and inward, for the first time on a whole record, to their lives and learning as boys on the way to uncertain manhood (and their band) in Dublin." (Fricke). Two years later, Carney's characterization of Bono and The Edge's involvement in *Sing Street* reflected their waning involvement in the project beyond the early development stage:

> They were actually very helpful early on… Unfortunately, our schedules didn't match up. I think they were on tour, and we were shooting back at home, and it didn't work out on a timeline. But Bono and Edge were both really helpful in terms of pitching story ideas, and talking about bands in the '80s, and talking about youth. They set up the ultimate pop band, really. So I'd be a fool not to pick their brains. You know, I was in school bands, and I was in The Frames, but I wasn't in a successful band in that sense that U2 is successful. Bono could give us a good idea of, "If this kid's band is to succeed, here's what it's like." Also, the point of my film is that these kids are in a good band. They do become good, and U2 did become good. I don't know what they were like as a school band, but I imagine they were always pretty good. (Robinson)

For his part, Bono remained complimentary of the project and his comments on the completed film suggest the degree to which U2's high school experience shaped the film:

> I remember the 1980s with somewhat of a blush. No man's hair should be bigger than his girlfriend's. But that was the time. Dublin in Technicolor. In reality it was monochrome and in the grip of a recession. But on videotape you could be transported. You could wear what you liked, and the more outrageous the better. Anything to wind up the jackbooted skinheads on Dublin's north side. Make-up on a boy drove rockers wild, and the teachers wilder. Thank God for Bowie, who made all the black eyes

62 J. V. ULIN

okay. And allowed people to find out who they were. My brother gave me the gift of music through my first guitar. We formed a band. In truth, at the same stage, U2 were not as good as the kids in Sing Street. In truth most films you'll see this year won't touch *Sing Street*. ("Bono's been talking about *Sing Street*")

Bono's discussion here of the capacity of video to facilitate escape from the monochromatic, the reactions of teachers and fellow students to boys wearing makeup, the influence of his brother, and the reference to Bowie serving as a model for self-reinvention likely echo conversations he had with Carney in the course of the film's development. These widely recognized elements of the story of U2 proved not only vital to the narrative development of the film but contribute to the "happy ending" that Levine identifies and the belief in a positive outcome for Conor and Raphina's journey and Sing Street's future.

In his most succinct summary of *Sing Street*, John Carney describes the film as "the story of just how [Conor] gets on that boat at the end, that's all it really is. How he gets over that year of his life" (Robinson). Adaptation is the key to that physical and mental journey; Conor's success in drawing upon existing visual, narrative, and musical models and structures to create alternative visions of Dublin, Synge Street's bullies and abusers, Raphina, and himself accounts for reviews of the film that are nearly universal in describing the film as joyous. Carney's reluctance to agree with these interpretations both in interviews and in the film itself, with its internal endorsement of art that is "happy-sad," arises from how such a characterization obscures a number of the film's darker currents, specifically references to childhood physical and sexual abuse, alcoholism and institutionalization, and entrapment within familial cycles. Conor both acknowledges these realities and resolves to "get on with it and make some art" that wages war against Synge Street's refusal to see the self as "a human work of art" (*Sing Street*). While for Carney *Sing Street* remains chiefly a deeply personal tribute to his late brother, the film achieves significance beyond that for its indebtedness to an Irish cinematic, literary, and cultural tradition in which the individual fights to create art, to live in a manner that resists imposed limitations, and to see anew spaces and selves that have been symbolically over-determined.

WORKS CITED

"Bono's been talking about *Sing Street*." U2.com, April 27, 2016, www.u2.com/news/title/sing-street.

Clarke, Donald. "John Carney goes urban musical once more." July 12, 2014, www.irishtimes.com/culture/john-carney-goes-urban-musical-once-more-1.1862099.

———. "The Reel Dublin: Best Movies about the Capital City." *Irish Times*, June 25, 2018, www.irishtimes.com/culture/film/the-reel-dublin-best-movies-about-the-capital-city-1.3542768.

———. "Sing Street Director John Carney: I knew that era so well I didn't have to research it." *Irish Times*, March 18, 2016, www.irishtimes.com/culture/film/sing-street-director-john-carney-i-knew-that-era-so-well-i-didn-t-have-to-research-it-1.2575462.

Collins, Jim. *Uncommon Cultures: Popular Culture and Post-Modernism*. Routledge, 1989.

de Bréadún, Deaglán. "'Synger': An Irishman's Diary on Synge Street CBS in the Sixties." *Irish Times*, August 25, 2016, www.irishtimes.com/opinion/synger-an-irishman-s-diary-on-synge-street-cbs-in-the-sixties-1.2767159.

Dunphy, Eamon. *Unforgettable Fire: The Definitive Biography of U2*. Warner Books, 1987.

Fricke, David. "Songs of Innocence." *Rolling Stone*, September 11, 2014, www.rollingstone.com/music/music-album-reviews/songs-of-innocence-118134/.

Gittens, Geraldine. "I find it very hard to be in the world without that kind of company: U2's Bono on his wife Ali." *The Independent*, November 3, 2017, https://www.independent.ie/entertainment/music/i-find-it-very-hard-to-be-in-the-world-without-that-kind-of-company-u2s-bono-on-his-wife-ali-36287692.html.

Hess, John Joseph. "Music Consumption and the Remix of Self in Colson Whitehead's *Sag Harbor*." *Write in Tune: Contemporary Music in Fiction*. Bloomsbury, 2014, pp. 169–81.

Joyce, James. *A Portrait of the Artist as a Young Man*. Penguin, 1993.

Lodge, Guy. "Sundance Film Review: Sing Street." *Variety*, January 25, 2016, variety.com/2016/film/reviews/sing-street-review-1201687683/.

Marks, Craig and Rob Tannenbaum. *I Want my MTV: The Uncensored Story of the Music Video Revolution*. Plume, 2011.

McCormick, Neil. *Killing Bono: A True Story*. Pocket Books, 2004.

Nolan, Larissa. "Why one of Ireland's most famous schools is going Gaelscoil." *Irish Times*, March 14, 2017, www.irishtimes.com/news/education/why-one-of-ireland-s-most-famous-schools-is-going-gaelscoil-1.3002628.

The Commitments. Directed by Alan Parker, 1991.

Report of the Commission to Inquire into Child Abuse. 2009, www.childabusecommission.ie/rpt/.

Robinson, Tasha. "Why Sing Street Director John Carney Regrets the Film's Ending." *The Verge*, April 21, 2016, https://www.theverge.com/2016/4/21/11477490/sing-street-john-carney-interview-once-begin-again.

Setoodeh, Ramin. "'Once' Helmer Faces the Music 'Again.'" *Variety*, June 24, 2014, p. 16.

Sing Street. Directed by John Carney, 2016.

Scott, A.O. "Review: *Sing Street* is an '80s Love Affair, Hair Gel Required." *New York Times*, April 15, 2016, www.nytimes.com/2016/04/15/movies/review-sing-street-is-an-80s-love-affair-hair-gel-required.html.

CHAPTER 4

The Women Incarnate of *Words Upon the Window Pane*

Matthew J. Fee

Such is the fate of female race
With no endowments but a face;
Before the thirti'th year of life
A maid forlorn, or hated wife.
    Stella to you, her tutor, owes
That she has ne'er resembled those[1];

Irish cinema certainly does not lack depictions of bygone eras, as its films very frequently evidence an "obsessive desire to reproduce narratives of history on screen" (Barton 130). While this abundance of film narratives set in the Irish past varies in its funding arrangements, historical content,

[1] Esther Johnson ("Stella"), "To Dr. Swift on his Birthday, November 30, 1721," *The Poems of Jonathan Swift*, vol. 2, edited by Harold Williams, Oxford University Press, 1937, p. 736.

M. J. Fee (✉)
Le Moyne College, Syracuse, NY, USA
e-mail: feemj@lemoyne.edu

© The Author(s), under exclusive license to Springer Nature Switzerland AG 2022
M. C. Conner et al. (eds.), *Screening Contemporary Irish Fiction and Drama*, Palgrave Studies in Adaptation and Visual Culture, https://doi.org/10.1007/978-3-031-04568-4_4

aesthetic strategies, ideological approaches, and box office success, certain dominant trends nevertheless emerge. Many of these films focus on the traumatic legacies attendant to Ireland's colonial history, its struggles for independence, and the development of the post-Independence State.[2] Within this corpus, a cycle of "Protestant/Big House" films, including *Ascendancy* (Edward Bennett, 1983), *Fools of Fortune* (Pat O'Connor, 1990), and *The Last September* (Deborah Warner, 1999), specifically chronicles the Anglo-Irish's anxious and uncertain perspective on its hybrid identity. Commonly adaptations of literary sources, and with women most often at the center of their narratives, these Big House films draw on the Irish gothic as they depict a present haunted by the memories of its past. Although set in Ireland during the 1920s, these cinematic works are better considered British heritage films, due to their focus on traumas specifically associated with the end of Empire. On the contrary, a different body of cinematic tales avoids explicit engagement with British-Irish relations, comprising what Ruth Barton defines as an "Irish heritage cinema." Similar to the tradition of British heritage films, these works highlight the past as spectacle; however, with the Irish heritage film, the past to which we nostalgically return is that of mid-twentieth-century rural Ireland (or to a more contemporary Ireland characterized by its appearance of "pastness") with traditional Irish musical underscore, conservative gender roles, and children regularly serving as harbingers of the future. Across both cinematic trends and characteristics of Irish film production in general for the past thirty years, co-productions dominate, with Irish, British, and American production companies providing significant funding. Whether focusing on history as trauma, or history as a timeless rurality, these films engage their audiences through connecting with long-standing popular tropes of Irishness that have been established and maintained across a variety of contexts, namely prior film and television works, literary sources, cultural nationalism, and tourism.

With events transpiring in both the eighteenth and early twentieth centuries, Mary McGuckian's *Words Upon the Window Pane* (1994) could be understood to doubly evidence such an "obsessive desire" to represent

---

[2] My overview of the variety of Irish historical narratives in film (i.e. films that prioritize Irish history as trauma, Big House films, and Irish heritage films) draws from Ruth Barton, pp. 130–156.

Ireland's past. A European co-production with a limited release during the 1990s boom in Irish heritage films,[3] McGuckian's *Words* features various elements of Irish historical films: its temporal settings harken to those films concerned both with costume dramas and drawing room grandeur and with post-Independence uncertainties. Its prioritization of women's experiences and memory recalls both Irish and British heritage films, not to mention the gothic hauntings of Big House adaptations—albeit in this instance, set within a Georgian townhouse. It evokes a hybridity at the core of Big House film adaptations: "borrow[ing] their generic formulae from the British period films but then re-work[ing] these to concentrate on local, Irish concerns" (136). *Words Upon the Window Pane*'s engagement with the historical film's cinematic tropes recalls how a defining characteristic of Irish film as a national cinema may be found in how "native themes and concerns are worked into an international style" (McLoone 90). Duly provocative in the case of Mary McGuckian's film is how these "native themes" are themselves brought more to the fore through her adapting a play by one of Ireland's most prominent writers.

However, contrary to heritage films in which the past simply provides a nostalgic—and, in the specific case of Irish heritage films, bucolic—backdrop that enshrines an ahistorical and idealized representation of gender, McGuckian's film and its blurring of cinematic temporalities challenges heritage cinema's frequently superficial engagement with Irish history. Moreover, it simultaneously presents the fantastic as a complementary strategy for contemporary feminist filmmaking practices in Ireland, and in particular their interrogation of women's (dis)placement within Irish history. *Words Upon the Window Pane* thus offers a complicated intervention into both cinematic and feminist histories of Ireland. Indeed, the film's post-Independence recuperation and, ultimately, reassessment of women's historical roles in defining Irishness proves highly significant to similar debates surrounding gender and Irish identity during the final decades of the twentieth century. Much as Stella lauds an alternate role for herself in this chapter's opening epigraph, in the possibility of being neither maid nor wife—lines that we will hear her repeat when she first speaks in the film—so too does this adaptation of one of the most famous chronicles of

---

[3] The film received funding from Ireland, the U.K., France, Germany, and Luxembourg. Following its limited festival and theatrical run, some video distribution, and brief availability to stream on Amazon.com, the film is now only available for private screening through the Irish Film Institute.

68   M. J. FEE

her relationship with Jonathan Swift grant us an additional cinematic lens through which to view gender in Ireland.

Adapted from W.B. Yeats' one-act play of the same name, Mary McGuckian's *Words Upon the Window Pane* focuses on a 1928 gathering of the Dublin Spiritualists Association.[4] Coordinated by group secretary Miss MacKenna (Geraldine Chaplin), the organization has brought the famous medium Mrs. Henderson (Geraldine James) over from England for its first séance. By way of an advertisement, Miss MacKenna has assembled Cornelius Patterson (Donal Donnelly), a watch fixer and gambler curious whether they race whippets in heaven, and Mrs. Mallet (Gemma Craven), a supposed widow who frequents séances as a means of consulting with her dead husband, and who now claims to want to know whether to open a tea shop in Sandymount. President of the Association Dr. Trench (Ian Richardson) has asked the Reverend Johnson (Gerard McSorley) to sit in his place, with the Reverend more than eager to join, as he seeks inspiration from the evangelist Moody.

Rather than assisting its members' pursuits of their own interests in the spirit world, however, the séance channels an "evil presence"—revealed to be the spirit of poet, churchman, and politician Jonathan Swift (Jim Sheridan). During their séances, Mrs. Henderson becomes possessed by the spirit of Swift, while Miss MacKenna channels the spirit of Esther Johnson—a former pupil of Swift's who fell in love with him, and whom Swift brought with him to Dublin—otherwise and affectionately known as Stella (Brid Brennan). As Mrs. Henderson and Miss MacKenna channel the spirits, those in attendance (and we as well) witness incidents from Swift and Stella's relationship, particularly those involving Stella's jealousy of Vanessa (Orla Brady), another of Swift's romantically inclined pupils more formally known as Hester van Homrigh, and for whom he wrote the poem "Cadenus and Vanessa." As the spirits possess Mrs. Henderson and Miss MacKenna, Dr. Trench is brought in to assist, along with Cambridge-educated skeptic (and, as fate would have it, scholar of Swift) John Corbet (John Lynch). Held in Stella's house, the séance replays the drama surrounding Stella's and Vanessa's rivalry toward each other for Swift's affection. With a final confrontation between Swift and Stella, the film concludes

---

[4] As there is a discrepancy between the spellings of some of the characters' names, I am using the spelling in the film (i.e. MacKenna) instead of that in the original play (i.e. Mackenna).

with the presumed laying of Stella's spirit to rest on the 200th anniversary of her death.

While director/screenwriter McGuckian has made a number of alterations and additions to Yeats' text, the core elements of the play remain intact. Specifically, both play and film concern a meeting of the Dublin Spiritualists Association led by the London-based (but Dublin-born) medium Mrs. Henderson that becomes hijacked by the ghost of Jonathan Swift. Also, both texts gather an assortment of Irish Protestants, each with their own unique reasons for contacting the spirit world—personal, individualized reasons that become sidelined by the drama of Swift's relationships with his pupils Stella and Vanessa.

Through the device of a séance, Yeats' play brings Ireland's eighteenth-century past—embodied, so to speak, via Mrs. Henderson's channeling the presence of Jonathan Swift, whom John Corbet characterizes as "the chief representative of the intellect of his epoch[,] free at last from superstition" (Yeats 222)—into its early twentieth-century present; Ireland's eighteenth-century Anglo-Irish heritage consequently haunts the post-Independence era inhabited by Yeats (and the play's characters) in *Words Upon the Window Pane*. As a result, the play is commonly interpreted as "a parable of...social and historical disintegration" (Archibald 194), as an expression of Yeats' disaffection with early twentieth-century Ireland, of his "disillusionment with...the failings of independent Ireland," for his "progressive enchantment with Swift...maps a parallel disenchantment with the Ireland of Yeats's [sic] own time" (Mulhall 17). The play explicitly articulates such claims not only through Corbet's "hope to prove that in Swift's day men of intellect reached the height of their power—the greatest position they ever attained in Society and the State—[and] that everything great in Ireland and in our character...comes from that day" (Yeats 204), but also by an actual, later inscription of Yeats that asserted: "I wrote this play as a help to bring back a part of the Irish mind which we have been thrusting out as it were foreign. Now that our period of violent protest is over we claim the Anglo-Irish eighteenth century as our own" (as qtd. in Fitzgerald xv). Even more so, Mrs. Henderson's channeling of an exchange between Swift and Vanessa, during which he refuses Vanessa's physical advances for fear of passing down his perceived madness to their possible progeny, allegorically "enables Yeats to use Swift's feared hereditary flaw as a symbol for his larger theme: the decline of contemporary society from its past greatness" (Fitzgerald 69). According to these readings of *Words Upon the Window Pane*, then, Jonathan Swift is thus "a

70   M. J. FEE

visionary who can foresee the dissolution which will eventually accompany democracy" (69).[5] Indeed, as John Corbet wonders, was Swift's avowed celibacy the result of his fear that his offspring would inherit his madness, or having "foresaw democracy" and thus "dread[ing] the future. Did he refuse to beget children because of that dread" (Yeats 222)?

Mary McGuckian's discussion of her 1994 film adaptation of the play likewise rehearses these allegorical interpretations. Regarding the Anglo-Irish legacy that haunts Yeats' play in the person of Swift—a legacy whose embrace she believes remains vital to addressing the 1990s Anglo-Irish conflict—she notes: "If it's not faced up to we're going to lose an incredible amount that we can discover about ourselves and bring to our cultural life" (Collins 19). However, although McGuckian denies "shifting the focus of the work in its adaptation" (Power 11), I would argue that alongside her adaptation's maintenance of the original text's dynamic tension between the eighteenth and twentieth centuries, the film's alterations in regard to gender—particularly via the film's significant enhancement of the characters of Stella and Miss MacKenna—provide an additional commentary of critical import when considering gender at the time of the film's mid-1990s release.[6]

Before focusing on what has been added, it should be noted that a number of the play's elements have been removed in McGuckian's adaptation. For example, gone is Lulu, the little girl spirit who serves in the play

---

[5] As Richard Taylor similarly interprets, the play offers "a telling commentary on the prevailing debasement of a once heroic culture" and a demonstration of "the conflict and tension between the age of reason and that of a debased modernity." See Richard Taylor, *A Reader's Guide to the Plays of W. B. Yeats*, St. Martin's Press, 1984, pp. 132–133, 136. Katharine Worth summarizes (and echoes): "Critics have tended to interpret Yeats's [sic] presentation of his low-life material in allegorical terms, as a disdainful vision of modern Dublin in sharp decline and decay from its great Augustan era." Katharine Worth, "The *Words Upon the Window Pane*: A Female Tragedy," *Yeats Annual*, vol. 10, 1993, p. 144. For the rare counter reading, see Derek Hand's "Breaking Boundaries, Creating Spaces: W.B. Yeats's *The Words Upon the Window-Pane* as a Postcolonial Text," in *W.B. Yeats and Postcolonialism*, edited by Deborah Fleming, Locust Hill Press, 2001, pp. 187–204. However, while Hand questions whether the play necessarily prioritizes an idealized Anglo-Irish past over a Catholic nationalist present disconnected from that heritage, he nonetheless acknowledges that the play's key meaning(s) involve a dynamic staging between the two historical eras.

[6] Paul Power's question to Mary McGuckian about whether she shifted the focus of the play is specifically in response to McGuckian's changing the words that Stella inscribes into the window pane. The words inscribed into the window pane in the play are instead spoken by Stella to Swift in the film during her first speaking appearance in the film, and replaced by the phrase "If the words become flesh, then the spirit has substance." See endnote 13.

4 THE WOMEN INCARNATE OF *WORDS UPON THE WINDOW PANE*   71

as Mrs. Henderson's "control" or spirit guide in the other world. The film adaptation also removes Yeats' foregrounding of the monetary compensation that Mrs. Henderson receives, a hint in the play that supports Mr. Corbet's belief that she is an "accomplished actress and scholar" only in it for the money. More significant than what McGuckian removes in the translation from stage to screen, however, are the numerous additions and expansions in her filmic version. Some of these changes may be attributed to the need to relay the story more cinematically and less stage-bound, with added scenes moving the tale outside of the original play's singular focus on one séance on one night in one location. Richly visualized locations such as rain-soaked Dublin streets, Trinity College's library, and St. Patrick's Cathedral (particularly the crypts of Swift and Stella), as well as the added scenes and settings of Mrs. Henderson's dockside arrival, Dr. Trench's rooms, Cornelius' watch stand, and numerous carriage-set conversations extend McGuckian's *Words Upon the Window Pane* across a two-day period throughout a host of Dublin locations both real and fictional. Moreover, when the action is confined to what is the sole location in the play (i.e. the lodging house's sitting room), this space becomes broadened through fluid and circular camera movements, mirrors that render the frame multi-dimensional, expressive editing, and cinematographic techniques such as the numerous rack focus pulls that shift attention between the frame's foreground and background, between the room's inside and outside as viewed through the window pane itself. Finally, the film's actual visualization of Swift's encounters with Stella and Vanessa in the same sitting room—albeit in the eighteenth century—extends the filmic space temporally as well as spatially and cinematically. In other words, the film depicts two cinematic versions of the play's singular setting: an eighteenth-century mise-en-scène that stages the action for Swift, Stella, and Vanessa; and an early twentieth-century figuration of the space as home to Miss MacKenna and the Spiritualists Association. Consequently, while *Words Upon the Window Pane* may have theatrical roots, the film adaptation's aesthetics assure us that we transcend the limited view of theatrical spectatorship into a more wide-ranging, cinematic perspective. Indeed, such additions enhance the text's dimensions as a work of heritage cinema by visually emphasizing a vibrant and ornate array of historical locations and details.

But the most important revisions that McGuckian's film makes to its source material can be found in its expansion of characters. In Yeats' play—which takes place during a single, fourth séance—Dr. Trench and

72 M. J. FEE

Mr. Corbet dominate the action. They have been brought in to assist the proceedings, given that the earlier séances have been overwhelmed by an as-yet unknown presence. In the play, conversations between Trench and Corbet serve an expository function, as they supply background information on the participants and their motivations for taking part in the gathering, as well as the prior séances' occurrences. In their roles as Spiritualists Association president and Swift scholar, respectively, Trench and Corbet are also able to provide necessary knowledge to the audience regarding theories of the spirit world as well as historical context important to understanding Swift and his relationships with Stella and Vanessa. Other characters in the play occupy very limited roles, and so alongside Trench and Corbet, it is only Mrs. Henderson (and her dual channeling of Swift's and Vanessa's spirits) who serves an additionally significant function to the narrative.

In Mary McGuckian's film adaptation of *Words Upon the Window Pane*, however, Miss MacKenna literally emerges at the film's start from the shadowy edges of the frame in order to assume a much more primary place. As the original play's "enthusiastic secretary" for the Association (Yeats 199), Miss MacKenna's main function is taking care of Mrs. Henderson and the event's spatial arrangements (for she has a room in the lodging house where the séance is held), and opening the door for the various participants. Although she performs these same roles in the film— responsibilities that are cinematically expanded upon via scenes of her picking up Mrs. Henderson at the dock, placing the announcement for the gathering, and methodically setting up the space—McGuckian greatly enhances MacKenna's role in the film, providing her with a more dominant voice and perspective on the proceedings than what she has in the play. Moreover, the film augments MacKenna's voice not only in and of itself, but also and more significantly through MacKenna's serving as a literal and direct conduit for Stella's voice—a voice completely absent in the play. In Yeats' play, we only "hear" Stella via John Corbet's and (channeled via Mrs. Henderson) Swift's comments either about or to her. When the play's Mrs. Henderson relays Swift and Vanessa's exchange, she speaks in both Swift's and Vanessa's voices. When she embodies Swift and Stella's conversation, though, she only speaks in Swift's voice, as Swift speaks *to* Stella, expressing what *he* perceives to be Stella's desires and concerns. Even if one were to argue that Stella "speaks" in the play through its quoting of her poems, here once again these words are recited via Swift, as channeled through Mrs. Henderson.

Stella's absence in the original play resonates with the ways that she has been commonly featured in discussions of her and Swift's relationship. As Louise Barnett notes regarding Swift's destruction of Stella's letters after her death: "Stella is ironically memorable for this erasure—for the absence of enough information about her to form an opinion or reach a conclusion, and, above all, for the silence of her own voice except for its intermittent reflection in Swift's" (23). Understood in terms of her supposed "compliance" and "tractability," Stella has provided critics with a convenient means for prioritizing Swift's over her concerns (Palumbo 431). By presencing a Stella who not only exists, but also speaks—and, as we will see, in fact bargains—McGuckian's figuration hence challenges perceptions of Stella as "marginalized" and "deliberately erased as an independent voice," as someone whom Swift "deprived...of autonomy" (Barnett 22–23, 37).

In McGuckian's film, Stella and her concerns become central, and she is given both body and voice alongside Swift and Vanessa.[7] In fact, her spirit resides at the heart of the séance's supernatural proceedings, as the hauntings are linked specifically to the anniversary of her death. Only spoken for and about in the play, the film, on the contrary, explicitly depicts Stella in three scenes. During the first séance, Mrs. Henderson becomes possessed by Swift, while Miss MacKenna is overtaken by the spirit of Stella. A dissolve from Miss MacKenna's reflection in the window to that of Stella transports us into the same room two hundred years prior, while Jonathan Swift questions Stella as to whether she is happy with their relationship. After reciting lines from her birthday poem to Swift, Stella shifts her attention to his poem "Cadenus and Vanessa," as they discuss Stella's jealousy of Swift's other paramour, Vanessa. The film's first presencing of Stella concludes with Swift and Stella secretly marrying, as Swift declares "Your fears for your own character's loss of face weighs so heavily on me that I have to allow some means of allaying them," at which point he "determine[s]" that they should be married—albeit under the condition that their marriage remain private. However, after the private ceremony is completed, Stella refuses Swift's physical advances, noting that she

---

[7] The film's foregrounding of women complements certain interpretations of the play, namely Katharine Worth's 1990 staging at the Yeats International Summer School at Sligo that she documents in the *Yeats Annual*. While that production maintained the play's single-room setting, the spirits of Swift, Stella, and Vanessa—as well as spirit guide Lulu—were seated in the shadows, off to the side of the stage, and they would emerge and venture toward the center of the stage during the appropriate moments in the play.

"cannot countenance the hypocrisy of a marriage unacknowledged in public being acknowledged in private."

Stella returns during the second séance sitting depicted in the film, as her and Swift's card playing is interrupted by Vanessa's arrival at the house. Although Stella initially refuses to receive Vanessa, Vanessa eventually gains entry, only to be chastised by Swift for writing to Stella in order to inquire whether Stella and Swift were married. Locking Stella out of the room, Vanessa attempts to seduce Swift. Her seduction of Swift occurs in both film and play—indeed, it is the only event in the film's multiple séance sequences to transpire in the play as well, with all other séance occurrences having narrative additions that were made by director/screenwriter McGuckian. It also represents one of the rare instances where narrative content has been abridged from Yeats' original work, as Vanessa's tempting of Swift proves more extensive in the play (although here we should recall that even with this somewhat more active role, Vanessa only speaks in the play through Mrs. Henderson, as she, like Stella, is not visualized). In the film adaptation, however, this sequence concerns itself much more with Stella's frustrated attempts to break into the room—along with her shock at discovering a partially undressed Vanessa once she finally bursts into the space—rather than with Vanessa's pleas for Swift to find comfort in her arms.

Stella's final appearance during the third séance finds her at the end of her life, expressing regret to Swift that he never publicly acknowledged their marriage. Swift counters that to have done so would have been hypocritical, given that Stella never permitted him to acknowledge Vanessa through the publication of his poem "Cadenus and Vanessa" while Vanessa was alive. The words we have witnessed Stella carve into the window pane next become visible—"If the words become flesh, then the spirit has substance"—and after physically struggling with Swift, Stella collapses to the ground. The window pane shatters as we view our last image of Stella, being carried in Swift's arms.

Since Stella neither appears nor speaks in the play, McGuckian's adaptation's extensive depiction of her in these scenes—not to mention numerous brief, silent appearances at other points in the film, when Stella's image is hauntingly juxtaposed with that of Miss MacKenna—notably revises Yeats' original text. It should come as no surprise that Stella's presence in the film consequently introduces multiple narrative elements absent from the play: Stella's jealousy of Vanessa, her secret marriage to Swift, her refusal of Swift's advances, and her death-bed request. However,

McGuckian's *Words Upon the Window Pane* does more than simply expand the scope of Yeats' play through introducing much debated biographical elements of Swift and Stella's relationship. If, as critics have convincingly argued, the introduction of Jonathan Swift enables Yeats' *Words* to comment upon twentieth-century Ireland's dismissal of its Anglo-Irish heritage, then what significance can be ascribed to the cinematic adaptation's addition of Stella? I would argue that given the degree to which it radically increases Stella's presence, the film *rewrites* Stella as an active agent in Swift's life—a rewriting of the eighteenth century's "frail and fatherless" love interest that proves consequential both to the play itself, as well as to our sense of its contemporary importance to figuring gender, particularly in an Irish context (Barnett 18). Specifically, by increasing the agency of female characters such as Stella (and, as we will discuss later, Miss MacKenna), McGuckian's adaptation not only contests prior understandings of gender within the context of Swift and his works, but also challenges the passive femininity typically rendered in Irish cinematic representation—not to mention incorporates concerns around women's agency within the domestic sphere that were prominent at the time of the film's 1990s release, especially in regard to debates around abortion and divorce.

Jonathan Swift's relations with, and representations of, women have generated considerable debate, with Swift's approach to women framed in relation to two distinct groups: women with whom Swift interacted, and women contained in his writings. Two dominant figures emerge in regard to the former: Esther Johnson (Stella) and Hester van Homrigh (Vanessa)—both of whom are central to McGuckian's *Words Upon the Window Pane*. An understanding of Stella and Vanessa "as moral opposites jelled early" in accounts of Swift (Barnett 21), a tension borne out in McGuckian's text not merely through a narrative that highlights their competition for Swift's affections, but aesthetically emphasized in the second séance, with its dramatic crosscutting between the two women during the sequence of heightened emotion when Vanessa visits—and attempts to seduce—Swift.

We must recall, however, that the adaptation's newly incarnating Stella across the three scenes in the film coalesces around one particular topic, and in relation to one particular character. More specifically, taken together and bearing in mind their narrative substance, these three scenes between Stella and Swift foreground marriage as an element uniquely central to our engagement with McGuckian's *Words Upon the Window Pane*, with marriage thus at the heart of the eighteenth century's haunting of the Spiritualists Associations' twentieth-century meeting. To be sure, the film's more ongoing focus on marriage recalls a couple of fleeting moments from Yeats' original work. First, in the play an enraged Swift ruptures the séance's "peace" by accosting Vanessa about her writing to Stella to inquire whether Stella and Swift were married—for if they are not married, then Vanessa fails to grasp why she and Swift cannot be wed. Similarly and during another instance in the play, Mrs. Henderson channels Swift's regretfully addressing Stella as to whether she was happy, in spite of their not marrying (for in Yeats' play, there is no mention of Swift and Stella being married).

The discrepancy between the film's marrying of Stella and Swift, and the play's choosing not to do so, rehearses a crucial, oft-deliberated topic in considerations of Stella and Swift's relationship. The very notion that Swift and Stella were married has generated substantial debate.[8] Regardless of what we ultimately believe regarding Stella and Swift's marital status, however, the romantic nature of their relationship foregrounds issues around gender. If we agree with the claim that they never married, there is thus a subversive agency afforded to both Stella's and Vanessa's relations with Swift, particularly in an Irish context. In an echo of the rhetoric of containment that animates analyses of the function that marriage assumes in an Irish context, Barnett states that "neither relationship was sanctioned by the legal recognition or social custom that *contained* the lives of most eighteenth-century women within the institutions of the family and mar-riage" (21).[9] And if Swift and Stella were married, the film nevertheless maintains such subversive agency through the active role given to Stella in this regard, in that she bargains with Swift to commit to marriage, yet withholds consummation of the relationship until he publicly acknowl-edges their relationship. The centrality of these thematic concerns around gender, agency, and marriage is borne out even more when we recall Stella's relation to the other character whose presence is more richly mani-fest in the film: that of Miss MacKenna.

[8] For an overview of some of the positions and sources regarding this debate, see Barnett pp. 39–42.

[9] My emphasis. For more on the rhetoric of containment in regard to gender and marriage in Ireland, see Kathryn A. Conrad, *Locked in the Family Cell: Gender, Sexuality, and Political Agency in Irish National Discourse*, University of Wisconsin Press, 2004; and James M. Smith, *Ireland's Magdalen Laundries and the Nation's Architecture of Containment*, University of Notre Dame Press, 2007.

4 THE WOMEN INCARNATE OF *WORDS UPON THE WINDOW PANE* 77

The connection between Miss MacKenna and Stella should come as no surprise. There is, of course, the primary supernatural connection that the film establishes between the two characters through MacKenna's channeling of Stella's spirit. But more than that, the cinematic strategies used to forge links between the two characters are varied and numerous. From the very opening of the film, once MacKenna emerges from the shadows of the frame, a pan across the frame (and centuries) from left to right joins her with Stella; similarly, MacKenna will look off screen, and the camera will follow her gaze, ultimately landing on an image of Stella. Editing also intertwines the centuries and characters, as the film expressively and abruptly cuts back and forth between past and present; for example, a match on action will unite the two characters, as a door opened by Miss MacKenna in the twentieth century is next closed by Stella in the eighteenth; or a shocked Miss MacKenna will react to a prone Vanessa, when Stella bursts into the seduction scene. And finally on other occasions, the two characters coexist visually and/or aurally, as Stella's image is faded up into MacKenna's image, or the image dissolves from one character's face to another's, or the characters' dialogue is overlapped.

In line with its expansion of characters, the cinematic adaptation of *Words Upon the Window Pane* produces an additional narrative association between the characters as well. Specifically, in the film, McGuckian develops MacKenna's relationship with Dr. Trench to parallel that of Stella and Swift, intimating that, as with the latter two characters from the eighteenth century, there is an unconsummated relationship between an older male teacher and his younger female charge in the twentieth century.[10] When Corbet recites a few lines of Stella's birthday poem to Swift, MacKenna immediately recognizes the text as something that Dr. Trench would read to her.

The connections that McGuckian's *Words* cinematically and narratively establish between MacKenna and Stella ultimately extend to the theme of marriage—or lack of—as well. For example (and, once again, it should be noted in scenes that McGuckian adds to Yeats' play), Mrs. Henderson clarifies that she recognized MacKenna at her dockside pick-up not through any "special powers," but rather since she was "the only single

---

[10] Expanding Dr. Trench and Miss MacKenna's relationship in this manner mirrors the commonality of a relationship such as that between Swift and Stella to their contemporaneous time: "women…were always to some extent in the position of pupil or daughter figures to adult males, to whom they were expected to be subservient and respectful" (Barnett 19).

78   M. J. FEE

woman there." Moreover, a scene between Corbet and Trench at Dr. Trench's apartments finds Trench sharing how MacKenna was left in his charge when her father died, to which Corbet responds that MacKenna must have been "handsome in her day," adding shortly thereafter that it is "strange she never married."

Through its character and narrative additions involving Stella and Miss MacKenna, Mary McGuckian's *Words Upon the Window Pane* thus significantly expands upon the role of women in its adaptation of Yeats' play. Consequently, the film's increased focus on women, particularly in the context of considerations of marriage, extends the original play's conversation between the eighteenth and twentieth centuries into one that articulates specific concerns involving gender.[11] The relationship between original play and film adaptation articulates an even richer dialogue between historical eras, particularly where gender is concerned. On the one hand, McGuckian's adaptation and its enhancement of the play's gendered dimensions remind us of women's concerns contemporary to Yeats' play that, while not explicitly articulated in the original work, nevertheless provide a noteworthy context to its production. Recalling that the play premiered at the Abbey Theatre in 1930 and was published in 1934, Sandra McAvoy's claim that "in the period 1929–1935, as Ireland was in the process of adapting to independence, sexuality became a focus for a paternalistic Church and government," particularly through legislation involving contraception and childcare as well as attendant concerns regarding the institutions of family and marriage (264)—not to mention the strong disappointment that Yeats explicitly vocalized to the Seanad in 1925 regarding the Irish Free State's legislation on divorce—then McGuckian's film and its enhancements to the play's gendered dimensions give voice to not just Stella, but also to the era's undertones.

But this dialogue between texts—theatrical and cinematic—and historical eras speaks in both directions, as by giving fuller voice to the Stella and Miss MacKenna of Yeats' *Words Upon the Window Pane*, McGuckian's film speaks to contemporaneous debates around gender in her own era—particularly in the context of marriage—that had likewise assumed

[11] While not as extensive as those revisions involving marriage in relation to Stella and Miss MacKenna, McGuckian's adaptation makes one additional alteration that likewise highlights marriage. Specifically, in the film adaptation, we discover that Mrs. Mallet has lied about being a widow seeking the advice of her dead husband, and is in fact a spinster, thus setting up the romance with Cornelius Patterson alluded to in the film. Such deception and romantic coupling are not present in Yeats' original play.

4 THE WOMEN INCARNATE OF *WORDS UPON THE WINDOW PANE* 79

prominence in political, social, and cultural discourses in the mid-1990s Ireland of the film's release. The film's 1928 narrative is hence not only haunted by events two hundred years prior, but also shadowed by more contemporary concerns with gender. Specifically, in the final decades of the twentieth century, considerations of gender underwent a period of particularly intense reassessment. The success in establishing a constitutional ban on abortion in 1983 via the Eighth Amendment, the Kerry Babies case in 1984, and the failure to repeal the existing ban on divorce in 1986 ensured that both the maternal and marital positions of women remained a topic of public debate. The election of human rights lawyer Mary Robinson as the first female president of Ireland in 1990 was hoped to inaugurate more liberating views on women and their roles in both Ireland and on the world stage (Smyth); however, the X Case in 1992 and subsequent failure to overturn the Eighth Amendment, along with the acrimonious debates that led up to the narrow overturning of the constitutional ban on divorce in 1995 revealed such optimism to be short-lived. Nevertheless, these events made certain that discussions around gender and in particular understandings around women's agency would provide a fertile context in which to consider the notable revisions made by McGuckian in her adaptation.

Understanding the film adaptation's Stella and Miss MacKenna as prioritizing women's experiences and addressing more recent historical contexts (and not simply those of their post-Independence creation), McGuckian's *Words Upon the Window Pane* thus shares in the feminist historical project of other works by Irish women filmmakers that have engaged with gender in Ireland. For example, Pat Murphy's *Maeve* (1981) and *Anne Devlin* (1984) along with Margo Harkin's *Hush-a-Bye Baby* (1990) were some of the earliest, canonical works that examined how Irish women's experiences were shaped by the intersections between nationalist and Catholic understandings of gender. In challenging not only cinema's stereotypical images of the feisty colleen and/or sacrificing Irish mother, but also the nationalist discourses that gave birth to many of those restrictive and conservative understandings of women in Ireland, these films overcame ongoing silences regarding the place of women in Ireland.[12] Yet unique in comparison to these earlier works, McGuckian's film specifically

---

[12] See, for example, Luke Gibbons, "The Politics of Silence: *Anne Devlin*, Women and Irish Cinema" and "'Lies that Tell the Truth': *Maeve*, History and Irish Cinema," in *Transformations in Irish Culture*, Cork University Press, 1996, pp. 107–127.

80 M. J. FEE

employs the fantastic as a means of giving voice and presence to Irish women. Thus much as Stella's letter to Swift speaks of another role for women, so too do the women incarnate in Mary McGuckian's *Words Upon the Window Pane* embody a provocative addition to Ireland's cinematic corpus, particularly when compared to the conservative depictions of gender frequently circulated via Irish historical films. And in this way, perhaps one final revision made in the film adaptation proves most telling. Specifically, in a change from the play, Stella cuts into the window pane: "If the words become flesh, then the spirit has substance."[13] Thus McGuckian's film does more than simply adapt Yeats' play; rather, it literalizes this demand for incarnation in its cinematic rendering of the fantastic.

WORKS CITED

Archibald, Douglas N. "*The Words upon the Window-pane* and Yeats's Encounter With Jonathan Swift." *Yeats and the Theatre*, edited by Robert O'Driscoll and Lorna Reynolds, Maclean-Hunter Press, 1975, pp. 176–214.

Barnett, Louise. *Jonathan Swift in the Company of Women*. Oxford University Press, 2007.

Barton, Ruth. *Irish National Cinema*. Routledge, 2004.

Collins, Pat. "Interview with Mary McGuckian." *Film West*, Spring 1995, pp. 18–20.

Fitzgerald, Mary. "Out of a Medium's Mouth": The Writing of "*The Words upon the Window-pane*". *The Colby Literary Quarterly*, vol. 17, no. 2, June 1981, pp. 61–73.

Johnson, Esther ("Stella"), "To Dr. Swift on his Birthday, November 30, 1721," *The Poems of Jonathan Swift*, vol. 2, edited by Harold Williams, Oxford University Press, 1937, pp. 736–739.

McAvoy, Sandra L. "The Regulation of Sexuality in the Irish Free State, 1929–1935." *Medicine, Disease, and the State in Ireland, 1650–1940*, edited by Greta Jones and Elizabeth Malcolm, Cork University Press, 1999, pp. 253–266.

McLoone, Martin. "National Cinema in Ireland." *Theorising National Cinema*, edited by Valentina Vitali and Paul Willemen, British Film Institute, 2006, pp. 88–99.

---

[13] In the play, the following words are carved by Stella into the window pane (an excerpt from one of her poems that, while not highlighted via the window pane, are nevertheless repeated in the film on numerous occasions): "You taught how I might youth prolong[,] By knowing what is right and wrong, How from the heart to bring supplies[,] Of lustre to my fading eyes" (Yeats 203).

Mulhall, Daniel. "Yeats, Swift, and Ireland's Contested Eighteenth Century." *"The first wit of the age": Essays on Swift and His Contemporaries in Honour of Herman J. Real*, edited by Kirsten Juhas et al., Peter Lang, 2013, pp. 17–27.

Palumbo, David M. "Death Becomes Her: Figuration and Decay in Swift's 'Birthday Poems' to Stella." *The Eighteenth Century*, vol. 51, no. 4, Winter 2010, pp. 431–450.

Power, Paul. "McGuckian's Travels." *Film Ireland*, February/March 1995, pp. 10–12.

Smyth, Ailbhe. "'A Great Day for the Women of Ireland...': The Meaning of Mary Robinson's Presidency for Irish Women." *The Canadian Journal of Irish Studies*, vol. 18, no. 1, July 1992, pp. 61–75.

Yeats, W.B. "The Words Upon the Window Pane." The Words Upon the Window Pane *Manuscript Materials*, edited by Mary Fitzgerald, Cornell University Press, 2002, pp. 198–224.

CHAPTER 5

Mouth Not Eye: On Jordan's Adaptation of Beckett's *Not I*

Eyal Amiran

Neil Jordan's 2000 adaptation of Samuel Beckett's *Not I*, with Julianna Moore as "Mouth," revises the priorities of the version of the play directed by Beckett and starring Billie Whitelaw. Beckett wrote the play with Whitelaw in mind, according to Beckett's London publisher John Calder (Wakeling 92), but its 1972 premiere was at the Lincoln Center in New York, directed by Alan Schneider, with Jessica Tandy in the role. Beckett directed Whitelaw the following year at the Royal Court Theatre in London. A Whitelaw performance of the role was filmed by the BBC in 1977; here a fixed camera shows only Whitelaw's mouth in the dark, approximating an idealized view of the actor on stage. Jordan's version

E. Amiran (✉)
UC Irvine, Irvine, CA, USA
e-mail: amiran@uci.edu

© The Author(s), under exclusive license to Springer Nature Switzerland AG 2022
M. C. Conner et al. (eds.), *Screening Contemporary Irish Fiction and Drama*, Palgrave Studies in Adaptation and Visual Culture,
https://doi.org/10.1007/978-3-031-04568-4_5

84   E. AMIRAN

was produced in 2000 as part of the ambitious *Beckett on Film*, a project conceived by Irish actor Michael Colgan, who had staged Beckett's nineteen plays originally in 1991 (all Beckett's plays but his first, the posthumously published *Eleuthéria*, written in 1947). In the late 1990s, Colgan teamed with Alan Moloney to produce film versions of the plays, each with its own director and cast. The directors recruited for the new project included John Crowley (*Come and Go*), Atom Egoyan (*Krapp's Last Tape*), and David Mamet (*Catastrophe*), and actors included John Gielgud and Harold Pinter (*Catastrophe*), Jeremy Irons (*Ohio Impromptu*), and Kristin Scott Thomas (*Play*), among other luminaries of stage and screen (Sierz 137–140). Ten of the films were screened at the 2000 Toronto International Film Festival (*Beckett on Film*), and the series, some of which had been shown on British television Channel 4, was screened in its entirety on September 13–20, 2001, at the Barbican Centre in London and released as a DVD box set. The producers have been explicit that film cannot reproduce theater directly, and have been interested to explore the cinematic features of the medium (Sierz 140–1), though, in the case of Jordan's adaptation, the result is a new sense of the work altogether, as I argue below. While Beckett and his estate have famously refused to let directors deviate from Beckett's prescribed staging of the plays, Beckett himself continually revisited his works, including when directing his plays (Gontarski 430), sometimes changing them significantly, as he did when he removed the figure of Auditor, a mute spectator on stage, from *Not I*, to focus solely on the figure of Mouth. In a sense *Beckett on Film*, which aims to preserve and disseminate Beckett's plays but cannot help but change them, reminds us and the Beckett estate that interpretation in the staging of plays is both inevitable and desirable.[1]

Jordan's adaptation recasts Beckett's drama in a specifically cinematic tradition. Where Beckett's version fixes a beam of light on Mouth in a dark space, flattening the plane of action and rendering the mouth as a nearly two-dimensional image, Jordan splices short cinematic cuts to show different sides of Moore's head, creating a visual experience that, to recall Walter Benjamin's distinction between theater and film, can only be seen on screen. As Benjamin says,

---

[1] As Gontarski notes, re-interpretation is essential to a living art, while "faith and accuracy" to the original remain impossible to pin down (448).

The artistic performance of a stage actor is definitely presented to the public by the actor in person; that of the screen actor, however, is presented by a camera, with a twofold consequence. The camera that presents the performance of the film actor to the public need not respect the performance as an integral whole. Guided by the cameraman, the camera continually changes its position with respect to the performance. (Benjamin VIII)

Hence cinema shows an object that cannot exist in theater. The interpretative tradition of cinematic cuts may seem to extend Beckett's career-long effort to show bodies that reference a missing whole, to reproduce a body as head, or to imagine it in parts. But despite Beckett's several experiments with media, including film (*Film*), television (*Eh Joe*), and radio (*All That Fall*), the reduction of the body in Beckett draws on a different kind of thinking than the cinematic. Jordan's adaptation helps bring into focus different assumptions about the dramatic space in Beckett and about the bodies, or body parts, that are almost inevitably found in it. For despite his interest in the image, and the flattening out of the body on stage in *Not I*, his body is not produced by a visual regime as a screen or a mental image alone. The body image in Beckett is "not an object but a 'process,'" as Gilles Deleuze says in his essay "The Exhausted," "neither that of names or of voices, but that of images, sounding, coloring," which Deleuze also calls a "pure image" (9). Bodies in Beckett draw on textual and linguistic traditions that see language as physical and bodily or as part of a physical and bodily process.[2] It is here that, to anticipate, the mouth is ready for its close-up.

The dramatic monologue in *Not I* consists of approximately 2300 words spoken by Mouth, presumably a woman's mouth but actually an ungendered mouth. The mouth is to appear eight feet above the stage (*Not I* 216), reinforcing the impression that Mouth is not a living person's mouth, but a disembodied presence. The stage is dark, except for a strong narrow beam that shines on the mouth. In the version Beckett directed, Whitelaw was draped in black and her head was restrained by "straps and braces" so her mouth would remain fixed in the light (Abbott 118). The beam allows only her narrow lips and the interior of the mouth to be seen, floating person-less in the dark. A second character in the play, the "tall standing figure" of "Auditor," is barely visible at stage left. Auditor is

---

[2] Audroné Žukauskaité suggests Beckett's characters should be read with Gilbert Simondon and Deleuze, as processes (275).

86   E. AMIRAN

"dead still" except when the figure raises and lowers its arms slowly three times during the play, but Auditor cannot be seen as separate from Mouth (see Worth, "Beckett's Auditors" 172), for as me, myself, and I she is her own object and also audits the affair. Auditor cannot be excluded from sight on stage, except by framing in representational media such as film.

Mouth's history is one mystery of the play. According to her monologue, delivered in the third person, she, or else the person about whom Mouth speaks, is or was a woman in her 70s who lived a loveless life, abandoned as a speechless infant by her father before and by her mother during her birth. She lived a solitary, traumatic, and disconnected life, and one day found herself in the dark, in the disembodied state we see in the play, "whole body like gone ... just the mouth." She appears to be dead and to consider her unexpected new experience. She is not in pain, she realizes, but hears a buzzing and sees a "ray or beam" of light—that is all. This condition contrasts with the afterworld she'd been brought up to expect, one in which a merciful God (the idea makes her laugh) might punish her. Instead it is a world without feedback, without distinct sensation, "all silent as the grave," except that she hears a stream of words, "certain vowel sounds," that must be her own, though in her life she avoided speech (on vowel sounds see below). The words come from far away—from her past. As often in Beckett, thought is rethought, remembrance of words that repeat, as in Krapp's tapes, each enunciation bringing the (or a) subject into being (hence they are recorded on Krapp's birthdays).

There seem to have been traumatic events, all of her life ultimately, that Mouth denies having happened to her, saying repeatedly it was not her—not I—to whom these events happened, about whom the story is told, but to the third person, "She." The narrator Marcel attributes this device to Albertine in Proust's *Remembrance*, an important text for *Not I* and the subject of Beckett's early study:

> She employed, not from any refinement of style, but in order to correct her imprudences, abrupt breaches of syntax not unlike that figure which the grammarians call anacoluthon or some such name. Having allowed herself, while discussing women, to say: "I remember, the other day, I ...," she would at once catch her breath, after which 'I' became 'she': it was something that she had witnessed as an innocent spectator, not a thing that she herself had done. It was not herself that was the heroine of the anecdote. (*Remembrance* 485)

What happened Mouth does not say, and the work hinges on this indeterminacy[3]: in Beckett identity is not so much negated or refused as found indeterminate, as Porter Abbott suggests (177). However unknowable her so-called life, some motivation for interpretation in *Not I* comes from the associations between Mouth's repeated phrases. She remembers lying face down in a field in April, and court proceedings in which she was asked "what had she to say for herself." She seems to have been the accused. Her gender is an explicit feature of this court proceeding: "guilty or not guilty ... stand up woman ... speak up woman" (221). There was "something she had to ... tell ... tiny little thing ... before its time" (221). Was this tiny thing herself, born before her time, or a fetus she had aborted and had to account for in court—or both? The narrative conflates her with this possible double of herself, and also identifies the rush of words with "something" pouring out into the lavatory, vomit but possibly something else that she has the urge to confess: "sudden urge to ... tell ... then rush out stop the first she saw ... nearest lavatory ... start pouring it out ... steady stream ... mad stuff ... half the vowels wrong ... no one could follow ... till she saw the stare she was getting ... then die of shame" (222). We will return to the conflation of words (and, in print, ellipses), objects, and the body's interior; for now, note that the work begins by invoking the out/in structure implied by birth: ".... out ... into this world ... this world ... tiny little thing" (216). The fetus is both outside its host and part of it, and when it comes "out" it goes "into this world," and likewise the fetus as body is both inside and outside the world, between mind and world, ear and mouth, like language.[4]

The plot, as it were, of the story is the same in Jordan's adaptation, but here the focus on cinematic cuts changes the location of Mouth. In Beckett's version, Whitelaw's mouth is surrounded by darkness and floats in a nether world. In Jordan's adaptation, Moore approaches an elaborate high-backed chair, part throne and part electric chair. We then see her

---

[3] When working on a 1972 Royal Court production of *Not I* with the actress Jessica Tandy, Beckett wrote in a letter that Tandy was "Bit bewildered by the text. Silly questions, 'What happened to her in the meadow?'" (letter to Avigdor Arikha and Anne Atik, *Letters* 304). Alan Schneider, the director, notes that he thought "the woman in *Not I* had been raped" (Beckett, *Letters* 305 n. 4).

[4] As "Mouth" is also "Mund," in German, there is a suggestion that the words enter or come out of the Earth, which is the planetary figure in the Unnamable's narrative that subtends *Not I*, discussed below. Beckett identifies and sometimes merges characters with a planet or with Earth, for example, Winnie in *Happy Days*.

88   E. AMIRAN

lower face as she speaks, the camera cutting quickly for discontinuous front and side views. These cuts require either several cameras or a post-production editing; neither is available to an audience in real time, as Benjamin notes. They belong to film, not to theater, and disrupt any imagined unity of Mouth. They also show enough of Moore's face and cheeks—a move supported up to a point by the mention in the script of the body parts needed to speak: the cheeks, teeth, tongue, and lips, whereas in Beckett's version we see no cheeks or skin—for us to recognize the person of Moore the actress, or at least to see she is a rosy, living person. Unlike Whitelaw's stark, terrifyingly mechanical mouth, Moore's full lips and smooth skin are the image of health. She is not the wandering woman nearing seventy recounted in the story, but a young person who may rightly deny the story is about her. Is she alive, and thinking of another person, as Mouth says ("she")? Or is she an actress playing Mouth? The adoption of a living, youthful figure as Mouth radically changes the meaning of the play, which hinges on producing the idea of flesh in its absence.

A reading that casts *Not I* in the afterworld is consistent with a line of thought that runs through many Beckett works (Gendron 49–50). (The most remarkable passage in Proust, he writes in *Proust*, is the one where Marcel imagines he sees his grandmother in the afterworld.) Many of Beckett's characters, beginning with his early protagonist Belacqua Shuah, seem to be dead, or else cannot tell how dead or alive they are, like Dante's characters, and recall a past world, not being able to find silence or to be silent. (Belacqua is a character in Dante's *Divine Comedy*.) After Beckett sent the publisher Chatto his collection of short stories (it came out as *More Pricks Thank Kicks* in 1934), the editor asked for another story to help justify the price they expected to charge for the book (*Echo's Bones*, "Introduction"). Beckett then wrote the strange and tortuous "Echo's Bones," in which his Belacqua, who had been killed off, continues his adventures in the afterlife, first sitting on a fence, then meeting a giant who wants him to sire an heir on his behalf, and finally investigating his own tomb. Chatto decided not to include the story in the collection, and it was published posthumously, in 2015.

Likewise in *The Unnamable*, often considered a precursor text for *Not I*, partly on account of its "not I" passages, the speaking voice imagines it is a series of characters that circle in the dark:

It's not I speaking, it's not I hearing, let us not go into that, let us go on as if I were the only one in the world, whereas I'm the only one absent from it, or with others, what difference does it make, others present, others absent, they are not obliged to make themselves manifest, all that is needed is to wander and let wander, be this slow boundless whirlwind and every particle of its dust, it's impossible. Someone speaks, someone hears, no need to go any further, it is not he, it's I, or another, what does it matter, the case is clear, it is not he, he who I know I am, that's all I know, who I cannot say I am, I can't say anything, I've tried. (*The Unnamable* 401–2)

The swirling dust motes are a common figure in Beckett's fiction for a glimmer of consciousness, as in the "ray or beam" in *Not I*. *Waiting for Godot*, to give another example of a work in which the liminal world may be read as an afterlife, is also a kind of fairytale in which Vladimir and Estragon must wait in a non-place or limbo for Godot, a bearded lord of the manor, according to the stable boy who meets them at the tree, meanwhile remembering episodes from a past life that is "all dead and buried" (35), when they swam in a river and climbed the Eiffel Tower. The boy messenger appears and disappears mysteriously, and time seems to pass in great leaps from the first act to the second.[5] As with Mouth, who now dismisses the idea of judgment and accounting with a horrible laugh (but keeps coming back to it), the tramps also invoke accounting on part of Godot, who they imagine might need to consult his books and make calculations before he knows what to do with them (*Waiting for Godot* 13), only to dismiss this idea, along with all the other ideas.

Here we should note the importance of accounting or of judgment more broadly in Beckett. Judgment is on Mouth's mind, and so is her own judgment of herself, but because we see Jordan's Mouth—Moore—as our object, the object seen only in the world of cinema and outside its presumed physical space, she is objectified, judged, by us, and not by her own internal position (which does not exist for Jordan). While Beckett owes a debt to Antonin Artaud, who saw immediate experience as a rejection of staged living ("The Theater and Its Double" and the 1947 radio play, "To Have Done with the Judgment of God"), a debt to which we will return in a moment, in Beckett there is an emphasis on measurement, though it measures spaces disconnected from a larger world. Along with his pervasive sense of uncertainty and indeterminacy, Beckett insists on measure, as in his geometrical television play "Quad" (1981) and the symmetrical and

---

[5] This prevailing reading of *Godot* puts it in mythical time; I've argued elsewhere the play can be read as an allegory of French modernity.

90   E. AMIRAN

rule-bound wanderings of the Dantesque "Lost Ones" trapped in a cylinder world (*Le Dépeupleur*, 1970). The relevant point for us is that these measures, a form of judgment, are not opposed in Beckett to the loss and uncertainty so palpable in *Not I*, but are their correlatives. Official documents and law courts Beckett rejects out of hand, as when Molloy tells the cop he uses his "papers" to wipe off with, or when Mouth remembers her, or She's, intractability in court. Excrement and official papers are at opposite poles for Beckett, as for Artaud. But government and judgment are not the same: a contract is needed to keep a sense of world intact, if only one that is ever in need of renewal. This is a point repeated in Beckett's essay on Proust:

> Life is a succession of habits, since the individual is a succession of individuals; the world being a projection of the individual's consciousness ... the pact must be continually renewed, the letter of safe conduct brought up to date. The creation of the world did not take place once and for all time, but takes place every day. Habit then is the generic term for the countless treaties concluded between the countless subjects that constitute the individual and their countless correlative objects. (*Proust* 8)

The language of contracts and treaties emphasizes the need to renew one's hold on objects and oneself.

These are treaties, arrangements one makes with oneself. But for Moore as a visual object on film there is a world, there are observers, if only in the nature of the cinematic work: we renew her as an object with each cinematic cut. In the imagined afterlife of Beckett's *Not I*, however, no one returns the ball ("Return the ball every once in a while," Vladimir tells Estragon in *Godot*). There is no one to treat with and no object with which to correlate. In the absence of a world of objects and of sensations, consciousness in Beckett's *Not I* is at the mercy of badly remembered people and events: "quick grab and on ... nothing there ... on to the next," as Mouth says (221). This habit is a projection of Mouth, caught five times during the play with the consciousness that she might be talking about herself, and so denying it. It requires a sense of losing oneself and then the threat of finding oneself. In Jordan's adaptation the viewer acts as this figure, looking at Moore from all angles. She cannot be seen projecting herself onto herself because it's the viewer who pauses, jumping to another angle. The film controls her pace too, as observers do not in theater. Moore can reject judgment and laugh at the courts, as the script says, but she cannot renew her treaties with the world of past objects, be overtaken by involuntary recall, only to snap out of it, because now her Auditor is embodied in the constitution of the film. She is undone—the term is a favorite of Beckett scholarship—but being cast again and again as an image, now seen from this side, now from that, she has no subjective position from which to grab memories or words, from which to then abruptly detach when they hit too close to home.

To return to the question of the voice that persists in the absence of a speaker in Beckett, the point is not that these voices, not able to fall silent, continue after death. As Beckett writes in his thesis on Proust, "Whatever opinion we may be pleased to hold on the subject of death, we may be sure that it is meaningless and valueless" (*Proust* 6). The dead, he also says, are only dead so long as we remember them (*Proust* 29). They do not have their own life or death: what they have, they owe to the living (and see Proust, *Remembrance* II.747). The status of Beckett's voices, rather, is undecidable in a way that conflates the living and the dead, present and past, the human being and disembodied consciousness. His voice belies the notion of Cartesian duality (at one time popular as a model for Beckett) because it denies the division of mind and body, dead spirit and living person. It renders ideas of death ideas of living. Thus in Beckett there is not, in Derrida's words, "pure life or pure death," either state being "always, infinitely, the same thing" (*On Touching* 291). Jordan's adaptation cannot share this structural undecidability because here Moore is very much alive, and so susceptible to death. Mouth, floating eight feet above the stage, is not something that can die.

Though sounds we hear in Beckett's *Not I* and in Jordan's adaptation are arguably similar, particularly if we see video reproductions of the works instead of seeing them in a theater, the idea of sound is different in the two works, and this difference is crucial to the status of the image in this work. Beckett's *Not I* relies on the idea of a physical mouth, not on mouth as mediated by cinema. The play, as Enoch Brater points out, takes the side of the mouth against the eye: *Not I* (Brater 49), and so in principle of sound against image. Words and sound, or their stand-ins, are explicit antagonists as two characters in Beckett's radio play, "Words and Music" (1962), a rivalry that echoes Proust's contrast between music and language staged in his discussion of Vinteuil's sublime late septet: what if humanity evolved to use music to communicate?—but humanity "developed along other lines, those of spoken and written language" (*Remembrance* II. 560). The antagonism of words and music is misplaced, for they are more exchangeable than the contest implies. Words are also music, just as music is words—a point not lost on Proust in his early discussion of the sounds and physical properties of place names (I.295–7). Examples of words in Beckett's work that are largely sounds, among many, include characters like "Bim" and "Bom" in *What Where*, whom Beckett tied to different colors (Albright 59–60), the discussion of the sound of the word "pot" in *Watt*, a sound that may be comforting (and see the discussion of the word "pot" in Proust's *Remembrance* II.619), and the musical prosody of *Not I* (Elam 140). (The characters in *What Where*— Bam, Bem, Bim, and Bom, or A-E-I-O—leave out "Bum," who would make the fifth vowel, connecting the vowels with excrement, as *Not I* also does.[6]) When asked about the relation between words and music, Beckett told Katharine Worth that "music always wins" (Worth, "Radio Medium" 210), echoing Proust again—Vinteuil's music is truer than all the books Marcel knew, he says (II.642)—perhaps because all words are musical, whereas in principle no music is wordy.[7]

As Brater says, Mouth is another of Beckett's characters whose name begins with M (49). The letter and its sound have a meaning connected with Mouth in *Not I* that Beckett's text surely knows: when in the Proteus episode of *Ulysses* Stephen composes a poem on the Strand—a poem actually borrowed from Douglas Hyde—he tells himself:

> He comes, pale vampire, through storm his eyes, his bat sails bloodying the sea, mouth to her mouth's kiss.
> Here. Put a pin in that chap, will you? My tablets. Mouth to her kiss.
> No. Must be two of em. Glue em well. Mouth to her mouth's kiss. (40)

These mouths in *Ulysses* require the M sound to produce the idea that love, or erotic contact, is vampiric and hence overly physical ("glue"). Beckett emphasizes the importance of sound in Joyce in his essay on "Work in Progress" (the working title of *Finnegans Wake*), which he said was not just to be read, but "to be looked at and listened to" ("Dante...Bruno.Vico..Joyce" 14). Asked about Joyce's interest in painting, he exclaimed, "But he couldn't see!"—but this literalism does not survive long. For example, in the same conversation he said that he and

---

[6] On Beckett's use of names ending with the letter "m" preceded by a vowel, see Banfield (13).

[7] In music, writes Proust, "the sounds seem to assume the inflexion of the thing itself" (*Remembrance* II.642), recalling Beckett's praise for the language of Joyce's *Work in Progress*.

Joyce were "*Jean qui pleure et Jean qui rit*"[8]: Beckett is the sad or crying one shown in *Krapp's Last Tape* as relinquishing artistic triumph, while Joyce is the epic winner: the eye loses, and the mouth wins. Neither organ, however, works in its sensory capacity: the eye does not see but sheds tears, the mouth does not speak but laughs, both reduced to rhetorically unreflective physical states. While the mouth wins, it is not in its capacity of making verbal sense but as part of the body's circulation of aliment and dispatch—"alimentation and defecation," as Lucky calls it in his speech in *Godot* (29)—with which Beckett is so often explicitly concerned.

It is with this capacity of the mouth to experience words as physical objects that *Not I* is engaged. In *The Logic of Sense* Deleuze writes that for Artaud, language is material, and "triumph" can only be achieved by "destroying the word" and replacing semantic and syllabic values with "breath-words and howl-words" (*Logic of Sense* 88). Here Krapp is turned on his head: *Jean qui pleure*, as it were, has the last laugh, except that it is not a happy laugh. Artaud's howl-words are the extreme case ("schizo-phrenic," Deleuze calls it) of the potential of language to interchange semantic meaning and sound. In ordinary use, language for Deleuze keeps symbols and things, sense and sound, apart, divided by what he calls a line or border between the two orders of things: "A line is the frontier between two series, propositions and things, or between dimensions of the same proposition. Along this line, sense is elaborated" (86). When we cross the line, as Artaud does, words become things, and things words, and sense dissolves. The mouth, for Deleuze, is the place where propositions and things threaten to interpenetrate because words and food share it.[9] The mouth is the locus where the speaker makes or loses sense. Hence Artaud mocks Surrealism for relinquishing what Deleuze calls depth for the surface of social action: Breton in the 1930s sought "in the realm of facts and of immediate matter the culmination of an action that could normally develop only within the inmost confines of the brain" (Artaud 139). For Deleuze, Artaud lives the permeability of language, while the Surrealists and Lewis Carroll only play at expressing it, particularly when they treat food as words and vice versa, as in the *Alice* books:

[8] In conversation with the author, Paris, August 1987.
[9] Maurice Blanchot, also a Paris contemporary, makes a similar argument about sound and image, as Adam Potts has argued.

94   E. AMIRAN

Artaud is alone in having been an absolute depth in literature, and in having discovered a vital body and the prodigious language of this body. As he says, he discovered them through suffering.... But Carroll remains the master and the surveyor of surfaces—surfaces which were taken to be so well-known that nobody was exploring them anymore. (Deleuze 93)

This line of thought in Deleuze (and its variation we have seen in Joyce) is a psychological idea that, in a remarkable turn, Proust too comes close to articulating. In a discussion of, among other things, M. de Charlus's inability to keep silent about his romantic attachments—here to Morel, his violinist protégé, whose allegiance Mme. Verdurin is just then drawing away from the Baron, the narrator Marcel notes that:

There are certain desires, some of them confined to the mouth, which, as soon as we have allowed them to grow, insist upon being gratified, whatever the consequences may be; we are unable to resist the temptation to kiss a bare shoulder at which we have been gazing for too long and at which our lips strike like a serpent at a bird, to bury our sweet tooth in a cake that has fascinated and famished it, nor can we forego the delight of the amazement, anxiety, grief or mirth to which we can move another person by some unexpected communication. (II. 595)

Language ("communication") is connected here to other desires located in the mouth, namely kissing and eating, where kissing is understood here as a version of eating through the analogy of the feeding serpent. The passage makes parallel eating and speaking, and so implies parallels between propositions and food: the sweet tooth sinks in the cake, the kissing mouth strikes the shoulder, the word moves another person. Deleuze's idea is already available in Proust and may be recalled when in *Not I* Beckett discusses Mouth's "sudden urge to ... tell."

Not I is, like much of Beckett's work, about the inability to get rid of the depth model. Like the Unnamable's condition which precedes hers, Mouth's indeterminacy and her loss of world express a condition in which, as Deleuze writes, "Other bodies always penetrate our body and coexist with its parts .... The inside and the outside, the container and the contained, no longer have a precise limit" (87). In this passage from *The Unnamable*, a part of one of the "not I" sequences in the book, words, images, and bodies interpenetrate:

> Looking out on the silence, straight out, why not, all this time on the brink of silence, I knew it, on a rock, lashed to a rock, in the midst of silence, its great swell rears towards me, I'm streaming with it, it's an image, those are words, it's a body, it's not I, I knew it wouldn't be I, I'm not outside. I'm inside. I'm in something. I'm shut up, the silence is outside, outside, inside, there is nothing but here, and the silence outside, nothing but this voice and the silence all round. (414)

The Unnamable imagines "streaming" with the world/words/body that is or is not the earth (the rock) or I, that is or is not outside or inside. The Unnamable goes on to imagine being punished, turning oneself in to authorities lying in wait, and also being a mouth into which the voice could enter—enter as it could not into the eyes:

> I need a prison, I was right, for me alone. I'll go there now. I'll put me in it. I'm there already [...] perhaps that's all they're waiting for, there they flare again, to give me quittance [...] I see nothing, it's because there is nothing, or it's because I have no eyes, or both, that makes three possibilities, to choose from, but do I really see nothing, it's not the moment to tell a lie, but how can you not tell a lie, what an idea, a voice like this [...] it's blind, it seeks me blindly, in the dark, it seeks a mouth, to enter into [...] it has no interest in eyes, it says I have none, or that they are no use to me, then it speaks of tears, then it speaks of gleams, it is truly at a loss, gleams, yes, far, or near, distances, you know, measurements [...] these gleams too, they were to save me, they were to devour me. (414–415)

Here several elements familiar from *Not I* come together: the "streaming" voice, the mouth, and judgment and punishment, together with the not-I and eye-lessness, and the light or glimmer. These are not a coincidental collection, but together help construct a logic ("piece it together," Mouth says [220]) of the two works. There is no question of reading Mouth's story as a direct adaptation or treatment of the Unnamable's story, but there are significant homologies between them, as though Mouth's story fleshes out a possible back story for the Unnamable.

Still more than this, in line with Artaud and Deleuze, Mouth in *Not I* conflates words and things, food that is vomited with words, or an aborted fetus with alimentary dispatch, toilet matter that renders the body inside

96 E. AMIRAN

and outside itself.[10] To return to the important passage in which she connects these logical dots, Mouth recalls a

> sudden urge to ... tell ... then rush out stop the first she saw ... nearest lavatory ... start pouring it out ... steady stream ... mad stuff ... half the vowels wrong ... no one could follow .... (*Not I*)

The words start pouring out in a steady stream, and they are mad or "wrong," or half the vowels are, allowing no one to "follow," as though a child cannot be born or follow.[11] The words that pour out then are food, or what you might vomit (wrong food), or else intestinal discharge that urgently seeks the nearest lavatory. Words (and particularly words for mother, Ann Banfield argues, with examples [9–11]) are interchangeable with food or its product, a confession of, possibly, the event for which the "woman" is indicted before a court (as Words and Music are before their Lord in "Words and Music").

Jordan's adaptation, as we have seen, severs the connection between the words and Mouth. The continuity of the soundtrack is unmasked by the necessary discontinuity of the image. It also negates what is mouth-like about Mouth's words, that they are aliment or dispatch, and that the mouth is the place where they interchange with their object, propositions with things, to cross the line of sense into "mad stuff." It is a world of images, not of things. Jordan's film threatens to restore sense to Mouth's narrative, not because the words are different but because they are understood as words apart from things, understood to keep their side of the line, on that side of their River Jordan. With clever cuts and slick editing, Jordan might be indicted as the Lewis Carroll of surfaces to Beckett's depth image, and Moore the actor, with breaks at the craft service table, to Whitelaw's palpable suffering on stage.[12]

Yet if Jordan violates Beckett's line of action, this violation can be read as an adaptation of the Deleuzian status of Beckett's language. Reading Moore's rosy flesh back into Whitelaw's mouth, we see the cheeks that Beckett's version left out for the words to tell, the physical matter that Mouth talks about but hardly seems to be. In this way Moore too is not just

---

[10] See Banfield on the "excremental mother" in Beckett; see Elam for a discussion of "the mouth-anus association" in Beckett, and of Mouth's "anal-verbal retentiveness" which "gives way violently and publicly to a kind of dia-logorrhea" (146).

[11] Madness is not to be confused with mental illness, as Thomas Bernhard says (42).

[12] Whitelaw blacked out during rehearsal and had to break away from the stage.

Mouth but also the subject of Mouth. The failure of Jordan's cinematic cuts to create what Deleuze calls the depth model likewise becomes one of the works' subjects. In the adaptation, it is not I that we see, but She—just like she said. Such a reading requires us to interpolate Beckett's work into Jordan's. The adaptation also loses the associations to food that, in an Irish context, invoke other kinds of loss, even national loss.[13] Beckett's language of national contracts and treaties supports such a reading. Instead it emphasizes the notion that the adapting apparatus, or suspension and indeterminacy produced by mediation, prevent Mouth from connecting with herself, moving from Mouth to I. Here cinema is the symptom of theater, broken and re-stitched in the wake of the disappearance of organic time. "Not She—I," it appears to say (not mouth, eye; not theater, film), and so to shadow Beckett's play as its obverse. Beckett's play ties consciousness to the body of the word, which cannot be undone; Jordan's film is cinema's reply to theater, not Beckett's play, as Jordan had said, but an adaptation. But that failure to be the body, I rather than she, is after all the point of Beckett's play, or one of them. And here Jordan is faithful to Beckett and indeed has Beckett as his subject, not despite but because he cannot reproduce the play.

WORKS CITED

Abbott, H. Porter. *Beckett Writing Beckett: The Author in the Autograph*. Cornell University Press, 1996.

Albright, Daniel. *Beckett and Aesthetics*. Cambridge University Press, 2003.

Artaud, Antonin. *Selected Writings*, ed. Susan Sontag. University of California Press, 1988.

Banfield, Ann. "Beckett's Tattered Syntax." *Representations* 84.1 (November 2003): 6–29.

Beckett, Samuel. "Dante...Bruno.Vico..Joyce." 1929. *Our Exagmination Round His Factification for Incamination of Work in Progress*. New Directions, 1962: 1–22.

———. *Echo's Bones*. Ed. Mark Nixon. Grove Press, 2014.

———. *The Letters of Samuel Beckett* vol. IV: 1966–1989, ed. George Craig et al. Cambridge University Press, 2016.

———. *Molloy, Malone Dies, The Unnamable*. Grove Press, 1955, 1956, 1958.

———. *Not I*. 1972. *The Collected Shorter Plays of Samuel Beckett*, 213–223. Grove Press, 1984.

———. *Not I*. Play. London: Royal Court Theatre, January 16, 1973.

---

[13] Mouth is about object loss, particularly of the mother figure, as Rina Kim has argued.

98   E. AMIRAN

———. *Not I*. Film. Dir. Neil Jordan. Shepperton Studios, 2000.

———. *Proust*. 1931. Grove Press, 1957.

———. *Waiting for Godot*. Grove Press, 1954.

Beckett on Film. Alchetron: *The Free Social Encyclopedia*. https://alchetron.com/Beckett-on-Film. Accessed December 14, 2019.

Benjamin, Walter. "The Work of Art in the Age of Mechanical Reproduction," trans. Harry Zohn. Random House, 1936. https://www.marxists.org/reference/subject/philosophy/works/ge/benjamin.htm

Bernhard, Thomas. *Walking*. 1971. Trans. Kenneth J. Northcott. University of Chicago Press, 2003.

Brater, Enoch. "Dada, Surrealism, and the Genesis of *Not I*." *Modern Drama* vol. 18 no. 1 (1975): 49–59. *Project MUSE*. https://doi.org/10.1353/mdr.1975.0015

Deleuze, Gilles. "The Exhausted." *SubStance* vol. 24 no. 3, Issue 78 (1995), pp. 3–28.

———. *The Logic of Sense*. 1969. Trans. Mark Lester with Charles Stivale. Columbia University Press, 1990.

Derrida, Jacques. *On Touching—Jean Luc Nancy*, trans. Christine Irizarry. Stanford University Press, 2005.

Elam, Keir. "*Not I*: Beckett's Mouth and the Ars(e) Rhetorica." *Beckett at 80/Beckett in Context*, ed. Enoch Brater. Oxford University Press, 1986. 1124–148.

Gendron, Sarah. "'A Cogito for the Dissolved Self': Writing, Presence, and the Subject in the Work of Samuel Beckett, Jacques Derrida, and Gilles Deleuze." *Journal of Modern Literature* 28.1 (Fall 2004).

Gontarski, S.E. "Reinventing Beckett." *Modern Drama* vol. 49 no. 4 (Winter 2006), pp. 428–451.

Joyce, James. *Ulysses*. Vintage Books, 1986.

Kim, Rina. *Women and Ireland as Beckett's Lost Others: Beyond Mourning and Melancholia*. Palgrave Macmillan, 2010.

Potts, Adam, ed. *Sounds of Disaster: Sonic Encounters with Blanchot*. *Angelaki* vol. 23 no. 3 (June 2018).

Proust, Marcel. *Remembrance of Things Past*, vols. 1 and 2. Trans. C.K. Scott Moncrieff. Random House, 1932.

Sierz, Aleks. "'A Relevant and Cinematic Environment': Filming Beckett's Plays." *Samuel Beckett Today/ Aujourd'hui* vol. 13 (2003), pp. 137–149.

Wakeling, Corey. "'Only Her Mouth Could Move': Sensory Deprivation and the Billie Whitelaw Plays." *TDR: The Drama Review* vol. 59, no. 3 (Fall 2015).

Worth, Katharine. "Beckett and the Radio Medium." *British Radio Drama*, ed. John Drakakis. Cambridge University Press, 1981.

———. "Beckett's Auditors: *Not I* to *Ohio Impromptu*." *Beckett at 80/Beckett in Context*. 168–192.

Žukauskaitė, Audronė. "Deleuze, Simondon, and Beckett: From Being to Becoming." In *Deleuze and Artistic Research*, ed. Paulo de Assis and Paolo Giudici. Leuven University Press, 2017: 272–278.

CHAPTER 6

"The Joyce of Filum: Cinematic Accounts of *Ulysses*"

Michael Patrick Gillespie

James Joyce first publicly demonstrated his interest in the motion picture industry with a brief stint, in 1909, as the manager of the Cinematograph Volta, Dublin's first permanent movie house. Although from the start he never intended this job to be more than a temporary position, it nonetheless marked "the beginning of a beautiful friendship" with motion pictures. Throughout his adult life Joyce maintained an avid interest in films. He enjoyed going to the movies when the problems he had with his eyes permitted it, and he even explored the possibility, in discussions in the early 1930s with both Warner Brothers and Serge Eisenstein, of a cinematic adaptation of his novel *Ulysses*. (For details of the Volta endeavor and the film negotiations a quarter century later, see Ellmann pp. 300–303 & p. 654.)

A number of scholars, noting Joyce's interest in film, have published traditional academic studies that examine connections between his writings and the motion picture industry. These efforts have touched on

M. P. Gillespie (✉)
Florida International University, Miami-Dade County, FL, USA
e-mail: mpgilles@fiu.edu

© The Author(s), under exclusive license to Springer Nature Switzerland AG 2022
M. C. Conner et al. (eds.), *Screening Contemporary Irish Fiction and Drama*, Palgrave Studies in Adaptation and Visual Culture, https://doi.org/10.1007/978-3-031-04568-4_6

99

100   M. P. GILLESPIE

several related areas: Some explored how an affinity for movies shaped Joyce's creative impulses. Others have traced analogues between Joyce's narrative structures and contemporaneous cinematographic elements. And still others have gone on to speculate on the influence Joyce's canon continues to exert on contemporary filmmakers. Thomas L. Burkdall has written specifically on how he sees Joyce's writing affected by the cinema. John McCourt has collected a number of essays along the same general lines. And Emily Tall has examined Eisenstein's November 1, 1934, lecture on Joyce.

Parallel to academic efforts to illuminate links between motion picture production and Joyce's narratives, filmmakers have continued to be drawn by the same aesthetic interests that attracted Eisenstein and Warner Brothers to Joyce's writings. Over the past fifty years several have demonstrated a particularly noteworthy energy for exploiting the cinematic potential inherent in Joyce's canon. Mary Ellen Bute's *Passages from James Joyce's Finnegans Wake* (1966) presents a literal, and sometimes surreal, visual rendering of portions of Joyce's final work. Joseph Strick's *Ulysses* (1967) and his *A Portrait of the Artist as a Young Man* (1977) use Dublin settings and Irish actors to offer naturalistic representations of the events of those novels. Michael Pearce's *Joyce's Women* (1985), adapted for film from Fionnula Flannigan's one woman theater show, features extended, episodic monologues drawing on material from several of Joyce's female characters as well as dramatized expressions of the opinions of his wife Nora, his benefactress Harriet Shaw Weaver, and his publisher Sylvia Beach. John Huston's *The Dead* (1987) offers not simply another naturalistic rendering, though in a number of scenes it does use the Usher's Island location where the actual Christmas parties upon which the narrative is based occurred. Huston's film dramatizes in a celebratory form the unique world that Joyce sought to recapture in his short story. And, most recently, Sean Walsh's *Bloom* (2003) articulates a stylized, some would say idiosyncratic, interpretation of one of the central figures of *Ulysses*. (There is also a feature length bio-pic, *Nora*, released in 2000 and directed by Pat Murphy, which chronicles Joyce's family life from the perspective of his wife, Nora.)

Analogous to these cinematic representations of Joyce's writings, over the last fifty years documentary filmmakers have undertaken a number of frankly interpretive projects aiming to enhance our understanding of Joyce's artistic efforts by giving visual grounding to the descriptive imagery of the persons, places, and environment that inform his works. There

6 "THE JOYCE OF FILUM: CINEMATIC ACCOUNTS OF *ULYSSES*" 101

are numerous documentaries which touch on Joyce's life and writings, but I will confine myself, in the following paragraphs, to offering context and comparison for *Imagining Ulysses* by providing brief summaries of key documentaries that also concentrate on Joyce's novel.

In 1968 Kieran Hickey directed *Faithful Departed*. It uses a compilation of contemporaneous photographs of Dublin's diverse geography and its active street life to present a comprehensive representation of the social ethos from which *Ulysses* emerged. The pictures—taken by the photographer Robert French at the turn of the last century and drawn from the William Lawrence Collection held by the National Library of Ireland—are accompanied by a voiceover by Irish actor Jack MacGowran whose descriptions put incidents from Joyce's life and the world he inhabited into the context of the photographs. The film remains particularly useful for readers who have never visited Dublin, and, as urban change continues, it has become a rich, animated archive of settings no longer in existence.

Other filmmakers, while retaining the documentary format, integrate dramatizations into their narratives. In 1988, for example, an American, Patrick Ryan, narrated a live-action, pedestrian tour across Dublin, *Walking into Eternity: James Joyce's Ulysses—a Dublin Guide with Patrick Ryan*. This documentary puts much of the ambiance described in *Ulysses* in a living context by visiting many of the then still-extant locations mentioned in the book. The commentary that Ryan offers as he walks touches on portions of the novel and of Joyce's life, and is punctuated by dramatic readings of selected passages from the novel.

Also in 1988, Nigel Wallace directed the *Ulysses* episode of *Ten Great Modern Writers* as part of a series for London Weekend Television. Like Ryan's film, Wallace's documentary makes some use of Dublin locations. However, it puts greater emphasis on dramatic re-enactments of selected events from the novel. These scenes are integrated with interviews with the writer Anthony Burgess and the Joyce scholar Clive Hart offering their opinions on the relevance of the novel.

All of these projects used cinematic conceptions to make Joyce's words clearer to both viewers and readers. They also offered articulate and urbane, though at times exclusionary, interpretations that sought to establish the primacy of often familiar though nonetheless sophisticated approaches to Joyce's writing. With that orientation, they all ended up following the traditional explicative pattern of imposing meaning from positions of authority. This meant presenting linearly, causal insights developed to show their viewers conclusively how to understand both

Joyce and *Ulysses*. While this is a legitimate, even time-honored, approach to documentary representations, all of these efforts left showed absolutely no interest in the way ordinary individuals might legitimately respond to Joyce's novel. The film that I take up in this essay offers a very different perspective.

Imagining Ulysses (2004) was written and co-directed by David Blake Knox, founder of Blueprint Pictures. (Information on the film credits multiple directors, including Knox, Dearbhla Walsh, Hilary Fennell, Neasa Hardiman, Shimmy Marcus. For the sake of expediency, I will just refer to Knox, and ask the indulgence of the others.) It does not concern itself with articulating a definitive interpretation or even with outlining a single, unified response to Joyce's text. Rather, Knox's documentary celebrates the subjectivity inherent in Joyce's writing by privileging any number of diverse, idiosyncratic reactions to all or part of the novel without any effort to tie them all together or even to see a clear link between each and the work that inspired it. In this fashion, it replicates the experiences of most readers with *Ulysses*, and it comes closer to capturing the multiplicity and non-linearity of Joyce's narrative than do the more conventional academic responses that have heretofore dominated documentaries about the novel.

Nonetheless, despite, or perhaps because of, the relentless innovation defining both the form of the documentary and of the novel upon which the film draws for its subject, it is useful before a specific look at *Imagining Ulysses* to keep origins in mind. Despite its radically innovative qualities, Joyce's creative approach owes much to his literary antecedents. Equally, the Blueprint Pictures production emerges from a rich tradition of Irish documentary cinema. That influence shapes both the construction of the film and the response that audiences can be expected to make to it. Consequently, before examining it, I will sketch the diverse features of a selected number of its predecessors so that one can understand more clearly the unique qualities of this project.

Imagining Ulysses emerged from an eighty-year documentary tradition that oscillated between Robert Flaherty's wildly unconventional (to a point bordering on fiction) *Man of Aran* (1934), to soporific public service films like *Safe Cycling* (1949) and innocuous, chauvinistic travelogues like *The Glamor of Galway* (1957), to the move controversial motion pictures like Peter Lennon's relentless critique of Irish urban life in *The Rocky Road to Dublin* (1968) and Steve Humphries' expose of Irish Magdalene Institutions, *Sex in a Cold Climate* (1998). One might trace the same pattern in the documentary history of any nation, but that similarity does not

6 "THE JOYCE OF FILUM: CINEMATIC ACCOUNTS OF *ULYSSES*" 103

give a full sense of the dynamic development of the genre in Ireland. As Harvey O'Brien has shown, films in this category have increasingly enforced their expectations of thoughtful responses from their viewers. The confident, eclectic approach of *Imagining Ulysses* highlights both the Irish documentary tradition and the sense that this genre is becoming the most innovative area of filmmaking in Ireland.

One of the most surprising areas of documentary films comes from the work of Catholic clergy. From the early years of the Irish Free State until well into the 1960s, parish priests made a surprisingly strong contribution to the documentary canon although their efforts have only attained significant appreciation among students of Irish film retrospectively. Amateur clerical filmmakers recorded the cycle of celebrations, liturgical and civic, and in the process provided an invaluable record of ordinary life in Ireland during the first half of the twentieth century. Most of these films did not receive general release, but as Sunniva O'Flynn has noted they were part of the fabric of middleclass and lower middleclass Irish life. They were often shown at church or community venues, and they became instruments for raising funds for parishes, sharing the experiences of local liturgical observances, celebrating the work of local priests and nuns, encouraging vocations, and celebrating the success of parish outreach projects. These films gained a breadth of distribution when they were shared among various parishes, social clubs, and community organizations to screen for their members. O'Flynn offers an excellent overview of this area of documentaries. She has also made a careful study of IFI records and ascertained that these clerical films had broad informal exposure.

To that end, *Imagining Ulysses* uses each of the eighteen chapters into which Joyce divided his novel as a starting point for a self-contained response, commentary, or meditation inspired by the section of the novel. By invoking the structure that Joyce gave to his writing, the documentary invites its viewers to reference the unity that readers find in *Ulysses* to enforce a cohesive sense of what is in fact a highly digressive film. In further emulation, just as Joyce used elements from Homer's *Odyssey* as touchstones or reference points for his narrative, Knox's motion picture plays off themes inspired by Joyce's novel—exile, love, paternity, nationalism, prejudice, pornography, anti-Semitism, and others—without taking prescriptive direction from them. In that fashion, each segment of the film explores independent, idiosyncratic associations given unity and coherence by the assumption of the validity of multiple possible reactions provoked by readings of *Ulysses*.

This episodic pattern of engaging diverse themes, attitudes, and impressions—in segments completely unrelated to one another—mimics the novel's digressive narrative impulses and diverse stylistic inclinations. From this perspective, and in the same manner as the novel, its heightened subjectivity frees viewers from the obligation to discern a single, privileged meaning. At the same time, while *Ulysses*, despite its wide-ranging stylistic experimentation, retains its connection to a strong, clear narrative arc that provides a unifying thread to anchor a reader's experience, the Knox production takes an avowedly subjective approach: jumping from interviews with famous and ordinary people, surveys of cultural artifacts, parodic vignettes that play off Joyce's works and life, and seemingly anything else that caught the filmmakers' fancy. It aims to capture feeling rather than present exposition.

In this way, *Imagining Ulysses* puts heightened emphasis on the first word of its title while feeling no imperative to offer a unified, linear response to the second word. The documentary gives us a cross-section of reactions provoked by Joyce's work. It does not presume to present a definitive explanation of the experience of reading the novel but instead offers a pastiche that surveys opinions of specialists, generalists, interested and indifferent readers, and whimsical reactions to the ethos that now surrounds Joyce's novel. In the process, it adopts protocols for representation analogous to the varied topics and forms that Joyce introduced into his narrative without in the least seeming to ape his efforts.

In this fashion, *Imagining Ulysses* presents a highly original approach to its documenting of Joyce's novel. On the one hand, like the novel, it frankly employs a range of digressive impulses to engage the interests of a range of viewers. At the same time, it eschews the unvoiced assumption, the one powering many of the films that preceded it, that its goal is to offer a correct, or corrective, interpretation of the novel. In consequence, the clearest response that viewers can make to this documentary will come from acknowledging its efforts to replicate cinematically the excursive, mutable stylistic framework of Joyce's novel while simultaneously showing no interest in offering a unified thematic response to *Ulysses*.

In this fashion and very much like Joyce's novel, *Imagining Ulysses* demonstrates an ongoing awareness of the importance of active viewer engagement with the film. In both the film and the book, a cross-section of attitudes, perspectives, and references uncouples narratives from traditional linear progressions. This frees readers and viewers from the burden of seeking any definitive meaning. In the process, the wide-ranging

6 "THE JOYCE OF FILUM: CINEMATIC ACCOUNTS OF *ULYSSES*" 105

approach followed by each helps one come to terms with his or her own understanding or interpretation. From the title onward, it reminds viewers of our responsibility to participate actively and creatively in what we see. By watching the film, we bring its text, in Roland Barthes' sense of the term, into existence, and we do so out of the subjectivity of our individual consciousness.

The film's first section establishes this organizational plan: by taking its title from the book's opening chapter, Telemachus, and by almost immediately straying from the issues and events of that episode, *Imagining Ulysses* introduces a pattern that will characterize each of its subsequent sections. The film begins with shots of the Martello Tower where the *Ulysses* chapter takes place while a voiceover offers a brief summary of the action. From there, the narrator briefly alludes to the conflicted attitudes that shaped Joyce's fictional renditions of life in his native city. Then, the scene shifts to short commentaries that will address the central concern of the segment: how Irish intellectuals feel about Joyce. A series of writers— Edna O'Brien, Roddy Doyle, Frank McCourt, Tom Paulin, Declan Kiberd, and Neil Jordan (also of course a filmmaker)—talk about the evolution of the country's responses to Joyce and his writings: they recall the initial Irish hostility, and then trace the gradual shift in opinion to its current state that mixes a sometimes grudging respect with a certain degree of misgiving for the adulation that Joyce now receives, particularly from non-Irish readers.

As will be shown in the next segment of the film, the writers' own views reflect far more intense attitudes than those held by the general reading public. This group admires Joyce's creative achievements, but implicit in several of the respondents' remarks is a sense of the burden any Irish author faces in writing fiction after Joyce. These contrasting feelings become particularly apparent in the remarks of O'Brien, who is sympathetic to Joyce's approach, and in those of Jordan, who struggles throughout the documentary with antagonism for much of what for him defines the Irish social and cultural context and seemingly for certain aspects of Joyce's creative life as well. Kiberd, a noted Irish academic with a sophisticated interpretive perspective, broadens the focus of discussion from the strictly literary to the societal context by putting these changes in Irish attitudes into an overview of the development of the Irish economy. McCourt, an expatriate like Joyce, blends a keen sense of the power of Joyce's language with a strong sympathy for the travails of composition. This opening section reflects a traditional form that documentaries invoke,

106   M. P. GILLESPIE

bringing in talking heads to lay out opinions, but by the filmmakers' careful selection of a group with markedly diverse opinions it orients viewers toward the real issue: how subjectivity largely informs how people chose to perceive Joyce and his writing.

(The chapter titles used here and in most discussions of *Ulysses* come from Joyce. He employed them throughout the process of composition, though he chose not to have them appear at the head of each of the chapters when the book was printed. Nonetheless, they remain a popular shorthand designation for identifying particular portions of the narrative.)

The next section, Nestor, which in the novel is set in a grammar school where Stephen Dedalus teaches young boys, takes up the antipathy, indifference, or apprehension that many Irish feel toward *Ulysses*. A series of ordinary Dubliners offer brief comments on their efforts, always unsuccessful, to read the work. They are interspersed by a nod toward closure in which Irvine Welsh (novelist), Dale Peck (novelist), Tom Paulin (poet), and Camille Paglia (cultural critic)—all of whom presumably did finish the book—talk about the book's importance.

These interpolations also nicely serve to remind us of the variety of responses provoked by *Ulysses*. The first two commentators alternate between positions of dismissiveness and hostility while the last two speak with enthusiasm and admiration. Viewers may find little in these contrasting between the responses of ordinary readers and of public intellectuals to contradict the impression that Joyce's novel remains a coterie rather than a popular attraction, but for me that misses the point. Just as all of those who finished the book offer varied responses so also among those who did not are feelings ranging from indifference to grudging respect to a desire at some point to get a fuller experience of the writing.

The Proteus section, named after the god of transformation, takes its name from the novel's chapter about aesthetics. The film gives that topic a nod, and then does some shape-shifting of its own, making the claim that some would find puzzling that Joyce was not considered a visual artist. Nonetheless, with unspoken irony it singles out a German sculptor, Joseph Beuys, to illustrate the impact that Joyce could have on someone working in another medium. Pronunciation of his surname makes homophonic connections with Joyce's, but the real link, presented somewhat histrionically by Richard de Marco, a Scots artist who was a friend of Beuys, comes through an articulation of the enthusiasm inspired by Joyce for the creative act.

This section elaborates on the idea that the words of Joyce could reinforce the artistic impulses of someone working in another medium like

6 "THE JOYCE OF FILUM: CINEMATIC ACCOUNTS OF *ULYSSES*" 107

Beuys, and de Marco underscores the point by speaking of them as "blood brothers." The emphasis on the catalytic impact that Joyce produced may seem clichéd to some long-time students of his writing. However, I think it is important for general viewers to be told that Joyce's novel has always had tremendous power to inspire others across a range of artistic media.

In *Ulysses*, Calypso marks the narrative's shift from a close examination of Stephen Dedalus to an equally intimate view of Leopold Bloom. This section of the documentary begins by emphasizing Bloom's isolation, and from that segues, not completely smoothly, into an account of the experiences of Joyce's Chinese translators, husband and wife Chua Cheng and Wen Jieruo. Much of its focus is on the travails of an intellectual in Maoist China, and *Ulysses* stands as an embodiment of the Western influence that the Red Guard, with Mao's encouragement, found so objectionable. This segment of the documentary traces key events that shaped the struggles, scholarly and societal, of the two translators while engaging with Joyce and his writing. In chronicling the persecution that the pair underwent and the ultimate triumph of their translation, the film both draws an implicit analogue to the harassment, less violent but equally insistent, that Bloom feels from other Dubliners, and, without trying to explain how it occurs, *Imagining Ulysses* gives us a sense of the profound impact that Joyce's writing can have on the lives of ordinary people.

The Lotus Eaters section of the film takes Bloom's peregrinations around Dublin as a basis for exploring Joyce's own displacement from city to city across Europe. Edna O'Brien speaks with great sympathy for Joyce's experiences. By celebrating his life of continual displacement, she underscores the impact on his writing of his frequent relocations: from apartment to apartment, city to city, and country to country. At the end of her commentary does she offhandedly compare herself to Joyce, saying "I have some idea of the price, spiritually and psychically, of the work he did." It would be a mistake for a viewer to see this is self-aggrandizement, for in fact it gives great insight into the impact of the novel as O'Brien movingly shares the personalizing process that her reading has gone through.

Hades, which in *Ulysses* describes the internment of Patrick Dignam at Glasnevin Cemetery, leads the film to an examination of Joyce's relation to Catholicism. That has been a long debated topic among literary scholars. However, *Imagining Ulysses* brings a fresh perspective to understanding the influence of the Church on his art. Specifically, it touches on the discipline that a Catholic heritage imposed upon his writing. Camille Paglia notes the impact of Catholicism on one's consciousness no matter what one comes to believe, and she sketches its lasting influence on writing. Tom Paulin points to the "patternmaking" quality of Catholic thought and ritual, and Declan Kiberd speaks of the ability to "order and judge" that Joyce derived from his Jesuit education. Neil Jordan, who seems to be using the segment as a way of dealing with his own Catholicism issues, provides a useful example of how we continually impose personal attitudes on the novel. Presuming an intimate sense of Joyce's spiritual priorities, he says that "Joyce was not interested in the afterlife." Whatever Joyce's beliefs, this range of views will touch on the equally diverse attitudes held by a great many readers as they struggle with appreciating a significant thematic core of the novel.

Just as the Aeolus chapter of *Ulysses*, dedicated to the god of the winds, disrupts familiar patterns of reading with unexplained headings, this section of the documentary abruptly offers a slice of pop culture. It presents The Gerry Show, a faux variety-TV program presumably echoing the long-running and extremely popular Irish telecast, *The Late Show*. It uses the now familiar audience engaged format of live TV, adding a literary twist that broadly parodies academic discourse by interviewing actors portraying Virginia Woolf and D.H. Lawrence. The burlesque is a wonderful contrast to the usual somber pronouncements that writers and critics (some recorded in this documentary) make about Joyce's work, and it reminds us of the irreverence at the heart of much of the novel's and the documentary's narrative.

The "Lestrygonians" episode in the novel emphasizes Bloom's efforts to distract his mind from his wife's impending adultery while *Imagining Ulysses* shifts the emphasis to Joyce's fascination with "his partner for life" and the woman he married twenty-seven years after they left Dublin together, Nora Barnacle. Frank McCourt talks with sympathy and understanding about the contrast in their natures and the force of attraction this produced. The segment then introduces passages from the sexually explicit letters that Joyce wrote to Nora in 1909, and in a subtle way suggests a connection between this physical desire and the inspiration that she gave his writing.

"Scylla and Charybdis," which Joyce set in the National Library of Ireland, gives the filmmakers the opportunity to reflect in a material way on *Ulysses'* impact on literary critics. It touches on Bloomsday celebrations in Dublin, offers fleeting images of Joyce critics presenting their work at various literary conferences, and provides comments from scholars from a range of countries—most of whom are non-native English speakers—about the universal appeal of Joyce's novel.

6 "THE JOYCE OF FILUM: CINEMATIC ACCOUNTS OF *ULYSSES*" 109

The section then turns to a longer discussion with Fritz Senn, director of the James Joyce Zurich Foundation. In a determinedly non-academic fashion, Senn discusses the attractions that Joyce's writings have for him and relates the early development of a group of Joyce scholars, including himself, who began the cycle of international conferences that continue to the present. The episode uses the examples of workshops and less formal gatherings presented at the James Joyce Foundation to make viewers aware of how Joyce's novel can change one's life, but its tone avoids the over-the-top enthusiasm that can make such examinations deadly boring.

In *Wandering Rocks*, Joyce presents a sometimes disruptive though nonetheless engaging tour of Dublin with nineteen vignettes highlighting the quotidian activities of a range of minor characters in the novel at locations all around the city. The film takes an equally unorthodox narrative approach to contextualizing Joyce's world. In this section it presents a charming view of what life was like for ordinary Dubliners living contemporaneously to the period of the novel by showing clips from early films of the city and by quoting from a series of postcards and other ephemera written in 1904 by diverse citizens. By recording their observations without editorial comment or condescension, *Imagining Ulysses* combines ordinary remarks with a few more serious statements to provide an overview of turn of the century Ireland that retains the unself-conscious charm of people who do not expect their private correspondences to come under public scrutiny.

The Sirens section of the film focuses, in a way that echoes the novel's chapter, almost completely on the motif of music. It mentions composers who have drawn on Joyce's works for inspiration and looks at Joyce's early ambitions to be a singer and at his wide-ranging taste in music—opera, music hall, traditional ballads. Both Edna O'Brien and Neil Jordan comment perceptively on how Joyce's aurality and interest in music informed his writing, and this segment also examines how this shaped the composition of this chapter of the novel.

The overt and virulent anti-Semitism of the "Cyclops" episode provides in this section a dual topic for examination. It points out Joyce's view of the similarities between Irish and Jews, and at the same time it indirectly acknowledges an Irish racism of a century ago with a musical performance by Gavin Friday of a popular ballad about a Jewish woman who lures a young boy into her house and murders him. It also mentions the Limerick anti-Semitic riots of 1904 with Frank McCourt providing local color. It also deftly puts the brake on any self-righteous inclination to rush to

110   M. P. GILLESPIE

condemning others from a distance. As contemporary Irish urban novelist Roddy Doyle notes, "racism is a condition in any city."

Naussica slips into a rather dry and somewhat defensive discourse breaking down along gender lines. Taking up the topic of sexual voyeurism, Neill Jordan focuses on Gerty McDowell, acknowledging her participation in Bloom's masturbatory fantasies as "both innocent and provocative." In contrast Camille Paglia puts the emphasis on Bloom's "violation of the young girl." Edna O'Brien offers a perceptive and balanced view, suggesting that the novel's narrative puts responsibility on both parties. In the end, as with any interpretation, their statements underscore the subjectivity of any effort to comprehend the inclinations of Joyce's characters.

The film makes a clever response to the structure of Oxen of the Sun, a long chapter that mimics styles of English writing from Roman times to the present. It uses Joyce's process of composition to introduce hypertextuality: the discursive stylistic gesture that moves one out of the immediate narrative and into the intellectual, emotional, and cultural context from which it emerges. Michael Groden, a textual critic, deftly describes the hypertextual-hypermedia experience and introduces Michael Joyce, an author who claims to have written the first hypertext novel, *Afternoon*. Like the chapter in the novel, this segment of the film may seem at first to have a limited appeal. However, like its literary counterpart it does underscore the overriding concern of Joyce's full narrative: both introduce the idea of wide-ranging and indulgently discursive it appeals to various readers at various points, so dissatisfaction with any segment will be balanced by deep engagement with another.

The section entitled Circe focuses directly on sexuality, as befitting that portion of the narrative that takes place in a whorehouse. There are references in the film to Joyce's dealings with prostitutes and to his reliance on pornography to write portions of the chapter (though no mention is made of Joyce's use of Flaubert, Goethe, and other literary figures as well). A number of authors who have appeared throughout the documentary talk about the conventional use of sex in literature, but some also offer a counterargument of sorts. Camille Paglia characterizes the chapter as wallowing "in sexual unconsciousness," and she sees the "fragility of the male ego and the difficulty of sustaining male identity in the world." All of the comments are set against a clip acting out faux sado-masochism that challenges viewers to decide on its level of satire.

The "Eumaeus" episode in *Ulysses* has Leopold Bloom and Stephen Dedalus in late night conversation in a cabman's shelter in Dublin. In

6 "THE JOYCE OF FILUM: CINEMATIC ACCOUNTS OF *ULYSSES*"   111

another dramatic set piece, with no obvious connection to that portion of the novel, the film presents a comic interlude depicting life in the Joyce household in Paris in the 1930s. It offers a slapstick version of family interaction with caricature representations, drawn to a degree on biographical material, of all the figures involved, including a cameo by Samuel Beckett as a frenetic defender of Joyce and his writing. The interchange with Lucia and Joyce is sweetly poignant as it touches on the love of the father and the daughter who are both highly strung solipsists, but more often the tone is farcical with Joyce shown as a bumbler much like the persona of Ozzy Osbourne in the early twenty-first-century reality TV show, *The Osbournes.*

The homecoming episode, "Ithaca," introduced by reference to Bloom bringing Stephen back to Eccles Street, becomes an occasion for examining issues of Irish fathers and sons. It draws upon clips from film versions of *The Playboy of the Western World, The Butcher Boy,* and *Angela's Ashes* to underscore its universality. Putting the topic in a broad social context, Frank McCourt tells us that "the theme of fathers and sons is very strong in Irish writing because of the lack of intimacy," except, as he says, when the father has had too much to drink. Declan Kiberd takes a more personal biographical view, seeing Joyce as attempting to relive the general conditions of his father's life "but this time [with the aim of] getting it right," though Kiberd does not elaborate on what Joyce might have meant. Several other writers lend pathos to the segment by pointing out that Joyce was devoted to his own father even as he felt guilt for his daughter Lucia's growing mental disability. The narrative takes some time to explore that relationship, but as McCourt points out it did not prevent Joyce from stepping away from domestic concerns so that he could continue to write: "the work was always there."

The Penelope chapter is a potpourri. After presenting viewers with the fact that this portion of the novel is devoted to Molly Bloom's monologue, the film has Neil Jordan talking about the achievement of the episode in terms so vague as to suggest that Jordan remains unconvinced by his own words. Edna O'Brien, on the other hand, offers a series of opinions that shows she has thought very carefully about Joyce's representation of women's libido. Martin Amis concludes this Trinitarian commentary by offering remarks that succeeds extraordinarily well in making all the talk of sex seem boring.

Then it shifts to a series of ordinary, unidentified women reading excerpts from the final chapter. There is much attention given to passages that use course language, and highlighting elderly women reading about orgasm and saying fuck. It culminates with these women reading the final passage of Molly's yes that for me goes on a bit too long, but of course that's only one of a range of possible reactions.

Where does all this lead? My own commentary affirms that, like Joyce's novel, *Imagining Ulysses* has various parts that will affect various viewers in different fashions and that any response to either will always be subjective. For me then, what it does most successfully is celebrate the multiplicity in Joyce's narrative not by trying to replicate what he has written but by imagining a range of responses that can grow out of engagement with Joyce's work. Most admirably, and again like Joyce's writing, it dares to be different. It takes the risk of being dismissed as trivial, unfocused, and even solipsistic. However, in fact the range of representations—this cacophony of voices—make it, like *Ulysses*, accessible to a variety of viewers with a variety of reactions. In the end it underscores the point that there is no single, definitive response to Joyce but a range of possibilities ensures a broad appeal if not of the entire work of a number of different portions.

Works Cited

Barthes, Roland. *S/Z*. Trans. Richard Miller. New York: Hill and Wang, 1975a.
———. *The Pleasure of the Text*. Trans. Richard Miller. New York: Hill and Wang, 1975b.
Burkdall, Thomas L. *Joycean Frames: Film and the Fiction of James Joyce*. New York & London: Routledge, 2001.
Ellmann, Richard. *James Joyce*. New and Revised Edition. Oxford: Oxford University Press, 1982.
McCourt, John. *Roll Away the Reel World: James Joyce and Cinema*. Cork: Cork University Press, 2010.
O'Brien, Harvey. *The Real Ireland: the Evolution of Ireland in Documentary Film*. Manchester: Manchester University Press, 2004.
O'Flynn, Sunniva. "Black and White and Collar Films: Exploring the Irish Film Archive of Clerical Films." In *Keeping It Real: Irish Film and Television*. Eds. Ruth Barton and Harvey O'Brien. New York and London: Wallflower Press, 2004, pp. 39–51.
Tall, Emily. "Eisenstein on Joyce: Sergei Eisenstein's Lecture on James Joyce at the State Institute of Cinematography, November 1, 1934." *James Joyce Quarterly* 24.2 (Winter 1987): 133–142.

CHAPTER 7

"One Beetle Recognizes Another": Translation, Transformation, Transgression in Cartoon Saloon's Film *The Secret of Kells*

Lisabeth C. Buchelt

If a viewer sits through the end credits of *The Secret of Kells* (Tomm Moore and Nora Twomey, 2009), they are rewarded with a rich voice reciting part of the medieval Irish poem, "Messe ocus Pangur Bán" in Old Irish. These few minutes bring a medieval poem learned as part of the Irish poetic canon by modern schoolchildren in translation but presented in its original language into a contemporary film; and they encapsulate the almost infinitely multifaceted glory of this extraordinary movie. It is not an adaptation in the conventional sense: that is, there is no single "original" or "base" prose work from which it draws its inspiration. In fact, the film produced its own "original" prose base as it was adapted into a young adult novel after it was released, the visuals translated into written text rather than the more customary text into visuals. Instead, *The Secret of Kells* is an adaptation of an aesthetic (early medieval Insular manuscript

L. C. Buchelt (✉)
University of Nebraska, Omaha, NE, USA
e-mail: lbuchelt@unomaha.edu

© The Author(s), under exclusive license to Springer Nature 113
Switzerland AG 2022
M. C. Conner et al. (eds.), *Screening Contemporary Irish Fiction and Drama*, Palgrave Studies in Adaptation and Visual Culture,
https://doi.org/10.1007/978-3-031-04568-4_7

illumination and metalwork) and an imagined historical epoch (the "Golden Age" of Irish civilization and art), as strained through a contemporary, multicultural collaborative group of artists, writers, and musicians. The result is an impressionistic, layered experience of medieval Ireland and the monastic scribal tradition that is neither entirely fictional nor entirely factual but is an entirely true insight to a culture over 1500 years removed and the ways in which that culture has been appropriated by the modern era.

The animation industry in Ireland is "regularly worth in excess of 80 million Euros" (Barton 41). Many, if not most, of the productions are not Irish-themed at all, and so most viewers of, for example, the late 1980s–early 1990s' television series *Teenage Mutant Ninja Turtles*, 2005's *Foster's Home for Imaginary Friends*, or 2007–2008's series *Skunk Fu*, both of which were broadcast on the Cartoon Network, have no idea that all these series were produced by animation studios in Ireland. It is an industry that was brought to Ireland in the late 1980s, when Don Bluth, whose two most well-known productions are *An American Tail* (1986) and *The Land Before Time* (1988), opened a studio in Dublin modeled on that of the Walt Disney Studios of the 1940s and 1950s. This company, called Sullivan Bluth, is credited with the introduction of commercial industry animation practices to Ireland; though film scholar Tom Walsh has argued that this model was another iteration of the colonization process in that Irish animators and artists "had to adopt an American commercial style" in order to work in this new-born industry (quoted in Barton 48). Although Sullivan Bluth was influential in the growth of animation in Ireland, this film genre did not have a chance to really develop into the highly successful local industry it is today until after Sullivan Bluth collapsed due to financial difficulties in 2000. This cleared the way for the foundation of more than twenty Irish animation companies, including Boulder Media, JAM Media, Brown Bag Films, and the studio whose film is under examination here, Cartoon Saloon.

Tomm Moore and Nora Twomey, who met at the Ballyfermot Animation College in Dublin, began developing *The Secret of Kells* in 1999 as they were building their company, Cartoon Saloon. The film took ten years to produce, utilizing the talents of over 200 artists in five countries and a budget of six million euros (about $8 million). Bucking the contemporary trend toward 3-D CGI animation, it is a unique 2-D, hand-drawn marvel which *Variety* called "absolutely luscious to behold" and that *Le Monde* said it "holds the spectator in a waking dream from beginning to end." *The Secret of Kells* won the Directors Guild of Ireland Directors

Series Award in 2008; was the first animated film to win the Edinburgh Film Festival Audience Award in 2009; and was named Best Irish Film at the Jameson Dublin International Film Festival in 2009, where it closed the Festival and received a standing ovation (http://www.cartoonsaloon. ie/work/the-secret-of-kells-animated-feature-film/). But when the film first opened to the general public in Ireland on St Patrick's Day 2009, it did not attract much attention. In 2010, it was nominated for an Oscar for Best Animated Feature, competing against films from Focus Features (*Coraline*), 20th Century Fox (*Fantastic Mr. Fox*), Walt Disney Animation (*The Princess and the Frog*), and Pixar (*Up*, which won). Moore remarked in an interview for the *New York Times* that he hoped "the attention from the Oscar race would propel the film to greater success [in Ireland]" (Ryzik, "Big Boys"). The attention seemed to have done so, and ultimately the film made $3.5 million worldwide, helping to establish Cartoon Saloon as an animation studio with an international reputation for astonishing creativity and quality.

For its first feature, Moore said that Cartoon Saloon "wanted to do something in [a] kind of Gaelic tradition … and we knew that a lot of people liked Celtic design, because you see it in people's tattoos and in Irish pubs—it's everywhere" (quoted in Ryzik, "Big Boys"). In another interview, Moore noted that "so much of the Celtic imagery around us could be traced to the Book of Kells," and so this medieval manuscript became the primary inspiration for the visual aesthetics of the film and the "stories and history surrounding [the manuscript] became the focus of the screenplay development" (quoted in Meltz and Dentz, "Illuminated Animation").[1] Bernard Meehan, retired Keeper of the Manuscripts at Trinity College Dublin and with whom Cartoon Saloon consulted as they worked on *The Secret of Kells*, comments that this collaboration between scholars and artists allows audiences "to engage convincingly with a remote intellectual world" (*Designing*, "Afterword"). *The Secret of Kells* is just such a product of the collaboration of an international group of artists and scholars. In it, we are given an imagined story about how the medieval manuscript of the Book of Kells was created that draws on historical facts behind its production and cultural milieu, and we learn that it, too, was the result of a medieval collaboration of international artists and scholars.

---

[1] See also Carnelia Garcia, "A Q & A with the Director of 'The Secret of Kells' Tomm Moore," 14 April 2010, www.blouinartinfo.com/news/story/34316/a-qa-with-the-secret-of-kells-director-tomm-moore.

116   L. C. BUCHELT

As the character of Aisling remarks in the film, "*aithníonn ciaróg ciaróg eile:*" one beetle recognizes another. The film's relationship to factual history and mythologized history is as equally nuanced as its relationship to historical Irish aesthetics.

For this viewer, steeped as I am in early medieval monastic culture as a result of my chosen field of study, from the moment the white cat, Pangur Bán, appears in the film in connection with the scribe and artist Brother Aiden, it is clear that this is more than just a series of pretty pictures exquisitely rendered and influenced by the visual aesthetic present in the medieval Book of Kells, which is, as Moore rightly noted, the seminal visual influence for what we consider today to be "Celtic" art. *The Secret of Kells* presents an image of early medieval Ireland that is simultaneously rooted in popular culture expectations of what constitutes "the medieval" as well as historical accuracy. The popular culture concept of the European Middle Ages is of different ethnicities and cultures existing more or less in isolation from each other, and of the monastic class as existing in further isolation from the rest of their secular cultures. In terms of the Irish Middle Ages, the popular historical narrative is of a unified "Celtic" culture dominated by hegemonic Catholicism. The monks lived and prayed in their monasteries with little to no interaction with the outside world beyond their walls, and all were equally devoted to studying nothing but the Christian religion without outside influences from anywhere else in the world. It is a picture of an Ireland that resists all comers until that initial moment of cultural trauma: the Viking invasions of the eighth and ninth centuries. In this version of Irish history, these incursions are the first of many subsequent cultural traumas perpetuated by foreigners (eventually mostly English), against which the Irish always fight valiantly but unsuccessfully until the early twentieth century.[2] And this is where *The Secret of Kells* diverges radically from the accepted conventions of the narrative of medieval Irish history. From within a viewpoint that accepts the popular (mis)conception of the medieval, the presence of the Book of Kells in the film is sometimes perceived by critics as presenting a "fictitious story"; a "playing with the truth" of history; a "challenging [of] the essence of the origin of an important Irish cultural symbol like the Book of Kells"; or a "questioning of the very origins of The Book of Kells" and so a rejection

---

[2] Burton places *The Secret of Kells* in her chapter devoted to Irish animation for obvious reasons, and it clearly belongs there. That said, it could easily deserve mention in her chapter entitled "Irish History and Trauma," depicting as it does the Viking attacks.

of "the dominant narrative of Christian Ireland" (Ramey 114; O'Brien 43; 35; 38). But what these critics are all missing because of their investment in, and acceptance of, the popular culture narrative about both the Middle Ages in general and the Irish medieval period in particular, is that this film is deeply erudite as well as being entirely enjoyable, presenting an imagined medieval world by freely transgressing the boundaries of time and place to provide viewers with its "true" vision of Ireland's Golden Age when it genuinely was the Island of Saints and Scholars. Ruth Barton in describing the concept of the transnational writes that "it acknowledges that global cultural exchange is not always a relationship of unequal power, but is just as often defined by straightforward mobility" (12). In her chapter on Irish animation where she examines *The Secret of Kells*, Barton applies the notion of the transnational to the literal production of the film without ever realizing that one of the messages of the film itself is that multiculturalism or transnationalism is not solely a modern phenomenon. The most obvious intellectual space that critics feel is clearly not historically accurate is the film's presentation of Irish medieval religion. In interpreting the film, many critics impose a false binary between "Christian" and "pagan" worldviews because this is the popular culture myth about medieval Christianity in Ireland: the Christian monks (bad) were working hard to eradicate completely indigenous pagan religion (good). Thus, some critics interpret the "lack" of "overt" Christianity in the film as perhaps a product of late-twentieth and early-twenty-first-century disillusionment and disgust with the Catholic church. But this notion of medieval Irish Christianity has little basis in historical fact.

The Secret of Kells is a film with a "gentle spirit of syncretism … which mixes folklore and history without too much piety or violence," and it is this willingness to transform and engage with not only folk tradition and history, but also the mythologizing of historical "fact" to arrive at a universal "truth," which contributes to the complexity of the film's deceptively simple narrative (Scott, "Fortified Walls"). Art historian Lynn Ramey, like Maria O'Brien and Barton, creates a dichotomy between "Christian" and "pagan" which simply does not exist in the film and so leads to a misreading of the characters and/or narrative.[3] O'Brien and Barton seem to feel that the film intentionally misrepresents "the original religious intent" of the manuscript of the Book of Kells to downplay its reality as a copy of the Christian gospels in order to "speak to a global viewer in universalist terms" (Ramey 117; O'Brien 34). Moore himself has said, "Didier Brunner [a co-producer] ... felt that we should stress the universality of the story" (quoted in Barton 57). But in doing so, *The Secret of Kells* does not undermine "the dominant narrative of Ireland as an Island of Saints and Scholars" allowing "the present [to question] the impossibility of an homogenous past" so much as provide a historically sound corrective to the present's acceptance of the popular cultural notion that medieval Ireland was not a multicultural, syncretic space through the film's complex interlacing of history, folklore, and popular mythologizing of Ireland's medieval past (O'Brien 37; 38).

As already noted, the name of the cat in the film, Pangur Bán, comes from the Old Irish poem, "Messe ocus Pangur Bán." But Moore has also said that Cartoon Saloon derived the film's central metaphor concerning the interaction of the forces of darkness and light, the transition from ignorance to knowledge, from this same poem. Moore quotes Celtic Studies scholar Robin Flower's 1931 translation of the Old Irish, which concludes, "Practice every day has made/Pangur perfect in his trade/I get wisdom day and night/Turning darkness into light" (180). Moore interpreted this last stanza as potentially describing the act of illuminating a manuscript as well as the act of learning. But this poem and the film's use and invocation of it is also a source for demonstrating the ways in which myths about history, although they may be strictly inaccurate, can capture a type of truth or authenticity about a distant culture.

Moore recalls learning the poem in school "along with the story that a monk had written it in the corner of a page he was illuminating" (*Designing*,

---

[3] In comments clearly influenced by popular culture's misconceptions about actual medieval culture, Barton remarks: "One of the most interesting aspects of this challenge was the filmmakers' determination to exclude all but the most unavoidable mentions of Christianity, which was a startling omission in a country still identified by its religious adherence. [...] The monks apparently spend little to no time in prayer and the Abbott is preoccupied with his fortifications. Instead, the film elevates craftsmanship and learning to the position of cultural identifiers" (54). For Ramey, this false binary leads to a complete misreading of the Abbot's concerns and so obscures the larger issue he represents: "The absence of an overt reference to the Christian content of the manuscript has ramifications in the fictional world of the film where the abbot does not see the book as a Biblical text but rather as a pagan-tainted obsession with abstract art" (117–118). This interpretation does much violence to the character of the Abbot, whose concern is in reality the time spent working on the book that takes away from time that could be spent on his wall—he has absolutely no issue with the book's visual aesthetic contents.

7 "ONE BEETLE RECOGNIZES ANOTHER": TRANSLATION... 119

"Foreword"). One of the charms of early medieval monastic poetry is that so much of it consists of one or two stanza poems that take the natural or secular worlds surrounding its monastic authors as its subject. Thus, we have delightful poems about a bird singing outside a scribe's window; the pleasure of resting under a tree in dappled sunlight; or how ink reminds the scribe of the iridescent color of a beetle's back. They present a religious voice that is happy, witty, secular, and not at all strict or staid or overly pious. And many of these poems are indeed written in the margins of the manuscripts in which they appear, where they seem to be irrepressible moments of joyful inspiration that simply could not be contained and had to be written down immediately. However, this is not the case with the poem "Pangur Bán." This poem is eight stanzas long, and takes up the entire bottom half of a verso folio in what is called the Reichenau Primer. It is clearly not a marginal outburst but is instead a carefully considered composition given a central spot within the larger manuscript of which it is an integral part. Additionally, the Reichenau Primer is an excellent microcosm of early medieval Irish intellectual culture in its mix of texts: it contains Latin hymns and grammar texts, Greek declension tables, astronomical charts and tables, and glosses on these various texts in Old High German. It too is a product of a multi-lingual and multicultural society. Thus, the story about "Pangur Bán" being scribbled in a margin in a codex that was the product of closed and insulated culture, though widely known and oft repeated, is not accurate. But this popular culture myth about the physical existence of "Pangur Bán" does describe a broader truth about the general corpus of early medieval Irish monastic poetry. Many of the poetic voices may be Christian, but they also appreciate the natural world in all its imperfection as another expression of the divine that exists outside humanity's dogmas; that is, for every severely strict Abbot Cellach there is a playfully irreverent Brother Aiden.

In the creation of the film *The Secret of Kells*, Moore and Twomey drew together Old Irish poems learned in school (such as "Messe ocus Pangúr Bán"); the visual stylings of the "UPA shorts of the 1950's [such as *Gerald McBoingBoing* and *Mr. Magoo*], Richard Williams' *The Thief and the Cobbler*, Genndy Tartakovsky's TV programs and Disney's *Mulan*" (*Designing*, "Introduction"). These are all juxtaposed with not only images from the medieval manuscript of the Book of Kells, but also recollected folktales about St Patrick and his arch-enemy, Crom Cruach/Crom Dubh; pre-Euro Irish coin design; Louis LeBroquy's famous pen and ink illustrations for Thomas Kinsella's 1969 translation of the medieval Irish epic saga *Táin Bó Cúailnge* (*The Cattle Raid of Cooley*); and the historical

120 L. C. BUCHELT

narrative of how Ireland's Golden Age—when it was the Island of Saints and Scholars—is interrupted and destroyed by the Viking incursions and raids that began with their fateful visit to Lindisfarne in Northumbria in 793.[4] But there are even more threads that are inspirations for this film.

Early Modern traditions and conventions of Irish *aisling* poetry are invoked in the character of Aisling and her relationship to the land; Irish saints' lives and mythologies, such as those of Saint Brendan the Navigator or Saint Aiden, the Irish founder of the monastery of Lindisfarne in Britain, in the characters of young Brendan and Brother Aiden; and historical abbots, such as the actual Abbot Cellach of the monastery of Iona in the character of Brendan's uncle Abbot Cellach. In addition to early medieval monastic poetry, pre-Christian Irish mythology is referenced in the character of Pangur Bán who reflects the idea of cats as guardians of the Otherworld and communicators with the *sidhe* (the faery folk of Ireland); the tradition of pre-Christian neolithic sites as entrances to the realm of the *sidhe*, or alternatively as entrances to hell, are referenced in the depiction of the cave of Crom Cruach. Furthermore, the historical tradition of the medieval Irish religious' reputation for undertaking difficult *peregrinatio*, or wandering, as an expression of piety is mirrored in the journey Brendan takes around Ireland after his home is destroyed. Finally, the film engages with the historical narrative of the Viking incursions into Ireland that has been created and recreated and adapted and repurposed and transformed in the historiography of medieval and modern Ireland for multiple political and cultural agendas over the last several hundred years. The interrogation of this narrative and its metaphorical possibilities forms the specific cultural experience on which the film can build a universal commentary on the nature of identity and art. Clearly, *The Secret of Kells'* list of potential references and sources of inspiration, both narrative and visual, is nearly infinite, and as such it could have been a convoluted muddle. But it's not. Instead, it is able to intertwine all these seemingly disparate threads and interlace them with a care and attention to detail and a sustainable intricacy that would make the late-eighth-, early-ninth-century artists and scribes of the Book of Kells smile in recognition of the twenty-first-century animators and writers as kindred spirits. I will first give a

---

[4] Moore has said about the use of folklore in his films, "I believe there is a strong underpinning in folklore that connects us to the past generations who retold these stories orally, and that the old stories contain links to our culture, to the past, and to universal truths" (quoted in Meltz and Dentz, "Illuminated Animation").

7 "ONE BEETLE RECOGNIZES ANOTHER": TRANSLATION... 121

quick thumbnail sketch of the history of connections between the monasteries of Lindisfarne, Iona, and Kells. Next, I will discuss current scholars' suggestions as to how the Book of Kells came to be and how it came to the monastic midlands from the island of Iona before giving a brief history of the public life of this most extraordinary of medieval manuscripts. Then, I will trace only a few of the potential thematic threads to demonstrate how complexly interwoven Cartoon Saloon's translation of the past into the present is in this film.

Christianity in Ireland, by the eighth century, was well established, and there were numerous monasteries throughout the island that had enormous power and wealth. For many of them, a portion of that wealth was spent on maintaining scriptoria, which require substantial raw resources to maintain: calfskin or sheepskin for parchment or vellum pages; goose quills and various inks with which to write; artists and scribes not only to produce the books, but also to train talented apprentices in both the drawing skills necessary and the knowledge of chemistry needed to produce the inks and continue the work. All of this was very expensive: it is estimated that the Book of Kells required the skins of approximately 185 calves, thus the monastery that produced such a luxurious volume needed a large herd in order to afford to kill so many of its young. The ink for the text is iron gall, a mixture of iron sulfate and tannic acids from oak galls that is relatively easy to obtain in Ireland; but much of the colorful ink for the images was made with imported materials from the Mediterranean, North Africa, even Afghanistan, which just like it is today can be an expensive proposition. The capacity to produce books of such outstanding quality contributed to Ireland's reputation in the medieval world as the Island of Saints and Scholars, which led to many people traveling to Ireland for their education and to many Irish scholars being invited to travel abroad as visiting professors. This produced even more avenues of potential revenue for the Irish monasteries, which created even greater wealth and this, in turn, led to their being integral parts of the secular political world as well as the religious landscape in Ireland.

The conspicuous consumption aspect of the great illuminated manuscripts and exquisite liturgical metalwork led many Irish religious to long for the simpler, more ascetic monastic life of the foundational years of Irish Christianity. Monasteries such as those of Finglas and Tallaght invoked the example of Columcille, among other early Irish saints, as more proper models for a Christian religious life. This movement came to be known as the Céili Dé. Those religious who chose to follow this stricter model were eventually taken into the communities of the larger religious institutions where they existed peacefully alongside the more easy-going monastic lifestyle followed by the majority of Irish religious. But monks of different levels of piety were not the only members of the monastic communities. The largest and most influential of the Irish monasteries—such as Clonmacnois or Kells in the monastic midlands, or Armagh or Iona in the north—were made up of diverse populations that included religious of varying degrees of piety as well as farmers, blacksmiths, carpenters, stone masons, sculptors, and many other artisans and craftspeople who had taken no religious vows at all but were nevertheless integral to the monastic community. The institutions like Kells or Clonmacnois were not established as places in which to live in pious isolation, but were instead more like small, pluralistic environments to which scholars and merchants from all over the world came to study or sell their wares, and which were actively engaged with their surrounding secular villages and communities. In the film, this international and cosmopolitan historical reality is depicted in the characters of Brother Tang, Brother Assoua, Brother Leonardo, Brother Friedrich, and Brother Jacques, who are from China, Africa, Italy, Gothic Germany, and France, respectively. It is also reflected in the active presence of secular villagers and their families, who live within the walls of the monastery. As Gearóid Mac Niocaill writes of the early medieval period in Ireland, "[i]t was a relatively stable and peaceful world, insofar as the eighth century was peaceful anywhere. Into this prosperous world the Norsemen irrupted … appearing off the Irish coast at the end of the eighth century" (31).

The monastery of Lindisfarne, founded in 634 by Saint Aidan, was raided by Vikings in 793; and the monastery of Iona, founded in 563 by Columcille, was raided in 795. These initial attacks were followed by more raids on Iona in 802 and 806, when 68 community members were killed. According to evidence from several Irish annals, once the Viking raids started, the island community at Iona seems to have often sought refuge at the inland monastery of Kells.[5] There is a record of an Abbot Cellach of Iona resigning and retiring to Kells in the early ninth century. There is an echo of this historical abbot and his movements in the film's character of Abbot Cellach, who is Brendan's uncle and the leader of Kells and who we

---

[5] The Viking raids on various monasteries, as well as specific references to Kells, can be found in the *Annals of Tigernach*, the *Annals of the Four Masters*, the *Annals of Loch Cé*, as well as the *Annals of Ulster*.

7 "ONE BEETLE RECOGNIZES ANOTHER": TRANSLATION... 123

learn used to work in the scriptorium at Iona. In 878 in the *Annals of Ulster* another abbot of Iona is recorded as bringing the shrine and "precious objects" of Columcille—scholars speculate that one of these objects may have been what would come to be called the Book of Kells— "to Ireland," apparently to Kells, in order to "escape the foreigners"; in other words, the Vikings. The character of Brother Aiden in the film, who arrives at Kells because he has fled the Vikings' raid on Iona and has in his possession an unfinished manuscript, is a clear reflection of this unnamed abbot from the annals. By the early tenth century, the monastery at Kells had grown and was prosperous enough to attract the attentions of the Viking raiders, and it too was repeatedly plundered in 920, 951, 970, and 991 (Mac Niocaill 32). It may have been during one of these raids that the Book of Kells had its posited jewel-encrusted covers torn off and taken. The Book remained at Kells until 1654, when it was moved to Dublin for safekeeping when the monastery housed Cromwell's cavalry. In 1661 it was presented to Trinity College Dublin, where it has lived ever since.

Although the Book itself has been around since the late eighth, early ninth century, the access of the general public to its visuals is relatively recent, as it wasn't put on public display until the nineteenth century. It wasn't until 1914 that the first substantial illustrated volume about the Book of Kells appeared—this is the one by Sir Edward Sullivan. This study was not a full facsimile and in fact included only twenty-four plates in color, with a number of the smaller drawings that are in the margins or form illuminated capital letters reproduced without the rest of their visual context. This somewhat dismembered version of the Book of Kells was the one used as a reference text by James Joyce, and has been reprinted many times up to 1986.[6] In the film, the manuscript is shown many times in this sort of dismembered state. We see only tiny moments of illustration, as we follow Brendan's visual experiments with translating his growing fascination and knowledge of the natural world outside the walls of the monastery into visual artistry. The tiny piece of manuscript that Abbot Cellach first rips in frustration, destroying the incipient visuals on what will become the magnificent Chi-Ro page from the Book, and then clutches at the end of the film can be read as a gesture to this partial knowledge of the book which the general public had for so long. Indeed, the public continues to have this partial knowledge of the Book of Kells through the pieces of it

---

[6] The first full-color complete facsimile of the Book of Kells was not produced until 1990. See Peter Fox "Introduction."

that are reproduced on postcards, posters, coffee mugs, refrigerator magnets, tea towels, scarves, bookmarks, and anything else on which an image can be slapped and sold. The film looks to restore a more holistic conception of the Book by providing the public with a space in which to experience visuals and narrative that interact in a complexly layered way that mirrors the experience of the medieval audiences of the Book of Kells. In doing so, *The Secret of Kells* successfully transposes the historical facts of the culture of early medieval Ireland into an imaginative truth about the broader art and culture of the period.

The Secret of Kells' narrative is told from the point of view of Brendan, a young, curious, and idealistic boy living in the tightly knit community at the Abbey of Kells, who is under the strict care of his stern uncle, Abbot Cellach. Cellach, once a talented illuminator, is obsessed with building a wall around the Abbey in order to prevent Viking attacks, and has spent his artistic skills designing and engineering the wall. An old friend of Cellach's from his time in the scriptorium at Iona, Brother Aidan, arrives at Kells after Iona has been sacked by the Vikings with his cat Pangur Bán and clutching an unfinished book on which he has been working. Seeing Brendan as a suitable apprentice, Aidan sends Brendan and Pangur Bán into the woods around the monastery to obtain gall nuts to make ink for the illumination of the book, although Cellach has expressly forbidden Brendan to venture outside the walls of the monastery. Here Brendan meets a member of the *sidhe*, Aisling, who helps him to see the beauty in, and draw artistic inspiration from, the natural world. After learning that Brendan has repeatedly left the monastery defying his orders, Cellach rips the page on which Brendan and Aiden have been working, and locks them both in the scriptorium. Shortly thereafter, the Vikings invade Kells, and Cellach watches in horror as they breach the wooden gate, destroying the monastery and killing most of its inhabitants. Brendan and Aiden escape from the scriptorium by making ink, the chemical process of which produces a smoke that allows them to flee unseen. Once free of the scriptorium, Brendan sees his uncle felled by a Viking arrow, but is dragged away by the frantic Aidan, who tells him that there is nothing that he can do. Cellach, although wounded, survives the attack with a small handful of those in his care, but believes Brendan has died and falls into a deep despair. Brendan and Aidan travel across Ireland, and, after many years, complete the book. After Aiden's death, the now-adult Brendan returns to Kells with Pangur Bán, where guilt-ridden Cellach clutches what he believes to be the only remaining piece of his nephew: the scrap he tore from the "book that makes the darkness light." Brendan displays the completed Book of Kells to his uncle, Cellach's overwhelming experience of which is indicated by an animated rendition of parts of the Book of Kells' Chi-Ro page.

In the film, the visual vocabulary includes the ending sequence in which images from the Book of Kells move into their positions—that is, the two mice holding the Host and the two cats holding the mice run; the bees swarm; the angels flutter; and the bearded face swirls into their final places on the Chi-Ro. Additionally, archeological sites or objects are brought together from all over Ireland and create the film's imagined monastic enclosure as well as the natural world around it. In the woods Brendan finds the Turoe Stone from Co. Galway; the Drom Beg stone circle from Co. Cork; the Dolman from the Burren in Co. Clare, and the pre-Christian statues from Co. Fermanagh. The objects the Vikings loot from the monastery are renditions of the Broighter Hoard torcs found in Derry, now on display in the National Museum of Ireland in Dublin; the doorway of Kells' scriptorium in the film invokes the Romanesque doorways at Clonfert Cathedral near Galway or the Nuns' Church at Clonmacnois in Co. Offaly; and Brendan and Aiden build themselves a beehive hut like those on the Ring of Dingle and on Skellig Michael in Co. Kerry. By bringing together all these actual, visual embodiments of Ireland into a single location, the filmmakers provide the viewer with an Ireland of the mind that may be geographically inaccurate (the beehive huts on Skellig Michael, off the far southwestern coast of Ireland are nowhere near the actual location of Kells, which is in the monastic midlands), but is nevertheless a true rendition of the intellectual and cultural world in which the artists and scribes of the Book of Kells moved and from which they drew inspiration. The film thus creates a multivalent visual Irish identity that participates in the well-established imaginatively manufactured and somewhat artificial "tourist" identity of medieval Ireland. It presents images that have been used for many years to promote the notion of medieval "Celtic" Ireland as a potential location of "authentic" Irishness, while simultaneously presenting modern audiences with an accurate representation of medieval Ireland's intellectual and cultural space. In other words, the film translates the highly recognizable, almost clichéd, aesthetic of the Book of Kells T-shirts, tattoos, and tea towels into a sly transmission of a cultural and historical truth about medieval Ireland. But *The Secret of Kells* does more than simply reproduce particular illustrations from the Book of Kells or specific archeological sites and objects from the visual history of

126   L. C. BUCHELT

Ireland. The film goes beyond the surface and integrates the two aesthetic styles present in the Book of Kells to convey several thematic tensions and the productive potential present when these tensions, which are set against the backdrop of the violent Viking invasions, are resolved into a creative whole.

There are two distinctive visual aesthetics present in the illustrations in the Book of Kells, likely the products of three artistic hands: one that is a more geometric, angular style; and one that has a more curvilinear flow. The more angular aesthetic in the Book of Kells can be represented by the "Tunc" page (f. 124r); or the "Temptation" page (f. 202v); the curvilinear most spectacularly by the "Chi-Ro" page (f. 14r).[7] When the angular aesthetic is the predominant visual vocabulary in the film, the colors used are primarily black, white, deep indigo blues, and grays contrasted with reds. These visual cues are consistently associated in the film with Abbot Cellach's blind and mistaken belief that his wall, and only his wall will protect the monastery; with his incapacitating fear for Brendan's and his community's safety; with his deeply rooted terror of the world outside the monastery walls; and with his forgetting that the monastic institution is not only a place of protection, but also the place of learning, of philosophical enquiry, and of artistic expression and that these efforts, too, can lead to the defeat of violence and the darkness. The angular aesthetic is also deployed to represent the violence of the Vikings and their singular, equally blind desire for worldly material wealth—"gold" is the only word we ever hear them utter (see Fig. 7.1). It is also used to depict the black wolf pack in the forest, which surrounds Brendan at the film's rendition of the Turoe Stone and threatens to attack him and Pangur Bán before called off by its white wolf leader. And when Brendan visits the lair of Crom Cruach, the entrance of which is framed by the two angular representations of the pre-Christian County Fermanagh statues, the snake-like beast he fights moves not in sinuous curves, but in jagged angles.

When the curvilinear aesthetic is the predominant visual vocabulary in the film, the colors used are greens, yellows and golds, lighter blues, earthy

---

[7] It should also be noted that the angular black devil which hovers near the church on the "Temptation" page makes a cameo appearance in the film when the brothers are discussing the mythology which is already growing up around Columcille and his abilities as an artist and scribe in producing the book that Brother Aiden is hoping to finish. The multiple ways in which the film creates imagined mythologies and then intertwines them with existing bodies of lore about its characters is yet another way *The Secret of Kells* engages with the narratives Ireland has generated about itself.

Fig. 7.1 Vikings on the march in *The Secret of Kells* (2009)

browns, pale grays, and whites. These visual cues are consistently associated with Brendan's curiosity and growing resistance to his uncle's nearly irrational fears about his community's safety. They are also associated with Aiden's view that a monastery is a place of safety, but that safety can also be produced by the work of intellectuals and artists within the monastic institution. The curvilinear aesthetic is used to describe the natural world as a location of benign and fruitful beauty, and is associated with its caretaker, Aisling, as protective and nurturing (see Fig. 7.2). But Aisling also has a capacity for extreme strength and aggressive violence when necessary; and it is this theme of combining seemingly antithetical worldviews that the film ultimately embraces to describe a philosophical and intellectual truth about the necessity to understand that darkness, evil, or fear are needed to fully recognize light, goodness, or courage: *Aithníonn ciaróg ciaróg eile*. Brendan's quest for an artistic tool that Brother Aiden has lost helps to draw these multiple threads representing darkness and light into a single interlaced design.

We learn that Aiden has lost what he calls the "Eye of Columcille," which is a crystal used to aid in the creation of the intricate designs of the illuminations. Brendan discovers that there is place to acquire another such crystal, and it is in the lair of Crom Cruach. In a dreamlike sequence, Brendan enters the lair with Aisling's help and is able to defeat the angular

Fig. 7.2 Brendan and Aisling in the oak tree

Crom Cruach by drawing curves to defend against the beast's jagged attacks, ultimately enclosing the snake within a circle (see Fig. 7.3). The "Eye of Columcille" was also taken from Crom Cruach, and so a link is re-forged between this creature of darkness and it being necessary to the production of enlightenment. Thus, the film points toward the necessary incorporation of risk with safety to produce knowledge and beauty. Visually, this idea is also conveyed in the aesthetic of the crystal Eyes themselves as they combine the angular and the curvilinear.

Like Crom Cruach, Aisling also combines the angular and curvilinear and so is multivalent in that she represents not only fertile, productive aspects of nature, but also the dangerous, destructive aspects of it. We learn that the white wolf who leads the black wolf pack to attack the Vikings when they threaten Brendan and Aiden is an incarnation of Aisling herself, the holistic depiction of the natural world represented by the angular black wolves being led by the curvilinear white one. And it is Aisling who, at extreme cost to herself, embodies the deeper powers of violent weather and earthquakes not only to allow Brendan to gain access to Crom Cruach's lair, but also to render the space benign once he has acquired the second Eye. Aesthetically, when Aisling is emphasizing the more dangerous aspects of nature (storms, earthquakes, or blinding fog), she retains her curvilinear structures but is surrounded by dark grays,

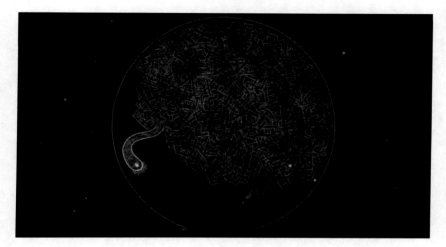

Fig. 7.3 Crom Cruach trapped

blacks, and whites. Calling upon the powers of the earthquake to move the enormous stones that guard the entrance to Crom Cruach's cave literally drains the life from Aisling. Although her long white hair still moves in curvilinear waves as if underwater, angular black, thorny vines entwine her arms as she lifts the stone, shifting her into what can be recognized as the Cailleach/Crone aspect of Ireland's traditional Tripartite Sovereignty Goddess. Nature's return to its benign aspect, and Aisling's survival despite her dangerous sacrifice, is indicated aesthetically by the addition of curved white snowdrop flowers around the toppled angular Fermanagh statues, and golden tones replace the blacks and grays that previously dominated Crom Cruach's cave entrance. At the end of the film, when Brendan returns to Kells to comfort his uncle and show him the completed book, we learn that Abbot Cellach has "seen the light" and come to understand that building a wall was not the permanent protection he envisioned, and that Cellach has remembered the value in the more immaterial protections of knowledge and beauty. His remembering and reintegration of what he once knew as a master illuminator, but had forgotten as an abbot, is indicated by the softening of the angular drawings with new curvilinear elements and the wash of golden light rather than dark indigo across the walls of his cell.

We see in the visual integrations of the curvilinear and angular aesthetics that the film underscores through the intimate connection of its verbal and visual elements a philosophically stance—perhaps a truth—that great knowledge and great beauty can only be produced by acknowledging the Dark, incorporating and transforming it so as to stay resolutely facing the Light. This is a theme that the novelization of the film underscores from its very beginning. Eithne Massey was tasked with the somewhat unconventional translation of visuals into written text, rather than text into visuals, when she wrote the novel version of *The Secret of Kells*. Like any good translator of an adaptation, she did not shy away from changing the narrative of the film if necessary to help to underscore the themes as the work moved from visual to written text. For example, instead of opening, as the film does, with Brendan chasing after a goose to catch it and pluck feathers from its tail to use for quills in the scriptorium, the novel begins with Brendan hiding and overhearing a conversation between his uncle and newly arrived Brother Aiden.

> The Abbot said abruptly, "We don't have time at the moment to be making books. Building the wall is the important work now. The walls will protect all of us from the attacks of the Northmen. And it will protect the refugees that come to us now; the pagans and the Crom worshippers. Through the strength of our walls they will come to trust the strength of our faith." [...] "Brother Cellach," [Aiden] said, "you must know that all the walls in the world will not be able to keep them out. Nothing can stop them. [...] Our work should be to make something that will outlast us, something that will still be there when all the walls are down, and all of us long gone. [Something] [t]hat will turn the darkness into light." (Massey 11)

The need to join seemingly antithetical worldviews, represented in the film by the union of the angular and curvilinear aesthetics, is here hinted at in Cellach's expressed desire to protect *all* the refugees that come to his monastery, whether they are Christian or not: "it will protect the refugees that come to us now; the pagans and the Crom worshippers." However, Cellach still needs to learn that protection comes in many forms, as Aiden suggests in his desire to continue his work on the book: "something that will still be there when all the walls are down." Thus, Massey introduces an underlying theme of the work textually which the film presents visually: "darkness" may be defeated only by joining it to "light." As in the film, the characters of Aisling, whose name means "vision," and Aiden are used as catalysts to forge the link necessary between darkness and light.

The explanation of some of the complex references to Irish mythology, folklore, and tradition and the potential ways in which they contribute to the elucidation of this theme is put in the mouth of these two characters. Aisling is given the task of explaining Crom Cruach and all he can represent:

> Crom Cruach is one of the Old Dark Ones … He has many different names, and many different lairs. Some people call him Crom Dubh, the Black One. Others say that his name means Bloody Head. There are those who think it means Bloody Mound. He has existed since the beginning of time. Through the ages, he has ruled by fear, and he has taken many forms. (Massey 68)

By allowing the single name, Crom Cruach/Crom Dubh, its full range of potential meanings, Massey permits the entity to be an individual ("the Black One"); a description of the result of a potential violent action ("Bloody Head"); or an archeological location of cultural trauma ("Bloody Mound").[8] The character of Aisling also points the reader to the ways in which the idea of Crom Cruach is threaded through the narrative in Cellach's incapacitating fear that blinds him to the futility of his wall-building despite his best intentions, and in the form of the violent Viking attacks: "he has ruled by fear, and he has taken many forms." By underscoring the multivalent verbal possibilities in this entity's name(s), Massey has translated into written text the multiple visual associations the film makes with the angular aesthetic's depiction of the Vikings, of the snake form of Crom Cruach and its lair, of the black wolves, and of Cellach's architectural drawings of his wall.

While Aisling explains the darkness in her world to Brendan, it is Aiden who explains Aisling's role in that world to Brendan:

> She is not like us. But she is not human. She's one of the Old Ones too, like Crom Cruach. But she is one of the bright ones, Brendan, the ones that walk in the light and do good rather than evil. I do not know very much about the Old Ones, but I do know that they do not go away entirely; they

---

[8] The name Crom Cruach can also mean "the Crooked One," and although Massey does not mention this possible meaning, I would like to do so as in its invocation of crookedness it is another connection to the angular visual representations that this entity and all it represents is given in the film.

only change their form. So she will come back, and she left the flowers as a sign for you. I am sure you will see her again some day. Maybe when you are least expecting it, maybe in some shape—an animal or bird—that you will not recognize at first. But never let anyone make you think she is anything other than good. She is part of the goodness of the trees and the wind, and of the creatures of the wood. (Massey 124)

The links that are made visually in the film between Aisling and productive Nature as well as between her and destructive Nature in the combining of the curvilinear and angular aesthetics in the drawings of her character are rendered textually in the words of Brother Aiden. Aiden does not shy away from the fact that she is not human, nor from her similarities to Crom Cruach, though she has made different choices: "[s]he's one of the Old Ones too, like Crom Cruach. But she is one of the bright ones … that walk in the light and do good rather than evil." That said, Aiden makes it clear that she is not controlled by Brendan or by anybody else in the human world and will come and go as she pleases. Indeed, Aiden admits to some ignorance regarding the pre-Christian denizens of Ireland, but emphasizes that ignorance need not lead to fear: "never let anyone make you think she is anything other than good." Aiden understands that creatures like her are often misunderstood by humans because, like nature itself, she has the capacity for destruction as well as production. Like Aisling's explanation of Crom Cruach, Aiden allows her to be an individual, an idea, a place that takes many forms across time. Massey's words in Aiden's mouth describe in written language the multivalent possibilities of Aisling that the film presents visually: she is the young girl, and the snowdrops, and the giant oak tree, and the fog, and the potentially dangerous or protective white wolf of the film.

Amanda Dillon, in her article about the ways in which the Book of Kells contributes to the visual identity of Ireland, comments on how the visual aesthetic of the Book of Kells is readily appreciated, accessible, and recognizable by anyone, but that the Latin text of the Book, "being Latin, [is] largely inaccessible to many viewers" (310). She suggests that this creates a disconnect between the potential Irish-identity formation possibilities of the visual aesthetics of the Book now and the Irish-identity formation possibilities of the Book at the time of its creation when the combined visual and verbal aspects of the book could be fully appreciated in all its intricacies by its audience. This modern disconnect breaks what is perhaps the Book of Kells' defining contribution to medieval book production and intellectual culture: its place as the apogée of Insular manuscripts' intimate intertwining of the verbal with the visual.[9]

The creators of *The Secret of Kells* seem to have noticed this disengaging of written text from image for modern viewers of the Book of Kells and have worked to restore the Book's complicated relationship between word, narrative, and image through the intricate connections between narrative and image in their film. *The Secret of Kells* provides modern audiences and appreciators of the Book of Kells with an insight into an early medieval understanding that image can do more than provide aesthetically pleasing embellishment to text or act simply as literal illustrations of the action described by words on a page. But that *The Secret of Kells* replicates this potential medieval relationship to the integration of visuals, narrative and meta-narratives is sometimes missed even by medieval art historians. So although Ramey is correct to suggest that the Book in the film "is not identical to the material book sitting in the Trinity College Library in Dublin" but is a "simulacrum," the Book in the film is not nearly as distorted a version of the original as she implies. She suggests that when filmmakers are confronted with an original in which "text and image seem to be doing different things" as often happens in medieval illuminated manuscripts, the filmmaker "may be forced to choose between remediating either the text or the images, but not both at the same time" (114). The beauty of *The Secret of Kells* is that Cartoon Saloon has in fact remediated not only text and image at the same time, but has included the multiple meta-narratives surrounding not only the Book of Kells' own history and production, but also the medieval history of Ireland and the popular (mis) conceptions and revisions of that history. By twining together iconic images of Ireland's past, popular narratives about Ireland when it was the "Island of Saints and Scholars," and documented historical references to events that occurred and people who existed, Cartoon Saloon presents, as Bernard Meehan remarks, "the imaginative recreation of the past"

---

[9] "Because the visual dimension of the Book of Kells is so strong and the text, being in Latin, largely inaccessible to many viewers, the aesthetics of the book dominate the collective imagination as they reach back to the early Irish-Christian monastic era. Pulliam notes perceptively that 'perhaps the most unique feature of the Book of Kells is the manner in which the imagery repeatedly invades the territorial domain of text.' This has happened in both the cultural and religious reception of the book. The aesthetics of the Book of Kells have become—through both genuine, popular-cultural evolution and marketing manipulation—a portal which promises entry to the timeless compounds of ancient Celtic consciousness" (Dillon 310).

(*Designing*, "Afterword"). Thus, the film allows us to experience a particular mindset and understanding of how to process information utilizing both text and image. *The Secret of Kells* becomes, as Umberto Eco has suggested of the Book of Kells, a

> model of language and, perchance, of the world. [...] It is a model of a universe in expansion, perhaps finite but still limitless, the starting point for infinite interrogations, for a maze of hermeneutics without end. It allows us to feel like men and women of our own times, even as we navigate across the same perilous sea that bore St Brendan. (16)

It has become a commonplace to think of the twenty-first century as more visually literate than cultures of past ages. *The Secret of Kells* reminds viewers that this is simply not true; that the modern age did not invent an intimate integration of word and image. It is true that much of the content and intellectual contexts are different for integrating the written text with the visual. About 1200 years ago, the contexts for the text and visuals of the Book of Kells were the Bible, biblical exegesis, medieval philosophy and theology, and knowledge of Latin. In *The Secret of Kells* today, it is instead the 200 years of historical narrative revisions and cultural identity formation that have appropriated the archeological and visual icons of Ireland. But the ways in which the Book of Kells and the film each ask us to engage with their respective information is nearly identical: each work allows us "to feel like men and women of our own time" even as each simultaneously allows us to engage with it as a person of the early medieval period would have done. The complex interlacing, the intervisuality and intertextuality performed by the Book of Kells and *The Secret of Kells*, as well as the film's translation into a novel—that is, these media's consistent "polyvalent aesthetic" and methodology—allows audiences to see there is more to be found in the past than objective facts to selectively spin or warp for particular cultural or political agendas; there is also a relevance and truth that speaks to contemporary culture.[10]

Roger Allers, animator and co-director of Disney's *The Lion King*, remarks, "*The Secret of Kells* is nothing less than an Initiation into the Mysteries. The mystery of Nature, of Art and Craft. To Seeing beyond the

---

[10] As Dillon remarks, this polyvalent aesthetic "looks set to prevail into the future. From handmade craft work [sic], to kitsch and political art...the ability of the Book of Kells to inspire artists of every ilk and medium endures undimmed" (311).

Surface while Making surfaces Beautiful. This film IS illumination" (*Designing*, "Afterword"). The same could be said of the Book of Kells itself. *Aithníonn ciaróg ciaróg eile*: one beetle recognizes another. Although it is true that the "Celtic" aesthetic of the Book of Kells continues to inspire artists, *The Secret of Kells* provides the insight that contemporary Irish artists may be influenced by the medieval past, but are expressing a version of that past in thoroughly modern visual vocabularies. This is most apparent through the film's visual nods to Louis LeBroquy's pen and ink illustrations for Thomas Kinsella's translation of *Táin Bó Cúailnge* in particular, but is also present in the more subtle nods to pre-Euro Irish coin designs and, arguably, the gestures toward Celtic-infused Irish contributions to the late-nineteenth and early-twentieth-century Arts and Crafts Movement.[11] But the film's engagement with the long continuum of Irish contributions to intellectual culture and the process and production of scholarship goes beyond the visual in the ways in which Irish literature and history is also remediated in the film. The most obvious example of this is the central position of Pangur Bán to the narrative of the film, remediating as she does the integral position of the character's source poem in its ninth-century manuscript. By purposefully transmuting and transforming ancient, medieval, and modern visual icons of Ireland, transgressing boundaries of both time and space and interlacing them together with the film's narrative, *The Secret of Kells* performs an act of translation between past and present in which artists and intellectuals 1200 years apart work together to entertain, to inform, and to inspire twenty-first century audiences.

Works Cited

The Secret of Kells. Created and directed by Tomm Moore and Nora Twomey. Produced by Cartoon Saloon, 2009. http://www.cartoonsaloon.ie/work/the-secret-of-kells-animated-feature-film/.

---

[11] Interestingly, not only will the film become part of the continuum of Irish visual identity, but the products of the process of making it have now been, in a way, canonized through their preservation in the archives of Trinity College: "When [Bernard] Meehan learned the drawings from *The Secret of Kells* were going to be destroyed and the paper recycled, the archivist offered to house them in Trinity College, where they'll be preserved. In a few years, or a few centuries, the 21st century drawings and the 8th century manuscript that inspired them may inspire future practitioners of the arts of animation and draftsmanship" (Solomon, "Foreword").

Allers, Roger. "Afterword." In Tomm Moore and Ross Stewart. *Designing The Secret of Kells*. Korea: Cartoon Saloon, 2014.

Barton, Ruth. *Irish Cinema in the Twenty-First Century*. Manchester: Manchester UP, 2019.

Dillon, Amanda. "The Book of Kells and the Visual Identity of Ireland." In Bradford A. Anderson and Jonathan Kearney, eds. *Ireland and the Reception of the Bible: Social and Cultural Perspectives*. London and New York: T & T Clark, 2018, pp. 295–312.

Eco, Umberto. Oscar Ratti, trans. "Foreward." *The Book of Kells: Trinity College MS 58/ Kommentar*. Luzern: Faksimile Verlag Luzern, 1990, 11–16.

Flower, Robin. *Poems and Translations*. London: Constable and Co., Ltd., 1931.

Fox, Peter. "Introduction." *The Book of Kells: Trinity College MS 58/ Kommentar*. Luzern: Faksimile Verlag Luzern, 1990, 17–21.

Massey, Eithne. *The Secret of Kells: The Novel*. Dublin: The O'Brien Press, 2009.

Mac Niocaill, Gearóid. "The Background to the Book of Kells." *The Book of Kells: Trinity College MS 58/ Kommentar*. Luzern: Faksimile Verlag Luzern, 1990, 27–33.

Meehan, Bernard, "Afterword." In Tomm Moore and Ross Stewart. *Designing The Secret of Kells*. Korea: Cartoon Saloon, 2014.

Meltz, Nathan and Shira Dentz, "Illuminated Animation: An Interview with Tomm Moore," *Tarpaulin Sky Press*, 1 February 2016, https://tskymag.com/2016/02/tomm-moore-2/.

O'Brien, Maria. "*The Secret of Kells*, a Film for a Post Celtic Tiger?" *Animation Studies 6* (2011).

Ramey, Lynn. "Immediacy, Hypermediacy, and New Media in *The Secret of Kells* (Moore 2009).' *Medieval Perspectives 29* (2014).

Ryzik, Melena. "An Indie Takes on Animation's Big Boys," *New York Times* 3 March 2010.

Scott, A.O. "Outside the Abbey's Fortified Walls, a World of Fairy Girls and Beasts," *New York Times*, 5 March 2010, https://www.nytimes.com/2010/03/05/movies/05secret.html.

Solomon, Charles. "Foreword." In Tomm Moore and Ross Stewart. *Designing The Secret of Kells*. Korea: Cartoon Saloon, 2014.

CHAPTER 8

Bad Da's: Rewriting Fatherhood in *Breakfast on Pluto*

Nicole R. McClure

> *In the first years of the new century the young Irish playwrights wrote about bad fathers.*
> —Colm Tóibín, "Selling Tara, Buying Florida"

And so did the novelists, and the poets, and the screenwriters. Bad Irish fathers have become a certainty in family narratives, a requisite inclusion as sure as green fields and country lanes. In the opening paragraphs of his autobiography, Frank McCourt remarks that "worse than the ordinary miserable childhood is the miserable Irish childhood" and in further reading, we learn that much of McCourt's childhood misery is inextricably linked to his alcoholic and eventually absent father (McCourt 11). While McCourt has been accused of writing more histrionics than autobiography, he has maintained a commitment to his initial story that his father was a scoundrel and a source for much of his aforementioned pitiful childhood.

N. R. McClure (✉)
Kutztown University, Kutztown, PA, USA

© The Author(s), under exclusive license to Springer Nature
Switzerland AG 2022
M. C. Conner et al. (eds.), *Screening Contemporary Irish Fiction and Drama*, Palgrave Studies in Adaptation and Visual Culture,
https://doi.org/10.1007/978-3-031-04568-4_8

138   N. R. MCCLURE

McCourt's imaginative portrayal is not an anomaly. Plenty of twentieth-century Irish writers have also included feckless and abusive fathers. Take for instance John McGahern's *The Dark*, which depicts the horrifying and dysfunctional relationship between a son and his violent father. The opening pages of the novel graphically illustrate physical abuse with a description of the "heavy leather strap he used for sharpening his razor," an ominous introduction to the tools of his father's cruelty (McGahern 7). The scene continues with a chilling depiction of psychological and physical terror; the young Mahoney weeps, pitifully apologizing to his father for uttering the word "fuck," while his father vows to "teach him a lesson." The younger daughters watching in terror (McGahern 8). Such a horrific introduction to the father figure frames the rest of the novel as a critical study of savage cruelty.

Edna O'Brien depicts several grim tales of abusive and drunken fathers in *The Country Girls* and *Down by the River* (and in nearly everything she writes); O'Brien's overt feminism is the resulting triumph caused directly by years of violent assaults, both physical and psychological, at the hands of men often in paternal roles. O'Brien's ghastly descriptions of fatherhood are explicit and prominent. Like McGahern, O'Brien describes the wretched father in *The Country Girls* within the first few pages as Caithleen and her mother consider what fate awaits them when the patriarch finally arrives home:

> She was thinking. Thinking where was he? Would he come home in an ambulance, or a hackney car, hired in Belfast three days ago and not paid for? Would he stumble up the stone steps at the back door waving a bottle of whiskey? Would he shout, struggle, kill her, or apologize? Would he fall in the hall door with some drunken fool and say: "Mother, meet my best friend Harry. I've just given the thirteen-acre meadow for the loveliest greyhound…" All this had happened to us so many times that it was foolish to expect that my father might come home sober. (6–7)

Caithleen's cavalier consideration that she could be murdered by her own father is a disturbing portrait of a then-unnamed toxic masculinity. Again using such characterization in the very early pages of the novel helps to normalize the behavior as an establishment of a particularly Irish story.[1]

---

[1] It should be noted that O'Brien's continued use of these tropes was written in an attempt to de-normalize such behavior, rather than reinforce it. The importance of the trope is the same, however, as the repeated patterns of recognizable "fatherly" behavior still remain.

Further evidence of dysfunction appears in William Trevor's 1994 novel *Felicia's Journey* when a young father, Johnny Lysaght, abandons his teenage girlfriend, leaving her heartbroken and their child fatherless; the resulting scenario leads the young mother into the arms of a dangerous serial killer. Mr. Hilditch is able to groom Felicia by taking on the role of a father, again reinforcing that fathers of any kind are dangerous, threatening, and eventually absent. John B. Keane's 1964 drama, *Year of the Hiker*, is an unapologetic tale of a father who suddenly walked out on his family, only to return in a haggard state 20 years later with little explanation or justification for his absence except to blame the women in the house for his own inadequacies. Hiker Lacey complains that his wife and sister-in-law are at the heart of his personal dissatisfaction in life: "Kate was a mouse, but I loved her. I couldn't make her into a woman with you around. We could do nothing with you. There was no peace or fulfillment in our lovemaking with you in the house" (Keane 31). Hiker Lacey's misogynist conflation of sex and happiness point to his lack of concern for his family; his unsatisfying sexual relationship is his ultimate reason for seeking happiness elsewhere.

Colm Tóibín's statement that "In the first years of the new century the young Irish playwrights wrote about bad fathers" illustrates a chilling trend among Irish writers that dads are just no good (11). Tóibín's larger context points to the juxtaposition of the tradition of an idyllic rural Ireland in which fatherly skeletons remained in proverbial closets, and a contemporary Celtic Tiger Ireland where global exposure illuminated such ghastly secrets in the Irish family. Yet, regardless of any Celtic Tiger optimism, Tóibín notes that Irish writers embraced the horror as an accepted part of Irish life and in doing so, the convention remains a standard part of the Irish canon. In short, there seems to be no other way to write the Irish father.

This literary phenomenon isn't accidental. In fact, the Irish father has a history of ill-repute long before contemporary writers adopted the trope. Early depictions of a fair Hibernia/Erin often also feature an ogre-like Fenian beast as a husband/father lurking in the corner. Either nineteenth-century *Punch* cartoons feature Hibernia being abused or subjugated by her Irish spouse or, rather, the images leave the father out of the image completely, implying that fair Hibernia raises her children alone. In many cases, Hibernia is either protected by a strong, military figure of Britannia, or lauded as a dominant maternal figure. Such gendered nationalism figures prominently in the historical, political, and social discourses surrounding the island nation. "Mother Ireland" and the feminized "Hibernia" and "Erin" are firmly embedded in the national vocabulary, appearing anywhere from the rhetoric of nationalism to the business of tourism. C.L. Innes traces the adoption of the motherhood and familial identities to the establishment of Home Rule (9). The role of a traditional and recognizable mother corresponds to an identity of national martyr, "in some sense representing the race as a whole in its suffering and in its yearning for redemption" (Innes 11). Thus the Irish mother is seen as an iconic figure symbolic of a national history, easily mapped on to the individual family home. She is both protected and assaulted by her sons/husband. These gendered identities become internalized by a nation which has begrudgingly accepted itself as a colonial subject.

Such established characterizations maintain a secure existence because they are continually unchallenged, repeatedly re-inserted into popular cultural products. While other ethnic minorities work hard to erase negative imagery from popular culture, this brand of Irishness has become a marketing tool, particularly with Irish-American audiences. The appeal of the hard-drinking, hot-tempered Irish family dynamic is evident with the success of Irish-American films like *The Departed* and *Boondock Saints* which function within the conventions of the classic gangster genre; the career criminal is only a hard man because he is a victim of circumstance, in these cases that circumstance is being Irish. The Irish-American father appears in similar modes to his Irish counterpart, although American ideals and influences evolve his still-present negativity. The television show *Rescue Me* features Denis Leary as Tommy Gavin, a "typical" Irish-American dad—alcoholic, hot-tempered, and frequently absent. His behavior is often justified *because* of his Irish heritage and further, Tommy achieves an idealized masculinity precisely because he fails at so many domestic responsibilities. The show continuously conflates unredemptive qualities with Irish heritage and there are numerous references to their Irish blood being the sole reason for his inadequate parenting. For all of these representations, Irishness functions as a legitimate excuse for poor masculine familial roles; while the experience of the Irish-American is quite different than the Irishman, Irish ethnicity, and more so, masculinity, appear as a non-geographically located essence that becomes a socialized excuse for behavioral patterns.

In a discussion with Colm Tóibín, film director Jim Sheridan excitedly noted that his film *In the Name of the Father* was the first film about a good

Irish father in a long time, but his exuberance falls short when it becomes clear that the standards for such are quite low:

> I asked him [Sheridan] why he had made the film and he said that he wanted to make a film about a good Irish father. He felt that it was time, that there was a change coming, and it was an image he felt needed to be embedded in the large array of other Irish images, many of which are of gruesome Irish fathers. That would be the test, he thought, of change—if good fathers began to appear like daffodils in spring, both casually and deliberately, on the Irish stage and in Irish film and in Irish fiction. Could I think of one in the whole body of Irish writing? he asked me. The only one I could think of was Goldsmith's *Vicar of Wakefield*, but that was set in Wakefield. Maybe in the early Roddy Doyle books, *The Snapper*, *The Van*. Sheridan nodded: "Maybe that is a beginning." Are you saying, I asked him, that the only good father you can come up with is in prison for something he did not do and dies there? Sheridan laughed. "Yes," he said, "that is what I am saying." (Tóibín 12)

Taking a closer look at fatherly representations from films in the several decades, it is evident that the stagnant stereotypes surrounding fatherhood that prevail in literature maintain a strong presence on screen as well. Irish psychiatrist and broadcaster Anthony Clare acknowledged this trend commenting simply that "contemporary images of [Irish] fatherhood are neither positive nor encouraging. Today's dad is likely to be portrayed as foolish and antiquated when he is not being abusiveness or feckless" (xi). Those extremes exist on a swinging pendulum of bad to worse and ultimately play out in film, literature, and as Kieran McKeown points out, "the public imagery of fatherhood and the private experiences of individual fathers mutually influence each other" (8). Despite progress in gender equality and progressive renderings of the family, the Irish father is still pictured as a farcical fall guy within the home.

There are several theories as to why Irish fathers are continually negated as substantial parental figures, many of which are tied up in political ideology. Fidelma Farley attempts to define the parameters of masculinity and fatherhood in Northern Irish film, particularly those about the Troubles, and correlates the violence of the Troubles with a problematic feature of masculinity and Irish fathers. She argues that violence is often written as a "legacy which is passed on from one generation of men to the next," implying that violence and partisan politics are the only real offerings a father can give his son (203). Further, Farley claims that even those fathers who maintain a tradition of violent politics are often "absent, and those who are present are weak and ineffectual, unable to provide their sons with an effective and appropriate (i.e., non-violent) model of masculine authority" (203). This kind of representation posits that fatherly ineptitude is as much a part of being Irish as the wearing of the green (or orange); it is an ethnic characteristic brought upon by the trauma of the Troubles regardless of an associative identification of north or south.

The political nationalism that has historically guided the family dynamic may not always be so overt. Farley's arguments identify active political involvement, but such entrenched activity is not the experience for all families. Yet such gendered politics runs deep, informing a systemic characterization of the family that while not always relevant, and often outdated, still relies on masculine service to the country to define familial roles. The negative attitudes toward Irish fathers were noticeably ingrained into Irish law in 1964, when unmarried fathers were denied automatic guardianship of the children regardless of the condition or state of the mother. Under the Guardianship of Infants Act of 1964, unmarried fathers could apply for guardianship but could not assume custody unless granted by the court. In 1966, slights against the father were confirmed with the clarification of the definition of family. The definition of a family in the 1939 Irish Constitution is vague, implying only that the family is "the natural primary and fundamental unit group of society" (www. IrishStatuteBook.ie). Further on in the same article, there is only mention of the protection of a mother against undue labor (her priorities should be to the home) and also that a woman (mother) "by her life within the home, woman gives to the State a support without which the common good cannot be achieved."[2] In this article, the father is not explicitly stated as a member of the family, and certainly not protected or considered as valuable to the health of the home/family as the mother.[3] The social climate of the mid-1960s further raised confusion in terms of defining Irish masculinity. While the culture does reflect traditional patriarchy, it does so through the structure of the church. Proper masculinity is defined through

---

[2] Such clear demarcations of male and female roles in the household allows for strategic assignation of men to accepted political involvement. Their role is to serve outside of the home and such language allows them to dismiss household duties for political ones.

[3] It should be noted that this very same law, in its attempts at canonizing motherhood, also denies women the right to a life other than maternity. This has only recently been challenged with the changes in the Marriage Act. Ironically though, work has been done to redefine same sex couples, but little change has been made that resists traditional domestic roles.

8 BAD DA'S: REWRITING FATHERHOOD IN *BREAKFAST ON PLUTO* 143

power and as such, through the clergy (Fathers with a capital "F"); the remainders of Irish men are simply functionaries in some capacity. As seen in Peter Lennon's Rocky Road to Dublin, it is the clergy that aims to redeem Ireland from the failures of the men who battled for independence. The film reflects the mid-century disappointment in the previous decades' leadership and Sean O'Faolain's remark that Irishmen are simply nothing more than "urbanized peasants" who lack moral courage is telling of the resentment toward nationalist masculinity.[4]

In 1966, the rhetorical absence of the father was clarified in the case of *The State (Nicolauo) vs. An Bord Uchtála* in which the Irish Supreme Court ruled that unmarried fathers are not part of the family unit: (i) a natural or biological father is not a member of a family within Article 41; (ii) a natural or biological father is not a parent within Article 42; and (iii) a natural or biological father has no personal right in relation to his child which the State is bound to protect under Article 40.3 (State [Nicolaou] vs. an Bord Uchtála). While the case was readdressed in 1996, and again in 2007, the language of the constitution still denies any full inclusion of fathers as legitimate family members and certainly contains no language regarding the importance of fathers to the social good. The reasoning behind such exclusion is couched in the rhetoric of safety. For example, excluding fathers from the definition of family occludes fatherhood that has resulted from rape and incest and/or domestic abuse and unstable parental relationships. Such logic seems noble, but is precariously balanced on the notion that all men are capable and/or likely to commit such acts. There have been numerous challenges to the custody laws, but little progress in re-evaluating the way the family is defined. In 2010, the European Court of Justice in Luxembourg denied any rights to custody for an Irish father whose former partner moved their children to England without his knowledge or permission. Irish Supreme Court Justice Nial Fennelly referred the case to the EU court, claiming that married families earn special privilege in Irish courts and, that while biological relationships between father and children are important, they are not deserving of

---

[4] There is, of course, an irony in that the film features Father Michael Cleary as an idealized "father" figure who prides himself on his ability to understand Ireland's youth population. Cleary was later the subject of a scandal in which it was revealed that he had a sexual affair with his housekeeper that also resulted in an illegitimate child. See David McKittrick's article for a discussion of the impact on his otherwise spotless reputation. The Cleary scandal was just further evidence that even priests don't get it right as fathers, an issue explored later in this essay.

special rights (Cahill). The courts have seen numerous cases of "child abduction" similar to the aforementioned case, all of which have ruled in favor of the mothers. The Children and Family Relationships Act of 2015 did provide some protections for unmarried fathers, but guardianship can only be achieved after a series of criteria are met including one that requires the father and mother to have lived together for 12 consecutive months and at least three months after the birth of the child.[5]

The first half of this study presumes a bleak recognition that Irish fatherhood is in danger and/or dangerous. Yet Jim Sheridan's aforementioned aspirations to instigate change through art suggests that if stereotypes and rigid social structures can become concrete because of their presence in art, then the ability to counter such characterizations can exist also. Yet, simply creating films about "good Das" oversimplifies the power of the original stereotypes. The activism required to overturn tradition would need to be substantial and powerful.

Adaptation seems to offer another opportunity to reestablish old narratives in new ways. As a prominent fixture in both the Irish literary and cinematic industries, it seems a hopeful place to search for this kind of artistic activism. Francesco Cassetti regards the medium of literature as a site for a discourse that is larger than the author alone in that it is a "symbolic construction[s] that refer[s] to a cluster of meanings that a society considers possible (thinkable) and feasible (legitimate) ... as discursive formations which testify to the way in which society organizes its meanings and shapes its system of relations" (82). Stereotypes and stock characters exist precisely because the audience expects them to exist, but adaptations of literature are a space for cultural narratives to transcend their original form and create space to interrogate and investigate the genesis of those expectations. These film adaptations are in no way benign or simplistic adjustments to form; in fact, the adaptations reveal a greater shift in social perceptions, positive or negative, providing an alternative to such stagnant cultural norms. The change in medium and the inherently new authorship allows for revision and quite possibly apology in terms of breaking the cycle. However, Cassetti would argue that the adaptation of literature into film must be viewed in the context of the social discourse that surrounds

---

[5] *The Irish Times* covered this very issue in July 2020, interviewing several unmarried couples and estranged fathers who have been attempting to navigate the system that is clearly designed to protect children against fathers rather than protect the paternal relationship. See Sheila Wayman's article on shared parenting from July 2, 2020.

both the original work and the film. Instead of simply retelling, the result is a "reappearance, in another discursive field, of an element (a plot, a theme, a character, etc.) that has previously appeared elsewhere" (82).

Thus the perpetual myth of a failed Irish father can be interrupted in a cinematic adaptation. Revised considerations of previously told narratives of fatherhood are not simply conspiratorial media that serve to bolster a recognizable social myth. The "reappearance" or desire to adapt such stories is indicative of the existence or reality of that myth in the later discourse that surrounds the film version. Dudley Andrew uses a metaphor of architecture to illustrate this. Buildings built in one period are not continuously demolished to make way for new buildings. Rather, those buildings are modified to reflect the contemporary design philosophy. The original building still stands as a reminder of the past, yet its facelift reveals a modern sensibility and acknowledgment of the future (Andrew 191). These film adaptations function in much the same way. While the stereotypes surrounding the failed father still exist in the previous narratives, there is an opportunity in film adaptations to revisit and rethink what it means to be an Irish father.

Pat McCabe's work on Neil Jordan's version of *Breakfast on Pluto* presents an important approach to this cinematic revisionism. The original novel and the subsequent film both explore the central discussion of fatherhood with characters that struggle within and against the social currents that define what it means to be an Irish father. While there is less than a decade between the two versions, McCabe's work on both the novel and the screenplay suggests his own efforts at revisiting the original story. There are marked revisions of Patrick's destiny and his relationship with his father, so much so that "revision" seems an inadequate term. The inclusion of a drastically more emphatic "happy" ending in the film insinuates a dramatic shift in the way McCabe understands his original work and possibly a personal reconciling with the notion of fatherhood and patriarchy.

McCabe published the novel in 1998, on the heels of the Good Friday Agreement, which means that its origin lies within the preceding decade of violence and upheaval. Recession, crime, and social oppression dominated the tableau. Divorce had only recently become legal and the state very much still controlled bodies. The last Magdalene Laundry had closed only two years prior (www.jfmresearch.com). McCabe's novel emerged as an ominous interlocuter of Ireland's dark history—a bleak and pessimistic view of the social and cultural regression, economic disparity, and political unrest. The core story narrates the life of Patrick "Pussy" Braden, a young transitioning teen in 1970s' Ireland on a quest to find her mother. Pussy's illegitimacy figures politically and socially into the tableau of the hostile Troubles, signifying McCabe's uneasiness with Republicanism and nationalist ideology as well as an examination of a conservative social structure that leaves little room for outsiders.

Like Roddy Doyle's *The Barrytown Trilogy* adaptations, one of the most significant comparisons between the two versions is revealed in the names of the lead characters. Patrick "Pussy" Braden remains as the protagonist, but his nickname and feminine identity shifts from Pussy in the novel to Kitten in the film. Further, Fr. Bernard, Pussy's father, becomes Fr. Liam in the film. There are likely mundane reasons for the name changes; the adjustment to Kitten rather than the sexually charged and coarse Pussy may strictly have been related to censor and audience comfort issues. However, the name changes seem more indicative of a separation between the novel character and the film character. Kitten lacks the viciousness and resentment of her literary counterpart, as evidenced in the way she approaches the search for her family which is discussed later in this analysis. Bernard and Liam offer no recognizable connections, allowing McCabe to completely depart from the original, vicious portrayal of the scandalous priest. Phonetically and sonically, Liam has a softer and more lilting tone than the harsher consonants of Bernard. Further there is a youthfulness attached to the name of Liam, a name only recently making its appearance as a common name in the twentieth century.[6] Separating the newly adapted father figure from the original one allows McCabe to completely disconnect the two, so much so that there is little to actually map on to the other aside from his paternity of the protagonist. This is underscored by the casting of Liam Neeson in the role. Neeson is a well-known and well-loved actor who is known for playing "good man" roles and thereby contradicting negative stereotypes of Irish men both in fiction and in reality—an attribute quite fitting for the new version of Patrick's father. If audiences are familiar with the novel, the complete name break

---

[6] There is only anecdotal evidence of this, but various "baby naming" sites attribute the name, originally a derivative of William, to only fully emerging in the UK in the 1930s and gaining massive popularity in the 1980s.

8 BAD DA'S: REWRITING FATHERHOOD IN *BREAKFAST ON PLUTO*   147

and connection with Neeson quickly diminishes the residual memories of the sinister Fr. Bernard and allows for the following re-characterization.[7] In the novel, Fr. Bernard is flatly described as evil, uncaring, and sexually perverse. As a literary tool, McCabe only offers Pussy's conception of his father; readers are given insight to Fr. Bernard's thoughts only as Pussy imagines what he thinks. There is little character development aside from the pantomime readers' experience via Pussy's imaginative diaries, leaving the priest as villainous anti-hero. The true depravity of Fr. Bernard is revealed in Pussy's description of the rape of his mother in the chapter, "Breakfast is Served." Even in Pussy's retelling, Fr. Bernard is denied much dialogue at all; Pussy oscillates back and forth between her own musings and what she imagined her mother had said that fateful morning. Instead, readers are given a detailed description of the physicality of the rape with Eily crying out that "'Ow! I'm being split in two!'" (28). It is in the description of the aftermath of the rape that Fr. Bernard is literally revealed as a monster:

> It was only when he fell back across the room with a Hallowe'en mask on him that she really became confused, thinking to herself; 'But it's not Hallowe'en!' How long it was before she realised that it was in fact her Employer's actual face she was looking at—and not a whey-coloured Egyptian mummy-type papier mâché affair... And that thing—that glaring red thing with its malevolent eye—what was that? (28)

While much of this description is laden with Eily Bergin's naiveté, the choice to use Hallowe'en and monstrous imagery explicitly casts Fr. Bernard as inhuman. Later in the novel, Pussy unequivocally expresses her vitriol for her father when she remarks that "there appears to be no similar generosity of spirit evident when it comes to my treatment of Fr. Bernard" (58). She is unapologetic in her anger and dismisses accusations that her actions may have caused pain to her biological father.

The film takes a startling different approach to the rape scene. Upon Eily's arrival at the house, Fr. Liam does shoot her a few salacious glances, but he ultimately softens his demeanor with a kind smile and bad joke. Eily is portrayed as partly responsible for her own circumstances as she coyly raises her skirts and acknowledges Fr. Liam's advances with the maternal

---

[7] For clarification purposes, I will use Pussy and Fr. Bernard to refer to the written narrative and Kitten and Fr. Liam to refer to the film.

148 N. R. MCCLURE

dismissal one might give a child.[8] The entire scene is accompanied by swinging music and caricatured actions (Fr. Liam literally flies across the room), adding a strangely dark humor to an otherwise grim scene. The screenplay takes several bits of dialogue directly from the novel, specifically references to Fairy Liquid, but intentionally eliminates all references to Hallowe'en masks and monsters. Fr. Liam is depicted as a fragile man who let his sexual desires get the best of him, rather than an abhorrent rapist.[9] It is also significant to note that later in the film, Fr. Liam reveals that he and Eily had spent time together as a couple, often visiting the ocean, indicating that the conception of Kitten was *not* the result of a violent rape, but rather the product of an unrequited love.

It is important to address Pussy's anger and violent sense of retribution. McCabe's novel directly embraces themes of revenge and vicious retaliation. In fact, much of Pussy's motivation throughout the novel is to enact such cruelty on Fr. Bernard in an effort to somehow reconcile her own troubled experience. The purpose of writing the vile rape scene as a class assignment is quite specifically meant to damage Fr. Bernard and the resulting establishment that has allowed his sexual perversions to go unpunished. Pussy is determined to topple the patriarchy that she sees responsible not just for her own illegitimacy, but also for her own inability to be Pussy rather than Patrick. There are no noble sensibilities here though; Pussy's concerns are hers and hers alone. She lacks meaningful relationships with most people (aside from Charlie, Irwin, and Laurence), again a phenomenon marked by the naming of characters through nicknames only. She cares little for those around her to connect to them by something so personal as a name and resorts to code names like Mrs. Whiskers and Mr. Dummy Teat.

Throughout the novel, Pussy continuously dismisses the excuses that Fr. Bernard could not take care of his illegitimate son because of his appointment as a priest: "I just genuinely felt that if you could bring

---

[8] This is likely meant as behavior only perceived by Liam; however, the line of where the fantasy begins and ends is unclear, and the humor of the scene complicates that intention.

[9] While there is no specific evidence for this, the rewriting of Father Liam's supposed rape coincidentally seems to co-opt the story of Father Michael Cleary. Cleary was a well-loved priest who was shockingly revealed to have had an illegitimate child with his housekeeper, Phyllis Hamilton. Unlike Father Liam and Eily, Cleary and his lover actually lived together along with their son, functioning behind the scenes as an ordinary family. The scandal only broke after Cleary's death in 1993, and even though the news was troubling to many, he is often still revered (McKittrick).

someone into this world then it is your responsibility to care for and look after them" (102) However, Kitten takes a more diplomatic approach in the film. While she doesn't completely forgive Fr. Liam at first, she comes to realize that the both of them are misfits within Tyreelin and have more in common than they know. Kitten's realization that Fr. Liam truly loved her mother reveals a new tenderness in the narrative as well as a dichotomous role of the father that is not investigated in the novel at all. Much like the casting choice of Liam Neeson, Cillian Murphy's performance as Kitten brings a vulnerability and near-optimism to the character, countering the literary Pussy who is full of vitriol and rage.[10] Unlike Pussy, Kitten wants reconciliation and love. She wants to be cared for and recognized as a part of something rather than destroy the systems that put her in this position in the first place. She even shows some concern for those who harm her, expressing an affective condition not at all seen in the novel. The polar shift in this characterization allows McCabe's wildly different re-imagining of the family structure all the more palpable and possible.

The film presents paternal responsibility as a schizophrenic identity. Fr. Liam must play both Father, the parish priest, and father, biological and paternal, to Kitten. It becomes evident that a man cannot be the F/father, but must choose one or the other. This duality of fatherhood is not evidenced anywhere in the novel, as Fr. Bernard and Pussy never reconcile their relationship. McCabe's rewrite of this relationship in the screenplay implies a reconsideration of illegitimate fatherhood, particularly in the context of societal tradition and secrecy.

---

[10] I do want to acknowledge the more recent problematizing of Murphy, a cisgender man, portraying a trans character. In some respects, the casting is a result of Jordan's consideration of performance on camera, rather than gender performance. Murphy is an accomplished and respected actor so his willingness to accept the challenge of such a role was applauded rather than criticized at the time. The casting of a trans actor may have brought authenticity to the experience of Kitten, but it is not insignificant to note that McCabe wrote this novel in the late 1990s prior to trans visibility and that Pussy/Kitten Braden were likely constructed more as drag than trans; his intentions were to imagine a character that simply did not fit in rather than interrogate gender equity. This discussion was reignited in 2020 when Fra Fee, also a cisgender man, was cast in a stage production of *Breakfast on Pluto*. A trans actress, Kate O'Donnell, was hired to play Ma Braden (not a trans character), but left the production when a trans actor was not cast in the role of Patrick/Pussy. See the BBC coverage of the West End production for more on why O'Donnell left. While this discussion is an important one in relation to the way gender equity is granted or denied, it does not figure significantly into the way the text was adapted to film and is better served in a separate discussion.

Fr. Liam makes the initial choice to be the spiritual father of the community and abandon his illegitimate son Patrick. His negotiation with Mrs. Braden to provide financial assistance for the child is quite acceptable among the community members. While many of the women, particularly Fr. Liam's housekeeper, maintain an air of ignorance about the situation, there is a sense that they do in fact know very well who fathered Patrick "Kitten" Braden. Silence is the preferred manner in which to handle the situation of Father turned father, so it is not surprising that Kitten's intentions to break the silence are met with resistance from the people of Tyreelin as well as Fr. Liam. It becomes clear that shedding light on the father/son relationship, no matter how well known it already is, will be figuratively and literally dangerous for both Liam and Kitten.

The community secrecy may keep the social climate in rural Tyreelin calm, but it is exactly what makes Kitten restless. Fueled by her intense curiosity and desire to stir up the stuffy village, Kitten embarks on a journey to find her biological mother. Kitten's journey to London ironically leads her back to her father rather than her mother. The scene in the gentlemen's club in London is a moving role reversal in which Fr. Liam confesses his sins, putting a spin on the earlier scene in which Kitten confesses his knowledge of his father's identity to Fr. Liam. Fr. Liam is a failed paternal figure in that he literally abandoned his son and denied him any information about his mother, but this scene offers a redemptive moment. In that his relationship with his son is already taboo, it is fitting that this "confession" takes place in a seedy strip club, foregrounding Fr. Liam's new dismissal of social and religious judgments. When Fr. Liam first enters the peep show booth, his voice is only heard through the speakers as Kitten hears him and his face is veiled in shadow. As Fr. Liam tells his "story" of a young boy who lost both his mother and father, he refers to himself in the third person, creating yet another identity for himself that is separate from his horrible reality. When Kitten asks how this shadowy figure knew the young boy in the story, Fr. Liam powerfully remarks, "I knew his father." The use of the past tense to utter this phrase illuminates Fr. Liam's own coping mechanism to treat his identity as a man that loved his son and lover as separate than his current self. With this confession, the lighting brightens just enough to reveal Fr. Liam's face; it is key to note that while Kitten still cannot see him physically, it is this moment in which Kitten also "sees" her father metaphorically. Fr. Liam dashes out of the strip club after giving Kitten the address of her long lost mother, the

Phantom Lady, disappearing into the seedy London neighborhood as somewhat of a phantom himself.

While an outright apology is not made explicit in the film, Kitten reconciles with her father by appearing on his doorstep a few weeks later. When Fr. Liam opens his front door, the two acknowledge their relationship for the first time and it becomes clear that Kitten was looking for the wrong parent all along. Fr. Liam challenges the status quo by attempting to wear both proverbial hats, telling Kitten to "Call me Father." However, this redemption is thwarted and impossible *because* it violates the expectations of the failed father. Fr. Liam does manage to regain some fatherly credibility by caring for Charlie after the death of Irwin and boldly transgressing against social mores; the scenes in which he openly takes Kitten shopping for baby clothes for an unwed mother visibly sends the town into hysterics, yet none of the three seem to care. But it is precisely this apathy toward established behavior that causes the community to turn their back on both of them. The church is burned to the ground and Fr. Liam is reassigned to another parish, forcing Kitten and the pregnant Charlie to return to London. The slightest attempt at having a happy and constructive family life is impossible for Kitten, Charlie and Fr. Liam as long as they stay in Ireland.

McCabe's changes to this part of the narrative are incredibly illustrative of the habitual dismissal of good fathers. While he does offer an apologetic rewriting of the father, McCabe also makes it clear that this vision, like much of the fantasy present in *Breakfast on Pluto*, cannot truly exist. Even attempts at becoming a good father are circumvented by social norms and myths. He shifts his earlier criticisms from the fathers themselves toward the social structures that prevent a positive and happy family experience. This transferal allows McCabe to offer a sense of hope by suggesting that familial and paternal bonds can still be successful if they are restructured. A move away from the traditional sense of family, and of Ireland altogether, is precisely where the father can become good again. Although the transgressive "family" unit of Kitten, Charlie and Fr. Liam cannot remain in Tyreelin, the film ends on a decidedly happy note. Father Liam's loss of his social and religious respect within the community and the literal loss of his religious position and authority is surprisingly what grants the fallen priest a sense of peace. Although he must transfer to "the only parish that will have me," this exclusion from the community serves as a symbol of Father Liam's freedom from his long-kept secret. The price of the transfer amounts to only a portion of the value of his newfound relationship with

152   N. R. MCCLURE

his son. Additionally, Kitten and Charlie perform as a functional nuclear family in London. The birth of Charlie's baby allows the "couple" to embrace a family dynamic that both had been denied while living in Ireland. Kitten has even exceeded his earlier dreams of merely finding his biological mother. By the end of the film, Kitten has in fact reunited with his mother, albeit not in a mother/son relationship, and is even on friendly terms with her step-brother, again as casual acquaintances and not siblings. As Charlie's partner he can now become both a father *and* a second mother to Charlie's baby, allowing him to be both the father he was denied and the mother he never knew in hopes to end a cycle of the broken home for the new baby that would otherwise be fatherless. For McCabe, it is not enough to simply write about a good father; rather, the father has to be reconceived altogether dismissing previously engrained social and religious structures in favor of new paternal identities.

As much as the novel reflected the time in which it was created, the film does so as well. The year 2005 was a remarkably different era in Ireland than 1998. The gloss of the Celtic Tiger was only just beginning to fade, and a renewed sense of optimism and prosperity was made clear in both economic and social systems. The early twenty-first century also witnessed a fury of social activism and the early rumblings of a new progressive social order. The first acknowledgment of the Magdalene Laundries abuses came in 2001, Pride celebrations had nearly tripled in size, and representations of gay characters began to appear prominently in film and television. Father's rights groups began to sprout up around Ireland, advocating for parental custody equality and fatherly consideration. Much of the groups like Fathers.ie and Unmarried & Separated Fathers of Ireland (USFI) primarily concentrate on custody battles, but the groups have also tried to advocate for positive reputations of fathers and helping men to become better dads.[11] While this is only a small extract of cultural production, this film adaptation still offers a genuinely important contribution to the consideration of the role of Irish fathers. According to anthropologist Kevin Nugent, "literature, poetry and history of a culture become, therefore, a rich source of hypotheses which can suggest appropriate empirical investi-

---

[11] Many of these groups are devoted to custody battles for divorced and/or single fathers rather than simply negotiating the negative stereotypes against fathers. The rise in this trend is largely due to the relatively recent legalization of divorce which created a vast amount of new custody trials. The lack of rhetorical inclusion of fathers can be traced to the aforementioned assumption that fathers will not be able to/want to take part in their children's lives.

gations and can, in turn, sensitize the investigator to the complex history of the behavior or institution to be studied" (169). McCabe's original narrative no longer held water in this new Ireland. His adaptation was urgent and necessary, adjusting the story to mirror and emerging progressive society that still greatly struggled with the demons of a dark history. Fr. Liam and Kitten couldn't exist in 1998, but they COULD in 2005. Their appearance signals an important reconciliation with the past and gestures at a future untold.

WORKS CITED

Andrew, Dudley. "Adapting Cinema to History." *A Companion to Literature and Film*, edited by Robert Stam and Alessandra Raengo, Blackwell, 2004, pp. 109–204.

Breakfast on Pluto. Directed by Neil Jordan, performances by Cillian Murphy, Liam Neeson, and Ruth Negra, Sony Pictures Classics, 2006.

Cahill, Ann. "'Sad day' as EU Court Rules Father Has No Custody Rights." *IrishExaminer.com*. Irish Examiner, 6 Oct. 2010.

Cassetti, Francesco. "Adaptations and Mis-adaptations: Film, Literature and Social Discourses." *A Companion to Literature and Film*, edited by Robert Stam and Alessandra Raengo, Blackwell, 2004, pp. 81–91.

Clare, Anthony. "Foreword." *Changing Fathers? Fatherhood and Family Life in Modern Ireland*, edited by Kieran McKeown, Harry Ferguson, Dermot Rooney, Collins, 2000.

The Departed. Directed by Martin Scorcese, performances by Matt Damon, Leonardo DiCaprio, Jack Nicholson, and Mark Wahlberg. Warner Bros. Pictures, 2007.

Farley, Fidelma. "In the Name of the Family: Masculinity and Fatherhood in Contemporary Northern Irish Films." *Irish Studies Review*, vol. 9.2, 2001, pp. 202–213.

Innes, C.L. "Virgin Territories and Motherlands: Colonial and Nationalist Representations of Ireland and Africa." *Feminist Review*, vol. 47, summer 1994.

Irish Supreme Court. *The State (Nicolauo) vs. An Bord Uchtála*. 1966.

Justice for Magdalenes Research, Justice for Magdalenes, jfmresearch.com.

Keane, John B. *The Year of the Hiker*. Cork, Mercier Press, 1964.

McCabe, Pat. *Breakfast on Pluto*, Harper Perennial, 1999.

McCourt, Frank. *Angela's Ashes*. Scribner, 1996.

McGahern, John. *The Dark*. Penguin, 2002.

McKeown, Kieran, Harry Ferguson, and Dermot Rooney. *Changing Fathers? Fatherhood and Family Life in Modern Ireland*, Collins, 2000.

McKittrick, David. "The Secret Life of Michael Cleary (Entertainer, Radio Show Host, Father of Two...and Priest)." *Independent.co.uk*. The Independent. 11 Sept. 2007.

Nugent, Kevin. "The Father's Role in Early Irish Socialization: Historical and Empirical Perspectives." *The Father's Role: Cross-Cultural Perspectives*, edited by M.E. Lamb, Taylor & Francis, 2013, pp. 169–194.

O'Brien, Edna. *The Country Girls*. Plume, 2002.

Oireachtas na hÉireann. *Article 41*. 29 Dec. 1937. *Irish Statue Book*.

Oireachtas na hÉireann. Children and Family Relationships Act of 2015. 6 Apr. 2015. *Irish Statue Book*.

"Punch." Vassar Victorian Studies Project. Vassar College, 1994.

Rescue Me. FX, 2004.

Rocky Road to Dublin, Dir. Peter Lennon, 1968.

Tóibín, Colm. "Selling Tara, Buying Florida." *Éire-Ireland*, vol. 43, no. 1/2, spring/summer, 2008.

"Trans Actress Drops Out of Breakfast on Pluto amid Trans Casting Row." *BBC News*, 11 Mar. 2020, www.bbc.com/news/entertainment-arts-51817383.

Trevor, William. *Felicia's Journey*, Penguin, 1994.

Wayman, Sheila. "Shared Parenting: Fathers Being Forced to Go Down 'Adversarial Route'" *The Irish Times Online*, 2 July 2020.

CHAPTER 9

What Richard Did: Sort of Adapting Irish History

R. Barton Palmer

Unlike his first two projects, *Adam and Paul* (2004) and *Garage* (2007), both of which engage poignantly, if fictionally, with the discontents of Celtic Tiger culture, Lenny Abrahamson's third feature, *What Richard Did* (2010), is a film of fact. However, it is by no means a "true story" in the sense of offering a faithful record of the Brian Murphy (or Club Anabel) murder case and its complex aftermath. Instead, central elements of this series of events are in the film reproduced and referenced, if in a slantwise fashion that renders them fictionalized. *Richard*'s allusions to the "true" are indirect, at the second degree, as it were, but—and this is crucial—they are unmistakable. Abrahamson and screenwriter Malcolm Campbell, working with the novelist on the script, produced a screen version, faithful to its main elements, of a docu-novel devoted to the case that was written in the wake of its final disposition. Kevin Power's sensational bestseller *Bad Day in Blackrock* was published in 2008 by Lilliput Press, one of Ireland's most prestigious independent houses, with a special

R. B. Palmer (✉)
Clemson University, Clemson, SC, USA
e-mail: ppalmer@clemson.edu

© The Author(s), under exclusive license to Springer Nature Switzerland AG 2022
M. C. Conner et al. (eds.), *Screening Contemporary Irish Fiction and Drama*, Palgrave Studies in Adaptation and Visual Culture,
https://doi.org/10.1007/978-3-031-04568-4_9

155

156   R. B. PALMER

interest in the national history, to which this book made a foundational and important contribution (see an early review in Boyne). For readers, as one academic blog reported at the time, the novel "certainly pinpoints the zeitgeist—and specifically the rottenness in wealthy Ireland that has brought us to our current state" (see SCC English; Alvarez; Brown).

In *Uncertain Ireland*, a collection of scholarly essays published in 2006 by the Institute of Public Administration in Dublin, the editors, sociologists Mary P. Corcoran and Michel Peillon, blame "the passing of the old orthodoxies" as creating in the new millennium a society "not quite sure where it is at, never mind where it is headed" (1, 3). A key symptom of that uncertainty was the Brian Murphy case, then still awaiting a final disposition, a provocative essay on which, written by cultural critic Tom Inglis, is featured as the lead piece in the collection. For Inglis, the Murphy killing and the subsequent inability of community, church, or judicial system to close out the trajectory of crime and punishment was about nothing less than "the breakdown of the social and moral order of elite Dublin society" (17). The privileged adolescent men involved in the shocking crime were members of a generation "uncertain of themselves," so says Corcoran, because, with the decline in the authority of the Catholic church and of traditional Republican values, they lacked a "moral anchor" that might prevent their slipping into "the nihilistic narcissism that, sociologists argue, is at the core of the postmodern condition" (5). Or, as Inglis puts it, the young men implicated in the crime found themselves "caught in a long-term process of change from a Catholic culture of self-denial to a consumer culture of liberal-individualism and hedonism" (17).

Given the popularity of *Bad Day* and its resonance with current cultural concerns, that a film version was soon planned by one of the country's leading directors was hardly surprising. The prospect that the Murphy case would thereby once again be a focus of public attention was met with considerable excitement, as Eithne Shortall, the arts and culture correspondent, observed in *The Irish Times*: "The controversy surrounding the death of a Dublin schoolboy 10 years ago is set to be rekindled. Lenny Abrahamson, the acclaimed director of *Adam and Paul*, is to make a film based on the killing of Brian Murphy, an 18-year-old who died of head injuries after a fight with a group of schoolboys from Blackrock College outside a Dublin nightclub in 2000" (Shortall). The film, she observed, would also be an adaptation of Power's novel. Abrahamson and Campbell follow *Bad Day* in imagining the killing as the end result of a bitter rivalry between two rugby teammates (here named Richard Karlsen and Conor

Harris) over the affections of the girl they both want, Lara (Laura in the novel). *Richard* also follows Power's lead in focusing on the back story of the murder and not on the complex judicial maneuverings that were its years-long aftermath.

Considering the pre-soldness of the event and the novel's bestselling re-structuring of it, that Abrahamson and his collaborators decided to abandon Power's title, with its provocative reference to one of Ireland's most famous men's colleges, was certainly surprising. It was more puzzling that Abrahamson attempted to persuade the public that the film is only loosely connected to Power's true story fiction. The film's legally mandated credits name the book as a source, and it was public knowledge that Power had been hired to work on the screenplay. No convincing explanation was forthcoming from the filmmakers about this seemingly bizarre attempt to undermine the fact that *Richard* is both a true story and an adaptation. According to Abrahamson, the film should be seen as having no connection to the events of the Murphy case. Barry Monahan, who has written the first study of his meteoric rise to prominence, reports that Abrahamson denied there was "any validity in attempting to make such connections," an assertion that makes little sense (110). Also, the film is not an adaptation because, according to Monahan in another dubious assertion, the director did not intend it to be so considered. Not surprisingly, however, what Abrahamson had to say on the matter deeply influenced the critical assessment of *Richard*. In interviews after the film's release, Abrahamson made no mention either of Power's novel or of the Murphy case, treating the film's narrative as if it were based on an original screenplay (see, e.g. Gilbey). Reviewers, even in Ireland, followed the same line, which is what was promoted by marketing materials (see Trailer).

The record needs correcting. It should be hardly necessary, but my intention in this essay is to shine a critical light on this mischaracterization, demonstrating how *Richard* is in fact a rather faithful adaptation of *Bad Day, mutatis mutandis*, and reproduces closely the main elements of Power's structuring as a conventional fiction that complex series of events known as the Murphy case. As Eithne Shortall's report implied, when announcing that the country's most successful new director would be adapting *Bad Day*, this also meant that he would be making a film "based on the Brian Murphy case." And so he did. It's just that the auteur was unwilling to proclaim this indebtedness. Similarly, Kevin Power's contribution to the project was kept on the down low. Unusually, no poster or trailer would brag that *Richard* was an adaptation of a book that had aroused enthusiasm and controversy only a couple of years earlier.

Thorny questions immediately arise. Why the choice to adapt for the screen a novelistic source so deeply connected to a national trauma and to the cultural politics many would invoke in order to give that trauma some kind of meaning? Why, having made that choice, would Abrahamson then work diligently with the film's producers to minimize, if not sever, any connection with both the event and its fictional versioning? It's hard to imagine any reason other than a radical change of heart on the part of the filmmakers. To deny what was obvious to anyone in the cultural know was to throw away the pre-soldness of the material as a hook to pump up ticket sales. An at least partial answer might be found in the film's production "moment," to which the filmmakers might be seen as responding. Abrahamson seems to have been concerned about the place of this project in his portfolio as he proceeded to build his career, which, tellingly, was moving away from national materials as source, as he himself announced in 2013 when *Richard* was still in release.

At the time that he was contemplating making a screen version of the Power bestseller, the Irish industry was in the midst of a significant transition that had begun in 1993 with the re-establishment of the Irish Film Board (Bord Scannán), which under its new operating charter provided substantial financial and other forms of support for the country's filmmakers. For some decades a wannabe player on the international scene, the Irish cinema suddenly found itself having substantial success in the first decade of the new century. Deeper connections were formed to the global marketplace and other national cinemas. Films that reflected contemporary Irish culture, and directed by native-born talents like John Crowley, Paddy Breathnach, John Michael McDonagh, as well as Abrahamson were shot and produced in Ireland to considerable acclaim at home and abroad, helping fund a solid infrastructure and providing experience to an expanding crew base. In these developments, the Bord played a key role, expanding its role into digital production in 2018, and leading from the front as the media arts sector in Ireland forged an exciting and profitable future. A key aim was promoting updated images, warts and all, of a vibrant, thoroughly Europeanized society willing to modify but not reject its unique cultural traditions.

In the early years of the new millennium, to be sure, domestic and global audiences continued to show an interest in the historical past that had long made for profitable cinematic exploitation, especially the War for

Independence (1919–21) and the subsequent Civil War (1922–23). Most significant in this regard, and supported by the Bord, was a trans-national production that was shot in Ireland and employed a mostly Irish cast and technicians. UK director Ken Loach's *The Wind that Shakes the Barley* (2006) not only looks back to the conflict-ridden 1920s, but in so doing also adapts a novel about that period written some four decades earlier, Walter Macken's *The Scorching Wind* (1964). This was material that had been most recently dramatized for the screen in Neil Jordan's 1996 film *Michael Collins*, with some investment from the Bord but major funding coming from US producers David Geffen and Warner Brothers. The film was registered in the US, the UK, and Ireland—a truly trans-national enterprise. Key roles were played by Hollywood veterans (Liam Neeson, Aidan Quinn, and Julia Roberts) and Brits (Alan Rickman and Ian Hart), supported by Irish actors (particularly Stephen Rea and Brendan Gleeson).

With no Hollywood stars and an almost all-Irish cast, and Ireland's Element Pictures playing a major role in production, *Wind* considerably altered the Jordan formula. The film went on to receive considerable acclaim, winning both the IFTA award for Best Film and the Palme d'Or at Cannes. For some years, *Wind* held the record of most profitable Irish release, but it was, legally speaking, a UK film. The Irish influence on world cinema in the early years of the new millennium can be measured in such trans-national productions. It can also be measured in those films that, even if they do not focus on Irish subjects, can claim to be Irish in terms of the involvement of Irish arts. Martin McDonagh is arguably the most acclaimed of contemporary Irish playwrights, but has in his film work regularly eschewed Irish themes as such, most recently in *Three Billboards Outside Ebbing Missouri* (2017). *Three Billboards* was hugely profitable, garnering considerable critical acclaim from nominations received for a number of Academy and BAFTA Awards. Despite McDonagh's high profile in the country, and its successful release there, *Three Billboards* received no notice at that year's IFTA. Financing was provided by the UK's Film Four and Blueprint Pictures, with no involvement from the Bord or Irish producers.

With their interest in contemporary Ireland, the emerging directorial stars of the early 2000s pursued filmmaking that was by contrast thoroughly Irish in terms of script, production, and in large part financing, of which the first three releases of Lenny Abrahamson furnish striking, successful examples. And yet the levers of global production soon became more available to those directors who, like Abrahamson, had shown

160 R. B. PALMER

themselves to be technically talented, intellectually astute, and ambitious for opportunities that were increasingly more trans-national or even post-national. Such projects would not be severed from, but be less determined by, the institutions of Irish cinema that had hitherto nourished their careers, rewarding their focus on what was happening in an Ireland roiled by the Celtic Tiger and other forces, including increased secularization.

Abrahamson's breakthrough success, *Room* (2015), is no more "Irish" than *Three Billboards*. To be sure, the project made use of Bord seed money and screened a novel written by Emma Donoghue, who is Irish but then resident in Canada. However, the film's narrative is set in North America, and there are no Irish characters or diaspora themes. Brie Larson, a rising star from the American Independent cinema, portrayed the main character. Even so, *Room* was named Best Film and Abrahamson Best director at that year's IFTA awards, nudging out John Crowley and *Brooklyn* in both categories (there's more to say on this further on). In contrast, Abrahamson's first two films, based on scripts by Ireland's Mark O'Halloran, had been praised for their engagement with the particularities of the national culture and its recent history. Production featured native talent and crew, not overseas name players. Provincialism of this sort could be seen as charming, and it proved to be appealing to both domestic and overseas viewers. However, such a filmmaking approach could also be thought an unwise rejection of the forms of storytelling (especially genre) and performance (the anchoring presence of star players). These elements of a film "package" had long since proven their reliable profitability in the international marketplace, as the successes of Neil Jordan and Jim Sheridan had proven. None of Abrahamson's first three films, it should be noted, was picked up by a major international distributor (the involvement of UPI/UIP with *Room* played a key role in the film's international success).

Abrahamson is too sharp an operator not to have been well aware, as *Richard*'s planning moved ahead, that the Murphy case, especially in the fictionalized shaping Power gave it, offered pre-sold material that would be especially attractive to domestic viewers and, if properly presented, would speak to cultural issues that, as recovery from the busted Celtic Tiger proceeded, were still very much *au courant*. It is the deep Irishness of the material, of course, that likely appealed to him in the first place, especially since the plight that besets the main character in Power's novel fits interestingly into the storytelling and thematic patterns of both *Adam and Paul* and *Garage*, both of which focus on men in crises that are mocked by urbanization and globalism. As it turned out, Campbell's script enhanced these similarities. Abrahamson's third film also would feature a conclusion that is both unconventional and puzzling, refusing the easy pleasures and unequivocal closure of the so-called happy ending in order to focus on the discontents of Tiger culture.

However, the Murphy case was not news beyond the Republic and the UK, and *Bad Day* was not marketed beyond the British Isles and Commonwealth of Nations (significantly, no US publisher was interested in producing an edition for the huge American market). To be understood as a film of fact overseas, the filmmakers would have to signpost that the film was based on actual events and then find some means to explicate the connections to the Murphy case and to the cultural politics of the Tiger boom. Would this effort be worth it in terms of box office and critical approval? The filmmakers evidently thought no.

There was no question that the film would appeal to domestic viewers. Murphy killing's connection to Irish politics, as Tom Inglis suggests, was intense and controversial, reflecting the alarming rise of homicides in Ireland during the preceding three decades (Inglis). Many of these had involved binge drinking, with those of a younger generation who were less inclined to live by traditional values often the victims or perpetrators. In the view of Inglis and other social commentators, this was a trend that had been intensified by the sudden prosperity of the Tiger and the astonishing speed with which the Catholic Church had forfeited its position of cultural and legal prominence after a series of horrific revelations about past and present practices (see O'Dowd). But these changes brought their own discontents. By the turn of the century, many young Irish men, including those at the upper levels of society, had come like Richard Culhane to inhabit a "culture of self-elimination" that was dominated by anomie, even as in conflicts with others they found themselves "struggling to attain and maintain honour and respect" (Inglis 18). Overindulgence in drink, a social ritual difficult to refuse, would empty out the self, allowing violent impulses to be freely and disastrously expressed (Inglis 20–21). Such was the destructive world of male camaraderie and competition so tellingly anatomized in *Bad Day*. What was different about the Murphy case, in addition to the unusual circumstances in which the murder took place, was that "it was about how nice, polite, civilised young men became violent thugs" in a permissive atmosphere that many thought reflected the moral laxity of nouveau riche materialism, so different from the plain virtues preached by the nation's founder Eamon de Valera (17; see also De Valera).

162   R. B. PALMER

Power's story, at its base, was animated by a politicized sociology, whose aim was to illuminate troubling aspects of Tiger culture on which the Murphy case was shining a harsh light. As it turned out, Abrahamson's adaptation would "essentialize" and thus de-politicize Power's story by not providing the film with an equivalent to the prolix and ever-curious narrator and thus attenuating its connections to an actual event by concentrating on Richard's loss of control (what he did) rather than the consequences of the murder for the cultural elite as set forth by the narrator (the bad day that Blackrock, as an ironic metonymy, experienced as a result). Contrary to Eithne Shortall's expectation, the film would not be acknowledged as bringing to the screen the national embarrassment that was the Brian Murphy case. Such an essentializing approach was perhaps adopted so that the film would succeed in worldwide exhibition, even as it testified to Abrahamson's ability to reach beyond, but also through, material that might have been too provincial to exert a wider appeal. *Richard*'s marketing created the impression that the film was "free-standing," and that seems to have become the intention of both Abrahamson and Campbell as they proceeded to write the screenplay. One wonders what Power, as he surveilled this process at least in part, thought of such an approach. Was he not disappointed that the novel's indictment of contemporary culture had been put in the closet?

(Un) Screening the National

By making the principal killer the protagonist, the novelist had anchored his version of the story to a transgressing figure, embroiled in a love triangle whose emotions he cannot handle, and afterward desperate for but failing to achieve relief from his guilt. Richard can be read as exemplifying a widespread national horror at and remorse (in some sense) for a "rottenness" that the country's dysfunctional institutions of justice and religion did not remedy or even adequately explain. Above all else, the novel offers a stark and disturbing commentary on that rottenness, exemplified by the heartless cruelty with which Richard snuffs out the life of his erstwhile friend and teammate, Conor, who has become a rival for the affections of the beautiful Laura, a misdeed that he feel inclined at first to confess. But then he keeps his silence, allowing the finest justice money can buy to keep him out of jail and thus officially untainted by what is beyond doubt a murder.

9 WHAT RICHARD DID: SORT OF ADAPTING IRISH HISTORY 163

In *Richard*, the killer is granted an extended private moment of agony, with Jack Reynor's portrayal of something close to all-consuming madness difficult to watch. But this *anagnorisis* is vitiated by uncertainty. Does Richard find it intolerable to take responsibility for such a terrible, irremediable deed? Or is he only out of his mind with fear that he will be identified as the killer, then to suffer the weight of public shaming as well as a lengthy prison term? It is easy enough to sympathize with his evident suffering since in an earlier sequence, not in the film's source, Richard confesses to his father (Lars Mikkelsen), who, visibly shaken, finds it impossible to deal with this revelation other than to suggest to his anguished son that he leave the city as the investigation proceeds. Not provided with parental counsel, Richard not surprisingly takes the easy way out as Lara (Róisín Murphy), who found herself in the middle of his murderous dispute with Conor (Sam Keeley), reprimands his behavior but stands by him even after his refusal to confess (Fig. 9.1).

The novel unabashedly flaunts its connection to the Murphy case, then just definitively resolved with some minor convictions on associated charges but with no one found guilty of what the coroner pronounced "an unlawful killing." In response to complaints that he was bringing up a sordid and painful chapter of recent Irish history, Power appealed to the socially critical function of fiction: "If you find something in a society that people aren't talking about, in a sense that is what fiction is for" (qtd in Horan). The novel speaks when society, out of shame and reticence, holds

Fig. 9.1 In an intimate moment, Richard (Jack Reynor) confesses to his father (Lars Mikkelsen), who cannot deal with the situation

its peace; it presents itself as a coda of sorts to events that never found their proper judgment. A screen version could have done much the same.

Bad Day offers the rambling first person meditation of an unnamed narrator, who suggests he knew the young men and women involved. Troubling questions remain for him and for Irish society in general, prompting the writing of this account that refers, often obliquely, to events of which for the most part, he has little direct knowledge. Uncertainty and unknowability deeply mark his account. What does Richard talk about with his family? Do they discuss justice, or money, or perhaps death? If curious, and more than a little outraged by a collective lack of closure, he admits to being "sanguine about the possibility of real knowledge" (Power 13). His fragmentary musings, not lacking in contradiction, advertise themselves as furnishing a provisional explanation, balanced previously between truth and inference, for how a young man wound up kicked to death. The tone of his account is at turns anxious, confused, and outraged, capturing perfectly the national mood as the case was investigated and made its tortuous way through the legal system to the worst of all solutions: a final "uncertainty" that was the last of a series of institutional and personal failures.

For prosecutors, the general facts of Murphy's death proved easy, yet also impossible, to establish, giving rise to the subjunctive referentiality that shadows their fictionalization in *Bad Day*. In the early hours of 31 August 2000, outside a nightclub located in a well-known Dublin hotel, 18-year old Brian Murphy, an 18-year-old from the Southside fees-paying school scene, was among the large crowd, mostly drunk, of similar others milling around outside the establishment. In the middle of this crowd, an argument broke out over a romantic rivalry of sorts, leading to a fight between Murphy and a group of perhaps ten altogether. The struggle was over very quickly as his attackers brought him down with a flurry of blows. But this did not end the fight. Shortly after he was taken to hospital, Murphy was pronounced dead from the severe head injury that came from a kick received after falling to the ground (see Keane and O'Halloran for details of this complex chain of events). The Garda quickly discovered that there were many witnesses, actually too many, to what had happened. After many weeks of investigation, four men from the crowd, all recent graduates of Blackrock College, were identified as responsible for the attack on Murphy. And yet the case against them was hampered by conflicting accounts of a fracas that had lasted only a minute or so in the midst of a hardly stationary crowd of perhaps seven hundred or so young people.

9 WHAT RICHARD DID: SORT OF ADAPTING IRISH HISTORY   165

The prosecution took three years to prepare, but the case was kept alive in the newspapers as developments in the courts required updating.

The separate trials in 2004 garnered intense national attention, particularly because the defendants were from a privileged upper middle class that, with the recent prosperity, had become more numerous and politically influential. Two of the group were convicted of "violent disorder" and served some time in custody, but neither one was found guilty of manslaughter. In 2006, legal proceedings ended on a note of supreme and disturbing irony as the long-delayed coroner's report determined that Murphy's death was an "unlawful killing" that took place in the presence of many and the plain sight of some. Responsibility for which could only be apportioned to those who could be proved to have delivered punches or kicks, though none of these could beyond a reasonable doubt be designated as responsible for the fatal brain injury the young man suffered (see O'Halloran).

Bad Day was Power's first novel, and it was selected for the prestigious Rooney Prize in 2009. A screen versioning of the book by Ireland's most successful young director (Abrahamson had won the IFTA best director awards for his first two releases) was in this small country a major cultural event, promising a melding of creative visions. As so conceived, the project certainly testified to the synergistic force that could be summoned up by the younger talents in the literary and film establishment (Power was only 27 when the book was published, Abrahamson 43 during production). Their collaboration on the adaptation of a book that shocked and intrigued readers in the Republic interestingly exemplifies the roles that adaptation and auteurism (two powerful and not always harmonious forces) had come to play within the national film industry since the re-founding of the Bord Scannán (BSÉ/IFB) in 1993 with a new remit to assist native production.

Within eleven years, over one hundred commercially released features, many of which achieved substantial commercial and critical success, had been produced with assistance from the Bord; a number of these were adaptations of Irish fiction and drama. Much the same was true for state-sponsored TV production, the RTÉ. The national cinema thus came to parallel the wider economy, generating its own "tiger" and based like many European "new waves" or "new cinemas" on star directors. In 2010, the Irish cinema could count at least ten internationally known auteurs, including such luminaries as Conor McPherson, John Michael McDonagh, Paddy Breathnach, Kirsten Sheridan, and John Crowley, all of whom had achieved considerable box office and critical success in exploring Irish subjects for the domestic and international markets. This carefully calculated intervention in the private sector, setting aside free market Friedmanism, was overseen by the Minister for Arts, Culture, and the *Gaeltacht*, Michael D. Higgins, who has served as president of the Republic since 2011 and is an author/politician in the exalted tradition of André Malraux (see O'Leary). An ardent nationalist and sociologist who was proud that the Republic had joined the EU, Higgins was an ideal leader for this period of boom, bust, and sustained global engagement, with a sophisticated governing philosophy best expressed in his public speeches, which were, unusual for a politician, reprinted in a book that became a national bestseller (see Higgins). The title he chose for the collection, *When Ideas Matter*, could have served equally well as a motto for the national cinema then coming into being with his assistance.

By the beginning of the new millennium, many in the business and arts communities had been concerned that during the previous decade or so major works of Irish fiction, or original scripts, had been adapted for the screen by foreign producers, often with substantial critical and box office success that shone only a reflected light on the power of the country's artists even when Irish filmmakers were involved. That scriptwriter and director Neil Jordan's *The Crying Game* became a Channel Four production, and thus officially a UK film, receiving five Academy Award nominations, including for Best Picture, in 1993, was particularly bittersweet, given the long history of British appropriation of Irish artistic talent. Higgins was eager to nationalize this trend by making initial financing and other development services readily available for important projects, making better use of the nation's considerable creative talents.

Late-century overseas adaptations—such as Jim Sheridan's *My Left Foot* and Alan Parker's *The Commitments* (1989 and 1991)—typify the "modern" period of the Irish literary cinema, that is, the 80 years or so of screen history that preceded the meteoric rise to prominence of film projects conceived and produced in the contemporary Ireland in the course of the later 1990s such as Paddy Breathnach's *I Went Down* (1997), a transnational partnership with BBC Films (see the chapter on *The Commitments* in this volume). As representations and as cinema projects, films like *Richard* mirror an era transformed by financial-sector prosperity, political Europeanization, and secularization, including greater freedom of artistic expression as formerly strict censorship protocols were relaxed or abandoned (on the modern period of adaptation, see the introduction and the essays in Palmer/Conner). In any event, it was important news on the international cultural scene that whiz kid cineaste Abrahamson and novelist Power, already acclaimed as an important new literary voice, teamed up on an adaptation of *Bad Day* (see Lavery). The project would help fulfill Higgins's vision for a vital, national film sector that drew for its power and international appeal on what had always been the country's most successful cultural production and export: its critically acclaimed fiction and drama.

The revamped Bord (in 2018 renamed Fís Éireann/Screen Ireland or FÉ/SI) played an indispensable role in the development of the Irish film industry during the first decade of the new millennium. This rags to riches tale is worthy of being turned into a film script in its own right (see Barton 2019 for a full account). An artistically marginal and chronically underfunded player on the international market became one of the most artistically and financially successful of the European national industries, gaining ready access to the global (mainly arthouse) exhibition market, often through trans-national co-production projects, most of which profited from FÉ/SI development money. A useful illustration of Cinema Ireland's clout is provided by the success achieved by John Crowley and screenwriter Nick Hornby with *Brooklyn* (2015), based on the Colm Tóibin novel. In a symbiosis characteristic of the production and presentation of adapted screen fiction, *Brooklyn*'s outstanding success (including three Academy Award nominations and a worldwide exhibition gross of more than $62 million) did much to promote Crowley and solidify the already impressive reputation of Tóibin as a novelist and cultural commentator (for details see the chapter in this volume by Costello-Sullivan/Grossman; box office figures from Box Office Mojo).

The complex trans-nationalism of the film's financing (involving 13 British and Canadian entities, including the BBC) not only suited the story's engagement with thorny questions of cultural allegiance and economic self-interest (these are perennial Irish themes), but exemplified how a nationalist efflorescence of both literary and cinematic excellence could be achieved through the canny transgressing of financial borders, working not against but with the productive capacities of global capitalization, all in service of the desire to provide a significant aesthetic experience with Irishness to a worldwide viewership. Tóibin provided the ideal material for such a project since for him the personal and particular are always inflected by the political, as Kathleen Costello-Sullivan has demonstrated. Crowley's film honored the writer's vision, shaping aspects of Irishness for knowledgeable domestic viewers, while clearly explicating the paradoxes of

168   R. B. PALMER

diaspora identity for those overseas (see Costello-Sullivan). Admittedly, this double rhetoric required complex gestures of adaptation, as Costello-Sullivan/Grossman suggest in their chapter, but the outstanding success of *Brooklyn* demonstrates that it is possible to reconcile these two functions of a national cinema in the global marketplace. In fact, it seems hardly radical to suggest that such reconciliation should be the most respected protocol guiding how the adaptation of Irish fiction and drama should now take place, if Higgins's vision for the native cinema is going to continue to be fulfilled. Note, however, that *Brooklyn* (even with changes to the story that rendered it more America-centric) was deemed by the IFTA jury to be less successful than *Room*, whose Irishness is a matter only of the nationality of the filmmakers involved.

As a project that drew on the creative participation of a talented director and author, both of whom were invested in fiction that engaged critically with Tiger culture, the film that became *What Richard Did* could perhaps have achieved the double success of *Brooklyn*, holding up a critical mirror to viewers in the Republic, who were then caught up in the gloomy aftermath of the busted Tiger, while introducing international viewers to an Ireland then surprisingly in the throes of a radical transformation that could turn mindlessly riotous and homicidal, as, due to a generally moral decline, to quote Inglis, "the taboo against killing is no longer as deeply ingrained in the psyche as it used to be" (26; see also O'Toole; Ó Riain; and Allen/O'Boyle).

Because it is a film of fact, however, this project also had the potential to achieve something along the lines of the cultural impact of Peter Travis's *Omagh* (2004), written by Paul Greengrass, or Jordan's *Michael Collins* (1994), both with a pronounced political rhetoric whose reconstructions of events, periods, and important personalities provoked intense discussion among many in the national audience, bringing history to disputatious life and, in the case of *Collins*, delineating for international viewers the vexed causes of "the Troubles." Consider, for example, the domestic controversy that erupted over the portrait of Eamon de Valera that emerged in Jordan's reconstruction of the War of Independence and its fratricidal aftermath because the film focused on his erstwhile rival Collins rather than on the official founder of the Republic (see Merivirta).

Promoted as fiction, Abrahamson's film did not "rekindle" the controversy that the Murphy case inspired, as Eithne Shortall predicted. In fact, at least to judge by the lack of newspaper coverage, the film did not inspire much in the way of public discussion. *Bad Day* is an angry, anguished account of a society in crisis; the fevered dissatisfaction, regret, and disgust of his account (as much an inventory of his own feelings as of the case) is what readers found appealing. And yet in his screenplay, Campbell generalized and weakened the general lines of the social critique he found in his source, never creating an equivalent for the narrator's strident voice. Instead, the film focuses on the general loosening of moral restraints, with the house party attended by a horde of young people at a private residence the last (and suddenly) the most tragic of scenes in which drink is abundant and parents absent.

Richard fits into the production trend that Martin McLoone disdainfully terms "hip hedonism," with its pervasive "strong language" and, more shocking perhaps, unembarrassed depiction of casual hook-up sex. Nudity is avoided but there are several sequences of simulated intercourse involving the very young. These would have been impermissible only a few years earlier; such material on screen, to quote McLoone once again, perhaps signals "the new cinema's final affront to the values of the old Ireland" (97). In 2012, when the film was released, the troubling behavior of privileged adolescents certainly connected in the popular mind with the moral and social changes wrought by the Tiger, as the Irish nation suffered under the austerity that was imposing deep economic pain in the wake of near financial collapse in 2008–09 (See O'Toole; Allen/O'Boyle). *Richard*'s finely grained survey of the Dublin southside college scene could have been even more timely had it been presented as a film of fact.

What Abrahamson produced was undoubtedly brilliant, making the most of his astute aesthetic choices and obsessive attention to details of performance and design, while showcasing both the emotional appeal of Power's fictionalization of a complex series of events and also Campbell's devising of a screenplay that gave dramatic life to the novel's fragmentary, inwardly focused monologue. And yet, with its critically successful (it earned Abrahamson his third IFTA best director award) and profitable national exhibition, but then less than satisfactory releases abroad, *Richard* shines a revealing light on the central difficulty threatening what Higgins imagined as foundational to a productive alliance of two national arts, literature and filmmaking, that through export would boost the country's GDP.

As the examples of Tóibín and Power suggest, Irish literature is to some degree resistant to symbiosis with filmmaking, being in general more political than philosophical, more engaged with the ebb and flow of particular histories than with the transcendent moral questions that are most often explored in the modernist narratives of other cultures. The form of modernism we could term philosophical deeply inflects the serious, character-driven films of contemporary global cinema, following a convention established early on in the international art film sector as it evolved during the 1940s (see Balio). McLoone argues that for the Irish film industry modernizing globalization means inhabiting an "ill-defined space between the particular and the universal, between essentialist irrelevance and global insignificance" (89). The artistic trick is to make the particular seem significant and engaging to overseas viewers, as Crowley had done with *Brooklyn*.

In his negotiation of this liminality, especially through the presentation to the public that he oversaw, Abrahamson might be seen as failing to avoid essentialist irrelevance ("wider existential questions," as Barry Monahan suggests) even though *Richard* is otherwise a signal artistic achievement that advertises the excellence of the contemporary Irish cinema (111). The danger, whose effects are exemplified in this instance of cultural and literary adaptation, is that what is most insistently national loses its purchase in stories that are emptied of their particularity in order to lay some claim to trans-historical significance. This seems especially true for the Irish cinema, which is not well served, as Ruth Barton suggests, by the de-historicizing cinematic conception of "Ireland" as "an all-purpose traumatic space," which it nearly becomes in *Richard* after the directorial decision to obscure the sense in which the film is true event fiction (Barton 2019 16).

Cultural incoherence shadows the film, which minimizes, but does not discard completely, the connections to its literary source and, through that source, to the historical real, which rates no mention of any kind in marketing materials. Even so, *Richard* follows its source (and the facticity of the Murphy debacle) by dramatizing the failure of society to provide a coda to an event that simply could not be closed. In *Bad Day*, Power recounts the failure of the justice system to make sense of a troubling criminal act committed in the presence of many, showing it also to be resistant to the reconstruction of a concerned witness who from the beginning of this meditative project forecasts his total failure to deliver the answers that he and his readers are most desperate to receive.

Instead of emphasizing, as does *Bad Day*, that the judicial inconclusiveness was obtained by expert legal assistance, Abrahamson and Campbell soft-pedal this indeterminacy through an ellipsis. The filmmakers had little choice, given the cinema's difficulty in incorporating a distinctive narrative voice. The screenplay lacks any equivalent of the novel's obtrusive and anguished narrator, who is the only source of social and moral analysis (which in *Bad Day* is never the subject of a dramatically conceived scene). Tense scenes of Richard discussing his delivery of a fatal kick to the head of his rival Conor (Sam Keeley) with both Lara and his father promise some kind of confrontation with the law. But then the film's closing sequences, without providing any information on intervening events, show Richard attending classes at the University; he has apparently skated free of any consequences for his act. The film ends with a puzzle rather than anything like the *aperçu* that closes out *Bad Rock*. Power's narrator imagines Richard and his family in an anguished isolation that perhaps portends a general moral crisis: "They are alone on a bleak and emptying island, receding and alone, alone at last where everything ends, sitting out their ruined lives on Inishfall" (235).

The resonance of Power's fiction derives from its granular, sociological anatomizing of a Southside Dublin culture that has lost its moral compass. It is a fiction that explores a group *mentalité*, constructing an inside outsider with the sufficient intellectual distance to offer a penetrating critique of the event and its participants. His narrator bewildered by a world that contains and repels him, Kevin Power shows that he is not intrigued by issues of individual conscience. Richard, his guilt-stricken protagonist, hardly speaks, and only occasional access is provided to his inner thoughts, whose lack of significant depth reflects Power's low estimate of this culture's capacity for self-understanding. And so he is afforded little narrative space in which to act out his transformation into a killer *malgré lui*, nothing like what Dostoyevsky and Camus provide to Raskolnikov and Meursault, turning them into the sources of wisdom about the human experience. Richard, to see this as a matter of form, is a main character only in a limited sense. His essential flatness renders difficult his transformation into the subject rather than the object of events that overwhelm him, with his arc of development constituting the plot. *Bad Day* can be fit into this pattern, but only by abandoning much of the novel's political tendentiousness, which plays out in the consciousness of the narrator and only tangentially contacts the main character.

Discussing his early career in an interview with Adam Dawtrey in 2013, Abrahamson proclaimed that "I wanted to make films that were culturally relevant in my own country, that challenged people and that people talked about." His decision to adapt *Bad Day* surely reflected that intention. But that conception of his artistic interests then changed: "in the past couple

172   R. B. PALMER

of years I've made a conscious decision to open myself up to bigger stories... really interesting and original projects that require a more expansive canvas" (qtd. in Dawtrey). *Room* (2015) and *The Little Stranger* (2018) materialize that change of focus fully; they reflect what John D. Hill calls the conventions of the post-national art cinema in that they entirely lack Irish themes (see Hill). Abrahamson initially pursued cultural relevance and a dialogue with the national audience, and brilliantly furthered that dialogue with his first two films, both of which end with tragic twists that engage the viewer's moral sensibility. The project that became *Richard* might have depicted how the toney enclave of Blackrock (with its eponymous exclusive college) came, in the most penetrating of understatements, to have a "bad day," with the twist ending reflecting on the failure of the judicial system. Instead, he narrowed the focus to *What Richard Did*, turning him into a fictional character rather than a fictionalized version of the actual killer.

The director's desire for a "more expansive" canvas seems to have affected the way in which the adaptation and marketing of *Bad Day* proceeded. Yet the material still required a certain amount of truth-to-the-facts. No room was left for Campbell to provide the kind of conclusion, with its crowd-pleasing measured hope for the future, that surely figured significantly in the huge success attained by *Room*, a film in which the issue of cultural relevance for Irish viewers was simply not put in play. As suggested earlier, the lack of "Irishness" in *Room* did it no harm with IFTA jury members. Abrahamson's biggest recent success has been with the Screen Ireland/Hulu/BBC 3 co-production, in 12 episodes, of Sally Rooney's novel *Normal People*, first broadcast on RTÉ in the spring of 2020. The at turns grim and triumphant portrayal of the love affair between two young adults, *Normal People*, if atmospherically Irish, engages only tangentially with the country's contemporary cultural politics (discussed at more length in the introduction to this volume).

The Irishness of an Irish filmmaking that screens the important texts from the national literature is most vibrantly and affectingly observed (and communicated) when it avoids such a universalizing, deracinating engagement with its story materials. *Richard* is impressively authentic (and perhaps even ostentatiously truthy) about the details that collectively constitute the feel of its world of unself-conscious adolescent privilege. Thanks to Campbell, the film's constant teenage banter, much of it incomprehensible, has a John Hughes ring of observed reality. And yet, Abrahamson insisted that the film should be marketed neither as the

9 WHAT RICHARD DID: SORT OF ADAPTING IRISH HISTORY   173

screen version of an important novel (whose cultural value it could have raised) or as a film of fact that memorialized more than it does of a usable past from a regrettable episode of communal history that demonstrably intrigued the national public and could easily have been marketed to do the same for international viewers.

PRODUCTION, AUTEUR, HISTORY

Such an emptying out, it seems likely, was not the approach taken in the beginning. Though this is a choice that screenwriters doing adaptations often do not make, Power was engaged by Abrahamson and Campbell to work on the project, receiving screen credit for his contributions, which were thus likely substantial. It is hard to read the hiring of Power except as a move to deepen the film's connection with the novel and, by extension, with the Murphy case. Abrahamson had worked successfully with writer Mark Halloran on *Adam and Paul* and *Garage*, but in this instance he partnered with Malcolm Campbell, who had had a good deal of experience writing for the small screen. This choice perhaps reflected the need to fashion effective and authentic dialogue as well as a clear, narrative through line for a story clearly divided into beginning, middle, and end. Though *Bad Day* contains a narrative that, if presented out of chronological order, can be pieced together from the different chapters, the text offered Abrahamson little in the way of usable dramatic encounters since "story" as such is minimized. Power clearly envisioned a readership well-versed in the major events of the Murphy case, to which he has only to allude under the guise of fiction. During the film's pre-production, it seems likely that Abrahamson's intention to emphasize the material's true event connection was abandoned.

In his third project, Abrahamson does not focus on those living lives of spiritual and material poverty who have been pushed to the margins of a newly prosperous society that is desperate to renew its moral center, now that its founding values (community and Catholicism) had been largely discredited. The protagonists for his first two films, by way of contrast, had found no places for themselves in a transforming Ireland: the eponymous self-destructive drug addicts in *Adam and Paul* (2004) whose odyssey to cop their next fix ends in a fatal overdose; the mentally challenged gas station attendant in *Garage* (2007), whose misguided attempts to escape from his loneliness ends in a public shaming that drives him to suicide. To be sure, with a tone that sometimes borders on the farcical, Abrahamson finds a way to find what is mildly comic in these stories, including the daring move to cast noted comedian Pat Shortt as *Garage*'s often pathetic, and finally doomed, protagonist. Nonetheless, these two films poignantly engage with the discontents of the current scene, avoiding both what Michael Patrick Gillespie identifies as the fanciful mythology of traditional Irish identity and also the comforting, if arguably equally fanciful, conventions of the commercial cinema (see Gillespie). David Clarke is surely on target when he suggests that "Adam & Paul is a work of naturalism. Where it differs from the films of, say, Ken Loach is not in its approach to verisimilitude, but in its capacity to extract humour from the grimmest incidents in the lives of the socially excluded" (Clarke).

As Clarke observes, like *Garage*, *Adam and Paul* sometimes reveals the lighter side of its bitter social critique, but there is nothing funny about the overdose that shockingly ends the film, radically altering its tone. In *Garage*, the turn toward tragedy comes as a similarly disturbing and for the spectator re-orienting surprise. One is certainly reminded of Ken Loach, but in terms of the social observation of detail, more perhaps of Émile Zola, who in his series of Rougon-Macquart novel similarly identifies with an often merciless critical eye the *habitus*, as well as the discontents and inequities, of a culture, Baron Haussman's Second Empire, then at its various class levels undergoing rapid change. *Richard* regards with cold objectivity the spectacle of a society cut loose from its moorings in religion and civic nationalism.

If it avoids the *déclassé* precincts of modern life, *Richard* otherwise shares more in common than might be first apparent with Abrahamson's two earlier grim *histoires*. Here again is a screen world haunted by a shocking and unnatural death that is not recuperated by either Republican or Catholic values, thus constituting an implicit commentary on a country in which these two established forms of guidance have lost their purpose. Here again in a naturalist vein, society is portrayed as wanting, as no authority emerges in the story world or off-screen as a source of political or ethical truth. *Richard* anatomizes the suburban landscape of South Dublin, shown to be inhabited by lost souls whose lives will soon be marked by particular forms of indelible moral failure that exemplify the spiritual vacuity of their class identity. *Richard* moves up the social ladder to dramatize the lives of those who have most profited from Tiger prosperity, as Abrahamson completes an unacknowledged cinematic triptych of the period, whose economic exuberance had found its comeuppance in the fraud-exposing crash of 2008–09.

To be sure, unlike *Adam and Paul* and *Garage, Richard* does not explore in unstinting detail the deprivation and anomie of those trapped hopelessly in the lower orders, where isolation has replaced community as the central social fact. Instead, in *Richard* Abrahamson limns the spiritual wasteland inhabited by the country's ostensibly successful establishment, the white-collar executives and professionals, thoroughly Europeanized, whose children attend the area's exclusive fees-paying schools in hopes of completing their education at either Trinity or University College. A focus on this high-flying youth culture is glimpsed in the film's opening images of three young men, Rugby teammates as it turns out, who have strapped themselves into a speeding luxury sedan that is taking them to the Wicklow shore for some vacation partying. Testosterone-fueled, they dispose of abundant spending money, and the unsupervised freedom to booze and hook up in their family vacation homes with their willing colleagues from the city's private women's colleges. This elite school culture, as Abrahamson evokes it, is rigidly stratified in gender terms; that the film's initial focus opening shots follow the experiences of an all-male group is predictive of the film's subsequent focus on adolescent discontents. This is the beginning of an at-speed journey that leads them to a murder they do not intend and will not acknowledge, despite the pleas of Conor's parents for justice during a memorial mass where the students and parents in attending remain embarrassed and silent. The camera only rarely observes the girls who, as it were, are simply along for the ride.

The film tells essentially the same story that had emerged from years of testimony and journalistic investigation. This much was obvious to most domestic viewers. A simple signposting would have confirmed *Richard* as a film of fact: "this film offers a fictionalized version of the Brian Murphy killing" or, more circumspectly, "though based on the Brian Murphy case, this film is fiction in that none of the characters is meant to reference any particular individual involved." Tellingly, the producers, and the director, also declined to make that connection in the trailer prepared for domestic release; it was only slightly modified for the film's limited international exhibition, making it very unlikely that audiences overseas, who were in any case largely ignorant of what had happened at the Club Anabel, would understand *Richard* as a film of fact (see "Trailer"). For them it would seem a self-contained fiction, like most screen narratives. The film's sourcing in Power's novel rated no mention.

What is puzzling is that Irish and UK reviewers (the film was only briefly given a US release) generally followed that same protocol, avoiding

176   R. B. PALMER

anything but the vaguest occasional reference to the Brian Murphy case or to *Bad Day*. This judgment is now the critical consensus. Consider, for example, the review of the DVD release in *Pop Matters*, which opines that Abrahamson's film starts out as a "fairly formulaic coming-of-age drama" but turns "particularly unsettling" when the killing occurs and concludes with a "lack of definitiveness" (see *Pop Matters*). For Peter Bradshaw, writing in *The Guardian*, *Richard* is "a complex, subtle drama about self-confident teenagers that draws on two traditions: American teen-noir such as *Carrie* or *Heathers*, and European dramas of group dysfunction such as those by Vinterberg and Haneke" (Bradshaw). Most misleading, perhaps, is Monahan's strangely illogical statement that Abrahamson's intention for the film *not* to be an adaptation determines whether the film *is* an adaptation, as if such a material fact would require the "author's expressed intention" for it to be so (111). It is no doubt illuminating to invoke, as he does, Sartre's notion of *mauvaise foi* in order to explain Richard's actions, but it is arguably more relevant in terms of the film's inevitable extratextual referencing to point out the origin of his ethical failure to engage appropriately with the painful facticity of the brutal death of an undeserving young man. Also significant is the failure of all involved to bring anything like justice to bear in the agonizingly long way in which Irish society processed this terrible death.

Of course, as is the case with all true event fiction, a "self-contained" reading of the film's story and themes is certainly possible. However, a strictly aesthetic approach to *Richard* is in fact political since it erases the cultural politics of the film's ineluctable invocation to a true story that the Irish themselves viewed as revealing, in a disturbing microcosm, developments that pointed toward a decline in the traditional values of the nation. For its original Irish audience, *Richard* remained as it were "in the closet," its extratextual referencing an open secret that producers and filmmakers were unwilling to acknowledge "as such." From a globalist perspective, such a presentation of the film contributed to what Ruth Barton calls the "continued dilution of the local in the face of the global," relieving the productions of a national cinema of the particularity and intriguing difference that largely constitute their trans-national appeal (1). Richard's limited success in overseas releases (as mentioned earlier, it was pulled from US exhibition after one disappointing week in NYC with a box office of under $3k) suggests that this was indeed a problem. Martin McLoone has said: "To jettison wholesale the narratives of Irish nationalism is to bow to the destructive power and cultural domination of international capital"

(90). This seems to be what Abrahamson and Campbell did as they set about adapting *Bad Day* for the domestic and then the international screen by attempting to scrub it clean of its deep connections to Tiger era cultural politics.

WORKS CITED

Allen, Kieran and Brian O'Boyle. *Austerity Ireland: The Failure of Irish Capitalism.* London: Pluto Press, 2013.

Alvarez, Lizette. "Suddenly Rich, Poor Old Ireland Seems Bewildered." *New York Times* 2 February 2005. https://www.nytimes.com/2005/02/02/world/europe/suddenly-rich-poor-old-ireland-seems-bewildered.html (accessed 11/15/2019).

Balio, Tino. *The Foreign Film Renaissance on American Screens, 1946–73.* Madison: University of Wisconsin Press, 2010.

Barton, Ruth. *Irish Cinema in the Twenty-First Century.* Manchester: Manchester University Press, 2019.

Boyne, John. "A Story that Breaks the Rules" (review of Power). *Irish Times* 11 October 2008 https://www.irishtimes.com/news/a-story-that-breaks-the-rules-1.894830 (accessed 7/8/2020).

Bradshaw, Peter. "What Richard Did: Review." *The Guardian* 10 January 2013. https://www.theguardian.com/film/2013/jan/10/what-richard-did-review (accessed 4/7/2020)

Brown, Terence. *Ireland: A Social and Cultural History 1922–2002.* Second Edition. London: Harper Collins, 2004.

Clarke, Donald. "Vein Spotting" Review of Adam and Paul. *Irish Times* 20 August 2004. https://www.irishtimes.com/culture/vein-spotting-1.1154211 (accessed 8/14/2020).

Corcoran, Mary P. and Michel Peillon. *Uncertain Ireland: A Sociological Chronicle 2003–2004.* Dublin: Institute of Public Administration, 2006.

Costello-Sullivan, Kathleen. *Mother/Country: Politics of the Personal in the Fiction of Colm Tóibín.* Bern: Peter Lang, 2012.

Dawtrey, Adam. "Director Lenny Abrahamson Poised for Breakout with *Frank.*" *Variety* 5 September 2013. https://variety.com/2013/film/global/director-lenny-abrahamson-poised-for-breakout-with-frank-1200599044/

De Valera, Eamon. "The Ireland that We Dreamed of" 1943 radio address. https://www.rte.ie/archives/exhibitions/eamon-de-valera/719124-address-by-mr-de-valera/ (accessed 9/15).

Gilbey, Ryan. "Lenny Abrahamson: 'Good guys can be complex, too'." *The Guardian* 3 January 2013. https://www.theguardian.com/film/2013/jan/03/what-richard-did-lenny-abrahamson (accessed 8/6/2020).

178 R. B. PALMER

Gillespie, Michael Patrick. *The Myth of an Irish Cinema: Approaching Irish-Themed Films*. Syracuse, NY: Syracuse University Press, 2009.

Higgins, Michael D. *When Ideas Matter: Speeches for an Ethical Republic*. Dublin: Head of Zeus, 2017.

Hill, John D. "The Rise and Fall of British Art Cinema: A Short History of the 1980s and 1990s." *Aura Film Studies Journal* 6, no. 3 (2000): 18–32.

Horan, Niamh. "Shock Novel Based on Anibel's (sic) Tragic Death." *Irish Independent* 5 October 2008. https://www.independent.ie/irish-news/shock-novel-based-on-anabels-tragic-death-26482088.html

Inglis, Tom. "Club Anabel" in Corcoran and Peillon, 15–27.

Keane, Fergal. "Never-ending Nightmare of Brian Murphy Murder". *Politico* 25 February 2005. https://magill.ie/archive/never-ending-nightmare-brian-murphy-murder (accessed 3/4/2020).

Lavery, Michael. "Movie Based on Annabel's (sic) Killing Sold Across the World." *Herald.I.E.* 23 October 2012. https://www.herald.ie/news/movie-based-on-annabels-killing-is-sold-across-world-28850802.html

McLoone, Martin. "National Cinema in Ireland." In Valentina Vitali and Paul Willemen, eds., *Theorising National Cinema*. London: BFI, 2006: 88–99.

Merivirta, Raita. "Like Cain and Abel: Michael Collins and de Valera in Neil Jordan's Film *Michael Collins*." *Wider Screen* 2001. https://www.researchgate.net/publication/282074901_Like_Cain_and_Abel_Michael_Collins_and_de_Valera_in_Neil_Jordan's_Film_Michael_Collins/citation/download (accessed 8/5/2020).

Monahan, Barry. *The Films of Lenny Abrahamson: A Filmmaking of Philosophy*. London: Bloomsbury, 2018.

O'Dowd, Niall. *A New Ireland: How Europe's Most Conservative Country Became Its Most Liberal*. New York: Skyhorse, 2020.

O'Halloran, Georgina. "Jury Returns Verdict of Unlawful Killing." *Irish Examiner* 19 September 2007. https://www.irishexaminer.com/ireland/icrime/jury-returns-verdict-of-unlawful-killing-42960.html

O'Leary, Jennifer. "Who is Michael D. Higgins?" *BBC News* 28 October 2011. https://www.bbc.com/news/uk-northern-ireland-15500225 (accessed 8/14/2020)

Ó Riain, Seán. *The Rise and Fall of Ireland's Celtic Tiger: Liberalism, Boom and Bust*. Cambridge: Cambridge University Press, 2014.

O'Toole, Fintan. *Ship of Fools: How Stupidity and Corruption Sank the Celtic Tiger*. New York: Public Affairs, 2010.

Palmer, R. Barton and Marc C. Conner, eds. *Screening Modern Irish Fiction and Drama*. London: Palgrave Macmillan, 2016.

Power, Kevin. *Bad Day in Blackrock*. Dublin: Lilliput Press, 2008.

SCC English. "Bad Day at Blackrock." 8 April 2009. http://www.sccenglish.ie/2009/04/bad-day-at-blackrock.html

Sheridan, Kathy. "The Nightclub Killing That Convulsed and Divided the Middle Classes." *Irish Times* 16 March 2004. https://www.irishtimes.com/news/nightclub-killing-that-convulsed-and-divided-the-middle-classes-1.1135594 (accessed 3/10/2020).

Shortall, Eithne. "Brian Murphy's Death to Become Film." *The Irish Times* 24 January 2010. https://www.thetimes.co.uk/article/brian-murphys-death-to-become-film-d2ph3stqn2z (accessed 8/7/2020).

"Trailer for *What Richard Did.*" https://www.youtube.com/watch?v=xXTcSCp8R6E (accessed 8/15/2020).

Warren, Adrian. "The Moral Conflict of *What Richard Did.*" *Pop Matters* April 2013. https://www.popmatters.com/170815-what-richard-did-2495761810.html

CHAPTER 10

Plagues of Silence: Adaptation and Agency in Colm Tóibín's and John Crowley's *Brooklyn*s

Kathleen Costello-Sullivan and Julie Grossman

Colm Tóibín's acclaimed 2009 novel *Brooklyn* explores the boundaries, national and imaginary, that limit and delimit main character Eilis Lacey's social interactions and self-perception. Tóibín's characters tend to be somewhat restricted emotionally, owing to Tóibín's crafting of their cultural origins in small-town Ireland. Eilis is a heroine whose inner life is accordingly limited, but who displays glimpses of evolution from her time in Brooklyn. The novel's use of silence generates a large part of this characterization by framing Eilis's family life, as well as her relationship with suitor Tony. Eilis's emotional restriction and tendency toward silence condition her and the narrative and prevent any simple analysis of emotional resolution by text's end.

John Crowley's 2015 adaptation of *Brooklyn*, at first glance, does not adhere to this equivocal representation of Eilis's fate. On the contrary, the

---

K. Costello-Sullivan • J. Grossman (✉)
Le Moyne College, Syracuse, NY, USA
e-mail: sullivkp@lemoyne.edu; grossmjj@lemoyne.edu

© The Author(s), under exclusive license to Springer Nature   181
Switzerland AG 2022
M. C. Conner et al. (eds.), *Screening Contemporary Irish Fiction and Drama*, Palgrave Studies in Adaptation and Visual Culture,
https://doi.org/10.1007/978-3-031-04568-4_10

film *seems* to adopt many mainstream filmic narrative conventions—best exemplified in the happier ending, for instance, or in Eilis's confident and assertive declaration, "I am Eilis Fiorello!"—to present a more one-dimensional conclusion than appears in the novel (Fig. 10.1).

As we know in adaptation, however, films are not beholden to their sources but are in conversation with them, participating in what Kate Newell has called "the dynamics of expansion common to all modes of adaptation" (19). As Julie Grossman argues elsewhere,

> sources and adaptations…are indivisibly connected. […] I want to endorse a way of thinking about adaptation that emphasizes its power to 'slant' (create a different viewpoint on) a source text, to shift our way of filing known literary works in our mental cabinets. […] Many…adaptations…are not interested in re-presenting [sic] other works but in engaging them in conversation from a new viewpoint and, often, a surprising context. (Grossman 2)

In such a context, Tóibín's fiction provides an eminently apt source for adaptation, because his novels are already part of an adaptive world in which characters and places appear and reappear across texts. Thus, in his 2014 Irish novel, *Nora Webster*, characters from *The Heather Blazing*,

Fig. 10.1 Eilis's assertion, "I am Eilis Fiorello!"

Brooklyn, and *The Blackwater Lightship*, as well as from the short story *The Name of the Game*, make cameos. John Crowley's act of adaptation effectively extends this world into cinema, continuing the porous boundaries characteristic of Tóibín's canon and marrying the verbal and visual fictional worlds of Brooklyn and Ireland.

This chapter explores what, we argue, is a kind of "conversation" in which the film engages with the novel. Neither simply regurgitating the 2009 text nor rejecting it, the film rather establishes an intertextual dialogue with it, at times expanding and elaborating, at others inflecting the prior text. The film harnesses its visual metaphors—the use of mirrors, screens, reflections, and slow-motion images of crossing thresholds, for instance—to engage with Tóibín's exploration of divided and multiplied selves in relation to place. It also employs a distinct *mise-en-scene* to signal the complexity of Eilis's interior life. Her shifting perspective is shown alternatively in long shots and closeups, the latter preoccupied with the face and performance of lead actor Saoirse Ronan; crowded and pastel-drenched shots of *Brooklyn* are set against a tear rolling down the doomed Rose's face. The silences haunting the text thus open up filmic possibilities visually to present—and subvert—the rigid parameters of place and Eilis's equivocal expressiveness, both of which extend the representations of the novel.

By collapsing the visual markers of place, the film works to undermine the strict binary of Ireland/Brooklyn and the restrictions such a binary entails.[1] The film's use of color delineates these issues, with director John Crowley adding repeated images of Eilis's eyes and mental activity to proffer a visual means of showing the protagonist's resistance to the oppressive forces of community, family, and place so often discussed in an Irish literary context. Both texts thus explore "Irelands" and "Brooklyns"—exemplifying not only how the film extends Tóibín's novel, but also how

---

[1] Michael Patrick Gillespie has raised the question of whether, given that films like *Brooklyn* are often an internationally produced, financed, and distributed, the phrase "Irish Cinema" is apt (see also Conner and Palmer, "Introduction"). Ruth Barton develops an alternative perspective through the use of the "transnational," "and the possibilities this term offers for retrieving, rather than dismissing, the national" (19), arguing more broadly in her recent volume for "[a recognition of] the continuing validity of the cinematic national imaginary within the global flow of finance and production" (12). We are not engaging questions of the "Irishness" of the film or industry per se, but rather interested in the ways in which such dichotomies break down in the filmic adaptation.

adaptations can multiply the meaning of a place to redefine its imaginary or intermedial spaces.

Adaptations that hew closely to their sources always run the risk of generating hackneyed analyses focused mainly on evaluation and one-to-one comparisons. From such a dyadic perspective, for example, readers might observe the erasure of Eilis's brothers in the movie, whose presence in the novel and emigration to England undergird the sense of her subordinate place in the Lacey family: "Since Jack, the nearest to her in age, had followed his two older brothers Pat and Martin to Birmingham to find work, Eilis had moved into the boys' room, leaving Rose her own bedroom, which their mother carefully tidied and cleaned each morning" (11). Similarly, and perhaps most pronouncedly, her confident declaration as "Eilis Fiorello," which we referenced above, makes for a potentially jarring change to what is, by all accounts, a persistently paralyzed character in the text. Consider novel-Eilis's response to Miss Kelly's knowledge of her marriage. Rather than boldly claiming and asserting her married identity as we see in the film, Eilis follows the novel's pattern of silence and allows Miss Kelly to dismiss her, just as she would have at the novel's beginning: "Is that all you have to say, Miss Kelly? [...] So is that all, Miss Kelly?" (256). Such side-by-side evaluations tell us how an adaptation changes a text and demonstrate a shift in Eilis's characterization in the film; however, these observations do *not* contribute very meaningfully to our understandings of the adaptation itself.[2]

In fact, even in an adaptation that appears to adhere in a fairly straightforward fashion to its source—showcasing the same characters, setting, and story arc—the film *Brooklyn* still re-orients viewers to the narrative, rewriting Tóibín's story with not only things left out or a different ending, but, more interestingly, with a varied tone and character pattern. On the one hand, the novel ends with an idea that is captured in the following shot from the film (Fig. 10.2).

While Eilis's glance seems to be directed mournfully out to the passing Irish landscape, her mirrored reflection suggests a more self-directed and ambivalent gaze. This is in keeping with the novel's ambiguous

---

[2] In *Irish Cinema in the Twenty-First Century*, Ruth Barton observes that the concluding gestures of the film *Brooklyn* "betray the tone of the novel" (132). We are suggesting that while the film does indeed make changes to the novel, more productive considerations of adaptation move away from the language of fidelity and betrayal to frame these relationships in terms of dialogue, rather than a dyad or binary that embraces hierarchy and invites generalized evaluation.

Fig. 10.2 Eilis on the train, gazing out the window

conclusion, as Eilis imagines her future in Brooklyn: "Eilis imagined the years ahead, when these words would come to mean less and less to the man who heard them and would come to mean more and more to herself. She almost smiled at the thought of it, then closed her eyes and tried to imagine nothing more" (262). In the novel's conclusion, Eilis "almost" smiles; rather than fantasizing enthusiastically about returning to her life with Tony, she is thinking about Jim Farrell, and then "tries to imagine nothing more." This is clearly an instance where visual markers capture the conceit of the novel, even though the film does not end there.

On the other hand, despite the ameliorative tone at the very end of the film with Eilis and Tony's joyful embrace, there are more compelling instances of adaptation that underscore the values and fascination of textual transformations, dialogue, and story extension. One immediate example offers a noteworthy qualification to the earlier point that the film might be seen to follow certain mainstream narrative devices (such as an unambiguously romantic happy ending). A conventional Hollywood narrative, as John Crowley suggests in his DVD commentary, might reveal some major flaw in Tony: some secret, for example, that keeps him from being an appropriate mate for Eilis, or a limitation of his that keeps the two apart for a time. Used to mainstream narrative conventions, viewers anticipate

> something bad to come out about Tony, that he's not quite what he seems to be. Of course it never really goes there in that direction. We always try to subvert the expectation of the next thing to happen, very gently as it goes forward and never rely on anything melodramatic.

Instead, the film abides by and deepens Tóibín's delineation of Tony's character as fundamentally stable. Tony is repeatedly described in terms that stress both his attractiveness and his fundamental decency: "His skin looked soft. When he caught her looking at him he twisted his mouth in amusement and this made his eyes seem even larger than before. [...] He looked happy and she liked that" (133). Tony does not develop as a challenge to Eilis or their relationship in the film, but rather just as a partner who falls in love with her. As played by Emory Cohen and owing to the actor's charisma and cinematic presence, Tony remains animated by his expressions and charm (see Fig. 10.3).

The film's introduction of an actor whose affect continually registers his joyful bewilderment that Eilis has chosen to be with him employs its own filmic nature to extend elements of the text—a mediation that highlights the act of adaptation while focusing our attention on what is distinctly cinematic. Borrowing from Gérard Genette, R. Barton Palmer recently observed that "Adaptations are not just *from* something, but *for* something, which can be put simply: they continue" (79). The insight is nicely exemplified in Emory Cohen's embodiment of Tony, which *continues* the film's source through performance.

Indeed, the film uses not only performance to interpret the characters but its imagery to continue Tóibín's emphasis on silence as a major force in Irish life.[3] Two examples are particularly notable. In the novel, Eilis's internal dialogue and a third-person narrative capture the silences that plague the Lacey family: "As she read and reread, her mother moved about the kitchen with her back to her, saying nothing. [...] She was, in fact, Eilis saw, making work for herself so that she would not have to turn" (27). As in so much of Tóibín's canon, the novel *Brooklyn* suggests that

---

[3] Silence is a dominant theme in much Irish literature and is, of course, a well-established element of Tóibín's oeuvre. For one reading of silence in his canon, see Costello-Sullivan, *Mother/Country* 20n67.

Fig. 10.3 Eilis and Tony, embodied charismatically by Saoirse Ronan and Emory Cohen

silence is a plague upon the Lacey family, conditioning their interactions and stunting Eilis's emotional life.

In the film, we do not have direct access to Eilis's interior monologue—but the visuals employed nonetheless convey this emotional restriction as well as indirect access to the intense quality of Eilis's thoughtfulness. In the same way, consider the stunning shot (Fig. 10.4) of Rose sitting at tea with her mother, eating and drinking without conversation, with a just barely noticeable tear running down her face. The tear reflects not only Rose's individual suffering, but also familial dysfunction that can't be discussed and emotions that can't be voiced or shared demonstrably. A visual correlate of an untranslatable sadness with no outlet, Rose's silent tear exemplifies filmically the crippling silences besetting Rose and her family.

The second, more resonating, visual trope connected with silence in the film is found in director John Crowley's repeated focus on Eilis's eyes—open, staring, or opening after being closed—which further expresses the quality of her mind and how alert she is to her experience, as in Fig. 10.5.

In the novel, as we have seen, Eilis is habitually silent and watching, failing to express her needs and concerns and succumbing to the pressures

Fig. 10.4 Rose's silent tear

Fig. 10.5 Eilis's eyes, her stare signifying an alert mind

10 PLAGUES OF SILENCE: ADAPTATION AND AGENCY IN COLM TÓIBÍN'S... 189

of small-town Irish life. She even recognizes that she is limited and wonders if this is a hindrance in her blossoming relationship with Tony:

> She discovered a vantage point from where, unless he looked directly upwards and to the left, he would not see her. [...] He was delighted by things, as he was delighted by her, and he had done nothing else ever other than make that clear. Yet somehow that delight seemed to come with a shadow, and she wondered as she watched him if she herself, in all her uncertainty and distance from him, was the shadow and nothing else. (150)

If watching is a sign of Eilis's passivity in the novel, however, the film's sustained attention to the activity of Eilis's eyes is different. It becomes a way to develop Tóibín's theme of silence and, finally, to *revalue* it as a source of energy and empowerment for film-Eilis in the film's end.

Indeed the film converses with the novel in its representation of Eilis's passivity. Tóibín repeatedly explores Eilis's habit of observation: she is unable to choose her life, but instead watches it unfold according to convention or by following the determination and will of others. Her response in the novel to her impending immigration is typical: "Eilis would have given anything to be able to say plainly that she did not want to go... [...] She ... would keep it from herself if she had to until she was away from them" (32–33). Similarly, novel-Eilis watches Tony constantly, as we have seen, which signals her uncertainty and passivity. The novel's Eilis watches rather than acts, often to her own detriment.

In contrast, the film appropriates Eilis's silent observation as a source of empowerment. This vibrancy in her silent presence in the film is largely effective because of actor Saoirse Ronan's intensity. An image of silence that registers Eilis's selfhood, Ronan's face and colorful blue eyes are in sync with a pastel-rendered Brooklyn and Long Island. The film not only adapts book-Eilis's penchant for observation, then, but also interprets and rewrites it visually.

With Eilis portrayed by Ronan, who has been described by Crowley as "one of the great watching faces in cinema," *Brooklyn*'s director considers the work "a film about a face" (DVD commentary). Tóibín, too, in a recent interview, observed that "John Crowley realized that [Ronan] would've made a great silent actress" (cited in Costello-Sullivan, Interview). Silence is an oppressive force of repression in Tóibín's oeuvre: in Saoirse Ronan's embodiment of Eilis, silence instead presents her not as passive, swept along in the wake of others' directives—but as an active thinker, working through her ideas and identity.

Repeated shots of Eilis watching, even staring sometimes at the ceiling, show that her silence affords her time to consider her options. She is clearly thinking about the different ways she might occupy the place, Brooklyn, that Crowley paints with colors that did not appear in Enniscorthy before Eilis came to this "new world" of America.[4] As an adaptation, the inclusion of these silent moments of Eilis's thinking follows Thomas Leitch's suggestion, borrowing Wolfgang Iser's discussion of gaps, that texts will always allow openings for interpretation for viewers to engage and fill (see "Mind the Gaps"). What, we wonder, is Eilis thinking? How does she imagine her place redefined as a space in which she can assert her individual desires? What different path does she conceive for herself versus the one determined by others? In the film's figuration, when Eilis opens her eyes, she isn't watching, but staring, as if her open eyes embrace a moment to which she is awake. As we have suggested, Crowley thus expands Tóibín's use of silence, suggesting that Eilis inhabits and utilizes these moments of silence rather than only being subject to them.

Interestingly, Crowley's visual attention to Eilis's intense thought processes also positions Tóibín's story in relation to a novelistic narrative tradition of valuing thought over action.[5] Certainly this harking back to a wider literary tradition is familiar to Tóibín.[6] But more specifically, he tends throughout his canon to privilege the movement of the mind over narrative action, as in the short story "One Minus One."

At the same time, through Ronan's silent stares, the film *Brooklyn* reminds us that viewers' own silence is, like the camera's attention to Ronan in these moments, not a passive but an active experience of

---

[4] As Ruth Barton observes, for Eilis, the "movement towards a more developed sense of self is further indicated by the ever-stronger colours of Eilis's dresses, their assertive cut, and her confident application of make-up" (132).

[5] Consider Austen's emphasis on the meaningful "action" taking place mainly inside her heroines' minds, or Henry James's enjoinder within his novels that an individual be an alert thinker—as he says in *The Art of Fiction*, "one of the people on whom nothing is lost!"

[6] Tóibín's 2017 novel *House of Names* is heavily intertextual, drawing not only on the Greek tragic tradition, but also on Shakespeare in its references and characterizations. In a recent interview, Tóibín notes of *House of Names*, "[O]bviously there are parts of *Macbeth* in it. When Clytemnestra kills the guards that have been sent by her husband to look after her on the way back, it's exactly the same trick, to badge them with blood so it seems like the others did it. [...] [S]he's also Gertrude [from *Hamlet*]. She has a whole lot of those [Shakespearean characters' traits] in her." Cited in Costello-Sullivan, "The Irish Oresteia" 5.

engaging with the film. We are, as Leitch suggests, adapting the film by filling these gaps of silence. Interestingly, this effect too is consistent with Tóibín's oeuvre: in his novels, Tóibín often leaves characters physically undescribed, allowing the reader to fill in such details, even as he often forecloses interiority and asks us to "read" characters' behaviors to try to ascertain their emotional inner lives. Such a strategy makes the novel more ripe for continuation—again, in Palmer's terms, whereby "all texts are fragments in the sense that they await gestures of continuation" (76).

In both novel and film, after the tragic death of her sister Rose, Eilis returns to Enniscorthy and gradually acclimates to home. While the force of home and the machinations of her mother pull Eilis into a paradoxically new and old (i.e., scripted) future in Ireland, she seems to swoon toward a life in Enniscorthy, attracted to Jim Farrell and seduced by the ease with which she might fall back into an alternate conventional life. Not presented, at least initially, as "the wrong choice," that conventional life might actually offer up contentment. As in the novel, Jim isn't simply a negative alternative to Tony, but increasingly her time with him is a source of pleasure for her.

Through the use of visual markers, however, Crowley suggests that such pleasures appear as part of what the director has likened to the Land of Oz. In an example of film adaptations drawing from cinema culture and history as well as its primary literary source, Crowley comments in the DVD audio commentary that he was thinking about Dorothy and her friends galloping through the poppy fields when filming Eilis's return to Ireland ("she gets a bit sleepy and dreamy in this section"). As with Dorothy, Eilis is likewise in a narcotic state back in Enniscorthy, drugged by the promise of what had been her life-long expectation of a life and a home in Ireland: "Eilis had always presumed that she would live in the town all her life, as her mother had done, knowing everyone, having the same friends and neighbors, the same routines in the same streets" (29). Crowley's allusion to *The Wizard of Oz*—his idea that Eilis may abandon the agency she had developed in America—becomes especially interesting and salient given both films' use of color to represent the other worlds to which these young women (Dorothy and Eilis) are exposed. If *The Wizard of Oz* seems to question whether Dorothy can bring some of the color and vibrancy of Oz back to Kansas, *Brooklyn* suggests that Eilis may do so to Ireland, when she wears her light blue dress and jaunty sunglasses on her return to Enniscorthy (see Figs. 10.6, 10.7, and 10.8).

Fig. 10.6 Eilis and her sunglasses, catching the attention of passers-by on her return to Enniscorthy

However, such brightness, Crowley suggests, reflects Eilis's impaired vision, her potential blindness to the threat that besets her in succumbing to the seductions of life back in Enniscorthy. For example, "the score and the imagery [at Curricloe Beach are] elegant and so different [from] the first section in Ireland because of course she sees a very different side to it now." As Crowley's emphasis on Eilis's subjective perception highlights, the film presents that perspective as chimeric.

Like the film's re-presentation of the landscape, Eilis's clothes similarly reflect her own self-refashioning. In the yellow dress with which we became familiar in Brooklyn, Crowley simultaneously invokes and subverts a long-standing literary trope—that of the "Returned Yank."[7] This element is also broached in the novel: Eilis-pre-Brooklyn refers to America's "compensating glamour" (33); when she returns after Rose's

---

[7] The "returned Yank" refers to the literary trope of Irish who immigrated to America and then return to Ireland. As Meredith Cary argues, usually in these texts "exiles' dreams make Irish life mythic…but the people they return to remember them as themselves." In contrast, Eilis is received not as herself, but as a reincarnation of Rose, and therefore a kind of cultural placeholder, as we discuss below. "Going Home" 66.

Fig. 10.7 Eilis and Jim Farrell (Domhnall Gleeson) on the beach in Ireland

Fig. 10.8 Eilis and her bright yellow dress

death, she believes that "[n]ow that she was back from America, ...she carried something with her, something close to glamour, which made all the difference to her" (236).[8] Whereas the Returned Yank is predicated on the notion that an immigrant can never really return home, instead being marked as "Other" by his or her American identity, Eilis's Americanness ironically becomes the vehicle that slots her back into her own life—only as Rose: "[I]t was hard not to think that she was Rose's ghost, being fed and spoken to in the same way at the same time by her mother, having her clothes admired using the same words as were used with Rose, and then setting out briskly for work" (227). Eilis's yellow dress marks her as American and yet surprisingly reclaimed as Irish at once, doubling her identification and making Eilis in Ireland not only a ghost of Rose, but also a ghost of her American self.

This develops what Tóibín presented in the novel. Throughout the 2009 text, Tóibín collapses the boundaries between Ireland and Brooklyn, suggesting that culture is a vehicle that binds these locations and uncannily doubles her history. As Kate Costello-Sullivan has argued elsewhere, "Eilis learns that her cultural experiences are permeable and interwoven, just as diasporic communities are intertwined and to a degree inextricable. Eilis cannot escape the influence of her past, as metaphorically embodied in Mrs. Kehoe and Enniscorthy, any more than she can pretend away the personal experiences and roots she has begun to accrue in Brooklyn" (*Mother/Country* 218). Eilis's wardrobe works to capture visually the impact of her time in America and to deconstruct any strict division between her lives in Brooklyn and Enniscorthy. Thus we see the intricately laced white blouse (covered by a white sweater) she wears in her confrontation with Miss Kelly in the film (see first image above), a reference to her identity as a Brooklyn bride—visually blurring the division between Brooklyn and Ireland's Eilises and at the same time reinforcing her decision to honor her vows to Tony.[9]

The collapsing of locales and selves that affects Eilis also applies to setting. With their green landscape and vistas, scenes in Ireland also ghost the earlier scene where Tony shows Eilis the land in Long Island, which he and his brothers have purchased. Uncannily displacing the paradigmatic green of Ireland with unspoken memories of Brooklyn, the film thus again

---

[8] For an analysis of the "Returned Yank" in *Brooklyn*, see Costello-Sullivan, *Mother/Country* 213-215.

[9] For an in-depth analysis of costuming, see "This is Where your Life is."

visually disrupts the unitariness of place, suggesting that the distance between the two is permeable or porous. Of course, this too is thematically consistent with the novel. Just as, in the novel, Eilis believes she sees her father in Brooklyn (90) and learns that Miss Kelly is Mrs. Kehoe's cousin in Ireland (255), the film disrupts the neat divisions between Ireland and Brooklyn, but again it does so visually. In this way, the film extends, even as it remakes and adapts, the novel.

Crowley uses other cinematic tools to show Eilis's acquiescence to a future that would erase her and render her Rose's replacement, especially for her mother—but here, too, Crowley subverts this easy elision by marking her visually as a "Returned Yank," which extends the conceit of the novel. When Eilis goes to her friend Nancy's wedding, the film represents the proleptic call of Eilis's possible future with Jim through the *mise-en-scene*. Cinematically reinforcing the seduction of returning for good to Enniscorthy and marrying Jim Farrell, Crowley's rack focus seen in Figs. 10.9 and 10.10 establishes a visual rhyme between Nancy and George and Eilis and Jim.

Visually shifting the viewer's attention from a medium closeup of Nancy to Eilis and Jim in the pews behind her, Crowley's camera work underlines the social and psychological pressure on Eilis to meet the community's expectations that she marry Jim Farrell and settle back in Enniscorthy. In the novel, this allure of the familiar is palpable:

> The idea that she would leave all this—the rooms of the house once more familiar and warm and comforting—and go back to Brooklyn and not return for a long time again frightened her now. [...] She would face into a life [in Brooklyn] that now seemed an ordeal, with strange people, strange accents, strange streets. (241)[10]

Yet, although film-Eilis is placed in the middle of the community in this way, directly in front of her approving mother, the film subverts this reading. Despite her placement literally in the center of Enniscorthy society, Eilis stands out with her pink-and-white-striped dress and her pink hat,

---

[10] Ironically, of course, readers familiar with Tóibín's canon would know that Eilis's friend Nancy does not live out a small-town fairy tale with George Sheridan; rather, we learn that he dies, leaving her financially strapped with children and burdened with the opinions and expectations of small-town Ireland. See Tóibín, *The Name of the Game.*

Figs. 10.9 and 10.10 Crowley using a rack focus to redirect viewer attention

makeup, and drop earrings. Once again, Eilis's visual markers seem to suggest that her very Americanness is what has placed her where she sits, but as an uncanny double of herself. As Alex Witchel asks in his cogent review of the novel, "A central question for Eilis Lacey in "Brooklyn" is: "Do you relinquish whatever identity you've built to collapse back into (what at least seems) the warm embrace of family and small town that long ago defined you as so much less? And if that is what "home" means, is that where you want to be?" ("Irish Diaspora"). Like her active mind and the linkage of Brooklyn and Enniscorthy through scenery, Eilis's emplacement here is both integrated and disrupted, thus capturing and deepening the sense of dual loyalties and identities we see in the novel.

In considering what the two *Brooklyns* can tell us about adaptation, perhaps the novel's positing of two realms—Brooklyn and Ireland—that are, on the surface, schematically opposed but, finally, deeply interrelated is most important here. Tóibín's story in *Brooklyn* may be seen as an analogue of ostensibly two worlds in adaptation studies—that of the novel and the film—that are revealed to blur inevitably, to extend one another, or to lead to other worlds or realms, contexts, and texts, which further illuminate the story and its aftermath. If Tóibín suggests in *Brooklyn* that culture is portable and that Eilis's journey across the Atlantic will find Irishness in Brooklyn and, later, carry Brooklyn back to Enniscorthy, sources and adaptations similarly cross-pollinate; they mutually inform. Like Eilis, sources travel the turbulent sea toward adaptations, extending the source text, blending with it. Sources and adaptations are the same and different, achieving the kind of uncanniness that Eilis experiences when she sees a ghost of her father in Brooklyn, or indeed, when she feels herself to be a ghost in New York, Rose's ghost, or a ghost of her American self in Ireland. That uncanniness also haunts her when she feels like Tony is a dream or apparition once she is back in Enniscorthy. *Brooklyn* offers in its content an allegory of the importance of discerning and describing the uncanny sameness and difference that characterize textual transformations through adaptation. Analysis of the contexts that inform both novel and film and the world-building achieved by imagining these texts in conversation not only with each other but also with other works of fiction and film highlights the value of thinking about the rich and multiple lives a text—and a self—can live.

WORKS CITED

Barton, Ruth. *Irish Cinema in the Twenty-First Century.* Manchester: Manchester UP, 2019.

Cary, Meredith. "Going Home": The 'Returned Yank' in Irish and Irish-American Fiction." *Colby Quarterly* 29:1 (March 1993): 57–67. Print.

Conner, Marc C., and R. Barton Palmer, eds. *Screening Modern Irish Fiction and Drama.* London: Palgrave Macmillan, 2016.

Costello-Sullivan, Kathleen. "The Irish Oresteia": An interview with Colm Tóibín." *American Journal of Irish Studies* 15 (2018). Print.

———. "The Irish Oresteia": An interview with Colm Tóibín." *American Journal of Irish Studies* 15 Unpublished portion of Interview with Colm Tóibín. May 15, 2017. Simon and Schuster Offices, New York City.

———. *Mother/Country: Politics of the Personal in the Fiction of Colm Tóibín. Reimagining Ireland series 44.* Oxford, Bern, New York: Peter Lang, 2012. Print.

Crowley, John. Audio Commentary. *Brooklyn.* Dir. John Crowley. Perf. Saoirse Ronan, Emory Cohen, Domhnall Gleeson. Fox Searchlight Pictures, 2015. DVD.

Gillespie, Michael Patrick. *The Myth of an Irish Cinema: Approaching Irish-Themed Films.* Syracuse, NY: Syracuse University Press, 2008.

Grossman, Julie. *Literature, Film, and Their Hideous Progeny: Adaptation and ElasTEXTity.* Palgrave Studies in Adaptation and Visual Culture. London: Palgrave Macmillan, 2015. Print.

Grossman, Julie, and R. Barton Palmer. *Adaptation in Visual Culture: Images, Texts, and Their Multiple Worlds.* London: Palgrave Macmillan, 2017.

James, Henry. "The Art of Fiction." *Longman's Magazine* 4 (September 1884), reprinted in *Partial Portraits* (Macmillan, 1888). https://public.wsu.edu/~campbelld/amlit/artfiction.html. Online.

Leitch, Thomas. "Mind the Gaps." In Grossman and Palmer, 53–72.

Newell, Kate. *Expanding Adaptation Networks: From Illustration to Novelization.* London: Palgrave Macmillan, 2017. Print.

Palmer, R. Barton. "Continuation, Adaptation Studies, and the Never-Finished Text." In Grossman and Palmer, 73–100.

Tóibín, Colm. *Brooklyn*. New York: Scribner, Simon and Schuster, 2009. Print.

———. "Name of the Game." *Mothers and Sons* . New York , London, Toronto, Sydney: Scribner, 2007. 51–107. Print.

———. "One Minus One." *Mothers and Sons.* 271–288. Print.

"This is Where Your Life Is: The Costumes of "Brooklyn" and How They Tell the Story in Clothing." *Tom and Lorenzo*, March 30, 2018. https://tomandlorenzo.com/2018/03/The-costumes-of-Brooklyn-movie-fasion/. Accessed 20 May 2018. Online.

Witchel, Alex. "His Irish Diaspora." Book Review, *Brooklyn* by Colm Tóibín. *New York Times Magazine.* April 29, 2009. https://www.nytimes.com/2009/05/03/magazine/03toibin-t.html. Accessed 28 May 2019. Online.

CHAPTER 11

The Program, Seven Deadly Sins, and Stephen Frears

Lesley Brill

Stephen Frears's *The Program* (2015) acknowledges its sources equivocally. The first nod to David Walsh's book *Seven Deadly Sins: My Pursuit of Lance Armstrong* (2012) occurs not in the credits, but in a closing wrap-up of such continuations as "Floyd Landis retired from cycling and is currently assisting the US Government in its case against Lance Armstrong," and "Michele Ferrari has been banned for life from involvement in all competitive sports." In every case, the information is accompanied by photos of the actual persons, not the actors who portrayed them. David Walsh's occurs near the end, just before a photo of a document accompanied by "USADA [United States Anti-Doping Agency]

L. Brill (✉)
English and Film Studies, Wayne State University, Detroit, MI, USA
e-mail: lbrill@wayne.edu

© The Author(s), under exclusive license to Springer Nature
Switzerland AG 2022
M. C. Conner et al. (eds.), *Screening Contemporary Irish Fiction and Drama*, Palgrave Studies in Adaptation and Visual Culture,
https://doi.org/10.1007/978-3-031-04568-4_11

Reasoned Decision Document ... was invaluable in the making of this film."[1]

When Walsh's turn comes, he receives a less than enthusiastic encomium: "David Walsh, whose book *Seven Deadly Sins* helped inform the making of this film ...." Given that Walsh plays a major role in *The Program*, his lukewarm acknowledgment is surprising. By contrast, the USADA document is never shown or quoted from directly; it is referred to only twice, once in a clip from a "Today" show and briefly in an intense confrontation between Lance Armstrong and several USADA officials.

During the closing credits, however, David Walsh and *Seven Deadly Sins* receive a warmer citation. "INSPIRED BY THE BOOK 'SEVEN DEADLY SINS' BY DAVID WALSH." Given this second acknowledgment and many direct borrowings from Walsh's work, *The Program* clearly counts as an adaptation of *Seven Deadly Sins*.

The additions and deletions the film makes to the book are nothing unusual for such adaptations, but *The Program* revises *Seven Deadly Sins* unusually by altering its structure and its genre: Walsh's work combines the genres of detective novels, memoirs, and narratives of discoveries. The screenplay that derives from *Seven Deadly Sins*, on the other hand, is structured as a tragedy, with Lance Armstrong (Ben Foster) the protagonist who rises only to fall. As a result, the roles of Armstrong and Walsh (Chris O'Dowd) change: Armstrong becomes the sole central figure while Walsh acts as a sort of combined Fury and Chorus—or, as Armstrong calls him, "that little troll." The trajectory of Walsh's action in the film contrasts sharply with Armstrong's, moving from his early frustrations and outright dismissals to eventual vindication. This aspect of his role, as one would expect, figures more importantly in *Seven Deadly Sins* than in *The Program*.

Despite a few setbacks and hints of trouble to come, the direction of Armstrong's career (en route to the final catastrophe) trends ascendant. We see him in the film's first sequence as an unidentified solitary bicyclist toiling up a steep hill. Not much later, he wins an important European race. That triumph is quickly followed by a potentially lethal setback:

---

[1] Released on October 10, 2012, the first paragraph and the beginning of the second read as follows: "Today, we are sending the 'Reasoned Decision' in the Lance Armstrong case and supporting information to the Union Cycliste International .... The evidence shows beyond any doubt that the US Postal Service Pro Cycling Team ran the most sophisticated, professionalized and successful doping program that sport has ever seen.

The evidence of the US Postal Service Pro Cycling Team-run scheme is overwhelming and is in excess of 1000 pages ...".

coughing blood in the shower, a diagnosis of metastasized testicular cancer, cranial operations, and chemotherapy. Soon thereafter, in one of only a few comic sequences, he begins his re-ascent. Struggling alone up another steep highway, he is briefly joined by a female bike rider. As she passes him, he attempts to keep up. "Are we racing?" she asks, increasing her pace. Disappearing from the frame, she calls back, "You've got a lot of work to do, buddy." An exhausted Armstrong flops onto the grass beside the road. (This incident and several others during his illness and recovery appear to have been entirely created for Frears's film.)

As the movie continues, Armstrong returns to bicycle racing with sensational rapidity. He and his team win the 1999 Tour de France. A montage sequence shows him winning the 2000 and 2001 Tours and getting married. Another montage covers his victories in the 2002–2004 Tours. In the last, he shares the podium with his small children.

In the midst of these athletic and personal successes, he becomes an almost mythic figure, one who can bestow life and ameliorate sorrow: "You made me live, Lance Armstrong," says an admirer. In a pediatric hospital, he takes time from his schedule to sit patiently on the bed of an acutely ill, depressed young boy undergoing chemotherapy. As Armstrong waits and speaks quietly, the boy finally smiles.[2]

The public ascent of Armstrong and his private successes chart a course for the tragic hero that structures Frears's film, but is only hinted at in Walsh's book. Those hints, nonetheless, are telling. Walsh writes, "His time for tears would come. What's meant to be always finds a way" (301). At the head of his final chapter, he inserts an epigram from F. Scott Fitzgerald: "Show me a hero, and I will write you a tragedy."

Armstrong's fall is foreshadowed by the insertion of a brief sequence in which a dozen rifle-bearing carabinieri confront Michele Ferrari (Guillaume Canet), the supervisor of Armstrong's drug regimen. More prefigurations of the hero's collapse are associated with Floyd Landis (Jesse Plemons), who hovers ambivalently and then disgustedly over the second half of the film. His change of "perspective" ultimately exposes, as he says, "everything."

During an inspirational talk to supporters of his anti-cancer foundation, "Live Strong," Armstrong describes "Dead Man's Hole ... a mineral

---

[2] Frears reuses this sequence, in most of its details, from his earlier film, *Hero.* (1992) There, however, the ironies are quite different: the inspirational fake hero becomes in his pretense a genuine one; Lance Armstrong, never a true hero, will eventually be revealed as a liar.

pool. ... And as I stood at the edge of the cliff, I could see, It's a long way down." (We have earlier seen that place when Armstrong, after his cancer diagnosis, gazes into it as he contemplates the likely end of his career and, perhaps, of his life.) Shortly following this speech, he makes the announcement that indirectly leads to his exposure, "I'm coming back." At the end of the film, a disgraced Armstrong returns to Dead Man's Hole, alone again, and puts to the test that "long way down" by leaping into the water below. Then, in the last shot of the narrative, he reprises the opening by riding slowly up another steep hill, by himself. One thinks of Macbeth, Oedipus, King Lear, and others, devastated and isolated (or dead) at the end of their tragedies.

The Program does not dwell on its protagonist's pain, but portrays it affectingly in Ben Foster's most powerful scene. At first defiantly confronting officials of the USADA, Armstrong is near tears in a speech as much to himself as to his auditors. Reflecting on his lifetime ban from all competition, he cannot imagine what reason he will have to get out of bed in the morning, "it's [competing] my whole life. It's what I do." As he then stands silent, Frears inserts an extraordinary shot: In medium closeup the camera pans to the left until Armstrong is in the extreme right of the frame; it then reverses that movement until he is in the extreme left. As it pans forth and back it underscores his solitude; no other human being appears on the screen.

Against the shape of Lance Armstrong's story, Frears and his screenwriter John Hodge set a countermovement, the David Walsh subplot. His story, the center of *Seven Deadly Sins*, has a comic trajectory. From an early enthusiasm for Armstrong's ambition and competitive personality, Walsh grows increasingly suspicious, then disillusioned. At the same time, the naivete of most of his colleagues in the media, the public adoration for the conquering, cancer-surviving hero, and counterattacks from Armstrong all serve to isolate and discourage him. The world's rejection of his warnings about Everyone's Hero are easily understood. As Walsh explained in a recent interview, the Armstrong saga was "the most feel-good story maybe we'd ever known in sport."[3] Walsh's career sinks as Armstrong's soars. But that will change, and he will not only regain what he has lost, but also emerge as entirely justified.

His first encounter with Armstrong—an interview conducted over a game of foosball, which he loses—would seem to presage future losses

---

[3] https://www.youtube.com/watch?v=bkARvYIwT8E.

when he attempts to persuade the cycling world of Armstrong's probable doping. Early on, however, he tells his journalistic colleagues that the young American has the makings of a winner. As he writes in *Seven Deadly Sins*, "I just got into the lift on the ground floor with a guy who was going up." (6) After Armstrong returns from cancer and turns into "the greatest climber I've ever seen," Walsh becomes convinced that such a transformation could not occur without pharmaceutical aid. His editor (Peter Wight) at *The Sunday Times*, however, needs proof, "What does it all add up to? Nothing." At the same time, the rest of the media, in the press and on TV, either ignore him or regard him as a Grinch trying to spoil Christmas. The Walsh subplot, the story of his Armstrong story, hits bottom when, acting on a clearly implied threat from Johan Bruyheel (Denis Menozhet), the manager of Armstrong's team, the sports reporters with whom he shares a car expel him. During a press conference, Armstrong skillfully turns Walsh's skepticism into an attack on Live Strong. Concurrently, *The Sunday Times*, having printed some of Walsh's allegations, loses a defamation lawsuit, has to pay a large fine, and is forced to print a humiliating retraction.

During this time, as Walsh writes in *Seven Deadly Sins*, the reporter can see only a dismal "road ahead [that] seemed to stretch forever." (285) He reports a level of discouragement greater than anything portrayed in *The Program*: His closest friend urges him to "get a bit more balance in your working life." (293) Shortly thereafter, when Armstrong retires from racing, he considers that to be "an opportunity for me to let go the story." (298) At the same time, Armstrong has attained the summit of his international celebrity.

From this nadir, in accord with the conventions of comic narratives, Walsh's prospects unexpectedly turn upward. An anonymous telephone informant urges him to "call Betsy Andreu (Elaine Cassidy)." When he does, she describes the hospital scene in 1996 when she heard Armstrong recite to a physician the list of performance-enhancing drugs he has taken in his career to date: "testosterone, EPO, growth hormone, other steroids." At this point in the film, Frears repeats and enlarges a scene he began forty-five minutes earlier. This surprising repetition fills in the details of Armstrong's long history of doping, and it marks the beginning of David Walsh's ascent and his quarry's ultimate downfall.

A voice-over further underlines the importance of the reporter's conversation with Betsy Andreu, "Now he starts to attract the dissidents. ...

And then there was Stephen Smart."[4] Smart was an early accuser. His accusations led Armstrong to call him "a liar with mental issues." Like David Walsh, he eventually attracts the attention of the Tailwind company, the corporate owner of Armstrong's United States Postal Service team. Tailwind is threatened with owing Armstrong huge bonuses if he continues to win The Tour—which, of course, we know he will. To guard against that risk, it brings in an insurance company headed by Bob Hamman (Dustin Hoffman), which assumes, for a premium, those risks. Thus two important entities have a strong financial incentive to reveal Armstrong's cheating, in order to recover the money he has received from them. Eventually, they succeed.[5]

The Sunday Times also recovers the funds it was forced to pay, and presumably retracts its original retraction and apology. Walsh's suspicions are fully confirmed and he is back in the good graces of his employer and his colleagues. "David Walsh continues to report on cycling and other sports," we are informed in the updates that follow the main film.

The second main subplot of *The Program*, Floyd Landis's, runs not in contrast to Armstrong's but parallel with it, as a sort of condensed version. It also becomes part of Armstrong's story. Introduced roughly half-way through the film, some of its details come from *Seven Deadly Sins* and some are invented in order to support the central story of Armstrong's tragic rise and fall.

Like Armstrong, Landis wins the Tour; and, like Armstrong in the end, he is "caught." When he joins the USPS team, Armstrong himself carefully instructs him in the details of their doping program, and the film follows with shots of Landis obeying Armstrong's orders. Again like Armstrong, he eventually recants his lies; not to Oprah on TV but to the USADA. When he arrives at their offices to confess "everything," he begins by stating his name and profession. The USADA official cuts him off, "I know who you are." His words repeat exactly those of Ferrari when Armstrong approaches him early in his career: "I'm Lance Armstrong." "I know who you are."

---

[4] This voice-over is unique in the film because it is not assigned to an obvious speaker. It may or may not be David Walsh's voice, but even if we assume it is, the use of the third person—"He starts to attract …"—argues against that hypothesis.

[5] Since his confession, Armstrong has faced myriad other financial consequences, but only one, Nike's canceling of its contract with him, is noted in the film.

After Landis wins the Tour, he is asked during a post-race television press conference if he used drugs. He hesitates before answering: "I'll say no to that."[6] As Walsh writes, "Floyd Landis was a bad liar, which suggested he might not be a bad person" (348), a view that *The Program* partly endorses.

Immediately after the shots of Landis applying the performance-enhancing drugs that Armstrong gave him, Frears flashes back to his youth in a pious, conservative Mennonite community. As a result of his upbringing—both *The Program* and *Seven Deadly Sins* imply—he remains uncomfortable with drug use and, especially, lying. He uneasily watches his team leader lie on TV, and he is angered when he discovers that the team has sold some of its bicycles to pay for pharmaceuticals—a way of keeping those purchases off its financial records. When Armstrong bullies another rider who has testified against Michele Ferrari, Landis has a brief argument with him, "I wouldn't have done that." After showing him strenuously protesting his innocence to a gathering of the people of Farmersville, his home town, the camera follows him into a private setting, in which he appears ambivalent and sad. A point-of-view closeup shows the embroidered wall hanging that we've seen earlier: THE RIGHTEOUS WILL RISE TO ETERNAL LIFE / WITH GOD / AND THE UNRIGHTEOUS TO HELL / AND SEPARATION FROM GOD.

Yet neither *Seven Deadly Sins* nor *The Program* paint Landis as wholly virtuous in his renunciation. Both show—*The Program* more emphatically—that he was willing to continue his denials and return to racing, until the fraternity of riders and Armstrong in particular reject him. His confession is thus partly a matter of clearing his conscience, partly a matter of anger at his rejection, and even revenge.

Although *The Program* changes the plot structure of *Seven Deadly Sins*, it takes to the screen Walsh's views of the characters. *The Program* offers three keys to its hero's personality: he's intensively competitive, he's a bully, and he's a liar. The opening credits are accompanied by a voice-over, which we can infer is Armstrong's, talking about the Tour de France and himself: "It's the hardest sporting event in the world. One-hundred-eighty riders ... and only one gets to wear the Yellow Jersey. ... Physically,

---

[6] He added, "The problem I have here again is that most of the public has an idea about cycling because of the way things have gone in the past. So I'll say no, knowing a lot of people are going to assume I'm guilty before I've had a chance to defend myself" (348). The film omits this explanation.

I'm not more gifted than anybody else; it's just this desire, this hunger. My mom didn't raise a quitter, and I would never quit. ... That's heart, that's soul, that's just guts." Cut to a young Lance Armstrong exulting in triumph at foosball over the journalist, David Walsh. When he wins, he raises his arms, precisely the same gesture he uses when he crosses the finish line in winning races and, for that matter, when he sinks a putt at miniature golf.

Armstrong's win-at-any-cost personality attracts Ferrari, despite his telling his future client that he was "born to lose" because of his limited VO2 Max (Cardio-vascular capacity to deliver oxygen to his muscles). Ferrari asks, "What matters to you, Lance?" "Winning." "What else?" "Love my Mom." "More than winning?" Revealingly, Armstrong doesn't answer the last question.

Besides his willingness to do anything to win, Armstrong's success depends upon his ability to lie, constantly and persuasively. We see him testing variations of his endlessly repeated line in front of a mirror, "I have never tested positive for performance-enhancing drugs." Frears cuts to a press conference where Armstrong delivers the favored version. Addressing followers of his anti-cancer foundation, he lies about an incident in which, recovering from his own cancer, he was struggling to walk down the hospital hall and was offered the relief of a wheelchair. "And I said, 'Thanks but no thanks, I'm going to walk.' And I did. I didn't give up." Here Frears inserts a shot of his audience nodding in approval, looking variously admiring, thoughtful, and deeply moved. But, as the film has already shown, Armstrong did in fact accept the nurse's offer.

Leaving his applauding audience, he enters another hall, where he remembers, in flashback, the real event. There he meets his future wife, who tells him, "You're brave." He seems about to confess his alteration of the truth when he notices that the speaker is a pretty young woman. He pauses and offers a more ambiguous response, "I just tell them what they want to hear," an explanation that applies equally to the media.

After his retirement from racing, he continues to raise funds by telling commercial lies. On an elaborate set, he praises "Scotch Whiskey" and takes an appreciative sip. Then, after the camera is turned off, he remarks, "This shit tastes like apple juice." Promoting "Flake o' Wheats," he declares, "Not only tastes great, it's good for you." He shovels a spoonful into his mouth, "Mmmm." "Cut!" He immediately spits it out, looking as if he's about to vomit.

Only rarely does he show any regret or ambivalence about his lying. The most notable occasion comes when the woman at a book signing says to him, "You made me live, Lance Armstrong. That's who you are." But, as in the hospital hall story, he knows otherwise. That's not who he is; and occasionally he seems to feel regret about pretending otherwise.

Another ameliorating aspect of his behavior comes when he decides that he'd like to set up a charity for helping cancer sufferers and funding cancer research. His altruism is uncomplicated by other motives, "I want to do something that helps people who are in the same situation that I was." His agent, Bill Stapleton (Lee Pace), shows little concern about Armstrong's making "a difference" but seizes on the idea as a public relations ploy, "Wow! That's good, that's great! ... If you're speaking for athletes and cancer, that's potent! ... You could be in a Pepsi commercial!" Sincere as Armstrong's philanthropic desire may be, he soon compromises his foundation by enlisting it to support his sterling, "never-tested-positive" public persona.

The third note in the tonic chord of Armstrong's personality is his inclination to bully. When another racer in the peloton (the entire group of riders) tells Walsh that doping remains endemic, Armstrong seeks him out during the next race to warn him against saying such things to reporters, "Maybe you just go home, get another job." Other members of the peloton join in the threatening that the man in the Yellow Jersey initiated: "Get to the back," "Keep your mouth shut," and unintelligible remarks evidently to the same effect. In another stage of the race, he approaches a rider named Simioni, "It was a mistake to testify against Ferrari. I have the money and the power to destroy you."

Given his wealth and influence, lawsuits offer Armstrong a further avenue for intimidation. As to Emma O'Reilly, who has also affirmed his doping, he tells his agent, "make her look like an alcoholic whore ... And if that doesn't shut her up, hit her with a lawsuit, and then another one, and then another one after that ... until she shuts her fucking whore mouth." He further instructs Stapleton to "Sue David Walsh, and his crummy little English newspaper."

Further flexing his bully's muscles, Armstrong sends surrogates to do his thuggery. He uses Stapleton to threaten Betsy Andreu through her husband Frankie (Edward Hogg). Confronted with the threat that doping officials might release the news that they have observed a "borderline" test result for Armstrong, he unleashes the fluent Stockton again, "Lance ... is single handedly transforming your shitty little Eurosport into a globally significant brand." Abashed, the official acknowledges, "No one appreciates Lance more than we do." The punches having been landed, Armstrong closes the meeting confidently, "I think you should do whatever you think is best for the integrity of cycling." The story is quashed. As has been noted, it is the team manager who bullies the reporters with whom Walsh has been traveling to get him expelled from their car.

Armstrong's last, futile attempt at bullying takes place during an interview with officials of the USADA. "I get a lifetime ban? Bullshit! I'm gonna help you clean up cycling and I'm gonna compete again. ... You're a bunch of amateurs!" The panel doesn't respond until they dismiss him, entirely defeated.

In addition to its tragic central story, *The Program* devotes considerable attention to what could be called its educational project, giving ordinary viewers the information they need to understand the Tour, its importance, and the specifics of performance-enhancing drugs. Walsh's book shares with the film the need to cater to a general audience, and so shares also its educational mission. Walsh, however, adds an interest in the history of sports doping more broadly, a topic the movie drops.[7]

The first words of the opening voice-over, and the accompanying images, begin the viewer's education. As the credits and the voice-over continue, a succession of action clips of the Tour, both contemporary and historical, fill the screen. Such montages will recur as representations of Armstrong's Tour victories, especially those of 2000 and 2001 and 2003 and 2004. Besides their narrative function, they steep the audience in the beauty, pageantry, and danger of the Tour de France. They include also images and words of an enthralled media. Even if most of its audience knew little of bicycle racing before seeing the film, they will understand the fascination of the Tour its worldwide reach by the end.

And its culture of performance-enhancing drugs. That aspect of the film's educational component begins as Armstrong waits with other riders at the beginning of his first important European race. A title announces "Belgium, 1994." Another rider, Johan Bruyheel, who will later manage Armstrong's USPS team, recognizes him, "Hey, you're the American. ... You won all those races in America. ... But you don't win here. See that

---

[7] For example, in *Seven Deadly Sins*, Walsh discusses with his editor the cases of two Olympic sprinters, Marlene Ottey and Marion Jones, who were eventually exposed as having doped and were stripped of their medals.

guy over there, and that guy, and probably that guy over there? They've got more red cells in their blood, more oxygen. You cannot win."

Indeed he does not. Nor does he finish second or third. Those places are occupied by members of the same team as the winner. Their doctor is Michele Ferrari. During a press conference after the race, a reporter asks the physician if his riders use EPO [Erythropoietin, a drug that stimulates red blood cell production]. Ferrari shrugs, "If a rider uses EPO, does not scandalize me. ... EPO is not dangerous, it's abuse that is."

After the race and press conference, Armstrong goes to Ferrari, asking to be on his "program." Ferrari rejects him because he has too much weight in the muscles of his chest and arms; his "ratio is all wrong."

Unable to enroll with Ferrari, Armstrong and his teammates set out on their own. In another of the rare comic sequences in the film, they go to a pharmacy in Switzerland, where EPO can be purchased without a prescription. Like bashful high school boys buying condoms, they attempt to make their purchase look "natural" by starting with other items: aspirin, a toothbrush, and diapers(!). Armstrong, wondering what is taking them so long, enters and cuts the camouflage, "Erythropoietin, EPO, Epogen, that's what this man wants." The salesgirl turns back to the tongue-tied team member, "So, how much would you like?" "I don't really—hesitates—a lot?"

The shots that follow this sequence show Armstrong winning his first race in Europe. The implication is clear; the visit to the Swiss pharmacy has everything to do with that victory.

After Armstrong's recovery from cancer—the chemo "diet" has thinned his upper body—he returns to Ferrari, who this time accepts him. As Armstrong pedals on a stationary bike, hooked to various monitors and a face mask with a tube to collect his exhalations, Ferrari explains to him how his drugs work. He begins by asking, "What's your VO2 Max?"

A: 84.
F: What does that mean?
A: It's my maximum Oxygen consumption
F: Literally, yes. But what it really means is that you were born to lose [to racers who can] deliver more fuel than you.

He continues by describing the application of science to athletic training. But "after a while, I thought we had exhausted the science." An inserted closeup focuses on a box of a dozen ampules of EPO. "And then, I tell you, Lance, it was like a heavenly vision."

Whence the vision? In the midst of these explanations, Frears flashes back to a conference on the medical use of Erythropoietin, with Ferrari in attendance. He asks the speaker "if any assessment has been made of the effect of this drug on healthy individuals ... athletes, for example." She is unaware of any such research, and Ferrari continues that such use "should equate to a corresponding improvement in athletic performance." "Doctor," she replies, "I think it would be unethical." Ferrari looks skeptical, "Would it?"

The film returns to the fictional present, as Ferrari continues his explanation. "No longer were we confined to the limits of physiology. ... No longer confined to earth; now we had learned to fly." We may, at this point, recall an earlier legendary figure, Icarus, who also learned to fly, and who finally flew too high and crashed back to earth. As Ferrari injects a sweating Armstrong with EPO, rock music takes over the sound track: "Mr. Pharmacist, can you help me out today?"

The illegality of sports doping and Armstrong's evasion of detection occupies significant space in *The Program*. That theme begins with the recreation of a notorious Belgian border crossing during the 1998 Tour. An inspector discovered massive amounts of EPO and other performance-enhancing drugs bound for one of the racing teams, a discovery that eventually implicated other teams and racers as well.

We hear Armstrong requesting that a doctor back date a prescription in order to generate an acceptable explanation for a positive test for steroids; he suggests treatment of "saddle sores." When he puts down the phone, he remarks to his masseuse, "Now you know enough to bring me down." The adulation of the media and its desire to assure everyone that cycling, and the USPS team in particular, is "clean" is cross-cut with shots of Armstrong and his team members injecting themselves, swallowing drugs, and discarding used syringes. When a testing official arrives unexpectedly at the team bus, he is stalled outside while Bruyheel infuses Armstrong with a saline solution in order to pass the test.

The alternative to doping? Talent. Ferrari tells Armstrong that the previous American winner of the Tour, Greg LeMond, had a VO2 Max of 93, far higher than his. In *Seven Deadly Sins*, LeMond gets substantial attention, both as a racer and as someone who publicly "regrets" Armstrong's association with Ferrari. As a result of the latter, Armstrong attacked him and his business, as Walsh reports, doing him significant financial damage.

In *The Program*, LeMond gets little attention, but the other time the film notices him is telling: If one watches the end of the opening montage carefully, one can see LeMond on the podium as the winner of an earlier Tour.

Any discussion of *The Program* would be incomplete without noting the many aspects that mark it as a film by Stephen Frears: deft storytelling, uniformly excellent performances by its actors, precise pacing, and the use of pop songs on the sound track as commentary. His most emphatic signatures are visual: dramatically slanted framings and consistent use of signifying colors.

Frears uses tilted frames dozens of times throughout *The Program*. He has used this visual trope in other films, but never so insistently. It is a technique he probably inherited from Alfred Hitchcock, who employed it more sparingly, usually to suggest that something is awry. For *The Program*, heavy use of slanted shots is fitting for a story of crooked behavior.

A few examples suggest the variety of the tilted scenes. The last shot of the 1999 Tour is strongly slanted, as are shots of the media coverage of the 2003 and 2004 Tours. When Armstrong meets Ferrari at his RV on an obscure country road in order to give blood for later re-injection, Frears inserts a tilted framing. A series of sharply slanted shots shows Floyd Landis telephoning Armstrong to ask that he be reinstated on Armstrong's team. But as the movie cuts between the speakers, Frears makes the sequence ironic: the once-caught Landis in tilts, the more guilty but never-tested-positive Armstrong sprawled in straightforward shots on a king-sized bed, watching television.

Insistently, Frears saturates *The Program* with blue, the signal color of Armstrong's "Blue Train." Yellow, the color of the jersey of Tour leaders and winners, is also deployed systematically. It is the hue of all of the credits and all of the numerous informative subtitles. Red, a color that dominates some of Frears's earlier films, appears prominently in only a few scenes, but they are important ones. As is usual for color films internationally, red in *The Program* signifies "danger," "alert."

After his team celebrates a winning race, a showering Armstrong coughs brilliant red blood, a symptom that leads to the diagnosis of metastasized testicular cancer. A second prominent use of red appears when, early in his recovery from the cranial surgery and chemo that follow, he is visited by Betsy and Frankie Andreu. A doctor asks Armstrong about any history he may have of using performance-enhancing drugs. Frears does not let us hear his answer—as we have seen, that comes later in a flashback—but instead he cuts to the couple descending a flight of stairs after ending their visit. "What is this?" asks a shocked Betsy, "You knew about that?" "Yes." "And what about you?" Frankie doesn't answer; his wife shakes her head in shocked disapproval and continues downstairs by herself. The entire scene takes place in front of a solid red wall.

"The dream," Armstrong says in the opening voice-over, is to wear the Yellow Jersey at the end of the Tour. In addition to using yellow exclusively for its credits and subtitles, *The Program* is replete with shots, both from media coverage and staged for the movie, of the present leader of the Tour in the "*Maillot Jaune*." The podium and the stage at the end of Armstrong's humiliating (for him) third place finish in his comeback Tour are totally yellow. The winner wears not only the yellow jersey but yellow shorts and socks as well. Two young women carrying flowers for the winners do so in yellow dresses.

In general, scenes with a predominantly yellow cast carry positive overtones. Notably, when Landis goes to the offices of the USADA to make his confession, the sign on the door has a yellow background; a painting behind the desk of the official who greets him has a predominately yellow cast. Next to the desk stands an American flag with a brilliant yellow fringe. The office furniture is yellow.

Most significant are the colors of a framed embroidery work that Landis grew up with in his intensely religious community. Its motto is on a yellow background, with a pair of lighter yellow flowers in the right lower corner and a similarly colored small house in the left. Its words are in a warning red. We see this motto when Landis gazes at it shortly before his "perspective has changed" and he makes his full confession. But the embroidery also contains some blue, which may remind us that Landis's decision to come clean was made with mixed motives.

Blue overwhelmingly tints *The Program*. A few instances: In darkness and wearing a blue sweatshirt, Lance Armstrong ponders whether to dope. Having decided affirmatively, he goes in the next shot to approach Ferrari, "I wanna be like one of your guys. I wanna be on whatever program they're on." He is wearing a blue jersey and blue jeans; Ferrari is dressed all in blue. Celebrating their first win, the members of Armstrong's team are wearing blue tee shirts.

Blue is associated with doping and lying; it also dominates the scenes of Armstrong's diagnosis and treatment of his cancer. Outlining his strategy for winning the Tour, he concludes, "We'll be a blue train," while images

11 *THE PROGRAM, SEVEN DEADLY SINS*, AND STEPHEN... 213

of ten blue clad racers fill the screen. The next shot is of the TV coverage of the race: "Welcome to the 86th Tour de France." On the screen, the words "Tour de France" appear in yellow, surrounded by a deep blue background.

Floyd Landis is wearing a purple sweatshirt when Bruyheel approaches him about joining the USPS team. He is dressed all in blue after he joins and Armstrong introduces him to the drug regimen. A little later, the movie flashes back to his youthful beginnings as a bike rider. He sneaks out of his home at night and rides through the woods, where he crashes. As he lies there, his father finds him. His parent reminds him that "riding a bike for pleasure is against the tenets of our religion." All in blue, in darkness Frears renders as blue, Landis can only answer, "I know that, Dad." A moment later, we see the framed motto describing the fates of "the righteous" and "the unrighteous."

An especially strong example of the association of blue with performance-enhancing drugs involves Dr. Ferrari. As he describes his researches into athletic training, his fear that science had gone as far as it could, and then his discovery of EPO, he tells Armstrong, "It was like a vision, a heavenly vision. When God spoke to Paul, that is how it felt to me. Lacrima Christi." While he speaks, Frears photographs him in semi-closeup, including the blue collar of his jacket. His teeth are tinted blue from the blue light pervading his laboratory, and his glasses and the pupils of his eyes have blue highlights. His words are religious, but the image approaches the demonic. Ferrari's knowledge has more to do with a snake in Eden than with God speaking to Paul. In the blue light of Ferrari's lab, with a blue mask covering most of his face, Lance Armstrong pedals on a stationary bike draped with a blue towel.

As this typical-for-Frears handling of color suggests, *The Program* remains a characteristic film for a strong director who has made at least seventeen movies adapted from works of fiction or memoirs. Among the better known are *Philomena* (2013), *High Fidelity* (2000), and *Dangerous Liaisons* (1988). Beyond its status as an adaptation, *The Program* stands as a work by a cinematic auteur, a significant portion of whose oeuvre consists of similar films, several based on contemporary Irish writers, including *The Snapper* (1993) and *The Van* (1996) from Roddy Doyle's The Barrytown Trilogy.

Like all of Frear's movies that have such origins, episodes in *The Program* condense, omit, or enlarge those in *Seven Deadly Sins*. The film also adds new material. The structure of the plot, though not its content, is radically altered from book to movie; *The Program* turns Walsh's straightforward account of his pursuit of Armstrong into a modern version of classical tragedy. In the relation between the two works, the film nonetheless remains true to the spirit of the book. More accurately than "an adaptation," *The Program* could be called a collaboration, the outcome of cooperation between Walsh's book and the screenwriter, cinematographer, editor, and the rest of the entire production crew of the film. Guiding that collaboration in its aspects large and small, we can identify the unseen figure of the director.

CHAPTER 12

The Immutable and Un-retrievable in the Diasporic Films of John Michael and Martin McDonagh

Eamonn Jordan

INTRODUCTION

John Michael McDonagh (b. 1967) and his brother Martin (b.1970) were born in London to parents who had emigrated from Ireland to England in the 1960s to find work. Whether to categorise the McDonaghs as second-generation Irish, English, London-Irish or Anglo-Irish writers is not as important as to understand that both brothers have strong diasporic connections and affiliations with Ireland, its history and culture. Still, as London-born, it is surprising that such a large amount of their creative output is dependent on Irish settings, mainly West of Ireland (Galway and Sligo) or is centred on Irish characters in non-Irish locations.

In works by both brothers set outside of Ireland, the films involve numerous first- and/or second-generation Irish characters, including the

---

E. Jordan (✉)
University College Dublin, Dublin, Ireland
e-mail: eamonn.jordan@ucd.ie

© The Author(s), under exclusive license to Springer Nature
Switzerland AG 2022
M. C. Conner et al. (eds.), *Screening Contemporary Irish Fiction and Drama*, Palgrave Studies in Adaptation and Visual Culture,
https://doi.org/10.1007/978-3-031-04568-4_12

215

216   E. JORDAN

eponymous Australian outlaw/rebel hero and his family central to John Michael's screenplay for *Ned Kelly* (2003) or his Irish hoodlum Pádraic Power who appears in *War on Everyone* (2016), a film set in Albuquerque. Martin's *In Bruges* (2008) has two Irish-born hitmen holding up in a Belgian city, and Los Angeles is the base for an Irish screenwriter in *Seven Psychopaths* (2012). And Martin's *Three Billboards Outside of Ebbing, Missouri* (2017) has a lead character with an Irish name, Hayes.

Both brothers share very complex diasporic, post-colonial, working-class and cosmopolitan identities, further complicated by the religious instruction they received in their early years. They were reared initially in London's Elephant and Castle, in pre-fabricated homes, where almost all of their neighbours were Irish, and where few of their friends were English. Both were educated in Catholic affiliated schools. John Michael served as an altar boy and Martin sang in the choir of their church, and both were encouraged to play Gaelic games, and spent their summer holidays in Ireland (Cummins, 2014 and Buckley 2014). On occasion, visiting family members spoke Irish in their home.

They were early school leavers, John at 17, and in 1994, he "won a fellowship to study screenwriting at the University of Southern California" (Chambers, 2018). Martin also finished school without sitting for final exams, had a series of part-time jobs, and did a lot of writing, including an estimated 22 radio plays rejected by the British Broadcasting Corporation (BBC). Literary influences are multiple, and film played a crucial role in their formation as writers as various interviews acknowledge (O'Toole, 1998, Chambers, 2018, and Cummins 2014).

The Irish diaspora in Britain is often (and sometimes incorrectly) associated with a peculiar nostalgia for an originary homeplace that regularly sits alongside an antagonism towards or rejection of that same place. Avtar Brah notes, "the intersectionality of Diaspora, border, and dis/location as a point of confluence of economic, political, cultural and psychic processes. It addressed the global condition of culture, economics and politics as a site of 'migrancy' and 'travel' which seriously problematizes the subject position of the 'native'" (181). How polyvocality and poly-locationality afford both McDonagh brothers subversive framing of the diasporic turn is evident in the combining of "multi-locationality across time and space" (190), "geographical, cultural and psychic boundaries" (194).

Accordingly, diasporic individuals tend to be more attentive to markers of diversity and face more challenges and greater difficulties in working through plural, comparative and rival modes of cultural and socio/

political consciousnesses and value systems. Specifically, diasporic communities are often more alert to the events of their history, and the implications of Ireland's 800-year history of colonial occupation, religious persecution, and political and military dominance. Collective and individual impacts on those subjugated would include humiliation, shame, hatred, anger, exclusion and revenge: the cultural, philosophical, economic and political violations that post-colonial scholars have variously mapped. The close proximity and mobility between both Ireland and Britain complicate the interconnection.

Traditionally, especially from the late 1940s forward, people moved from Ireland because of adventure, opportunity, exclusion, banishment or poverty to the place of the traditional enemy/occupier. Marked in many instances as distinctively and prejudicially "other" in the towns and cities of Britain, meant that for Irish migrants assimilation, if that was an objective, was not easily achieved in a society structured and keen to maintain differential, discriminatory and ranked relationships that benefitted themselves. Each of these complicating factors created particular obstructions, inequalities and uncertainties but also opportunities, inciting self-invention and self-determination. If somewhat deemed alien and other, the Irish did their own stereotyping, partially as an act of resistance, partly out of a reflexive need to strike back. Such dynamics were often complicated by friendships, work, cultural and leisure activities, and interpersonal relationships. That prejudicial socio/political landscape changed over time.

For first- and second-generation Irish, living with comparative, rival and contradictory sets of values, ideologies and belief structures ensure that there is little that is singularly uniform or normative about socio-cultural, political and economic identity formation. (That summation applies not only to the Irish, but to migrants from all other nations.) Both writers similarly and differently exploit the historic, modern and popular cultural linkages between conceptions of Irishness and the moral imperatives of Roman Catholicism, while also exploring how various markers and iconography of this Christian faith prompt questions about values, morals and social obligation in a twenty-first century, globalised world. Both writers make no claim or call on Catholicism as practising members of that faith (See Cummins 2014 and O'Toole 1998).

The primary focus of this essay is the sensibilities of sacrifice and the sacrament of penance; actions where characters chose to die on behalf of others in ways that link to notions of altruism, redemption, salvation or transcendence, or make unfiltered or unadorned admissions under the seal of confession, associated with moral conscience, guilt, judgement, penance, purification and absolution. Moreover, associated issues of disclosure linked to internal reflective narratives (voice-overs), interpersonal revelations or mock confessions reiterate the linkage between language and symbolic acts of truth utterance.

Larger arguments about individual and collective culpability are partially grounded in the revelations about clerical sexual abuse that have, more broadly, haunted the global Catholic Church. The types of revulsion that such violations draw out, more particularly as markers of definitive differentiation, in terms of the harm done to the innocent, is one often denied under the umbrella notion of postmodernism's relativism that provokes, prompts and haunts popular culture. The reflexive inclusion of sacrificial impulses alongside the reliance on fragments and residuals of a penitential consciousness shape world views of their characters. There is also the referencing of other faiths/belief systems (Buddhism, Hinduism and Quakerism) to be considered.

THE SECOND DEATH: LAST RITES

John Michael's *The Second Death* (2000) has an isolated rural Ireland setting and three locations, a cottage, a pub and a narrow, unlit road between the pub and the home of James Mangan (Liam Cunningham). (A British character named Lord James Mangan features in *War on Everyone*.) On his way to the pub James had heard the disembodied sound of a giggling schoolgirl from the enveloping darkness. In the pub, pool players (Aidan Gillen and Owen Sharpe) and chess players (Dermot Healy and David Wilmot) interact with knowing familiarity with local police officer, Gerry (Gary Lydon), and the bar's proprietor, Aisling (Michelle Fairley). Although this is rural Ireland, customers are not just there for the alcohol, they share cocaine.

The suicide of a teenager, who had previously gone missing on the day of her First Holy Communion some years back is discussed in the pub. James encounters two images of the young Helen Rainey (Roxanna Williams), wearing a communion dress and veil, lying on a blanket or bed; the first has her with her eyes closed and motionless, in the second she has her eyes open. On the way home, James again hears giggling, and sees a fully embodied Helen. James runs to flee this phantom presence, which is of a child and not the teenage Helen. It is an innocent laughter of sorts, but it causes distress and not a mirrored response of gaiety.

As James sits in his chair, consuming more whiskey, the camera lingers on two notable images, one of the Sacred Heart of Jesus Christ, and the image of St Francis of Assisi. Both images are presences that serve to protect and to remind people of their Christian beliefs, shared values and moral obligations.

James falls half asleep, and stirs as if prompted by the girl, who simultaneously awakens. Is Helen an apparition, forewarning him of his own death or is it her presence that prompts his death? The notion of a child being kidnapped, then returned unharmed is an interesting choice. Something obliged Helen to stay silent. As James dies, he is looking at her image in the doorway, and partially the camera pans close to the image of Christ, but just as it gets there, the focus stalls and fades.

Earlier in the pub, Townes van Zandt's "St. John the Gambler" and "Highway Kind" are heard, and later Hank Williams' "Alone and Forsaken" plays over the film's final credits. The amplification of guilt is brought about by religious belief and the songs' lyrics, as well as by the appearance of the young girl in a communion dress.

Helen's embodiment trumps the power of the inanimate iconography. The suspicion is that religious values are merely paid lip service, in a world where the legal system fails to investigate, charge and convict an abduction, and where victims are obliged to internalise their own trauma. The guilty are only punished by hauntings that are summoned from within and without. The appearance of Helen's ghost, by way of suicide, effectively serves as James' admission of responsibility, even if there is no verbal articulation of his guilt, his physical body betrays his past deeds. The ghost's presence ensures that he dies without last rites.

SIX SHOOTER: "AGAINST GOD"

Martin's early career as a playwright is marked by a series of plays set in rural Ireland. *The Beauty Queen of Leenane* (1996), *The Cripple of Inishmaan* (1997), *A Skull in Connemara* (1997) and *The Lonesome West* (1997) are steeped in Catholic sensibilities; sometimes religion is treated ambivalently, sometimes superstitiously, but most importantly religion is used to signal the anomalies and contradictions of public expressions of morality, justice and the common good, informed by a Catholic ethos. "Against God" is a refrain expressed again and again in these four plays, but as a marker of distinction it loses its importance when it becomes a catch-all term, incapable of signalling moral differentiation.

Six Shooter (2005) is a 28-minute short, which won the 2006 Academy Award for Best Live Action Short Film. The film's opening exchange is between a doctor (David Murray) and Donnelly (Brendan Gleeson), after his wife (Ann McFarlane) has just passed away. A shot of her remains in a hospital ward has her lying with rosary beads placed over her hands. In the background, there is a crucifix and a bottle of holy water in the shape of the Virgin Mary, items that affirm the religious affiliation of the hospital. When a photo of a pet rabbit, David, is placed alongside the rosary beads, the film's tragi-comic intent is signalled. All Donnelly musters by way of grief is: "I don't know where you are now" (2:28).

On a train journey, Donnelly encounters Kid (Rúaidhrí Conroy), who is on the run, having killed his mother. When Kid observes the interaction between a couple (Aisling O'Sullivan and David Wilmot), Kid intuits that there is something seriously amiss. Alone with the mother, he starts insulting their dead child's physical looks, remarking, "no wonder you banged it on something" (11:38). Earlier he had called the grieving couple, "Fred and Rosemary" (West), after the notorious Cromwell Road serial killers (8:19).

After the distraught mother jumps from the moving train, Kid's lack of emotional response bears all the hallmarks of psychopathological behaviour. Donnelly asks: "Have you no respect for the dead," which gets the response: "I haven't, no. Black fella stole mine" (16:05). When Donnelly shares with Kid that his wife has just died, Kid asks: "Did she get murdered too" (16:51), and his advice is "Don't cry auld fella. She's up with God now, she's up with God now" (17:13). Donnelly responds by saying that he has lost his belief in God, and that Mrs Dooley was the last straw. "That was not God's fault, he can't be everywhere at once," is Kid's reply, in effect denying the doctrine of omnipresence (17:32).

Now, in possession of a gun, following Kid's death during a shoot-out with the police, Donnelly plans to end his life in a living room, adorned with religious iconography, a crucifix, a Sacred Heart, and statues of saints that are not discernible. Looking towards the picture of his wife, Donnelly states: "Hope I see you soon babe. If I don't I don't," re-confirming his uncertainty about an afterlife (23:50).

Suicide is not something Donnelly can attempt with a picture of the Sacred Heart watching over him, so he faces the image down on the dresser. A bullet to the head ensures the mercy killing of the rabbit; however, when the gun breaks apart on the second shot, Donnelly is left alive, with the headless rabbit in his lap. Comic absurdity is key to the mercy killing that has unintended consequences. The film's final line, "Oh Jesus, what a fucking day" (25:58), marks Donnelly's sense of grief and existential bewilderment, and as David Clare notes, it is "half prayer half blasphemy" (342). The White Stripes' "St James Infirmary Blues" plays over the final credits, re-affirming the bewildering and chaotic situation, the dead rabbit ensures that attempted suicide falters. Mercy and sacrifice are denied significance.

IN BRUGES: RENDERING AND SURRENDERING

In Martin's *In Bruges*, two London-based Irish gangland figures, Ray (Colin Farrell) and Ken (Brendan Gleeson), are sent to the Belgian medieval city of Bruges by their crime boss Harry Walters (Ralph Fiennes). This is a consequence of Ray's execution of a Catholic priest, Fr McHenry (Ciarán Hinds) and the unintentional death of a young boy (Theo Stevenson). The film does not confirm the reason why the priest is assassinated in the way that deleted scenes in part of the DVD extras do. The priest's killing takes place in a confessional box, and the young boy is outside, kneeling and preparing to confess to innocuous sins. Diasporic characters, Ray and Ken, have discernible Dublin accents, and they acknowledge through conversation their Irish heritage and the upshots of childhood religious instruction.

The film opens with shots of church spire, gargoyle, cherub, saint, grotesque half-moon, bridge, cobbled streets, bell tower and canal. The gothic backdrop variously speaks to the issues of accountability, guilt, salvation and damnation that concern Ray. In addition, Carter Burrell's score, production design by Michael Carlin, Jon Gregory's editing, and Eigil Bryld's cinematography create a specific gothic-inspired, dream-like, "other worldly" atmosphere, delivering a sense of a disorientated elsewhere. Margitta Rouse notes how "The film creates a sense of visual strangeness in a temporal, spatial, and meta-cinematic sense" (174). And Irina Melnikova identifies "how the textual and cinematic Bruges" is transformed and reappraised in terms of the concept of "cinematic city" (213).

While visiting the Groeninge Museum, Ray has an unsettling encounter with Jan Provoost's "De gierigaard en de Dood" (The Miser and Death). Then the museum's gruesome diptych the "Judgement of Cambyses" and "The Flaying of the Corrupt Judge Sisamnes" by Gerard David unnerves Ray further. Flaying is the punishment for Sisamnes' corrupt judgements.

Rouse notes that "The Judgement of Cambyses" "is presented in hard cuts from photographic still to still; the limited camera movement after the series of stills simulates Ray's way of quietly taking in every single detail— the flaying of an arm, a face in agony, a cut chest and a skinned leg. Rolling his eyes, he moves past scenes from the Legend of St George by an unknown [Flemish] master, depicting St George being tortured in various ways" (117).

Hieronymus Bosch's "The Last Judgement" is admired by Ray, a day when salvation or damnation are determined, with heaven and hell the ultimate sanctions/rewards. Only the middle canvas of Bosch's triptych is featured, corresponding to the idea that we ever only get quick and partial glimpses of that world. Lapsed Catholics or otherwise, the religious iconography and symbolism resonate for both Ray and Ken.

Ken ignores Harry's kill order and takes Ray's side; instinct trumps duty when Ken stops Ray from killing himself. The moment is a miracle of sorts, however temporary. Ken's failure to see through on Harry's principled, obligated, consequential and retributive form of justice prompts Harry to Bruges. Ken effectively admits to his wrongdoing and surrenders to Harry in the bell tower. Harry remarks: "Like I'm not gonna do nothing to ya just 'cos you're standing about like Robert fucking Powell!" (80:34). (Powell played Jesus in Franco Zeffirelli's *Jesus of Nazareth* (1977)). Here, religious influence is remediated through a remembered television series.

When a badly wounded Ken plunges from the bell tower to warn Ray of Harry's presence, even at the moment of poignant, Christ-like self-sacrifice, there is the obstinacy of McDonagh's comic impulse, when the gun that Ken has stored in his pocket intended to help Ray with his self-defence, falls apart. Steven Pinker's overall analysis of empathy suggests that altruistic self-sacrifice goes against the notion of natural selection and self-beneficial behaviours (712). Despite Ken's aspiration to frame his sacrifice as a protective, altruistic and highly empathetic act, irony counterpoints intentionality, sacrifice is perverse if not "abject," in the Kristevan-usage of the word (1982, 1–3).

If the British police have not tracked them, and if Harry's system of justice is found wanting and suspiciously contrived around principles and honour, without any alertness to its selective thinking, then the propositions of a religious frame, in terms of penitence, pilgrimage, celestial salvation and damnation are also determined as instructive, but fundamentally inadequate. The grievously wounded Ray lies in an ambulance and evokes an alternative system of moral accountability.

In the quasi-confessional voice-over that mirrors the one that opens the film, he offers to visit the mother of the child he has killed and to be open to whatever form of punishment she chooses. This unambiguous admission of liability, and acceptance of reparative justice made by Ray is a form of confessional surrogation. The "found space" of Bruges has incited him into a form of admission of responsibility, without preconditions. The reckoning figure is human rather than divine or celestial substitute. Here there is no guarantee of forgiveness or absolution, even if the sinner is penitent. Ray's final remarks "Prison, death, it didn't matter. Cos at least in prison, and at least in death, y'know, I wouldn't be in fucking Bruges" (98:30) counter any sense of profundity. It is an irony from which the work cannot escape.

Earlier, over dinner, Ray and Chloë (Clémence Poésy) joked about their professions. She is a drug dealer and he a novice contract killer: they confess as well as transgress: the child murderer casually jokes about Belgian sexual abusers and killers of children, and his comments rely on a self-differentiation between him being an accidental killer and the premediated and sadistic actions of paedophiles. Yet, how often are cinema audiences invited to express empathy/compassion for the killers of children? Regardless, genre expectations demand that Ray must pay for what he has done, and, apart from leaving him close to death, another aspect of his punishment is the unconsummated relationship with Chloë. (See Jordan 2014, 171–84. for a broader analysis in relation to psychopathology, empathy and altruism.) *Bruges* is a decisive and original exploration of culpability in a world increasingly disinclined to take responsibility, happier to blame others for their own actions, content to side-line culpability and justice and prioritise victimhood.

THE GUARD: PROVISIONAL ERASURES

Set in County Galway, John Michael's *The Guard* pitches local police sergeant Gerry Boyle (Brendan Gleeson) and FBI agent Wendell Everett (Don Cheadle) against an international crime syndicate which is smuggling cocaine into Ireland with the assistance of corrupt policemen. As antagonists this cohort offers the full gamut of crazed, disturbed, seedy and greedy figures. While the relationship between the Irish and American law enforcement officers is non-compliant with the usual buddy movie

224   E. JORDAN

formula, there is a degree of provocative offence in Boyle's racist language as well as a countering in Everett's ability to fight back and challenge him. Everett has anything but a "Projects" background, and instead is one of privilege, including holidays in Aspen and the Hamptons, prep school, Yale University and a Rhodes Scholarship.

Boyle is not the typical, bachelor, with a mother-complex, Irish character, but is the "maverick" cop that people expect in such types of work: he takes and uses LSD from the bodies of young men who have just died in a road crash, has relationships with prostitutes and returns a discovered cache of guns to the Provisional Irish Republican Army. Boyle is a film buff, a Gogol-reading law-man with knowledge of various Russian novelists and is also someone who indulges in video shooting games, and is possibly an Olympian: this is neither the west of Ireland nor the rural police officer one might expect, even if backdrop shots of Connemara affirm many traditional tropes.

The opening murder scene sees the body of James McCormick (Declan Mannion) with pages from the Bible stuffed in his face, a flowerpot on his lap and 5½ is scrolled on the wall in blood. The scene is staged to confuse the investigation, to suggest "occult overtones," according to Liam O'Leary (David Wilmot) (9:15).

When the action first moves to Galway for an FBI briefing, the cathedral in Galway becomes a signifier of the transition to the city. However, it is a rural church that is the site of the most intimate exchange between Boyle and his terminally ill mother, Eileen (Fionnula Flanagan). There is a quick shot of Christ on a cross, then a focus on Boyle, who waits outside the confession box. The sacramental exchange proves unsatisfactory:

Eileen: He was no use.
Gerry: So, what have you got to confess anyways at your age?
Eileen: What's my age got to do with it? Pol Pot was in his seventies when he died.
Gerry: I think Pol Pot's shenanigans were a little bit more malicious than anything you might have got up to.
Eileen: Shows what you know.
Gerry: Really. You took part in a sex orgy or something, did you? One of them Bachanals (50:16).

When the priest comes out of the confessional, he partially overhears the exchange and is perturbed. Eileen wants to get cocaine, for its reputation as a "great get up and go" (51:09). Then she discusses Amyl nitrite and the feeling of missing out on the drug and on life more broadly: "You are not alone there" is his response (51:39). Instead of the penitential experience allowing her to focus on sin and transgression, it brings up for her a sense of loss, a regret at missing out.

Later Boyle extracts a confession from O'Leary by chatting through his previous murders, including that of his colleague, Aiden McCormick (Rory Keenan). Not knowing that Boyle has a concealed firearm, O'Leary's admissions have no remorse, and are rubbing in the failings of the police. If Boyle shoots O'Leary in self-defence, he allows a wounded Francis Sheehy-Skeffington (Liam Cunningham) to die. The fires surrounding Sheehy-Skeffington on the boat are almost biblical in terms of retribution. Indeed, there is suicidal recklessness in Gerry's attack on the boat.

Seven Psychopaths: Serial Narrators

In Martin's *Seven Psychopaths*, alcohol-addicted Marty Faranan (Colin Farrell) is an Irish writer suffering with writer's block, both of which are adding to his troubled relationship with Kaya (Abbie Cornish). Apart from Farrell's mid-Atlantic Irish accent, Marty is predominantly signalled and received by others as Irish. Billy Bickle (Sam Rockwell) is an out-of-work actor and wishes to inspire Marty's creativity, but it is merely a pretext to act out the personae of Jack of Diamonds, a serial killer of criminal gang members.

Marty struggles to move his writing away from violence-derived narratives. He has a story about a vengeful Vietnamese soldier (Long Nguyen) who plots the destruction of members of Charlie Company, some of whom were involved in the Mỹ Lai massacre of civilians (See BBC, 1998). Marty's other story features a killer (James Hébert), who a year after murdering a young girl, hands himself in, repents, finds God during his captivity and benefits from pastoral care in prison provided by a Catholic priest. Although pacifism informs the beliefs of the Quaker community, Marty's fictional Quaker figure (Harry Dean Stanton) unrelentingly stalks this killer, during his 17-year stay in prison and during the 11 years after his release. The killer decides that the only way to evade such remorseless pursuit is to take his own life, for at least in hell he will have repose from the Quaker. To commit suicide is to renounce salvation, according to a Catholic tract he has come upon. However, he has not anticipated that the

Quaker's commitment to vengeance would lead him to copycat his actions, and the damnation of his own soul.

The Quaker story belongs to Hans (Christopher Walken) and his wife Myra (Linda Bright Clay), who carried out the stalking together; Hans survives the suicide attempt, unlike what happens in Marty's version. The non-intervention of their deity is reflected on by Hans and Myra. Myra asks: "You ever worry that we was wrong all of those years and there ain't no heaven and there ain't no nothing" (17:11). Hans disagrees: "[...] God loves us but he has a funny way of showing us sometimes [...] He's had a lot to contend with in his time. Bastards killed his kid too" (17:36).

Seven Psychopaths pushes the notion of vengeance/sacrifice in alternative directions, with Hans' re-configuring of the Vietnamese narrative, where various voices urge the soldier to "desist" (96:33, 97:24, 98:30). The scenario switches from Phoenix to Saigon, circa 1963, with sacrifice configured as self-immolation; pain and suffering self-inflicted in the name of a greater political justice.

If Hans sees this act as a protest against the "War," the real-life incident that his Buddhist priest's actions mimic, occurred in advance of the Vietnam War. In an iconic moment from 11 June 1963 the Vietnamese Buddhist monk Thich Quang Duc, according to James Verini, self-immolated, not in protest against the Vietnam War as commonly thought, but against the "persecution of Buddhists by the Catholic (and US-backed) Diem regime" (2012). The act of self-sacrifice that Myra and Hans had made by passively stalking the killer of their daughter is re-configured by Hans' final re-imaginings. Self-sacrifice has strong religious, altruistic and self-destructive associations, even when carried out for a greater good.

When Marty comes across the body of Hans, Marty reflexively blesses himself, signalling an innate Catholicism. However, unconscious Catholic stimuli can be seen in Marty's imagining that the Buddhist solider disguises himself in the garb of a Catholic priest or that prisoner pastoral care in the Quaker story is provided by a Catholic clergyman. Marty's Catholicism is embedded and his quest to move his screenwriting away from violence towards peace and love is captured in the interrogation and unravelling of Gandhi's Hindu-inspired belief, "An eye for an eye leaves the whole world blind." This is a counter-response to an "eye for an eye and a tooth for a tooth," the vengeful iteration of an old-testament God.

In the film's final moments, during the interruption of credits, Marty confesses his failings to a vengeful-inclined Zachariah (Tom Waits) who is

12 THE IMMUTABLE AND UN-RETRIEVABLE IN THE DIASPORIC FILMS... 227

in an almost confession box-like phone booth. It is the unqualified and non-ironic nature of Marty's admission that contrasts with Ray's last line in *In Bruges*. Zachariah as vengeful victim of Marty's broken promise has a change of heart, the serial killer dispenses absolution.

CALVARY: PATRIARCHAL PURIFICATION

Aerial shots of an estuary on the Atlantic Ocean, mountains, Ben Bulben, and of surfers in the sea establish Ireland's north-west, and specifically Easkey, County Sligo, and nearby locations as *Calvary*'s setting. The scenery evokes the pastoral sensibility with which Ireland is often associated, but visual beauty is partly countered by the vileness and dysfunctionality of many of those living there. Place and people are not in alignment. There is little hankering back to the glories and fallacies of a cosy pastoral past in *Calvary*.

Calvary mixes different genres, part dark comedy and part suspense thriller, it is less a whodunit, and more a who-will-do-it. *Calvary* can also be seen as a "dark comedy, Western or noir," as Michael Stewart notes (3) or as he also proposes, as a combination of melodrama and gothic. Stewart signals Anglo-Irish gothic, in terms of terror and engulfment, hauntings, absences, the missing and the lost, and then its interlinking with "pathetic" family melodrama (4), which he sees as veering towards, Gledhill's term, neo-melodrama (15), in that it retains elements of the moral occult and "tries to return itself to innocence, but also fails to dispel discomfort and guilt" (15). Importantly, for Stewart, the film's melodramatic sensibility is not "structured via villainy and virtue" (3) and not driven by "moral legibility" (4), key components of traditional melodrama.

Calvary addresses the significance and residuals of Catholicism to the lives of its many characters, and particularly the film's central character Fr James Lavelle (Brendan Gleeson), who appears dressed in an old-fashioned soutane. In the aftermath of his wife's death, James had become a late vocation and has a daughter, Fiona (Kelly Reilly), who comes to visit, with her own traumas in tow. Anthony Lane comments that "in Brendan Gleeson—in his proud bearing and his lamenting gaze—we see the plight of the lonely believer in a world beyond belief" (2014).

Fr James engages in a range of daily acts of service, says mass, visits parishioners in their homes, workplaces, hospitals and prison. Fr James encounters a French woman, Teresa (Marie-Josée Croze), who is widowed, by a road accident that left five dead, and an elderly American writer

(M. Emmet Walsh) who is thinking about taking his own life. Fr James visits Freddie Joyce (Domhnall Gleeson), a mass murderer in jail.

Fr James turns a blind eye to rent boy activities, and his views on masturbation and sex outside of marriage are not in line with the teachings of his faith. Veronica Brennan (Orla O'Rourke) wants to confess to the sin of adultery before she does the deed, but guilt will not stop her, nor will threats of damnation. When Fr James tries to intervene in issues of adultery, incited by a black eye suffered by Veronica, the situation is far more complex than he can know. Doctor, Frank Harte (Aidan Gillen), gives expression to an atheistic world view.

Michael Fitzgerald (Dylan Moran) urinates on Holbein's *The Ambassadors* (1533), a painting that connects the Church and emerging capitalism (Stewart, 16). He does so to prove what he can do with wealth, signalling waste, disdain, irresponsibility, insensitivity as to how the value of the painting could be alternatively deployed. In response, Fr James remarks that the "wealthy have pissed on everything else, so why not that [the painting] too? (36:30). Fitzgerald links Fr James with the wealth of the church, and Fr James declines the connection.

Bar owner Brendan (Pat Shortt), whose business is about to be foreclosed by the bank, points out that the church took money from the Jews and is guilty of collaborating with Nazi Germany (50:10). Migrant, Simon (Isaach De Bankolé) asks: "Are you going to chop off my hand if I disobey you" (18:16), connecting race violence, slavery and imperialism with missionary activities. Simon rejects Fr James' sermonising and flicks a cigarette at him, nothing here of the subservient migrant. Fr James is somewhat dismissive of Simon's viewpoint. The Church's connections to imperialism, mass exploitation and capitalism are variously signalled. The police Inspector Stanton (Gary Lydon, who also played a corrupt police officer with the same name in *The Guard*) wonders after the church is razed to the ground, if this is the future. (Lt Gerry Stanton also features in *War on Everyone*.)

This priest's relationship with Fiona is complex; his absence around the time of his wife's passing and his negligence of his daughter's emotional well-being in its aftermath are signalled. A conversation between them in a confession box is a discussion about the moral implications of suicide, God's mercy, but it is not a confession per se, even though he is garbed for that purpose.

Equally, various arguments, discussions and debates establish a strong anti-relativism, seen in the following exchange. During a conversation with Milo Herlihy (Killian Scott), who wants to join the army, and who has murderous feelings because he is not getting sex, Fr James makes the following point: "Thou shalt not kill, does not have an asterix beside it, referring you to the bottom of the page," with exemptions listed (30:02). Again, apart from the notion of reasonable self-defence that leads to a death, which Milo raises, a point on which Fr James concedes, here there is the attestation of a rigorous belief system that stands firm in terms of valuing life and prohibiting murder. Earlier, Veronica wonders, "They say you can find beauty in everything" and Fr James counters, "And I'd say, you can find beauty in most things. Not everything. That's nonsense" (14:07).

However, it is a pre-credit sequence in a confessional box where that sense of the vocation and life's sacredness faces its most thorough interrogation. Fr James is told that he has seven days to get his house in order, before he will be murdered, not for crimes for which he is responsible, rather for the deeds committed by others. The film's opening line from the victim of abuse is that he was seven when he got the "first taste of semen" (01:07), after that oral and anal abuse occurred every other day for five years.

Gleeson's acknowledging face is lit by yellow light coming through the confessional box's opaque grille, while the other character remains unseen: he is not an anonymous penitent, but someone intent on revelation. Notably, the voice of the unseen person is not that of a single character, as Stewart notes, it is an "amalgamated voice" (8).

The priest who did wrong is now dead, and the victim of the abuse does not want specific justice against a perpetrator but wants to punish someone else, to lay down a marker of dissent, protest and unruly justice. It would be easy to kill a bad priest, "What would be the point of killing the bastard" (3:16), but to kill a good one, that serves not only a perverse form of justice, but something to awaken people to the systemic horrors of clerical sexual abuse and the ongoing impacts that such traumas have had on the lives of victims. It is summarised simply: "I am going to kill you father. I am going to kill you cos you did nothin' wrong" (3:35).

For Stewart, "As we hear the confessor leaving the confessional, a haunting, soft but powerful female voice accompanies the image of the priest's face, fearful and confused. The screen fades briefly to black and then lightens to reveal a romantic, beautiful pastoral scene" (7). Gleeson's mesmeric presence (*in persona Christi*) is robust, even in his hesitancy and fear.

230   E. JORDAN

Fr James in a conversation with his bishop, Garret Montgomery (David McSavage)—another cleric named Montgomery appears in *Billboards*—teases out whether the exchange between the priest and his potential slayer is bound by the seal of confession. As the person was neither contrite nor seeking absolution when he entered the confessional box, "the inviolability of the sacramental seal does not apply," (10:19) as it had in Alfred Hitchcock's *I Confess* (1953).

An unnamed bishop is paying a rent boy for sexual services, rather than honouring his vows of chastity. Gay police officer, Stanton, recounts investigating allegations of sexual abuse of a girl by a clergyman in Dublin 20 years previously, only for Stanton to be transferred to the country by way of reprimand, and the priest was shipped to the missions. Such evasive and irresponsible actions capture what in most instances, the Catholic Church did, cover its tracks, disbelieve and silence victims, and close down investigations, through its formal and informal channels of influence, demonstrating an utter contempt for the law. Africa is not simply a place to evade the law but a place where he "could do what he wanted over there" (26:55). The instinct of the younger priest, Fr Leary (David Wilmot, who played Liam O'Leary in *The Guard*), is inclined to view the cases of abuse currently written about in the papers as predominantly legacy issues, incidents that happened 40 or 50 years ago. His blatantly untrue perspective is a suitably self-deceiving and unconscionable one. The issue of the Church being in need to pay compensation to victims is also signalled in the film, particularly in the aftermath of the Ryan Report (2009).

Leading up to the film's denouement, someone in the community burns down the church and someone slays Fr James' dog (Bruno). On the beach, Fr James comes face-to-face with his accuser/slayer, revealed to be local butcher, Jack Brennan (Chris O'Dowd), who admits he burned down the church. Jack asks the priest a precise question, if he cried when his dog died? He answers "Yes." But, had he cried when he "read about what all your fellow priests did to all the children down through the years …? (90:56). Fr James answers that he had not. For Jack, he himself is one of the "lucky ones," who were not "buried back there, buried like dogs" (91:34).

Fr James' inability to express enough empathy or compassion is a signal not so much of his indifference, but an inability to respond to all such violations, partly based on a distancing from the bad eggs, and partly based on a capacity to distinguish abusers from the Church and its ministry. In that way, Fr James is culpable by way of his incapacity for empathy and by way of not seeing abuse as systematic, something that he condones almost by default, by belonging and remaining part of a corrupt organisation.

If there is a certain inadequacy or lack in his response to Jack's question, Fr James is honest in his admission, and not like those that blatantly, sinisterly and actively cover things up. His initial advice to the unseen person in the confession box was to get help and make a formal complaint. So, although his responses to the abusive revelations are not entirely empathetic, his moral instruction is driven by a desire to do the right thing by the victim, to make it a matter of the courts and not Canon Law.

By Jack's rationale, because the victims of clerical abuse have been positioned marginally and invisibly in many respects, Fr James becomes culpable by default, and this approach is somewhat consistent with the way that Mildred positions Fr Montgomery in terms of his culpability by association in *Billboards*. Fr James dies for the sins of others, and in that way his Christ-like death is quasi-sacrificial and quasi-scapegoat-like in orientation. Fr James considered escaping and not facing his fate and he armed himself but flings the gun into the sea.

Donald Clarke is hostile to the nihilistic leanings of the writing, arguing "McDonagh employs a scattershot nihilism that admits little hope, optimism or reasoned analysis" (2014, a). For Laura Canning, "the inability of the film to manage theoretical or psychological disjunctures between Lavelle as a man and Lavelle as priest start to crack it open" (2014). In contrast, Xan Brooks suggests that "*Calvary* touches greatness. It crawls clear through the slime and comes out looking holy" (2014), a perspective far closer to my own. *Calvary* is less about Fr James' hypocrisy and more about him doing the best he can in the face of an avalanche of revelations, of behaviours utterly at odds with the Christian message, love and protection of the innocent. Jack's disclosures in the confession box are not of the sins of his own doing, and he does not seek absolution, penitence, restitution and least of all forgiveness for the sins of others. Admission, sorrow, acquiescence to penance and the humble seeking of absolution were not instincts of the Catholic Church in the face of abuse revelations. Fr James' death re-formulates the notion of penance by way of perverse surrogation, and his murder is a suicide/sacrifice-by-victim in many respects.

232   E. JORDAN

THREE BILLBOARDS OUTSIDE OF EBBING, MISSOURI: CRIPS AND BLOODS

While the real Missouri is more associated with other forms of Christianity, the Catholic ethos evident in Ebbing's community is important to Martin's *Billboards*. Officer Dixon (Sam Rockwell) interrupts the Easter family meal of Chief Willoughby (Woody Harrelson) to tell him about the installation of Mildred Hayes' (Frances McDormand) billboards of protest against the inertia of the investigation into her daughter's death, seven months previously. As Mark Kermode observes, "From the opening morning-mist shots of those lonely billboards to the flames that evoke the burning crosses of the KKK, cinematographer Ben Davis perfectly captures the film's knife-edge balance between humour and horror, mayhem and melancholia" (2018).

Mildred's billboards are less a public confession and more a public accusation; they incite local resistance, and official complaints are made to the police. Willoughby, Connolly (Željko Ivanek) and Dixon intimidate advertiser Red Welby (Caleb Landry Jones) and threaten legal proceedings on Mildred that will tie her up in the courts and stop her earning a living. Mildred's specific targeting of Willoughby is also problematic, because of his terminal illness.

High School students and the local dentist variously express their disdain for her billboards. Father Montgomery (Nick Searcy) heads a religious community that is confident that it offers support to Mildred in terms of compassion, understanding and that the comforts of a God are abundant in the aftermath of her daughter's death. Mildred's grief is to be consoled, contained and offset by religious faith. Fr Montgomery drops by to admonish her for not attending services, his greater reprimand being reserved for the billboards and how much the town is against them. Mildred rejects his pleadings, because she disavows the church itself, particularly what it has done to cover up clerical sexual abuse.

Mildred attacks the Catholic Church by way of an example of laws passed to combat the rise in the street-gang activities of the Crips and the Bloods in Los Angeles.

> Mildred: ... Which got me thinking, Father, that whole type of situation is kinda similar to you Church boys, ain't it? You've got your colours, you've got your clubhouse, you're, for want of a better word, a gang ... And I don't care if you never did shit or never saw shit or never heard shit. You joined

the gang. You're culpable. And when a person is culpable to altar-boy-fucking, or any-kinda-boy-fucking, I know you guys didn't really narrow it down. (21:55)

Mildred is referencing The California Street Terrorism Enforcement and Prevention Act (1988), which deals with the substantive crime of gang membership. Mildred has the substance of that law correct, but it is a bit more nuanced than Mildred suggests on the nature of active participation (See First District Appellate Project).

For Mildred, it is not just the despicable priests, whose deviance and crimes shame the faith, but individual members of the clergy are singularly and jointly accountable by means of affiliation and association. Accordingly, Fr Montgomery "forfeits the right" to comment on her basic constitutional right to protest (21:50).

Vengeful rage displaces Mildred's pacifist inclinations and unwillingness to transgress the laws when the billboards are burned down. Revenge is seen in quasi-religious terms: "I'll crucify the motherfuckers. (*Crying.*) I'll crucify the motherfuckers" (71:43).

Mildred asks in a conversation with a deer, near where Angela was murdered: "Cos there ain't no God and the whole world's empty and it don't matter what we do to each other? Ooh, I hope not" (44:24:). If hers is a world where there are no rules, no meaning to existence, what should govern lives? In that hope there is responsibility and culpability. Pain distorts her capacity for empathy, which is only seen in fragments, in her upturning of a beetle on its back, or when Willoughby coughs up blood, a moment that contrasts to an earlier encounter between both.

Crop Haired Guy (Brendan Sexton III), who had been ruled out as a suspect in Angela's killing by way of DNA testing, may be held responsible and punished for other unspecified crimes, based on the policing intuitions of the reformed, sacked and offensively racist Dixon. Dixon's belief in Crop Haired Guy's culpability is based on a deeply belligerent story he overhears about a gang rape and the setting alight of a victim. Even unintentionally, self-incriminating narratives are prone to exaggeration and untruths. It is a story told in confidence, the bar booth and its opaque glass divider serves almost as a quasi-confessional situation, with Dixon as eavesdropper rather than confessor. This highly racist character was in a police force dominated by racist practices. Responses associating Dixon's changing behaviours as somehow redemptive within the arc of the film are way off the mark.

234   E. JORDAN

Guilt by association carries low-grade penalties for LA street-gang members, but culpability established by way of an over-heard story takes potential vigilante actions away from legal objectivity, impartiality, burden of proof and due process, the presumption of innocence and the rights to fair trial, a defence and appeal. The extra-judicial impulses signalled by Mildred and Dixon take the film into perverse, inconclusive and abject territory, based on a disclosure that only maybe has some ring of truth, and nothing like the necessary and valid confession of a suspect, substantiated by corroborating evidence. Vigilantism sacrifices the responsibility of proof. Mildred and Dixon take the logic of culpability into ever more fraught territory, which is at least tempered by their uncertainty.

CONCLUSION

John Michael and Martin have used Irish locations, worked with a shared pool of actors, many Irish, have used Irish music alongside anything from classical to country, evident in Martin's usage of "On Raglan Road" in *In Bruges*, and "The Last Rose of Summer," in *Billboards*, and John Michael's use of "Carrickfergus" or "The Parting Glass" in *The Guard*. Both brothers refer to the Birmingham Six's miscarriage of justice; Martin in *The Beauty Queen of Leenane* and John Michael in *The Guard*.

The motif of self-sacrifice seen variously in the actions of Ken in *In Bruges*, Fr James in *Calvary* and the Buddhist priest's self-immolation in *Seven Psychopaths* connects religion and political protest and altruism. The sacrifices of the Quaker couple make it an impressive if perverse commitment to justice, love and pacifism in *Seven Psychopaths*. If Martin's male characters like Donnelly, Ray and Ken are suicidally inclined, it is female suicides or attempts at such that feature more in John Michael's work, Helen in *Second Death*, Fiona in *Calvary* and Eileen in *The Guard*. Fr James' death is suicide-by-victim in *Calvary* and, Kid's is suicide-by-cop in *Six Shooter*. Willoughby's letter to Anne (Abbie Cornish) opens up the issue of an afterlife, and a hope of an existence beyond the grave tempered by the joys and virtues experienced. He kills himself not to avoid suffering but to save his family from witnessing his demise through illness. Suicide is the one unforgivable sin remarked upon in almost all the works discussed, and accordingly connects to the notion of damnation, complicated when it is linked to sacrifice, or framed as a sacrifice. Heaven and hell feature as consistent markers in the works of both McDonaghs, but that does not necessarily signal a belief in an afterlife, more it is a way of signalling end game clarity, a sense of purpose out of purposelessness.

Confessional boxes, revelatory spaces or substitutes thereof ensure that issues of admission, remorse, guilt, liability, penance, forgiveness and restitution are persistently interrogated. For increasingly secular audiences, the engagements with the iconography, symbolism and values of Christianity can be seen as twee, reactionary, something to be side-lined, disparaged or radically dismissed, given its increasing irrelevance to the contemporary lives of many. It would be too easy to suggest that both brothers consistently include religious motifs, structures and values as merely advantageous writing conveniences, or as exploitative contrivances apposite to their anarchic writing dispositions. Equally, it would be too simplistic to say that such practices were callous, careless, cynical, parasitic or an ironic/free-floating way of creating work from a postmodern, post-religious perspective.

It could be argued that the appeal to such religious-informed world views is an attempt to mine traces, fragments and residuals of traditional values in order to highlight a world less and less fortified by any values, a sort of dead cat bounce. Their endeavours to emphasise some will towards truth and accountability can also be taken to suggest that there is a lack of viable alternatives through which to situate and validate an ethical positioning that has relevance.

While Christianity in the determination of salvation and damnation often functions parallel to rival or alternative systems of morality and justice like Harry's principles of honour in *In Bruges*, more often than not, it serves as something beyond simply confounding, countermanding or reinforcing alternative points of view and ethical stances. Martin talks about his "pacifist rage" in relation to *The Lieutenant of Inishmore* (O'Hagan, 2001), and in more recent pronouncements he talks about "pure moral outrage" (Chambers, 2018).

Accordingly, religious beliefs, iconography and moral tenets stalk the work, not like some spectral presence or haunting by traditional values, but more by way of the heightened mores of a seemingly bygone era, even when such values may be increasingly regarded as unadvisable, irretrievable, offensive and tainted by sentiment and superstition.

Religious concepts serve as a means to signal inequities, interrogate the rule of law and the moral codes of gangland, without serving necessarily as an affirmation or disambiguation of these or any alternative set of values. Virtue, compassion, redemption and forgiveness are re-purchased in their

236 E. JORDAN

works, as are dignity, responsibility and culpability. Through the interfacing of sacrifice and confessional actions, judgement, liability and accountability are keys to both writers, even if they seem to be tentative, precarious, misplaced, mal-practised, ironised, anarchic and irretrievable values.

WORKS CITED

BBC News. "Mỹ Lai", Monday 20 July 1998. http://news.bbc.co.uk/2/hi/asia-pacific/64344.stm. Web.

Brah, Avtar. *Cartographies of Diaspora: Contesting Identities.* London: Routledge, 1996.

Brooks, Xan. "Calvary review—'a terrific black comedy that touches greatness'." *The Observer*, 13 April 2014. https://www.theguardian.com/film/2014/apr/13/calvary-review-terrific-black-comedy. Web.

Buckley, Cara, "His Turn with the Past." *New York Times*, 28 July 2014. https://www.nytimes.com/2014/07/29/movies/john-michael-mcdonagh-carves-his-own-niche-with-calvary.html. Web.

Canning, Laura, "Calvary." *Electronic Journal of the Spanish Association for Irish Studies* (AEDEI). 2015, Issue 10. 200–3. https://www.estudiosirlandeses.org/reviews/calvary-john-michael-mcdonagh-2014/. Web.

Chambers, Robert. "Martin McDonagh, interviewed by an *In Bruges* obsessive." *GQ Magazine*, 12 January 2018. https://www.gq-magazine.co.uk/article/martin-mcdonagh-interview. Web.

Clare, David. "The Intertextual Presence of Samuel Beckett's *All That Fall* in Martin McDonagh s *Six Shooter*". *Irish University Review*, 2015. Vol 45 no.2: 335–351.

Clarke, Donald. "Film Review: *Calvary*." *Irish Times*, 11 April 2014a. https://www.irishtimes.com/culture/film/film-review-calvary-1.1755673. Web.

———, "John Michael McDonagh responds to furore concerning that interview." *Irish Times*, 19 September 2014b. https://www.irishtimes.com/blogs/screenwriter/2014/09/19/john-michael-mcdonagh-responds-to-furore-concerning-that-interview/. Web.

Cummins, Steve. "John Michael McDonagh on Calvary, 'Plastic Paddies' and being Second-Generation Irish." http://www.stevecummins.com/features/john-michael-mcdonagh-calvary-plastic-paddies-second-generation-irish (previously published in *The Irish Post*, 2014). Web.

First District Appellate Project, https://sites.google.com/site/fdapwiki/main_page/gangs/substantive-gang-offense. Web.

Jordan, Eamonn. 2014. *From Leenane to LA: The Theatre and Cinema of Martin McDonagh.* Dublin: IAP; 2014.

Kermode, Mark. "*Three Billboards Outside Ebbing, Missouri* review—a search for justice writ large." *The Guardian*, 14 January 2018. https://www.theguardian.com/film/2018/jan/14/three-billboards-outside-ebbing-missouri-review-frances-mcdormand. Web.

Kristeva, Julia. *The Powers of Horror: An Essay on Abjection*. Trans by Leon S. Roudiez. Columbia: Columbia University Press, 1882.

Lane, Anthony. "Big Men: *Calvary and A Master Builder.*" *The New Yorker*. 28 July 2014. https://www.newyorker.com/magazine/2014/08/04/big-men-2. Web.

McDonagh, John Michael, *The Second Death*, 2000. (Written and Directed by John Michael McDonagh) (Reprisal and Rogue Films)

———, *Ned Kelly* 2003. (Directed by Gregor Jordan, screenplay John Michael McDonagh) (Endymion Films and Australian Film Finance Corporation)

———, *Calvary*, 2014, (Written and Directed by John Michael McDonagh) (Reprisal and Octagon Films, Fox Searchlight Pictures, Bord Scannán Na hÉireann/Irish Film Board, British Film Institute)

———, *The Guard*, 2011, (Written and Directed by John Michael McDonagh) (Reprisal Films, Element Pictures, Hindsight Media, UK Film Council, Bord Scannán Na hÉireann/Irish Film Board)

———, *War on Everyone*, 2016, (Written and Directed by John Michael McDonagh) (Bankside Films, Head Gear Films, British Film Institute)

McDonagh, Martin, *Six Shooter*, 2005. (Written and Directed by Martin McDonagh) (A Missing in Action, Funny Farm Films Production, Film Four, Bord Scannán Na hÉireann/The Irish Film Board))

———, *Six Shooter*, 2008. *In Bruges* (Written and Directed by Martin McDonagh) (Blueprint Pictures, Film4, Focus Features, Scion Films).

———, *Six Shooter*, 2012. *Seven Psychopaths* (Written and Directed by Martin McDonagh) (Film4, Blueprint Pictures, British Film Institute).

———, *Six Shooter*, 2017. *Three Billboards Outside of Ebbing, Missouri*. (Written and Directed by Martin McDonagh) (Hanway Films, Blueprint Pictures, Film4, British Film Institute).

Melnikova, Irina, "In(visible) Bruges by Martin McDonagh." *Journal of European Studies*. 2013, Vol 43.no 1, 44–59.

O'Hagan, Sean. "The Wild West." *The Guardian*, 24 March 2001. https://www.theguardian.com/lifeandstyle/2001/mar/24/weekend.seanohagan. Web.

O'Toole, Fintan, "Martin McDonagh." *Bomb*, 1 April 1998. Spring 63. https://bombmagazine.org/articles/martin-mcdonagh/. Web.

Pinker, Steven. *The Better Angels of Our Nature: A History of Violence and Humanity*. Penguin Books: London. 2011. Web.

Rouse, Margitta. 2011. "'Hit Men on Holiday Get All Medieval': Multiple Temporalities and Media Theory in Martin McDonagh's In Bruges." *European Journal of English Studies*, 2011. Vol 15: no. 2. 171–182.

The Ryan Report (The Commission to Inquire into Child Abuse). 2009, http://childabusecommission.ie/. Web.

Stewart, Michael. "Horrible beauty and (un)easy submission: melodrama and the gothic in *Calvary.*" *Studies in European Cinema.* 2017. Vol 16. no. 2: 108–25.

Verini, James. "A Terrible act of Reason: When Did Self-Immolation Become the Paramount Form of Protest", *New Yorker*, 16 May 2012. http://www.newyorker.com/online/blogs/culture/2012/05/history-of-self-immolation.html. Web.

CHAPTER 13

"How should we remember what happened?": Cultural Representations of Institutional Abuse in Jim Sheridan's *The Secret Scripture*

Tara Harney-Mahajan

INTRODUCTION

A two-day State-sponsored event for Magdalene Laundry survivors, the first of its kind, took place in Dublin in June of 2018. This vitally important event was organized only after a condemnatory November 2017 report accused the Ombudsman of the Magdalene Restorative Justice Scheme (outlined by Justice John Quirke in 2013) of maladministration. The November 2017 report speaks to the persistent, overt cycle of apathy and forgetting that often follows governmental reviews of its own historic abuses. As reported by Katherine O'Donnell, the event for Magdalene survivors included a "listening exercise" where women were given the public and private space to share their experiences, and they were asked to

---

T. Harney-Mahajan (✉)
Caldwell University, Caldwell, NJ, USA
e-mail: tharney@caldwell.edu

© The Author(s), under exclusive license to Springer Nature
Switzerland AG 2022
M. C. Conner et al. (eds.), *Screening Contemporary Irish Fiction and Drama*, Palgrave Studies in Adaptation and Visual Culture,
https://doi.org/10.1007/978-3-031-04568-4_13

239

share their thoughts in response to three questions: "What should we know about the Magdalene Laundries?," "What lessons should we learn from what happened there?" and, "How should we remember what happened?" (O'Donnell n. pag.).[1] Given the Irish government's continued refusal to make public the official records of this history of incarceration for thousands of women and children in twentieth-century Ireland, this last question, in particular, is critical and clings to any cultural representation of Ireland's "architecture of containment."

James M. Smith's landmark book, *Ireland's Magdalen Laundries and the Nation's Architecture of Containment*, published in 2007, was one of the first book-length studies to investigate this State and Church system of enforced confinement. His analysis underscores how and why cultural representations of this system are the only "records" we have, and function, therefore, as an urgent reminder of Ireland's ongoing "obligation to the survivors of the nation's architecture of confinement" (183). While activists and survivors of these institutions have mobilized around a number of key issues,[2] we can also see elements of the "architecture of containment" in its modern-day counterpart, Ireland's system of Direct Provision, which

---

[1] Fulfilling one of two important aspects of the Magdalene Restorative Justice Scheme, this was the first *state-supported* event for Magdalene Laundry Survivors (see McGarry for funding breakdown). It should also be noted, however, that researchers have collected oral histories from survivors for years. Two of these survivor oral histories projects, for example, are the Waterford Memories Project led by Jennifer Yeager and the Justice for Magdalenes collaborative oral history project, led by Katherine O'Donnell. See Yeager and Culleton for background on these projects and why they are an imperative part of creating a "community's collective memory," particularly given the fact that many Church archives and State records remain closed to researchers and survivors (143).

[2] In the last few decades, a number of activist groups have worked to aid and advocate for survivors of Magdalene asylums (and their families). For example, see Justice for Magdalenes Research, the Adoption Rights Alliance, and the Clann Project (JFMR/ARA). For survivors of Mother and Baby Homes, the Facebook group the "Coalition of Mother and Baby Homes Survivors (CMABS)" serves as a nexus for several survivor groups. The "Tuam Survivors Network" consists of "survivors helping survivors" relating to the site in Galway.

controls the fate of thousands of asylum seekers.[3] Any cultural representation of institutionalized women and children, therefore, is politically and ethically charged and must attempt to draw attention to the immense suffering of the individuals who were—and are—forced to make their way through these institutional spaces.

One of the most recent of these cultural representations is Academy Award-nominated director Jim Sheridan's 2017 film, *The Secret Scripture*, which he co-wrote and directed and is adapted from Sebastian Barry's 2008 novel of the same title.[4] Sheridan's adaptation of Barry's novel was much anticipated—yet, upon its release, was widely panned, with reviewers expressing outrage, dismay, and outright confusion about it—particularly in relation to the novel, which was critically acclaimed, commercially popular, and short-listed for the Man Booker Prize. But in the context of adaptation studies, where we would read the film as a "new original," as G. Jellenik, translating Walter Benjamin, phrases it, Sebastian Barry him-

---

[3] Many scholars have noted the connections between Ireland's twentieth-century architecture of containment and its contemporary system of Direct Provision, a system that houses asylum seekers in centers for years while adjudicating their citizenship applications. This system has been in place since 2000 and provides "full board in accommodation centres and a small weekly allowance" to asylum seekers, but individuals are not allowed to work or make meals for their children (Atkins 425). Designed to be "temporary," for some it takes seven years or more for their citizenship applications to be decided (Atkins 425). This system is increasingly under media and scholarly scrutiny, with activist-led (e.g., see MASI: Movement of Asylum Seekers in Ireland) protests bringing much needed attention to the isolated, very poor conditions at many centers, which "lack appropriate facilities" and are "situated at considerable distances" (Atkins 426).

For some recent scholarship about the Direct Provision system and its twentieth-century foundations, see Steven Loyal and Stephen Quilley for connections between Direct provision's "coercive confinement" and institutions of confinement from earlier decades, including workhouses, Country Homes, Magdalen Laundries, and reformatory and industrial schools (77); see Clara Fischer in relation to institutionalizing women and the politics of shame; despite many differences, for some of the similarities between "unmarried mothers" in the past and asylum seekers in the present, see Garrett; building upon research by Sara Ahmed, Patricia Hill Collins, Ronit Lentin, Eithne Luibhéid, and others, see Nilimini Fernando's article which focuses on the plight of African women seeking asylum in Ireland; see co-editors Nessa Cronin's and Karen E. Till's special issue of articulations on the relationship between art and geography and questions of belonging in relation to the Irish body politic. For contemporary literary representations of Ireland's punitive and carceral system, see Melatu Uche Okorie's outstanding fiction; for visual and artistic representations, see the arresting work of Vukasin Nedeljkovic.

[4] Some of Sheridan's most well-known films—*My Left Foot*, 1989 and *The Field*, 1990—are also adaptations.

self draws a distinct boundary between the two ventures (39). Barry, obliging us to consider the film as an object of inquiry in its own right, has insisted that not a line from the novel ended up in the film, and deemed the film, instead, "Sheridan's Scripture" ("Zozimus" n. pag.). Barry's position aligns with recent important interventions into adaptation studies, a field which has increasingly moved away from compare-and-contrast style readings (where fidelity to the source text is sacrosanct), and instead considers the adaptation as a cultural text in its own right, with as few connections to the so-called source or text as any other.[5]

In one of the countless differences between the novel and the film, the novel foregrounds Roseanne Clear/McNulty's 40-year incarceration in an asylum, whereas in Sheridan's film, in addition to a decades-long incarceration in an asylum ("St. Malachy's"), Rose Clear/McNulty is *also* committed against her will to a Mother and Baby Home ("St. Ignatius") when she becomes pregnant, from which she unsuccessfully attempts to escape after a nun threatens her unborn child with a life sentence in the Home, if not premature death. These distinctive plot elements connect to the timing of the film's release in March of 2017—just days after additional horrifying details were reported about St. Mary's home for unmarried mothers and their children, run by the Bon Secours Sisters in Tuam, Galway. By way of background, St. Mary's, or the Bon Secours Mother and Baby Home, operated "between 1925 and 1961, [and] was one of Ireland's numerous 'Mother and Baby' homes" (Burke 1). Illegitimate Irish children throughout the twentieth century, often referred to as Ireland's "stolen children" or "lost babies" were heavily stigmatized—along with their unmarried mothers—well into the latter-half of the twentieth century. Thousands of unmarried Irish women, ostracized by their families for becoming pregnant, were sent—often times unwillingly—to these institutions to have their babies, and many of the children were then placed for adoption by Church officials. Some babies and toddlers were malnourished and "failed to thrive," and never made it beyond their early years. Others stayed on in the Homes, as unpaid workers, or were moved to Industrial schools, often experiencing gruesome and appalling conditions across these institutional spaces.

---

[5] There are many recent collections and interventions in the fields of adaptation studies and literature on screen, and I mention just a few of them here: *Film Adaptation* edited and with an introduction by James Naremore; *Adaptation Studies: New Challenges, New Directions; The Cambridge Companion to Literature On Screen*, and the introduction by Deborah Cartmell and Imelda Whelehan, in particular, and *Adaptation in Visual Culture: Images, Texts, and Their Multiple Worlds.*

In the summer of 2014, the Bon Secours Mother and Baby Home made international news as reports of a "'septic grave tank' containing the skeletal remains of '800 babies' had been discovered within the grounds of a former home for 'unmarried mothers'" (Garrett 358). In 2014, the Irish Government ordered an investigation into the Bon Secours Mother and Baby Home, along with 13 other institutions like it. Just days before the release of Sheridan's film, the Commission confirmed that "[a] mass grave containing the remains of babies and children" had been found on the excavation site, aged between 35 weeks and to 3 years old, with the bodies dating to the 1950s (Grierson n. pag.). The investigation is currently ongoing; the Commission was due to issue its report in 2018 but has been given several extensions—with the final report due in February of 2020. The Commission's fifth interim report, published in April of 2019, "found that the burial locations of hundreds of children who died in the State's mother-and-baby homes remain unknown" (Horgan-Jones, n. pag). In December of 2019, Cathleen Corless, the local historian who is credited with bringing this entire episode to the nation's doorstep, implored the current President, Michael D. Higgins, "to visit Tuam as a gesture of solidarity with the infants buried there and the survivors of the home" and to "say it is horrific and Ireland as a nation must do something about this if we are to move forward. It would be healing for the survivors and for Ireland itself" (MacDonald, n. pag).[6]

Following the screening of the film at the Irish Film Institute in March of 2017, the host Chris Donoghue asked Sheridan about the film in relation to the recent reports about Tuam and Ireland's long history of incarcerating women and children.[7] Sheridan's response is revealing as he

---

[6] MacDonald further reports that Corless added: "'an awful lot more could be done if the people of Tuam got together on this, but it is all whispers...People tell me I am wonderful and tell me to keep going and that I have great courage. That is nice—but it is doing nothing.' 'You can see the state we are in with those babies, trying to get them recognised; trying to get something done; trying to get something for the survivors. If they won't look after these babies, they don't give two hoots about the survivors who are still with us.' 'I wonder is there still a stigma with illegitimacy—are they still lesser people down the scale that are not important. That is the very strong message I am getting from all sides,' she added" (MacDonald, n. pag.).

[7] Chris Donoghue's complete question is as follows: "...the week that I had watched the film, I had just been heavily dealing with Tuam babies and Mother and Baby Homes in work, and very heavy week [sic], and that story of an injustice done to Irish women for nothing that they did keeps coming up, and I'm sure the audience here, maybe it's crossed more than one or two minds, that same parallel, that an injustice and punishment that lasts a long time, for attention that they didn't seek, or something as innocent as having a child, was that in your mind making it?"

discusses the impact of Corless' investigations into Tuam's Mother and Baby Home on the making of the film as well as the film's conclusion, particularly in relation to the conclusions of two other recent mainstream films (*The Magdalene Sisters*, 2002 and *Philomena*, 2013) which portray Ireland's "architecture of containment." It also potentially points to a more ethically engaged turn in his filmmaking:

> Yeah, you know myself and Jack Reynor were going to do a documentary on the Tuam babies back then, and so that became a big part of my thinking in the film and drove me to change the past quite a bit. Like in the movie that I made, I had Eric Bana, like discover dead bodies of kids, and I had it much more, much heavier like, the head nun was letting them freeze to death, isn't that right, but then it's so fucking heavy you know, that I was like you know the reality is so heavy that I can't put that in. Em, and you know I think there's been a few movies made—you know, the *Magdalen Laundries* [sic], *Philomena*—you know I suppose I just wanted to make a movie where the woman at the end gets something out of it, you know. ("Jim Sheridan Q&A for *The Secret Scripture*")

The film, its release, and the "Tuam babies" are thus inextricably linked,[8] even as Tuam's past continues to be revealed in the present and future in ways that are difficult—if not impossible—to digest. As these historical realities are uncovered and made public in the present, they necessarily change our understanding of texts, films, and adaptations that purport to represent these human rights abuses. Given the ongoing revelations about Tuam, the film therefore implores us to consider it not simply as an adaptation of Barry's novel, but to consider it and Barry's novel in relation to Tuam. Building upon Brian McFarlane's idea that although we are "used to the idea of viewing an adaptation in the light of what we know of its

---

[8] In other interviews for the film's press tour, Sheridan continued to make connections between the film and the lives lost at Tuam, and other institutions like it. The *Belfast Telegraph* notes the "bizarre twist of fate" that connects the events at Tuam with Sheridan's film, reporting that "Sheridan shares the belief of campaigner Catherine Corless, who helped uncover the babies' remains in a sewage area near the Bon Secours home in Tuam, that similar mass graves are hidden around Ireland. 'I think there are a lot more. And the more that are exhumed and examined, the better,' says Sheridan, who describes the mother and baby homes scandal as 'insane'" (n. pag). Given all of the power the Church was given by the State in the decades after Independence, Sheridan added, "I think all that needs to be examined. Part of the thing that fascinates me is that examination between personal responsibility and communal responsibility" (n. pag).

13 "HOW SHOULD WE REMEMBER WHAT HAPPENED?": CULTURAL... 245

literary forebear," we must also be open to the notion that "the reverse process is also a possibility," I argue that the film and its unpublished screenplay (which I will discuss further)[9] ultimately compel us to revisit Barry's novel, particularly in the context of the unfolding crisis at Tuam (27). This adaptive, intertextual model insists that we revisit cultural representations of Ireland's architecture of containment in light of recent events, and that ephemeral traces—such as those found in the screenplay—become visible in order to prompt us to revisit our own ethical engagement as readers, viewers, and critics. Given these cultural representations are the only "records" we have, it remains of vital importance to dissect the ways in which they attempt to represent the experiences of tens of thousands of individuals who were committed to institutions for some portion of their lives.

In the essay that follows, I will consider the film as a relative departure from Sheridan's oeuvre as it attempts to narrate the marginalized trauma of a woman institutionalized for most of her adult life, and in the process, exposes deeply troubling episodes from Ireland's not-too-distant past. Despite the indisputably muddled final cut of the film, it still possesses powerful, resonant moments, particularly when read alongside one of the film's sources—its screenplay, which was finalized in 2015.[10] Given the controversial nature of the conclusion of the novel, and Sheridan's own framing of the film in relation to its conclusion, I will then turn to the conclusion of the film and consider it in relation to Barry's novel as well as to two peer films: *The Magdalene Sisters* (2002) and *Philomena* (2013). In the novel's conclusion, Barry insists on the main protagonist's happiness, a move that is re-imagined and amplified for the film's main protagonist, and these turns to happiness, I argue, require more sustained examination, particularly in relation to the unfolding nature of the Mother and Baby Homes investigation.

---

[9] I want to thank Jim Sheridan and his team for sharing the film's unpublished screenplay with me.

[10] Thomas Leitch, in "What Movies Want," notes that "surprisingly little has been written about screenplays as a distinctive mode of writing" (156). Building upon the work of Pier Paolo Pasolini, Leitch deconstructs the "agency" of the screenplay and argues that screenplays might be characterized as "structures that want to be other structures with a new and enriched understanding of the ways other discursive structures do and do not participate in the agency Pasolini reserves exclusively to screenplays—and would incidentally open the terms 'structures' and 'want' to productive debate" (173).

SHERIDAN'S SCRIPTURE

Sheridan has been characterized as a director who "makes films to an unashamedly mainstream formula...without apology" (Barton 4). Ruth Barton, writing about Sheridan in 2002, elaborates that,

> As Sheridan has discovered, if you want people to watch your work in large numbers, then you have to present it in a populist manner. Undue complications of theme and plot only distract the attention, hence his tendency to strip existing narratives of their peripheral characters and focus on one or two key protagonists. His films are text-based and actor-driven. They seldom obfuscate the issue and offer themselves to unambiguous readings that generally hinge upon a tale of triumph in the face of adversity. (4)

In this vein of appealing to a "populist" audience, she adds that "[h]is is, indisputably, entertainment cinema" (14). Sheridan has affirmed this reading of his films, declaring in an interview with Barton: "You just make things that make it easier for people to get up and go home after the cinema. You just make it to make life easier" (146). With the film *The Secret Scripture*, however, we see a more ethically engaged position from Sheridan—instead of making "life easier" for the audience, he argues that films should show people "things that they don't want to see" ("A heartbreaking secret..." n. pag.). Indeed, he predicted that the film would be received unfavorably because it brought historical circumstances too sharply into focus, commenting that "[the film is] not showing Ireland in roses. I think there's an element of people here who will feel that I am showing up things that they don't want to see. But the job of movies is to do that" ("A heartbreaking secret..." n. pag.). Countering Barton's analysis and indeed his own view regarding what films should do, Sheridan here amends his position about the "job" of movies. And while the conclusion of *The Secret Scripture* includes the familiar Sheridan move of "triumph in the face of adversity," the rest of the film diverges from "entertainment cinema" in the sense that it examines the politics of female trauma.

The film opens with Rooney Mara in an asylum, a young Rose Clear/McNulty, writing in the margins of a bible that will serve as her "scripture"; we see her rewrite "The Book of Job" to read "The Book of Rose." In a voiceover, Mara asserts, "My name is Rose McNulty. I did not kill my child." From here, we see modern-day, older Rose ("Lady Rose"), played by Vanessa Redgrave, as she makes her way through the halls of the same asylum—now in a state of great disrepair. The scenes move back and forth between young Rose, who seems to commit infanticide just after she gives birth by herself after her failed escape from the Mother and Baby Home, to older Rose in the asylum, and we are then quickly introduced to Dr. Grene (played by Eric Bana), who is in the process of selling his parents' house. The asylum, Rose's home for the last 40 years, is about to be demolished and turned into a hotel and spa. All of the current "patients" are in the process of being reassessed so that they can be moved to the new facility, and Dr. Grene's expertise has been officially requested in Rose's case, although we do not find out the mysterious source of this request until the conclusion of the film. From here, Rose's story is revealed, through brief, close-up shots of Rose's scripture and voiceovers by Mara and Redgrave, as we are taken to a small Irish 1940s' town that Rose throws into chaos because of her beauty and her direct manner with the local men of Ballytivan.

The opening shot features the hallway of the asylum, moving to Mara beginning to write her scripture by writing over the bible, and the soundtrack moves from Mara's voiceover to brisk, powerful piano music timed with staccato-like shots of the scripture and then finally to intercuts of Redgrave and Mara walking down the asylum hallway as the piano music continues. This fierce, non-diegetic music continues for some time, but about four minutes into the film, we see that the piano is being played by none other than older Rose herself, in an empty room. Sheridan here blurs the lines between diegetic and non-diegetic sound, and between the past and present, to emphasize the trauma that Rose has experienced as well as her powerful presence and vibrant lifeforce.

Harnessing the immense charisma of Vanessa Redgrave is one of the most dynamic ways that Rose's story is given voice in the film. Indeed, the film seems almost overpowered by Redgrave's performance at times—not only in the gravitas and import that she brings to older Rose, but also in the sense that Mara's performance seems to pale by comparison. One of the greatest challenges for Sheridan in adapting Barry's novel was surely how to visually represent Rose's scripture—in the novel, her scripture is an urgent piece of testimonial writing which features her deepest thoughts and feelings and most cherished, although necessarily inconsistent, memories. Part of Sheridan's strategy here, I argue, is that in addition to having Redgrave read the scripture in voiceovers, the film also utilizes Redgrave's cinematic presence to actually position Redgrave herself *as* the scripture, thus imbuing the scripture with incredible depth and allowing it to function as an integral part of her character. In effect, Redgrave performs the scripture in her authoritative interactions with the other characters in the present of the movie.

Older Rose's strength is bolstered by the account of her in the screenplay. In the scene where she first meets Dr. Grene about her reassessment, older Rose insists, "I am staying here until justice is done. I am finished speaking now." In the film, the lines change, but the impact is largely the same—Rose is not a powerless, frail old woman. Rather, she is an energetic force actively shaping the trajectory of her life:

Older Rose:	"No, I'm staying here."
Dr. Grene:	"Until when, Roseanne?"
Older Rose:	"Until I want to leave."
Dr. Grene:	"They're turning this place into a hotel and spa."
Older Rose:	"Then I will stay in the hotel. I'm finished speaking now."

Moreover, in the screenplay, Rose "actually controls the hospital," with other inmates looking to her for advice and aid, a role she seems eminently comfortable with (8). While her control over the asylum is less overt in the film, as she is more under the purview of the powerful "undertaker," when her room is prematurely cleared out, she puts the entire asylum in disarray when she rushes out to the front of the asylum, stops a massive moving lorry with her body, and removes the keys from the ignition. Dr. Hart's (the "undertaker") only recourse is to sedate her, at which point Dr. Grene takes "responsibility" for her.

Beyond these powerful moments which function with older Rose *as* the scripture, the literal scripture is represented in the margins of the bible or as illustrations across entire pages of the bible. There are quick shots of the scripture throughout the film: at times, the shots linger long enough to allow the viewer to read Rose's testimony (written as marginalia), or to contemplate the illustrations she has drawn. Taking the figure of Rose and representing her testimony in the margins of the bible emphasizes both the degree to which she has been marginalized—the marginalia signify her marginalization—as well as her subversive insistence in writing back and documenting her traumatic experiences. Rose's testimony literally defaces the bible and writes back, to the degree that she is able, to the religious and societal forces that determined her fate.

The scripture, and Mara's and Redgrave's voiceovers, repeat two main points: Rose did not kill her child and the hope that he will one day come

13 "HOW SHOULD WE REMEMBER WHAT HAPPENED?": CULTURAL... 249

to claim her. The need for this repetition becomes imperative as we learn, later in the film, that part of Rose's "treatment" in the asylum includes a mid-century version of Electroconvulsive therapy. To counterbalance the violent electric shock scenes and the memory loss the treatments induce, and in order to maintain some record of her life, she often verbally repeats these key details, and documents them as well, in her scripture:

> **Opening of the film (voiceover by young Rose/Rooney Mara):**
> "My name is Rose McNulty. I did not kill my child. My name is Rose McNulty. I did not kill my child."
> **Shots of bible concurrent with voiceover:**
> "The Book of Job to the Book of Rose."
> "I did not kill my child."
> Other shots of bible/scripture (date of 1942, music notes, drawing of Fr. Gaunt, dried flowers)
> **Shots of bible/scripture throughout film:**
> "I write these words in secret, in fear and in terror. I need to find a relative to claim me, otherwise I am here forever, condemned to a living death." (written in bible)
> "I did not kill my child. One day my son will come to claim me." (written in bible)
> **Near conclusion of film (Lady Rose voiceover, Vanessa Redgrave):**
> "I committed my memories to the book of Rose. They became me, and I became them. My secret scripture and me. There is no difference. I accept now that Michael is dead. I don't accept my son is dead. This has left a hole in my heart that can only be filled if my son comes to claim me."
> **Shots of bible/scripture concurrent with voiceover:**
> "The Book of Rose / January 4th, 1942: I write these words in..." / "This is my bible my secret scripture..." / "Michael McNulty R.I.P. I will live for his child" / "I believe that one day my son will come to claim me."

The full significance of these details is explained by older Rose in a scene from the screenplay, one that did not make it into the film, as she asserts: "My Secret Scripture. Without that I did not know who Rose McNulty was. Without that I did not know the name of the father of my child. The Secret Scripture became me and I became a vessel to hold and protect it. It calmed me down and gave me my dignity back" (82). Here, Rose imagines a symbiotic, mutually reinforcing relationship with the scripture where she becomes it and it becomes her—it animates her and gives her

250   T. HARNEY-MAHAJAN

life, dignity, and protection—a salve for the immense suffering she experiences over her many decades spent in the asylum.

In the screenplay, the scripture is less fully realized in that it is imagined as a series of copybooks, not a repurposed bible. Crucially, however, in the screenplay, Rose *also* uses her scripture to document the names of the babies and children who prematurely lost their lives at the Mother and Baby Home. When she is taken back to the asylum after supposedly committing infanticide, she gets herself "confined to a cell" and immediately begins to write at night "without stopping": "First my own name and then the names of all the little children I had baptised. 'Michael O'Brien, Anthony Flanagan'" (82). This project of using the scripture not just as a testimonial to record personal details, but also to document the names of the babies and children who were subjected to cruelty and violence (who Rose then subversively baptizes), is one of several moments in the screenplay that speaks directly to the "Tuam babies." The inchoate screenplay, entirely different from the film in many ways, is again and again marked by the influence of the Tuam controversy, with references to babies being buried in unmarked graves (17), infants being sold for the Church's profit (71–72), an "amazing" number of children with vague or suspicious causes of death (84), and the possibility of exhuming babies' bodies because of suspicion of neglect or wrongful death (84). The screenplay's scripture points to a more direct speaking out against the Church—particularly with Rose's moment of self-baptism and her baptizing of "illegitimate" children.

Rose's appropriation of baptism for herself and for the illegitimate children whose names she archives derives from her time spent in St. Ignatius, the Mother and Baby Home. In the film, following the screenplay, a central moment of plot development is Rose's committal to the nearby Mother and Baby Home once she is found to be pregnant. As Rose is moved from the asylum to the Mother and Baby Home, it takes her some time to understand the fate of her unborn child. In the spare, brief moments she finds to speak to the other pregnant and incarcerated women, she is incredulous as she learns that she has no choice about whether or not to keep her baby. A fellow inmate explains to her: "If he's well, will be sent to America. But if not, he'll have to stay here for the rest of his life." On the heels of this revelation, Rose is tending to some of the babies and children in the Home's nursery (as they await adoption) and it is here that a nun threatens Rose's unborn child with a lifetime in the Home, if not premature death. When Rose maintains that her baby will not be taken away, the nun replies:

Nun:	"No. It'll be staying here. How long have you been with us, Teresa?"
Teresa:	"Since I've been born."
Nun (to younger Rose):	"Since she was born. That's if it's lucky. Some of the poor mites don't make it."

In the film, the children in the nursery of the Mother and Baby Home look relatively well nourished and taken care of. This is in contrast to the description of the children in the screenplay, where they are described as "malnourished," "desperate," and Rose becomes overwhelmed by their "desperation" (71). These darker descriptions lend credence to Rose's desperate escape attempt. In the next scene of the film, as Rose folds laundry by herself in the basement of the Home, Teresa conveniently—and wittingly?—asks Rose to lock the back door for her as she briskly walks past her. Sensing a moment of opportunity, from here Rose undertakes a harrowing escape across the Ballytivan Causeway, just moments before she gives birth.

Vanessa Redgrave as Lady Rose, a powerfully imagined scripture, representing a Mother Baby and Home, and a screenplay that provides some direct references to the unfolding events at Tuam are all moments in the film and its sources that speak to the politics of female trauma within Ireland's "architecture of containment." Ultimately, however, perhaps in Sheridan's efforts to streamline Johnny Ferguson's screenplay, viewers are left with a convoluted plot—a film that is not text-based enough—and with too many competing key characters often delivering clunky dialogue. Instead of remaining focused on Rose's story, Sheridan turns to something that he has said he has always wanted to film—an Irish love story. When Rose evacuates back to her hometown because of the WWII raids in Belfast, the man she falls in love with is the character she has the least amount of chemistry with, as well as the most stilted exchanges (Michael McNulty, played by Jack Reynor). In the film, McNulty, a shopkeeper, almost immediately volunteers for the RAF (Royal Air Force)—an unforgivable offense from the perspective of local IRA members—and as he departs, he is marked by the local men as a traitor. But the real unrequited love story in the film is between Fr. Gaunt (Stephen/Theo James) and

Rose—and Sheridan seems unsure which love story he wants to pursue as the scenes between Fr. Gaunt and Rose shine with compelling dialogue and are far more electric than those between Rose and Michael. In the film, Fr. Gaunt is Rose's contemporary in age, and their initial chemistry is undeniable. But as he pursues her in an increasingly predatory fashion, Rose is warned by her Aunt to stay away from him. Yet Rose falters under her own powerlessness—Fr. Gaunt is a formidable religious figure in the community, and his relentless pursuit of her is not something she has any control over.

In an angle that Sheridan might have profitably pursued, this film seems to be about, in Rose's phrasing "a priest who also wants to be a man." Sheridan convincingly begins to explore how male and female desire have no means of expression, and this collective repressed desire mutates into a community mired in punitive surveillance, control, retribution, and secrecy. But this exploration is abandoned by returning to the main love story: in the first of two narrative twists that had reviewers absolutely howling, Rose's savior from Fr. Gaunt is in the form of Michael, whose fighter-plane is shot down just outside of Rose's cottage. In a matter of 72 hours, they consummate their relationship, are secretly married, and Michael then flees for his safety from the local thugs (unsuccessfully, we later find out). Fr. Gaunt, in a jealous rage and unaware that Michael and Rose have actually married, has Rose committed to an asylum by her Aunt. And although he later regrets his hasty actions, Rose is by then visibly pregnant (by Michael).

After Rose's attempted escape, we see that the scene from the beginning of the film is really just Rose cutting her newborn's umbilical cord, before passing out from exhaustion and exposure. Fr. Gaunt, right on her heels, steals the baby away, tells the authorities that Rose committed infanticide, and thereby sentences her to life in the local asylum. Rose never believes she killed her son, but her ravings sound like those of a mad woman, further fueled by rumors that the child was actually Fr. Gaunt's. At the end of the film, via a letter from Dr. Grene's deceased adoptive parents, we learn that Fr. Gaunt revealed the truth to Dr. Grene's parents late in life, and that Dr. Grene is in fact Rose's biological son. We learn, also, that Fr. Gaunt is behind Dr. Grene's assignment to Rose's case. Dr.

13 "HOW SHOULD WE REMEMBER WHAT HAPPENED?": CULTURAL... 253

Grene rips the "For Sale" sign from his parents' front-lawn and races to tell the elderly Rose that he is her son. In the final moments of the film, scenes of young Rose and Michael McNulty's brief relationship (imagined and real) are intercut with mother and son embracing:

Conclusion of film:
> Older Rose: "Michael sent you, didn't he?"
> Dr. Grene: "He did. Let's go."
> Older Rose: "Where to?"
> Dr. Grene: "Home."

Mother/son embrace; interspersed with scenes of young Rose and Michael McNulty ("real" and imagined):
> Young Rose to Michael McNulty, as she dreams of it: "Have you come to take me home?"
> Michael McNulty: "I have."

Back and forth scenes continue to end / Kelly Clarkson song closes the film.

The film closes with mother and son returning to Dr. Grene's childhood home, where Rose can presumably live out the rest of her days. Sheridan doesn't have Rose proclaim her happiness outright, but her happiness is plainly demonstrated through reunification with her son. It is certainly possible to read this as a fulfilling moment—one that Rose "deserves" and has "earned," given her incredible trauma. Even further, one might argue that Rose's happiness and reunification with her long-lost son function as a subversive commentary: in an uplifting, magical realist mode, it paradoxically calls attention, in its singularity and exceptionalism, to the thousands of individuals who remain in the dark about the status of the children they were forced to give up or the adults who may have no idea that they were adopted as children.

Critics and reviewers, however, remained unconvinced. During the press tour for the film, Sheridan defended the highly implausible conclusion of the film where Rose and her long-lost son are mawkishly reunited. Regarding the conclusion of the novel, he said, "I tried to make that work. And the biggest criticism we got was the part that actually stays true to the book. People maybe thought that you can't have such an 'up' ending in such a heavy story. But that's the whole book. That's the reason I did it" (Horan n. pag.). In another interview, he elaborated, "I thought that the ending, while some people have problems with it, at least it gives the woman a victory for once, y'know?" and "I was so fuckin' tired of all these movies

254 T. HARNEY-MAHAJAN

about the poor put-upon women in the Magdalenes and all. It was like, let's hit back for a change" (Roy n. pag). In Sheridan's desire to "hit back" and to stay "true to the book" in the conclusion of the film, it instead falls victim to cliché and sentimentality. Rose's unification with her son/husband and their return to his childhood home point to the preservation of traditional roles and social order and insists upon heteronormative domestic stability as the only resolution for these two characters. This implausible outcome—where mother and husband/son return to the traditional familial home—looks away from the ongoing nature of the past in the present for the survivors of these institutions and instead focuses on a recurrent atemporality where present and past are overlaid in a normative resolution.

When Barry's novel *The Secret Scripture* was awarded the prestigious Costa Prize in 2009, the selection committee simultaneously objected strenuously to its conclusion. Matthew Parris—the chair of the awards panel—stated that all of the judges "agreed that it was flawed, and almost no one liked the ending, which was almost fatal to its success" ("Interview" n. pag.). But Barry has always stood behind the plot twist, and according to Sheridan, the conclusion of the novel is what drew him to the project in the first place. In an article I wrote in 2012 on the novel, I tried to make sense of the conclusion of the novel, as well as the main protagonist's inexplicable insistence on her happiness—despite being institutionalized against her will for 65 years. In the novel, one of the three narrative threads is Dr. Grene's, who has been tasked with assessing Roseanne's mental state, and the novel is as much his as it is hers, with Dr. Grene's "Commonplace Book" interspersed with Roseanne's "testimony of herself"—her "Secret Scripture." Some of the most powerful moments in the text, Roseanne's "testimony" allows the reader to learn how radically her life story diverges from official records written by Fr. Gaunt—records that condemned Roseanne to an asylum for almost seven decades. In the novel's conclusion, when Dr. Grene finds out that he is Roseanne's biological son, he does not divulge this information to Roseanne and the novel remains open-ended as to whether or not he will tell her. Regardless, Dr. Grene proclaims happiness for both of them in the end of the novel: "...I smiled like a boy, that's what it felt like, and I gave a laugh of happiness. It was only then that it hit me. I am content to report that at the centre of it all, given everything, the nature of her history and mine, there was a very simple emotion" (298). Beyond this final declaration of happiness for Roseanne in the novel's conclusion, Roseanne's happiness is something she too insists on at various times throughout the novel. Today, given the film, its screenplay, and in the specter of the forthcoming findings at Tuam and institutions like it, the tensions in Barry's novel have become manifold, and perhaps insurmountable. I had previously suggested that the novel proposes the path forward must be predicated on an engagement with official history (which remains unavailable to the survivors), as well as the opportunity to voice one's own story. Since the publication of the novel and with the release of the film, the extent of the burials—of bodies, of histories, and of memories—that may be forthcoming, as well as the persistent cycle of apathy and forgetting that attends these historic abuses, complicate Barry's text all the more. In sum, both narratives—the film and the novel—investigate the politics of female trauma by concluding with a turn to happiness. How can we understand this insistence on Roseanne's and Rose's happiness?

Enforced Happiness

In Sara Ahmed's *The Promise of Happiness*, she asks not what happiness *is*, but rather what does happiness *do*?[11] Extending the "work of feminist, black, and queer scholars," Ahmed investigates further "how happiness is used to justify oppression" (2) and "how happiness is used to redescribe social norms as social goods" (2). She writes that "[w]e might even say that [certain] political movements"—women's movements, in particular—"have struggled *against* rather than *for* happiness" (2). Ahmed reminds us how Simone de Beauvoir has probed what lurks behind happiness, as de Beauvoir writes: "It is not too clear just what the word *happy* really means and still less what true values it may mask" (2). The questions for the film and the novel, then, are: how is happiness being used in these texts? What true values is it masking? And, why is happiness being demanded for Roseanne and Rose? Ahmed advises us to be suspicious of this compulsion. As she writes, "[t]he demand for happiness is increasingly articulated as a demand to return to social ideals, as if what explains the crisis of happiness is not the failure of these ideals but our failure to follow them. And arguably, at times of crisis the language of happiness acquires an even more powerful hold" (7). The film depicts a crisis—a societal and cultural crisis—whereby women were held against their will, crises that

[11] For a wide-ranging and even more recent analysis of the complex, gendered nature of happiness, see the special issue *Gendering Happiness and Its Discontents*, edited by Suzanne Clisby.

entire communities were complicit in. After the film's exploration of an entire town's complicity in the incarceration of women, one might argue that one way to "fight back," in Sheridan's phrasing, would be to give Rose a happy ending at the end of the film. This move to happiness, however, potentially obscures real women's experiences in that it represents Rose's narrative as resolved—something that is *over*.

To apply Ahmed here, to accept these narrative closures of happiness is to rest upon our own privileged position. It allows us to witness the trauma and read the suffering of these women in a comfortable way—as something that happened in the past, with their now ameliorated suffering in the present a welcome relief to us as readers and viewers. Moreover, building upon de Beauvoir, Ahmed importantly notes that happiness is tied to value (11): using this frame in relation to the novel and film, Roseanne and Rose are no longer the marginalized, or the wretched—they have been claimed by their biological sons and they now fit within a heteronormative paradigm of "valuable personhood:" a mother defined in relation to her child, and *specifically* her son. This logic is circular: Rose's life acquires value at the end because she has managed to find "happiness," and her hard-won "happiness" makes her life valuable. Her value is tied directly to her ability to claim personhood in the moment where her claim to motherhood is validated. Put another way, "happiness" is the only affect that can be imagined with the restoration of the normative maternal bond. The film then takes one step further, by insisting upon the domestic space of the home as the only place where the mother and son/husband bond can be reclaimed and fulfilled.

Ahmed calls upon us to "rewrite the history of happiness from the point of view of the wretch" (17). She elaborates: "If we can listen to those who are cast as wretched, perhaps their wretchedness would no longer belong to them. The sorrow of the stranger might give us a different angle on happiness not because it teaches us what it is like or must be like to be a stranger, but because it might estrange us from the very happiness of the familiar" (17). In Ahmed's articulations here, the audience would sit with the character who has been cast as wretched, with her irredeemability, with her shame, her trauma, her inability, and indeed her refusal, to be happy after a life spent involuntarily institutionalized. Instead of relying on the all-too familiar "happy" stereotype of reunited mother and son, the novel and the film might have estranged us from this easy resolution and invited us to consider "how to remember what happened" to Rose, to circle back to one of the introductory questions in this essay. Perhaps more importantly, they would resist closure where past and present are neatly forged, and instead point to the ongoing nature of the "Tuam babies" and institutions like it.

ALTERNATIVE APPROACHES

With two contested conclusions, it is fruitful to consider them in relation to *The Magdalene Sisters* (2002) and *Philomena* (2013). *The Magdalene Sisters*, written and directed by Peter Mullan, is very loosely based on the 1998 documentary *Sex in a Cold Climate*, which was directed by Steve Humphries. Written by and starring Steve Coogan and directed by Stephen Frears, *Philomena* was "inspired by true events" from the nonfiction book *The Lost Child of Philomena Lee*, written by Martin Sixsmith and published in 2009.[12] *The Magdalene Sisters* and *Philomena* largely succeed in excavating and representing the immense trauma of countless women without offering a "happy" ending to the audience. Instead, both films manage to signal to the ongoing nature of these human rights abuses.

For example, in *The Magdalene Sisters*, two out of the four main characters succeed in a triumphant, if entirely unrealistic, breakout scene from their confinement. Bernadette and Rose barrel through a door with a bed-frame, and Bernadette engages in hand-to-hand combat with Sister Bridget in order to escape. The film also gestures, however, to the documentary from which it is loosely based: *Sex in a Cold Climate* centers on the ongoing trauma of four older women, as they testify about how their lives were irrevocably damaged, and they delve into the shame and secrecy that shadowed their entire lives. In the conclusion of *The Magdalene Sisters*, the "futures" for all four main characters are foretold with the on-screen text explaining:

---

[12] Sixsmith also made a documentary in 2015, *Ireland's Lost Babies*, which investigates the Catholic Church's Ireland-to-United States adoption trade. Mary Burke and Jim Smith both presented on the adoption network between Ireland and the United States at the 2019 American Conference for Irish Studies. The panel, "Irish Complicity: Disremembering Institutionalized Women," was chaired by Rachael Sealy Lynch and included Mary M. Burke's "'A surprise for the wife from Ireland': Irish Products and Postwar Traffic(king) between Ireland and America," James M. Smith's "Knowing and Unknowing Tuam: Ireland Past, Ireland Present" and a third paper by me, "'How should we remember what happened?': Questioning the Ethics of Representing Institutional Abuse in Jim Sheridan's *The Secret Scripture*."

258 T. HARNEY-MAHAJAN

"Bernadette soon moved to Scotland where she opened her own salon. She has been married and divorced three times. She now lives alone." / "Rose married and had two children, both girls. She found her son in 1996, thirty-three years after he was taken. She remained a devout Catholic until she died in 1998." / "Margaret settled in Donegal, where she became a primary school teacher. Today she is an assistant headmistress. She never married." / "Crispina, real name Harriet, died of anorexia in 1972. She was 24 years old."

In Smith's chapter on the film, he argues that "[i]t courageously pans the camera lens out and documents the collusion among, and thereby establishes the culpability of, church, state, family, and community in maintaining the open secret of the laundries and the abuse of thousands of women confined therein" (158). Building upon Smith's analysis, Jessica Scarlata discusses how the "film…pay[s] homage to the fact that women who survived the laundries did so primarily only in body" (245), emphasizing how "[e]ach of the closing shots ends in a freeze-frame, a formal device that works as a visual refusal to move on. The freeze-frame in this context mimics the dynamics of trauma, which arrests its victims and holds them hostage to the past" (246). But I would argue that Mullan also establishes that while Margaret, Rose, and Bernadette are "freed in body," the institutional violence to which they were subjected is marked on their bodies, even if no visual remnants remain (Scarlata 247). For example, just prior to Bernadette's concluding freeze-frame shot, she seeks refuge from the rainstorm and finds herself momentarily stranded alongside two nuns. This physical proximity to women in habits triggers a physical reaction, and Bernadette begins to relive when her head was brutally shaved at the laundry, with the rain dripping onto her forehead simulating her blood. Bernadette, however, resists her embodied response in the moment by taking down and tousling her hair, also using her body to shake itself out of the triggered memory.

Therefore while the women survive "in body," it is also where, the film demonstrates, they remain forever marked from their time in the laundry. After the freeze-frame shots in relation to the four main characters, the film closes with statistics relating to the widespread and diffuse nature of these institutions throughout Ireland, allowing the film to widen its temporal reach: "It is estimated that as many as 30,000 women were detained at Magdalene Asylums throughout Ireland. The last laundry closed in 1996." Having treated its characters as though they are historical personages, the film here lays further claim to documentary reality in its

13 "HOW SHOULD WE REMEMBER WHAT HAPPENED?": CULTURAL... 259

transition from images to text and people to numbers, stressing the wide-spread nature of the abuse, as well as its relevance in the present moment as an ongoing situation, one that is still unfolding.

While *Philomena*'s conclusion is not exactly heart-warming (when she finally finds her son, he has been dead for years), Philomena does learn that her son had searched for her for much of his adult life. This much hoped for revelation is represented as one of the main reasons for Philomena's quest. Perhaps more problematic, the character of Philomena is made out to be a bit of a "dumb clock" throughout the film—another version, I argue, of making the film palatable for audiences (Lee n. pag.). And although Judi Dench pulls off these elements of "comedic relief," one also has to wonder why Philomena must be presented in such an infantilized way.[13] The ending, however, similar to *The Magdalene Sisters*, pays tribute to Philomena's ongoing pain and the unresolved cases of thousands of other women like her, with the on-screen text displaying: "Martin Sixsmith published 'The Lost Child of Philomena Lee' in 2009. Thousands more adopted Irish children and their 'shamed' mothers are still trying to find each other." This is not to say that something as basic or prescriptive as on-screen text referencing wider historical circumstances is all that is required at the end of a film which portrays the aftermath of human rights abuses. Rather, it is one final framing element in the overall trajectory of the film which repeatedly addresses the ongoing nature of Philomena's story, and therefore women like her. In her analysis of the film, Auxiliadora Pérez-Vides argues that *Philomena* functions as evidence of abuse as well as a reminder of the ongoing nature of this abuse, as she theorizes the idea of "Magdalene Otherness" (13). The film, she argues, demonstrates that this otherness is not "simply a historical gap to be filled," but given the "continuum of abuse and contempt experienced by these women," a past and present that Irish society has yet to fully reckon with—and in my reading, the more expansive conclusion is part of this continuum (13). By framing the abuse experienced by individuals within a

---

[13] Writing for the *Daily Mail*, Philomena Lee shared her experience of watching the film. In the piece, she considered the amount of exposure it will likely bring her, and she responded to initial reactions to the film. Of her character, played by Judi Dench, Lee commented: "I saw the film a few weeks ago and it still doesn't feel real. I come across as a bit of a dumb clock in it—an Irish term for a silly billy—and I suppose that's what I am really. I know they had to put some humour in it and they say 'There is no way we think you are silly'" (Lee n. pag.).

260   T. HARNEY-MAHAJAN

temporal continuum—a continuum with a future we cannot yet come to terms with—we can see that both of these films register the ongoing nature of historical institutional abuse for its survivors, and for society at large.

Refusing Happiness

While *The Magdalene Sisters* and *Philomena* offer alternative approaches, in refusing Rose and Roseanne's happiness, we still face the question of how to represent—and how to witness—these women's experiences. The field of human rights and literary studies offers some suggestions about how to represent and witness immense suffering without exploiting or marginalizing the experiences of those affected by it. In *Gender, Narrative, Human Rights*, Elizabeth Swanson Goldberg builds upon the work of Elaine Scarry and others who consider how to represent the unrepresentable, and she considers the genre of what she calls "witness literature." "Witness literature," Swanson Goldberg writes, is different from the historical novel or film,

> because of its dedication to an ethic of telling atrocity for the same reasons associated with testimonial: not simply a dramatization of history, but rather an honoring of those lost to the atrocity; an aiding of survivors by legitimating their experiences; a restoration of accounts denied by hegemonic or official narratives of events; a gesture toward prevention of such events in future. While witness literature does not gesture toward the truth in an experientially authentic or evidentiary model it does share many of the representational ethics that characterize the testimonial form. (158)

Given Goldberg's definition, witness literature attempts to honor, aid, restore, and prevent. Under this paradigm of potential outcomes, and perhaps even in an attempt to meet some if not all of them, Sheridan and Barry insist on the happiness of their main protagonists, ostensibly as "a way of measuring progress" (Ahmed 4). But upon deeper engagement, I think we can see how happiness potentially "becomes a disciplinary technique"—both for Rose and Roseanne and for us as readers and viewers in the sense that the move to happiness resolves their present *and future* trauma and marginalizes the ongoing nature of the past in the present and future (Ahmed 8).

Goldberg's scholarship analyzes how certain novels and films manage to "disrupt conventional narrative forms that reproduce fixed—predictable, and thereby often intractable—identity positions of victim and oppressor" (16). Still, Goldberg concludes her study with a question about audience and action. She writes that the question "of what audiences will do with information gathered and emotion generated by these narratives haunts the work of literary or cinematic artist and of scholar/critic" (193). This is a question that remains open for Goldberg, but she argues that the ethical work of representing immense suffering must generate "energy" in the audience's witnessing such that a visible "trace" is left "in return" (193). While Sheridan's film might ultimately fail in the end, for a variety of reasons and perhaps not only because of its conclusion, it succeeds as an adaptation because of the "energy" it creates and the "traces" it leaves as it connects with the "Tuam babies" and with Mother and Baby Homes in twentieth-century Ireland. These connections, a network of relations, create an adaptive, intertextual model whereby we might revisit cultural representations of Ireland's "architecture of containment." While the conclusions of the novel and film do not necessarily speak to the ongoing nature of the past in the present and future for the survivors of these institutions, the adaptation model itself acknowledges that each revelation about these homes and institutions in twentieth-century Ireland begs evermore questions and introspection. This adaptation model works toward cultural representations that incorporate some sense of the far-reaching and traumatic ongoing consequences of this culture of containment and recognizes the continual cycle of forgetting and effacement that real survivors of these institutions must continue to combat, along with their lifelong battles with shame and trauma.

WORKS CITED

Ahmed, Sara. *The Promise of Happiness*. Duke: Duke UP, 2010.

Atkins, Sarah. "Poverty, race and vulnerability: effects of children growing up in the Irish asylum system." *International Journal of Children's Rights*, 2015, vol. 23, no. 2, pp. 425–475. https://doi.org/10.1163/15718182-02302005

Barry, Sebastian. *The Secret Scripture*. New York: Penguin Group, 2008.

Barton, Ruth. *Jim Sheridan: Framing the Nation*. Dublin: The Liffey Press, 2002.

Burke, Mary. "Clandestine Pregnancies and Child Burial Sites in Tom Murphy's Drama and Mary Leland's *The Killeen*." *Irish University Review* 49.2 (2019): 245–61. https://doi.org/10.3366/iur.2019.0404

Clisby, Suzanne. "Gendering happiness and its discontents." *Journal of Gender Studies* (2017): 26:1, 2–9, https://doi.org/10.1080/09589236.2017.1273362

Collins, Liam. "Zozimus: Author Barry does not recognise his book in film version." *Indepentent.ie* 6 Nov 2016. https://www.independent.ie/opinion/comment/zozimus-author-barry-does-not-recognise-his-book-in-film-version-35191582.html

Cronin, Nessa and Till, Karen E. "Embodied Geographies of the Nation. " *Irish Review* 54 (2018). pp 1–7.

Fernando, Nilmini. (2016) "The Discursive Violence of Postcolonial Asylum in the Irish Republic." *Postcolonial Studies*, 19:4, 393 408, https://doi.org/10.1080/13688790.2016.1317390

Fischer, Clara. "Gender, Nation, and the Politics of Shame: Magdalen Laundries and the Institutionalization of Feminine Transgression in Modern Ireland," *Signs: Journal of Women in Culture and Society* 41, no. 4 (Summer 2016): 821–843.

Garrett, Paul Michael. "Excavating the past: Mother and Baby Homes in the Republic of Ireland." *The British Journal of Social Work*, Volume 47, Issue 2, March 2017, Pages 358–374, https://doi.org/10.1093/bjsw/bcv116

Goldberg, Elizabeth Swanson. *Beyond Terror: Gender, Narrative, Human Rights.* Rutgers, Rutgers UP, 2007.

Grierson, Jamie. "Mass grave of babies and children found at Tuam care home in Ireland." *The Guardian.* 3 Mar 2017. https://www.theguardian.com/world/2017/mar/03/mass-grave-of-babies-and-children-found-at-tuam-orphanage-in-ireland

Harney-Mahajan, Tara. "Provoking Forgiveness in Sebastian Barry's *The Secret Scripture." New Hibernia Review* 16.2 (2012): 54–71.

"A heartbreaking secret... and the need for healing." *The Belfast Telegraph* 18 March 2017. https://www.belfasttelegraph.co.uk/life/features/a-heart breaking-secret-and-the-need-for-healing-35541905.html

Horan, Niamh. "Irish director Jim Sheridan reacts to author's criticism of his movie." Feb 19 2017. *Independent.ie* https://www.independent.ie/entertainment/movies/irish-director-jim-sheridan-reacts-to-authors-criticism-of-his-movie-35462861.html

Horgan-Jones, Jack, Fiach Kelly, and Marie O'Halloran. "Mother-and-baby home inquiry: hundreds of burial plots unknown." *The Irish Times* 18 April 2019. https://www.irishtimes.com/news/ireland/irish-news/mother-and-baby-home-inquiry-hundreds-of-burial-plots-unknown-1.3863904

Jeffries, Stuart. "Interview: Sebastian Barry reveals the secrets of his Costa prize win." *Guardian* 29 Jan 2009. https://www.theguardian.com/books/2009/jan/28/sebastian-barry-costa-prize-winner1

Jellenik, G. "The Task of the Adaptation Critic." *Adaptation in Visual Culture: Images, Texts, and their Multiple Worlds.* Edited by Julie Grossman and R. Barton Palmer. Palgrave: Palgrave Studies in Adaptation and Visual Culture, 2017.

"Jim Sheridan Q&A for The Secret Scripture." *YouTube,* uploaded by Irish Film Institute, 26 Mar 2017, https://www.youtube.com/watch?time_continue=36&v=zraCXC9BRhs

Lee, Philomena. "I forgive the nuns who stole my boy: Played by Judi Dench in a heart-rending new film, PHILOMENA LEE reveals the search for her love child who was given away to strangers." October 31 2013. *DailyMail.co.uk* https://www.dailymail.co.uk/femail/article-2482269/Philomena-Lee-played-Judi-Dench-new-film-forgives-nuns-stole-son.html

Leitch, Thomas. "What Movies Want." Edited by Jorgen Bruhn. *Bloomsbury Publishing,* 2013. Kindle Edition. pp 156–176.

———."Mind the Gaps." *Adaptation in Visual Culture: Images, Texts, and their Multiple Worlds.* Edited by Julie Grossman and R. Barton Palmer. Palgrave: Palgrave Studies in Adaptation and Visual Culture, 2017.

Loyal, Steven, and Stephen Quilley. "Categories of State Control: Asylum Seekers and the Direct Provision and Dispersal System in Ireland." Social Justice, 43.4 (146), 2016, pp. 69–97.

MacDonald, Sarah. "President needs to visit Tuam babies site and tell nation to act, says Corless." December 30, 2019. *Independent.ie.* https://www.independent.ie/irish-news/president-needs-to-visit-tuam-babies-site-and-tell-nation-to-act-says-corless-38820985.html

McFarlane, Brian. "Reading Film and Literature." Edited by Deborah Cartmell and Imelda Whelehan. *The Cambridge Companion to Literature on Screen.* Cambridge University Press, 2007. Kindle Edition. pp 15–28.

McGarry, Patsy. "Hundreds of Magdalene women gather in Dublin for event in their honour." *The Irish Times.* 5 June 2018. https://www.irishtimes.com/news/social-affairs/hundreds-of-magdalene-women-gather-in-dublin-for-event-in-their-honour-1.3519343

The Magdalene Sisters. 2002. Produced by Francis Higson, Written and Directed by Peter Mullan. Dublin: A PFP Films Production in association with Temple Films.

O'Donnell, Katherine. "Let's listen attentively to survivors of Magdalene Laundries." June 5 2018. *The Irish Times.* https://www.irishtimes.com/opinion/let-s-listen-attentively-to-survivors-of-magdalene-laundries-1.3519069

Philomena. 2002. Produced by Gabrielle Tana, Steve Coogan, and Tracey Seaward, Written by Steve Coogan and Jeff Pope, Directed by Stephen Frears. A coproduction of BBC Films, Baby Cow Productions, BFI, Magnolia Mae Films, and Pathé.

Pérez-Vides, Auxiliadora. "Magdalene Otherness and Ethical Turns in Stephen Frears's *Philomena.*" *Nordic Irish Studies* Vol. 15, No. 1, SPECIAL ISSUE: Discourses of Inclusion and Exclusion: Artistic Renderings of Marginal Identities in Ireland (2016), pp. 11–26.

Roy, David. "Jim Sheridan on making The Secret Scripture in Ireland." March 25 2017. *The Irish News.* https://www.irishnews.com/arts/2017/03/25/news/jim-sheridan-on-making-the-secret-scripture-in-ireland-976705/

Scarlata, Jessica. *Rethinking Occupied Ireland.* Syracuse University Press: 2014. Kindle Edition.

The Secret Scripture. 2013. Produced by Noel Pearson, Written by Jim Sheridan and Johnny Ferguson, Directed by Jim Sheridan. Dublin: A Ingenious Senior Film Fund Production in association with Voltage Pictures and Ferndale Films.

Sheridan, Jim and Johnny Ferguson. "The Secret Scripture." 19 March 2015. Unpublished Screenplay.

Smith, James M. *Ireland's Magdalen Laundries and the Nation's Architecture of Containment.* Notre Dame, Indiana: U of Notre Dame P, 2007.

Yeager, Jennifer and Jonathan Culleton. "Gendered Violence and Cultural Forgetting: The Case of the Irish Magdalenes." *Radical History Review* 1 October 2016; 2016 (126): 134–146. https://doi.org/10.1215/01636545-3594481

Index[1]

A

Abbey Theatre (Dublin), 12, 78
Abbott, H. Porter, 85, 87, 118n3
Abrahamson, Lenny, 8, 155–162, 165, 167–177
Academy Awards, 9, 166, 167, 220
Adam and Paul (2004, Lenny Abrahamson), 155, 156, 160, 173–175
Afternoon (1990, novel), 110
Ahmed, Sara, 241n3, 255, 256, 260
Aiden, Saint, 116, 119, 120, 123–125, 126n7, 127, 128, 130–132
Aisling (poetry genre), 116, 120, 124, 127–129, 131, 132, 218, 220
Albright, Daniel, 92
Allen, Kieran, 168, 169
Allers, Roger, 134
All That Fall (1957, radio play), 85

"Alone and Forsaken" (song), 219
Amadeus (1979, play), 49
Ambassadors, The (1533, painting), 228
American Tail, An (1986, Don Bluth), 114
Amis, Martin, 111
Anderson, Michael, 12
Andreu, Betsy, 203, 207, 211, 212
Andreu, Frankie, 207, 211, 212
Andrew, Dudley, 145
Angel (1982, Neil Jordan), 3
Angela's Ashes (1999, Alan Parker), 111
Anne Devlin (1984, Pat Murphy), 79, 79n12
Antigua (Lesser Antilles), 51
Anti-Semitism, 103, 109
Archibald, Douglas N., 69

---

[1] Note: Page numbers followed by 'n' refer to notes.

© The Author(s), under exclusive license to Springer Nature Switzerland AG 2022
M. C. Conner et al. (eds.), *Screening Contemporary Irish Fiction and Drama*, Palgrave Studies in Adaptation and Visual Culture, https://doi.org/10.1007/978-3-031-04568-4

265

266　INDEX

Armagh (monastery), 122
Artaud, Antonin, 89, 90, 93–95
Ascendancy (1983, Edward
　　Bennett), 66
Assimilation (2013, Paula Kehoe), 17
Atkins, Sarah, 241n3
Atlanta (Georgia), 7
"At the Dark End of the Street"
　　(song), 37, 38, 39n14

B

Bad Day in Blackrock (2008,
　　novel), 155
BAFTA Awards, 159
Ballyfermot Animation College
　　(Dublin), 114
Ballytivan (Causeway), 251
Bana, Eric, 244, 247
Banfield, Ann, 96
Barbican Centre (London), 84
Barnacle, Nora, 108
Barnett, Louise, 73, 75, 76, 77n10
Barry, Sebastian, 241, 242, 244, 245,
　　247, 254, 255, 260
Barrytown Trilogy, The (book series),
　　15, 23, 46, 146, 213
Barthes, Roland, 105
Barton, Ruth, 8, 9, 41, 65, 66, 66n2,
　　114, 117, 118, 118n3, 167, 170,
　　176, 183n1, 184n2, 190n4, 246
BBC3 (TV station), 7
Beach, Sylvia, 100
Beauty Queen of Leenane, The (1996,
　　play), 56n8, 219, 234
Beckett on Film (2000, project), 84
Beckett, Samuel, 11, 18, 83–97, 111
Begin Again (2013, John Carney), 45,
　　48, 49, 57
Benjamin, Walter, 84, 85, 88, 241
Bennett, Edward, 66
Bernhard, Thomas, 96n11

Birch, Alice, 8
Birmingham Six (trial), 234
Blackrock College (Dublin), 156, 164
Blackwater Lightship, The (1999,
　　novel), 183
Bloom (2003, Sean Walsh),
　　57, 58, 100
Blueprint Pictures (studio), 102, 159
Bluth, Don, 114
Booker Prize, 23, 241
"Book of Job" (bible), 246
Boondock Saints (1999, Troy
　　Duffy), 140
Bord Scannán (Irish Film Board), 3,
　　158, 165
Bosch, Hieronymus, 222
Boulder Media (animation
　　studio), 114
Boxer, The (1997, Jim Sheridan), 15
Boyne, John, 156
Boyton, Lucy, 51
Bradshaw, Peter, 176
Brady, Orla, 68
Brah, Avtar, 216
Brando, Marlon, 60
Brater, Enoch, 91, 92
Breakfast on Pluto (2006, Neil
　　Jordan), 18, 137–153
Breathnach, Paddy, 158, 165, 166
Brendan, Saint, 47, 49–51, 55–57, 59,
　　60, 120, 122–132, 134
Brennan, Brid, 68
Breton, André, 93
British Broadcasting Company (BBC),
　　83, 149n10, 166, 167, 172,
　　216, 225
British heritage films (genre), 66, 67
Broighter Hoard (gold artefacts), 125
Brooklyn
　　2015, John Crowley, 18, 160, 167,
　　　168, 170, 181–197
　　2009, novel, 181, 186

INDEX   267

Brooks, Xan, 231
Brosnan, Pierce, 16
Brown Bag (animation studio), 114
Brown, James, 21, 33, 34, 36, 50, 51
Brown, Terence, 10, 11, 13, 14, 22, 23, 30, 31
Bruyheel, Johan, 203, 208, 210, 213
Bryld, Eigil, 221
Buckley, Cara, 216
Bulben, Ben, 227
Burgess, Anthony, 101
Burkdall, Thomas L., 100
Burke, Mary, 242, 257n12
Burrell, Carter, 221
Butcher Boy, The
  1997, Neil Jordan, 111
  1992, novel, 15
Bute, Mary Ellen, 100

C
"Cadenus and Vanessa" (1726, poem), 68, 74
Cahill, Ann, 144
Calder, John, 83
California Street Terrorism Enforcement and Prevention Act (1988), 233
Calvary (2014, John Michael McDonagh), 15, 227–231, 234
Campbell, Malcolm, 155, 156, 160, 162, 169, 170, 172, 173, 177
Campbell, Martin, 15
Camus, Albert, 171
Canada, 160
Canning, Laura, 231
Carlin, Michael, 221
Carney, John, 18, 43–62
"Carrickfergus" (song), 234
Carroll, Lewis, 93, 94, 96
Cartmell, Deborah, 44n3
Cartoon Network, 114

Cartoon Saloon (animation studio), 113–135
Casey, Bishop Eamonn, 14
Cassetti, Francesco, 144
Catastrophe (1982, play), 84
Cellach, Abbott, 119, 120, 122–126, 129–131
Celtic Tiger (economic boom), 3, 16, 24, 40, 139, 152, 155, 160
"Chain of Fools" (song), 37
Chambers, Robert, 216, 235
Chan, Jackie, 16
Channel 4 (British network), 84
Chaplin, Geraldine, 68
Chatto (publisher), 88
Cheadle, Don, 223
Cheng, Chua, 107
Cinematograph Films Act (1927), 13
Cinematograph Volta (movie house), 99
Clare, Anthony, 141
Clare, David, 221
Clare (Irish County), 125
Clarke, David, 174
Clarke, Donald, 43, 44n2, 61, 231
Clay, Linda Bright, 226
Clisby, Suzanne, 255n11
Clonmacnois (monastery), 122, 125
Club Anabel (murder case), 155, 175
Coen, Ethan, 5
Coen, Joel, 5
Colgan, Michael, 84
Collins, Jim, 46
Collins, Pat, 70
Come and Go (1966, play), 84
Commitments, The (1991, Alan Parker), 5, 14, 18, 21, 22, 24, 28, 31, 44–46, 44n2, 50, 51, 166
Connemara (region), 224
Conner, Marc C., 4–6, 10, 14, 16, 18, 167
Conner, Rearden, 12

268 INDEX

Conrad, Kathryn A., 76n9
Conroy, Rúaidhrí, 220
Coogan, Steve, 257
Coraline (2009, Henry Selick), 115
Corbet, John, 68–72, 77, 78
Corcoran, Mary P., 156
Cork (Irish County), 125
Corless, Cathleen, 243, 243n6, 244
Cornish, Abbie, 225, 234
Costa Book Awards, 254
Costello-Sullivan, Kate, 18, 167, 168, 189, 194
Country Girls, The (1960, novel), 138
Craven, Gemma, 68
Cripple of Inishmaan, The (1997, play), 219
Cronin, Nessa, 241n3
Crowe, Eileen, 12
Crowley, John, 18, 84, 158, 160, 165, 167, 170, 181–197
Croze, Marie-Josée, 227
Crying Game, The (1992, Neil Jordan), 5, 166
Culleton, Jonathan, 240n1
Cummins, Steve, 216, 217
Cunningham, Liam, 218, 225
Cure, The (band), 46

D

Dáil (Irish Parliament)
  Dáil Éireann Debate (1997), 4
Dangerous Liaisons (1988, Stephen Frears), 213
Dante Alighieri, 88
Dark, The (1965, novel), 138
David, Gerard, 221
Dawtrey, Adam, 171, 172
Dead, The (1987, John Huston), 10, 100
De Bankolé, Isaac, 228
De Beauvoir, Simone, 255, 256

De Bréadún, Deaglán, 48
Deleuze, Gilles, 85, 85n2, 93–95, 97
Dench, Judi, 259, 259n13
Dentz, Shira, 115, 120n4
Departed, The (2007, Martin Scorsese), 140
Deportees, The (2008, book), 16, 24, 39, 40
Derrida, Jacques, 91
Derry (Irish city), 125
"Destination Anywhere" (song), 37, 39n14
De Valera, Eamon, 10–12, 14, 161, 168
De Valera, Vivion, 4, 8
Directors Series Award (Directors Guild of Ireland), 114
Divine Comedy (1320, narrative poem), 88
Donnelly, Donal, 68, 220, 221, 234
Donoghue, Chris, 243, 243n7
Dostoevsky, Fyodor, 171
Down by the River (1996, novel), 138
Doyle, Maria, 43, 45
Doyle, Roddy, 6, 14–16, 21–41, 23n2, 23n3, 24n4, 26n6, 27n7, 31n13, 43, 48n6, 50, 105, 110, 141, 146, 213
"Drive it Like You Stole It" (song), 49, 59
Dublin (Irish capital)
  DART Line (transit service), 34
  Kilbarrack (suberb), 25, 34, 35
  Liffey (river), 43
  north-side, 61
  South, 171, 174
Dún Laoghaire Harbour (East Pier), 54
Dunphy, Eamon, 60
Duran Duran (band), 46, 50–52, 55

INDEX 269

E
Easkey (village), 227
Eco, Umberto, 134
Edinburgh Film Festival, 115
8th amendment (1983), 14, 79
Egoyan, Atom, 84
Eh Joe (1965, play), 85
Eisenstein, Serge, 99, 100
Elam, Keir, 92
Element Pictures (studio), 159
Elephant and Castle (London), 216
Eleuthéria (1947, play), 84
Ellison, Ralph, 22, 22n1
Ellmann, Richard, 99
Empire Marketing Board, 12
Employment Equality Act (1977), 14
England, 54, 68, 143, 184, 215
Enniscorthy (town), 190–192, 194,
    195, 197
Erythropoietin (hormone) (EPO),
    203, 209, 210, 213
European Court of Justice, 143
European Tour (1998), 210
"Europudding" (cinema), 9
"Exhausted, The" (1995, essay), 85

F
Fairley, Michelle, 218
Faithful Departed (1968, Kieran
    Hickey), 101
Fantastic Mr. Fox (2009, Wes
    Anderson), 115
Farley, Fidelma, 141, 142
Farmersville (Texas), 205
Farrell, Colin, 221, 225
Fathers.ie (online resource), 152
Felicia's Journey (1994, novel), 139
Fennell, Hilary, 102
Ferguson, Johnny, 251
Fermanagh (Irish County), 125,
    126, 129

Fernando, Nilmini, 241n3
Film (1965, Samuel Beckett), 85
Film Board Act (1993), 4
Financial crisis (2008–2009), 4
Finnegans Wake (1939,
    novel), 92, 100
First District Appellate Project, 233
Fischer, Clara, 241n3
Fis Éireann ("Screen Ireland") (FE/
    SI), 4, 167
Fitzgerald, Barry, 12
Fitzgerald, Mary, 69
Flaherty, Robert, 102
Flanagan, Fionnula, 224
Flaubert, Gustave, 110
*Flaying of the Corrupt Judge Sisamnes,
    The* (1498, Diptych), 221
Flower, Robin, 118
Focus Features (studio), 115
Fools of Fortune (1990, Pat
    O'Connor), 66
Ford, John, 12
Foreigner, The (2017, Martin
    Campbell), 15
Foster's Home for Imaginary Friends
    (TV Series), 114
Fox, Peter, 123n6
Frears, Stephen, 19, 199–214, 257
French, Robert, 101
Fricke, David, 61
Friedman, Milton (Friedmanism), 166
Fuller, Louise, 14–15

G
Galway (Irish County), 12, 125,
    215, 223
Garage (2007, Lenny Abrahamson),
    155, 160, 173–175
Garcia, Carnelia, 115n1
Garrett, Paul Michael, 241n3, 243
Gaye, Marvin, 29

270 INDEX

Geffen, David, 159
Gendron, Sarah, 88
Genette, Gérard, 186
Gerald McBoingBoing (animated
series), 119
Germany, 7, 55, 56, 67n3
Gibbons, Luke, 79n12
Gielgud, John, 84
Gillen, Aidan, 218, 228
Gillespie, Michael Patrick, 9, 11, 15,
16, 18, 28n10, 31, 32,
174, 183n1
Gittens, Geraldine, 59
"Glamor of Galway, The" (1957,
travelogue), 102
Gledhill, David, 227
Gleeson, Brendan, 159, 220,
221, 227
Gleeson, Domhnall, 193, 228, 229
Goethe, Johann Wolfgang von, 110
Goldberg, Elizabeth Swanson,
260, 261
Goldsmith, Oliver, 141
Gontarski, S.E., 84, 84n1
Good Friday Agreement
(1998), 15, 145
Good Friday Peace Accords
(1998), 2
"Grace" (1914, short story), 29n11
Great Britain, 1
Greendale Community School
(Kilbarrack), 25
Greengrass, Paul, 168
Gregory, Jon, 221
Gregory, Lady Augusta, 10
Grierson, Jamie, 243
Grierson, John, 12
Groden, Michael, 110
Grossman, Julie, 18, 167,
168, 182
Guardianship of Infants Act
(1964), 142

Guardian, The (publication), 176
Guard, The (2011, John Michael
McDonagh), 223–225,
228, 234

H
Haneke, Michael, 176
Hansard, Glen, 43n1
Hardiman, Neasa, 102
Harkin, Margo, 79
Harney-Mahajan, Tara, 19
Harrelson, Woody, 232
Harris, Conor, 156
Hart, Clive, 101
Hart, Ian, 159
Haussman, Baron Georges-
Eugène, 174
Healy, Dermot, 218
Heather Blazing, The (1992,
novel), 182
Hébert, James, 225
Hess, John Joseph, 53, 53n7
Hickey, Kieran, 101
Higgins, Michael D., 3, 5, 6,
166–169, 243
High Fidelity (2000, Stephen
Frears), 213
"Highway Kind" (song), 219
Hill, John D., 172
Hinds, Ciarán, 221
Hitchcock, Alfred, 211, 230
Hogg, Edward, 207
Holbein, Hans, 228
Holohan, Conn, 7
Holyhead (Wales), 54, 56
Horan, Niamh, 163, 253
Horgan-Jones, Jack, 243
Hornby, Nick, 167
Hulu (streaming service), 7
Humphries, Steve, 102, 257
Hurston, Zora Neale, 22, 22n1

INDEX   271

Hush-a-Bye Baby (1990, Margo
  Harkin), 79
Huston, John, 10, 100

I
I Confess (1953, Alfred
  Hitchcock), 230
Imagining Ulysses (2004, David Blake
  Knox), 101–105, 107–109, 112
In Bruges (2008, Martin McDonagh),
  216, 221–223, 227, 234, 235
Inglis, Tom, 156, 161, 168
Innes, C.L., 140
Institute of Public Administration
  (Dublin), 156
In the Name of the Father (1993, Jim
  Sheridan), 140
Into the West (1992, Mike Newell),
  28, 28n10
Iona (monastery), 120–122
Ireland
  abortion amendment debates
    (1980s), 14, 30
  animation industry, 114
  Civil War (1922–3), 1, 159
  Direct Provision, 240, 241n3
  Golden Age, 117, 120
  Irish Catholic Church, 14, 29
  Irish Cinema, 1–7, 9–11, 13, 17,
    24, 65, 158, 160, 165,
    170, 183n1
  Irish divorce referenda
    (1985-1986), 14, 30
  Irish Film and Television Awards
    (IFTA), 159, 160, 165, 168,
    169, 172
  Irish Film Institute, 4, 10,
    67n3, 243
  Irish Free State, 78, 103
  Irish heritage cinema, 66
  Irish Sea, 54

"lost babies," 242
National Library of, 101, 108
National Museum of, 125
"New Ireland," 2, 16, 23,
  24, 40, 153
Papal visit to (1979), 30
"stolen children," 242
Supreme Court, 143
"Troubles, the," 2, 141, 142
War for Independence
  (1919-21), 159
*Ireland's Magdalen Laundries and the
  Nation's Architecture of
  Containment* (2007, book), 240
Irish Times (publication), 44n2,
  144n5, 156
Irons, Jeremy, 84
Iser, Wolfgang, 190
Ivanek, Željko, 232
I Went Down (1997, Paddy
  Breathnach), 166

J
Jackson, Michael, 46, 53
James, Geraldine, 68
James, Henry, 190n5
James Joyce Zurich Foundation, 109
Jameson Dublin International Film
  Festival, 115
JAM Media (animation studio), 114
Jellenik, G., 241
Jesus of Nazareth (1977, Franco
  Zeffirelli), 222
Jieruo, Wen, 107
Johnson, Charles, 22n1
Johnson, Esther, 68, 75
Jordan, Eamonn, 18, 223
Jordan, Neil, 3, 5, 16, 18, 83–85,
  87, 89–91, 96, 97, 105,
  108–111, 145, 149n10, 159,
  160, 166, 168

272 INDEX

Joyce, James, 10, 18, 29n11, 44, 55, 57, 92–94, 92n7, 99–112, 123
Joyce, Michael, 110
Joyce, Nora, 57, 100, 108
Joyce's Women (1985, Michael Pearce), 100
Judgement of Cambyses (1498, Diptych), 221

K
Karlsen, Richard, 156
Kavanagh, Patrick, 26n6
Keane, John B., 139, 164
Keeley, Sam, 163, 171
Keenan, Rory, 225
Kehoe, Paula, 17, 194, 195
Kells (monastery), 122, 123
Kelly, Fiach, 184, 194, 195
Kermode, Mark, 232
Kerry (Irish County), 12, 125
Kerry Babies (1984, legal case), 79
Kiberd, Declan, 105, 108, 111
Killing Bono: A True Story (2004, memoir), 59
Killing Bono (2011, Nick Hamm), 59
Kim, Rina, 97n13
Kinsella, Thomas, 119, 135
"Knock on Wood" (song), 37
Knox, David Blake, 102–104
Krapp's Last Tape (1958, play), 84, 93
Kristeva, Julia, 222
Kunz, Don, 31

L
Land Before Time, The (1988, Don Bluth), 114
Landis, Floyd, 199, 201, 204, 205, 211–213
Landry Jones, Caleb, 232
Lane, Anthony, 227

Last Judgement, The (1482, triptych), 222
Last Orders with Gay Byrne (TV series), 48
"Last Rose of Summer, The" (song), 234
Last September, The (1999, Deborah Warner), 66
Lawrence, D. H., 108
Leary, Denis, 140
LeBroquy, Louis, 119, 135
Lee, Philomena, 259, 259n13
Leitch, Thomas, 17, 44n3, 190, 191, 245n10
Lemass, Sean, 23
LeMond, Greg, 210, 211
Lennon, Peter, 102, 143
Levine, Adam, 57, 62
Lieutenant of Inishmore, The (2001, play), 235
Lilliput Press (publisher), 155
Lincoln Center (New York), 83
Lindisfarne (island), 120–122
Little Stranger, The (2018, Lenny Abrahamson), 172
Loach, Ken, 159, 174
Lodge, Guy, 43
Logic of Sense, The (1969, book), 93
London (England), 215
London Weekend Television (TV network), 101
Lonesome West, The (1997, play), 219
Lost Child of Philomena Lee, The (2009, book), 257, 259
Lydon, Gary, 218, 228
Lynch, John, 68

M
MacDonald, Hettie, 8
MacDonald, Sarah, 243, 243n6
MacGowran, Jack, 101

INDEX   273

Mac Niocaill, Gearóid, 122, 123
Madame Bovary (1934, Jean
  Renoir), 11
Maeve (1981, Pat Murphy), 79, 79n12
Magdalene Laundry (asylums), 145,
  239, 240n1
Magdalene Restorative Justice Scheme
  (2013), 239, 240n1
Magdalene Sisters, The
  scandal, 14
  2002, Peter Mullan, 257
*Making of Alan Parker's Film 'the
  Commitments,' The* (1991,
  Edward J. Adcock), 27n8
Malraux, André, 166
Mamet, David, 84
Man of Aran (1934, Robert
  Flaherty), 102
Mannion, Declan, 224
Maoist Era (China), 107
Mara, Rooney, 246–248
Marcus, Shimmy, 102
Marks, Craig, 51
Massey, Eithne, 130–132, 131n8
Mauvaise foi ("Bad Faith"), 176
McAvoy, Sandra L., 78
McCabe, Patrick, 15, 145–149,
  149n10, 151–153
McClory, Séan, 12
McCormick, Neil, 48, 59, 60
McCourt, Frank, 105, 108, 109, 111,
  137, 138
McCourt, John, 100
McDonagh, John Michael, 4, 15, 158,
  165, 215–236
McDonagh, Martin, 18,
  159, 215–236
McDormand, Frances, 232
McFarlane, Ann, 220
McFarlane, Brian, 244
McFarlane, Noel, 25, 26
McGahern, John, 138

McGarry, Patsy, 240n1
McGuckian, Mary, 18, 66–75, 77–80
McKeown, Kieran, 141
McKittrick, David, 143n4, 148n9
McLoone, Martin, 67, 169,
  170, 176
McPherson, Conor, 4, 165
McQuaid, Archbishop Charles, 10
McSavage, David, 230
McSorley, Gerard, 68
Meehan, Bernard, 115, 133, 135n11
Melnikova, Irina, 221
Meltz, Nathan, 115, 120n4
Merivirta, Raita, 168
"Messe ocus Pangur bán" (poem),
  113, 118, 119
Metro Eireann (newspaper), 16,
  23, 24, 40
"Metro Eireann" (short stories), 23,
  24n4, 40
Metro Publishing and Consultancy
  Limited, 40
Michael Collins (1996, Neil Jordan),
  159, 168
Middle Ages, 39, 116, 117
Mikkelsen, Lars, 163
Ministry for Arts, Culture, and the
  Gaeltacht, 6, 166
Minnelli, Vincente, 11
Moloney, Alan, 84
Monde, Le (publication), 114
Mooney, Paschal, 6
Moore, Julianna, 83, 84, 87–91, 96
Moore, Tomm, 113–116, 118,
  119, 120n4
Moran, Dylan, 228
More Pricks Thank Kicks (1934,
  novel), 88
Motion Pictures Association
  (MPA), 3
Mount Temple Comprehensive School
  (Dublin), 45

274 INDEX

Mozart, Wolfgang Amadeus, 49
Mr. Magoo (animated series), 119
Mulan (1998, Tony Bancroft & Barry
  Cook), 119
Mulcahy, Russell, 50
Mulhall, Daniel, 69
Mullan, Peter, 257, 258
Mullen, Larry Jr., 60
Mumbai (India), 7
Murphy, Brian, 155–157, 160–162,
  164, 165, 168, 170, 173,
  175, 176
Murphy, Pat, 79, 100
Murphy, Róisín, 163, 164
Murray, David, 220
My Left Foot (1989, Jim Sheridan), 5,
  166, 241n4

N

Ned Kelly (2003, Gregor
  Jordan), 216
Neeson, Liam, 146, 147, 149, 159
Newell, Kate, 182
Newell, Mike, 28
New Irish Cinema, 5
New Waves (1960s European
  cinema), 5, 165
New York Times (publication), 115
"Night Train" (song), 33, 35,
  36, 39n14
Nolan, Larissa, 59
Nora (2000, Pat Murphy), 100
Nora Webster (2014, novel), 182
Normal People (2020, miniseries),
  7–9, 172
Norman/Viking Invasions, 17
North America, 7, 8, 160
Northumbria (Anglo-Saxon
  Kingdom), 120
Not I (2000, Neil Jordan), 18,
  83–97
Nugent, Kevin, 152

O

O'Boyle, Brian, 168, 169
O'Brien, Edna, 10, 14, 105, 107,
  109–111, 138, 138n1
O'Brien, Harvey, 103
O'Brien, Maria, 117, 118
O'Casey, Seán, 10
O'Connor, Pat, 66
O'Donnell, Katherine, 239,
  240, 240n1
O'Dowd, Chris, 200, 230
O'Dowd, Niall, 2, 10, 161
Offaly (Irish County), 125
O'Flynn, Sunniva, 103
O'Hagan, Sean, 235
O'Halloran, Marie, 164, 165
O'Halloran, Mark, 160
Ohio Impromptu (1981, play), 84
Omagh (2004, Peter Travis), 168
Ombudsman (Irish official), 239
Once (2007, John Carney), 43n1,
  45, 49, 57
"On Raglan Road" (song), 234
On the Waterfront (1954, Elia
  Kazan), 60
Onyejelem, Chinedu, 24, 40
O'Reilly, Emma, 207
O'Rourke, Orla, 228
Osborne, Ozzy, 111
Osbornes, The (TV series), 111
O'Sullivan, Aisling, 220
O'Toole, Fintan, 168, 169, 216, 217

P

Pace, Lee, 207
Paddy Clarke Ha Ha Ha (1993,
  novel), 23
Paglia, Camille, 106, 107, 110
Palm d'Or (Cannes Festival), 159
Palmer, R. Barton, 4–6, 10, 17, 19,
  167, 183n1, 186, 191
Palumbo, David M., 73

INDEX 275

Parker, Alan, 5, 6, 21, 22, 24, 26–32, 27n7, 27n8, 28n9, 29n11, 35–41, 39n14, 45, 166
Paulin, Tom, 105, 106, 108
Pearce, Michael, 100
Peck, Dale, 106
Peillon, Michel, 156
Pérez-Vides, Auxiliadora, 259
Philomena (2013, Stephen Frears), 213, 244, 245, 257, 259, 260
Phoenix (Arizona), 226
Pickett, Wilson, 26, 37, 38
Pinker, Steven, 222
Pinter, Harold, 84
Pius XI, Pope, 10
Pixar (animation studio), 115
Play (1963, play), 84
Playboy of the Western World, The (1962, Brian Desmond Hurst), 111
"Please, Please, Please" (song), 50
Poésy, Clémence, 223
Portrait of the Artist as a Young Man (1977, Joseph Strick), 100
Potts, Adam, 93n9
Powell, Robert, 222
Power, Kevin, 155–158, 160, 162–165, 167, 169–171, 173, 175, 216
Power, Paul, 70, 70n6
Princess and the Frog, The (2009, John Musker & Ron Clements), 115
Procol Harem (band), 29
Program, The (2015, Stephen Frears), 19, 199–214
Promise of Happiness, The (2010, novel), 255
Proust, Marcel, 86, 88, 90–92, 92n7, 94
Provoost, Jan, 221
Psalm 98 (bible), 39
Punch (cartoon series), 139

Q

Quảng Đức, Thích, 226
Quiet Man, The (1952, John Ford), 12
Quill, Máirín, 6
Quinn, Aidan, 159
Quirke, Justice John, 239

R

Ramey, Lynn, 117, 118, 118n3, 133
Rea, Stephen, 159
Redding, Otis, 26, 36, 37
Redgrave, Vanessa, 246–248, 251
Reilly, Kelly, 227
Remembrance of Things Past (1927, novel), 86, 91–92
Renoir, Jean, 11
Report of the Commission to Inquire into Child Abuse (2009), 47
Rescue Me (TV series), 140
Reynor, Jack, 163, 244, 251
Rhodes, Nick, 51
Richardson, Ian, 68
Rickman, Alan, 159
"Riddle of the Model, The" (song), 52
Ring of Dingle (peninsula), 125
Roberts, Julia, 159
Robinson, Mary, 79
Rockett, Kevin, 3, 4, 13, 24, 25
Rockwell, Sam, 225, 232
Rocky Road to Dublin, The (1968, Peter Lennon), 102
Rolling Stone (publication), 61
Ronin, Saoirse, 183
Room (2015, Lenny Abrahamson), 8, 9, 160, 168, 172
Rooney Prize for Irish literature, 165
Rooney, Sally, 7, 8, 172
Rougon-Macquart (book series), 174
Rouse, Margitta, 221, 222
Royal Air Force (RAF), 251
Royal Court Theatre (London), 83
Roy, David, 254

276 INDEX

RTÉ (broadcaster), 48, 165, 172
Ruffalo, Mark, 49
Ruffin, Jimmy, 34
Ruspoli, Reema, 51, 54
Ryan, Liam, 31
Ryan, Patrick, 101
Ryan Report, The (2009, Commission to Inquire into Child Abuse), 230
Ryzik, Melena, 115

S

Sacred Heart of Jesus Christ, 219
"Safe Cycling" (1949, public safety film), 102
Saigon (Vietnam), 226
St. Francis of Assisi, 219
St. Francis Xavier's Church (Dublin), 29n11
St. Ignatius (Mother and Baby Home), 242, 250
"St. John the Gambler" (song), 219
St. Mary's Home for Unmarried Mothers, 242
St. Patrick's Cathedral (Dublin), 71
St. Patrick's Day (holiday), 115
St. Patrick's Day Radio Address (1943), 10
Scarlata, Jessica, 258
Scarry, Elaine, 260
Schneider, Alan, 83, 87n3
Scorching Wind, The (1964, novel), 159
Scott, A. O., 50
Scott, Killian, 229
Screen Ireland (agency), 4, 167, 172
Seanad debate (1997), 6
Searcy, Nick, 232
Second Death, The (2000, novel), 218–219, 234
Second Empire (Renovation of Paris), 174
Secret of Kells, The (2009, Tomm Moore & Nora Twomey), 18, 113–135

Secret Scripture, The (2017, Jim Sheridan), 19, 239–261
Selznick, Barbara Wilinsky, 9
Senn, Fritz, 109
Setoodeh, Ramin, 48
Seven Deadly Sins (2012, novel), 199–214
Seven Psychopaths (2012, Martin McDonagh), 216, 225–227, 234
Sex in a Cold Climate (1998, Steve Humphries), 102, 257
Sexton, Brendan III, 233
Shaffer, Peter, 49
Shake Hands with the Devil (1959, Michael Anderson), 12
Sharpe, Owen, 218
Shaw, George Bernard, 10, 11
Shaw Weaver, Harriet, 100
Sheridan, Jim, 5, 15, 19, 28, 68, 140, 141, 144, 160, 166, 239–261
Shields, Arthur, 12
Shortall, Eithne, 156, 157, 162, 168
Shortt, Pat, 174, 228
Sierz, Aleks, 84
Sing Street (2016, John Carney), 18, 43–62
Sisters of Bon Secours (religious order), 242
"Six Shooter" (2005, short), 219–221, 234
Sixsmith, Martin, 257, 257n12, 259
Skellig Michael (island), 125
Skull in Connemara, A (1997, play), 219
Skunk Fu (TV series), 114
Sligo (Irish County), 8, 9, 73n7, 215, 227
Smithfield Market (Dublin), 26
Smith, Iain Robert, 9
Smith, James M., 76n9, 240, 257n12
Smyth, Ailbhe, 79
Smyth, Brendan, 14
Snapper, The (1993, Stephen Frears), 141, 213

Soderbergh, Steven, 5
Solomon, Charles, 135n11
Song for a Raggy Boy
  1999, novel, 15
  2003, Aisling Welsh, 15
Stanton, Harry Dean, 225
State (Nicolauo) vs. An Bord Uchtála
  (1966, legal case), 143
Stevenson, Theo, 221
Stewart, Michael, 227–229
Strick, Joseph, 100
Sullivan Bluth (animation studio), 114
Surrealist Movement, 93
Swift, Jonathan, 68–77, 70n6, 73n7,
  77n10, 80
Synge, John Millington, 10, 48
Synge Street Christian Brothers School
  (Dublin), 43, 47

T
Táin Bó Cúailnge (epic), 119, 135
Tall, Emily, 100
T.A.M.I. Show (TV series), 50
Tandy, Jessica, 83, 87n3
Tannenbaum, Rob, 51
Taoiseach (Irish prime minister), 10
Tartakovsky, Genndy, 119
Taylor, John, 51, 52
Taylor, Richard, 70n5
Teenage Mutant Ninja Turtles (1980s,
  TV series), 114
Ten Great Modern Writers (1988, TV
  series), 101
*Ten Years After: The Irish Film Board
  (1993–2003)*, 3
Thief and the Cobbler, The (1993,
  Richard Williams), 119
34th amendment (2015), 14
36th amendment (2018), 14
Thomas, Kristin Scott, 84
*Three Billboards Outside Ebbing
  Missouri* (2017, Martin
  McDonagh), 159

3-D CGI (animation), 114
Till, Karen E., 241n3
Tóibín, Colm, 18, 139–141, 167,
  169, 181–197
Top of the Pops (TV series), 50–52, 59
Toronto International Film
  Festival, 84
Travis, Peter, 168
Trevor, William, 139
Trinity College (Dublin), 8, 71, 115,
  123, 135n11
"Try a Little Tenderness" (song), 37
Tuam (Town in Galway), 242–245,
  243n6, 243n7, 244n8, 250,
  251, 255
20th Century Fox (studio), 115
Twomey, Nora, 113, 114, 119

U
Ulysses
  1988, Nigel Wallace, 101
  1967, Joseph Strick, 100
  1920, novel, 18, 57, 92, 99–112
Uncertain Ireland (2006, essay
  collection), 156
United International Pictures (UPI/
  UIP), 160
United States (US), 3, 6, 8, 11, 50,
  159, 161, 175, 176, 257n12
University College (Dublin), 175
Unmarried & Separated Fathers of
  Ireland (USFI), 152
Up (2009, Pete Docter), 115
U2 (Band), 14, 45, 57, 59–62

V
Van, The
  1991, novel, 25, 141, 213
  1996, Stephen Frears, 213
van Zandt, Townes, 219
Variety (publication), 114
Vatican II, 14, 30

278 INDEX

Verini, James, 226
Vicar of Wakefield, The (1766, novel), 141
Vietnam War (1955-1975), 226
Vigilanti Cura (Papal Encyclical), 10
Vikings (Scandinavia), 17, 122–128, 131
Vinterberg, Thomas, 176

W

Waits, Tom, 226
Wakeling, Corey, 83
Walken, Christopher, 226
Walking into Eternity: James Joyce's Ulysses – a Dublin Guide with Patrick Ryan (1988), 101
"Walkin' in the Rain" (song), 36
Wallace, Nigel, 101
Walsh, Dearbhla, 102
Walsh, Maurice, 12
Walsh, M. Emmett, 228
Walsh, Sean, 57, 100
Walt Disney Animation Studios, 115
Warner Brothers (studio), 99, 100, 159
Warner, Deborah, 66
War on Everyone (2016, John Michael McDonagh), 216
Wayman, Sheila, 144n5
Welsh, Irvine, 106
"What Becomes of the Brokenhearted?" (song), 34
What Richard Did (2012, Lenny Abrahamson), 19, 155–177
What Where (1983, play), 92
Whelehan, Imelda, 44n3, 242n5
"When a Man Loves a Woman" (song), 29, 30n12
When Ideas Matter (2017, book), 166

Whitelaw, Billie, 83, 85, 87, 88, 96, 96n12
Wicklow (shoreline), 175
Wilde, Oscar, 10
William Lawrence Collection (National Library of Ireland), 101
Williams, Hank, 219
Williams, Harold, 65n1
Williams, Richard, 119
Williams, Roxanna, 218
Wilmot, David, 218, 220, 224, 230
Wind That Shakes the Barley, The (2003, Ken Loach), 16, 159
Witchel, Alex, 196
Woolf, Virginia, 108
Words Upon the Window Pane (1994, Mary McGuckian), 18, 65–80, 70n5
World War I (Great War), 12
Worth, Katharine, 70n5, 73n7, 86, 92

X

X Case (1992, legal case), 79

Y

Yeager, Jennifer, 240n1
Year of the Hiker (1963, play), 139
Yeats, William Butler, 10, 18, 68–72, 70n5, 73n7, 74–78, 78n11, 80, 80n13

Z

Zeffirelli, Franco, 222
Zola, Émile, 174
Žukauskaitė, Audronė, 85n2

Printed in the United States
by Baker & Taylor Publisher Services